Through the Years

A Lifetime of Good Food

by

Bettye Rabb VanderVeen

ISBN 0-9672948-9-4
Library of Congress Catalog Number: 99-094007

First Printing, December 2002

VanderVeen Publishing
11916 Hickory Drive
Bentonville, AR 72712-8789
(479) 273-3388
1-800-982-2568
e-mail: VanPublishing@aol.com

Cover painting by Clo Ann Rabb
Meridian, Mississippi

Bettye's photograph on back cover by
bob's of Fayetteville, Fayetteville, Arkansas

A portion of the proceeds will be donated to
The American Cancer Society and/or other
designated charities.

The author has personally tested every recipe, many
of them several times. Contributor's recipes may
have been edited or changed upon testing.

WIMMER
COOKBOOKS

ConsolidatedGraphics
1-800-548-2537

to my husband—*Art*

Acknowledgments

Many people have helped to make *Through the Years — A Lifetime of Good Food* a reality for me. I want to thank all of you for your interest, encouragement and assistance, and though I know I will not remember everyone, the following are some, whom I would like to mention.

To my husband, Art, for his patience and fortitude in formatting and preparing this publication for print.

To our daughter, Terry VanderVeen Bright, for her encouragement and willingness to be our grammatical consultant.

To our son, Arthur, for his support and encouragement and for his technical advice in helping his dad become a "desktop publisher."

To my mother from whom I learned so much and whom I revere dearly.

To my sister-in-law, Clo Ann Rabb, a noted artist in Mississippi, whose painting, which is on the cover of this cookbook, hung over the mantel in our dining room as I was growing up and reminds me of the good food we ate as a family.

To Miss Maude Thompson, of Lexington, Mississippi, who prepared great after-school snacks for her daughter, Helen Thompson Baird, Eleanor Patterson Weathersby and me. She sparked a desire within me to cook.

To our friends in Burlington, North Carolina, who were our first friends in our first real home after college. I started my serious recipe collecting there.

To our friends in Annandale, Virginia, who contributed many of the recipes and are still lifelong friends.

To our friends in New Jersey, Jackie and Andy Andrishok, Patsy and Frank Minter and Doris and Clarence Brasfield, whom we met in the early 1960's. We were all transplanted southerners with the Bell System. They have given us encouragement in the huge undertaking of writing this cookbook.

To our friends in Colorado, especially the monthly duplicate bridge group with whom the bridge playing became secondary after cocktails, good camaraderie and dinner. To Beth Huffman and the Longmont First Friday Bridge Group, whose warmth is captured in their motto, "Once a member, always a member." To Patty Hogan of Boulder, a recipe contributor, who volunteered at the Boulder Humane Society, and through whom we found Dudley, our Olde English Sheepdog. To Midge Bartlett of Boulder, a wonderful cook and my

"Miss Daisy," an astute octogenarian, who maintained a great sense of humor and with whom I enjoyed discussing politics. To Kirk and Dody Martin of Lake of the Pines, who hosted the picnics for another one of our bridge groups. To Kat Forsyth, who was my very dearest friend, "sister" and "other mother," and to her husband "Easy George" Forsyth, who is Art's favorite bridge partner and confidant.

To our friends at the Valley Presbyterian Church in Scottsdale, Arizona, whose many cooks have shared their recipes with me, especially to Fran Fee, an incredibly creative hostess, originally from Mississippi, from whom I learned "hospitality with a flair." To Martha and Boyd Tompkins from South Carolina, whom we met in Scottsdale and who shared their southerness with us.

To our friends in the mountains of Colorado, those in Winter Park, Fraser, Tabernash, Granby and Grand Lake, with whom we enjoyed the many extraordinary activities that only the mountains could offer, during the beautiful summers and severe winters from 1989 to 1993.

To friends in Bella Vista, Arkansas, many of whom were pressed into service to taste-test my recipes when I brought them to bridge; many have contributed recipes and suggestions. Some wished I would finish the cookbook and others hoped I would just continue having them taste-test the recipes. To our friends at the Presbyterian Church of Bella Vista, who have encouraged me and contributed their special recipes. To friends at doctors' and dentists' offices, drug stores, banks, beauty salons and other shops and stops while running errands in Bentonville and Rogers, Arkansas, who also taste-tested my recipes.

To Ruthie Warnall, of Overland Park, Kansas, author of many cookbooks, who encouraged me to write my cookbook, saying, "Just go for it!"

To our "fresh eyes," Mimi Lyons, Mimi Tyte, Nancy Sherbondy, Bev Lehmann, Shirley Lausen, Jackie Andrishok and Martha Tompkins, who read and proofed all or portions of the book at different stages.

To Sheila Thomas, Connie Morgan and Ardith Bradshaw at Wimmer Cookbooks for guiding us through the development and production phases of getting this cookbook into print.

To all of you whose names are woven throughout this collection of treasured recipes, thank you for sharing your good food and friendship.

Bettye and Art VanderVeen

Introduction

My most vivid memory of cooking while growing up in Lexington, Mississippi, was the noonday dinner that Mama would prepare, full of traditional southern dishes. She would fix peas, fried corn, squash, okra, sliced fresh tomatoes, green onions, green beans and, of course, a skillet of cornbread and maybe a piece of beef or a chicken (we mostly had chicken, since we raised our own). Mama would have all the food ready when my daddy came home at noon. Looking back, I am still amazed by what Mama accomplished in one morning's time, from plucking the chicken to having a table set with piping hot food!

Not until Art and I married in 1957 did I realize my lack of preparation in the kitchen and that, all of a sudden, I was now to be the cook. I called Mama quite often for recipes and instructions. Taking good notes, I began to enjoy cooking, and I anxiously read cookbooks and collected recipes from friends; forty-plus years later I am still taking notes and collecting recipes. Today, my son and daughter call me frequently, sometimes daily, to ask for a much-desired recipe or tip. The cycle continues.

Sharing good recipes is great fun and compliments those who give them. During the last ten years or so, I have been transferring my handwritten recipes to the computer, including many tips and techniques learned from my mother and friends. I have finally put this wealth of knowledge into this cookbook.

Alice Waters, a well-known chef and cookbook author, claims, regarding cooking, "Nothing happens the same way twice ... it's always an experiment." Cooking is more than following recipes; cooking is an adventure. By trying new recipes and learning new techniques and experiencing new tastes, a person discovers that Waters is right.

I have tried to include something for everyone in this cookbook: quick-and-easy dishes for those on the run; make-ahead dishes for easier entertaining; a few light recipes; and a recipe or two that call to remembrance a favorite recipe long forgotten. These are not all original recipes; they are mostly my favorites. I have tried to adjust some of the good old familiar standbys to today's method of cooking and today's ingredients.

Recipes evoke particular memories, memories of friends and events that are all the richer because they include the smells and tastes of good food. So, these are some of my favorite memories, and this cookbook is like a diary of my life "through the years."

Bettye Rabb VanderVeen

Contents

About This Book

Unless otherwise stated:

- Use large eggs.
- Use all-purpose bleached flour, fluffed and then measured.
- Use fresh lemon juice.
- Sugar is granulated.
- Use clear glass pie plates for best results.
- Beat with mixer on medium speed.
- Preheat oven.
- Bake on middle rack of oven.
- Broil with oven selector and temperature set to BROIL (550°) in upper third of oven with door ajar at broil stop or as directed in the stove manual.
- Crush dried herbs and pepper flakes before adding to release flavor.
- Shortening means solid vegetable shortening. It is now packaged in 1-cup sticks for convenience; butter and margarine are packaged in *½-cup* sticks.
- Weigh cheese before shredding or grating: 4 ounces Cheddar-style cheese is equivalent to 1 packed cup of shredded or grated cheese, while 3 ounces of hard cheese, such as Parmesan or Asiago, equals 1 packed cup of grated cheese.

For your information:

- Bold, italicized titles refer to other recipes in this book.
- The term "spray" or "sprayed" refers to the use of nonstick cooking spray.
- *Appendix A – Tips* contains one hundred twenty suggestions and shortcuts I have learned over the years. Superscript numbers in recipes indicate a tip is available–find it in the appendix.
- *Appendix B – Tips* Index has been provided to help you search for a tip.
- *Appendix C – Glossary* contains definitions and pronunciations for possibly unfamiliar terms used in this book. A superscripted word, such as jicama[G], indicates an entry in the glossary.
- *Appendix D – Equipment* lists many sizes and types of utensils I use.

Appetizers & Beverages

Appetizers

Beverages

Still A Favorite Crab Mold

I was first introduced to this crab mold in 1957 when Mrs. Ellison served it at a bridal luncheon in my honor. It is still a favorite.

¼ cup plus 2 tablespoons cold water	⅛ teaspoon white pepper
1½ envelopes unflavored gelatin	1 teaspoon Worcestershire sauce
1 (8-ounce) package cream cheese, softened	Dash hot pepper sauce
	1 teaspoon lemon juice
1 cup mayonnaise	¾ cup pasteurized crabmeat or red sockeye salmon
1 tablespoon grated onion⁵⁵	
1 (10¾-ounce) can cream of mushroom soup	1 cup finely chopped celery, or ½ cup celery and ¼ cup each red and green bell pepper
¼ teaspoon salt	

Pour water into 1-cup glass measure, sprinkle in gelatin and let stand 2 minutes. Microwave on HIGH 40 seconds; stir thoroughly and let stand at least 2 minutes. Beat cream cheese in medium bowl with mixer until fluffy. Blend in mayonnaise and onion. Heat soup in medium saucepan until almost boiling. Mix in salt, pepper, Worcestershire sauce, pepper sauce and lemon juice. Remove from heat. Beat in gelatin and cream cheese mixture until smooth. Fold in crabmeat and celery. Pour into sprayed 4-cup mold. Refrigerate overnight or until firm. Unmold onto serving platter;⁵⁴ place lettuce around edge of platter and garnish with parsley. Serve as spread with round buttery crackers or *Toast Points*.

Makes 32 servings   Evelyn Ellison, Lexington, Mississippi

Per 2 tablespoons: 54 calories, 5 g fat, 1 g protein, 3 g carbohydrate, 16 mg cholesterol, 176 mg sodium.

Pepper Jack Cheese Toast

Great spur-of-the-moment appetizer. I helped at a reception where these were served. They were going like hot cakes–so fast we were mixing, spreading and baking, no time to refrigerate!

4 tablespoons dried parsley flakes, crushed	1 (12-ounce) loaf party rye bread
4 tablespoons dried minced onion	8 Pepper Jack or Swiss cheese slices, broken into 4 squares
2 cups regular or light mayonnaise	Paprika

Stir parsley flakes, dried onion and mayonnaise together in plastic container. Cover and refrigerate several hours. Spread bread slices with enough mixture to cover. Top each slice with cheese square and sprinkle with paprika. Bake at 375° for 10 minutes. Transfer to serving plate. Serve warm or at room temperature. Spread will keep for weeks refrigerated. Stir well before using.

Makes 32 pieces

Per piece: 89 calories, 7 g fat, 2 g protein, 5 g carbohydrate, 9 mg cholesterol, 204 mg sodium.

Cheese Straws

It would not be a southern Christmas or a southern wedding without cheese straws. Fran Fee, also from Mississippi, showed me how to make these when we both lived in Scottsdale.

1½	(10-ounce) packages *extra sharp* Cheddar cheese (red package)	1¾	cups flour
½	cup (1 stick) margarine,[50] *softened* (do not use butter)	¾	teaspoon salt
		½	to 1 teaspoon cayenne pepper (1 teaspoon is hot!)

Finely grate cheese into large bowl (Fran used a Mouli grater[G]). Blend in margarine with mixer until well combined. Whisk flour, salt and cayenne pepper in separate bowl.[2] Gradually beat into cheese mixture on low until thoroughly mixed (I squeeze dough through my fingers). Gather into ball and divide into four portions. Roll into cylinders to fit cookie press.

Fit star-shaped disk into cookie press and add cylinder of dough. Squeeze dough through press into five 10- to 12-inch long "ropes" about 2 inches apart on ungreased baking sheets (use light baking sheets–dark ones will cause cheese straws to burn on bottom). Straighten with table knife. Score lightly at 3½ to 4 inches. Bake *one sheet at a time* at 375° for 13 to 14 minutes or until edges just begin to brown. Cut at score marks and slide straws onto racks. Cool. Continue with remaining cylinders. Always use clean, cool ungreased baking sheets. Store in airtight containers or freeze.

Makes 90 to 100 cheese straws   Fran Fee, Scottsdale, Arizona

Per cheese straw: 34 calories, 2 g fat, 1 g protein, 2 g carbohydrate, 5 mg cholesterol, 59 mg sodium.

Patsy Minter's food processor method: Cheese and margarine must be soft–let stand at room temperature several hours or overnight. Blot cheese with paper towel if oily and cut into ½-inch cubes. Place steel blade in work bowl. Add cheese and pulse until coarsely chopped. Whisk flour, salt and cayenne pepper in medium bowl. Add to work bowl, covering cheese. Cut margarine into chunks over flour. Pulse and run until dough almost comes together. Remove and gather into ball. Continue as directed above.

Celeste Hors d'oeuvre

1 cup mayonnaise	1 tablespoon Worcestershire sauce
¼ cup finely chopped onion or ¼ cup chopped green onions, including some tops	6 slices bacon, cooked and crumbled[14]
	½ cup toasted[5] slivered almonds
8 ounces sharp Cheddar cheese, grated (2 cups)	16 slices firm white sandwich bread, crusts removed

Mix mayonnaise, onion, cheese, Worcestershire sauce, bacon and almonds in large bowl with fork. Add salt and pepper to taste. Spread bread slices with enough cheese mixture to cover. (May assemble ahead to this point; cover and refrigerate or flash freeze.[26]) Cut diagonally into fourths (easier if flash-frozen). Place on ungreased baking sheets. Bake frozen or unfrozen at 400° for 10 minutes or until puffed and golden.

Makes 64 pieces   Jackie Andrishok, Destin, Florida

Per piece: 70 calories, 6 g fat, 2 g protein, 3 g carbohydrate, 6 mg cholesterol, 103 mg sodium.

Lake George Clams Casino

In the 1970's we vacationed at Candlelight Cottages on Lake George in upper New York State. Eight families reserved cottages the same two weeks every August—some still return each year. One summer Jimmy made Clams Casino, his grandfather's recipe.

¼ cup (½ stick) butter, melted	1 teaspoon fresh lemon juice
1 tablespoon vegetable oil	¼ teaspoon salt
1 garlic clove, minced[20]	⅛ teaspoon pepper
2 tablespoons snipped flat-leaf parsley	¼ teaspoon chicken bouillon granules (optional)
½ to 1 teaspoon dried oregano, crushed	Seasoned dry breadcrumbs
1 (6-ounce) can *minced* clams, undrained	12 sprayed clam shells or sprayed medium-size mushroom caps
	12 (1-inch) pieces uncooked bacon

Combine butter and oil in small saucepan. Add garlic, parsley and oregano. Heat on low 1 minute, being careful not to brown garlic or it will be bitter. Remove from heat and mix in clams, lemon juice, salt, pepper and bouillon granules. Stir in enough breadcrumbs to make moist stuffing (about ½ cup).

Fill shells with clam mixture and top with bacon pieces. Place on sprayed foil-lined jelly-roll pan and bake at 400° for 10 to 12 minutes.

Makes 12 appetizers   Jimmy Corsello, New Brunswick, New Jersey

Per piece: 70 calories, 6 g fat, 1 g protein, 4 g carbohydrate, 12 mg cholesterol, 277 mg sodium.

Mushroom Aïoli Tapas

1½ tablespoons olive oil	2 to 3 teaspoons dry sherry
14 fresh medium button mushroom caps, thinly sliced[3]	½ *Baguette*, or purchased baguette
⅛ teaspoon salt	½ recipe *Aïoli*, or 1 recipe *Quick Aïoli*

Heat oil in skillet and add mushrooms, salt and sherry. Simmer covered until mushrooms release their juices, about 7 minutes. Uncover and cook until juices evaporate. Set aside.

Slice baguette into eighteen ¼-inch rounds. Place rounds on baking sheet and bake at 350° for 4 to 5 minutes to dry out. Remove and set oven to BROIL.[13] Spread rounds with aïoli and top with sautéed mushroom slices. Broil tapas on baking sheet until aïoli bubbles, about 1 minute. Transfer to platter and serve. Recipe may be doubled.

Makes 18 tapas

Per tapa: 67 calories, 7 g fat, 1 g protein, 2 g carbohydrate, 6 mg cholesterol, 82 mg sodium.

Green Olivada

Marianne loves green olives. I worked for her in the Season Pass Office at Winter Park Ski Area in Colorado. She would often bring in a jar of olives for snacks—no wonder she would send me a Green Olivada recipe!

¼ cup blanched almonds	2 teaspoons dried basil, crushed
1 (10-ounce) jar pitted Spanish olives, well drained	1 teaspoon dried thyme, crushed
1 teaspoon dried oregano, crushed	¼ cup olive oil

Put almonds, olives, oregano, basil and thyme in food processor and pulse until coarsely chopped. Scrape down sides. With machine running, pour oil through feed tube in continuous stream until mixture becomes a thick puree. Cover and refrigerate at least 3 days. Olivada will keep 2 weeks refrigerated. Serve at room temperature on melba toast or *Crostini*.

Makes 1 cup   Marianne Klancke, Fraser, Colorado

Per tablespoon: 69 calories, 7 g fat, 1 g protein, 2 g carbohydrate, 0 mg cholesterol, 392 mg sodium.

Green Olivada Cheese Spread: Mix several tablespoons Green Olivada with 4 ounces cream cheese. Spread on crackers or use to stuff celery; sprinkle with paprika.

Goat Cheese Crostini

Quick and easy.

5 ounces soft goat cheese	3 ounces Asiago or Parmesan
3 tablespoons snipped fresh chives	cheese, grated (1 cup)
60 *Crostini*	

Stir goat cheese and chives together in small bowl. Season with salt and pepper. Cover and refrigerate.

Preheat oven to BROIL.[13] Spread crostini[G] with enough goat cheese mixture to cover. Sprinkle with Asiago cheese and place on foil-lined baking sheets. Broil until cheese begins to brown.

Makes 60 pieces

Per piece: 26 calories, 2 g fat, 1 g protein, 0 g carbohydrate, 3 mg cholesterol, 36 g sodium.

Southwest Cheesecake

2 (8-ounce) packages cream cheese, softened	1 (4-ounce) can diced green chiles, drained
1 (1.25-ounce) package taco seasoning	2 tablespoons snipped flat-leaf parsley
2 cups sour cream, *divided*	¼ cup sliced ripe olives
3 eggs, room temperature	½ cup chopped green onions, including some tops
8 ounces sharp Cheddar cheese, shredded (2 cups)	1 cup chopped fresh tomatoes

Beat cream cheese in large bowl with mixer until smooth. Mix in taco seasoning and 1 cup sour cream. Add eggs one at a time, beating well after each addition. Stir in Cheddar cheese and green chiles. Pour mixture into sprayed 9-inch springform pan. Bake at 350° for 40 minutes or just until center is firm. Remove cheesecake. Maintain oven temperature. Carefully run sharp knife around top edge of pan. Cool 10 minutes. Spread remaining 1 cup sour cream over cheesecake. Bake 5 more minutes. Cool completely on rack. Refrigerate uncovered overnight.

Run knife around edge and remove sides of pan. Leave cheesecake on pan bottom for support. Place on serving plate. Top cheesecake with parsley in center, surrounded by circles of ripe olives, green onion and chopped tomatoes. Cut into wedges. Serve on small plates with *Salsa* and tortilla chips or corn chips.

Makes 20 servings   Pauline Friend, Chandler, Arizona

Per serving: 196 calories, 17 g fat, 7 g protein, 4 g carbohydrate, 79 mg cholesterol, 387 mg sodium.

Brie and Chutney

1 (8-ounce) round of Brie, chilled	8 slices bacon, cooked and
1 (9-ounce) jar chutney, your choice	crumbled[14]

Cut circle of rind from top of Brie, leaving small rim around edge. Place Brie on microwave-safe plate and microwave on HIGH 1 minute. Cover with chutney and sprinkle with bacon. Serve with baked whole wheat wafers, water crackers, pear slices and grapes.

Makes 6 to 8 servings   Jackie Andrishok, Destin, Florida

Per serving of 8: 350 calories, 24 g fat, 8 g protein, 23 g carbohydrate, 47 mg cholesterol, 662 g sodium.

Clam Salsa

Jerry says, "Make sure you add enough garlic salt!"

4 (6½-ounce) cans *minced* clams, drained	4 plum tomatoes, seeded[53] and diced
½ cup thinly sliced green onions, including some tops	1 teaspoon garlic salt, or to taste
1 garlic clove, minced[20]	Dash of hot pepper sauce

Mix clams, green onion, garlic and tomatoes in large bowl. Stir in garlic salt and pepper sauce. Refrigerate 4 hours to blend flavors. Serve at *room* temperature with round buttery crackers or saltines and beer.

Makes 4 cups

Anne Dartt, Bella Vista, Arkansas
Jerry Johnson, Roswell, New Mexico

Per ¼-cup serving: 30 calories, 0 g fat, 4 g protein, 4 g carbohydrate, 9 mg cholesterol, 284 mg sodium.

Salmon Spread

1 (14-ounce) can salmon	3 tablespoons sweet pickle relish
½ cup finely chopped celery	½ teaspoon hot pepper sauce
2 tablespoons mayonnaise	1 teaspoon liquid smoke, or to taste
3 tablespoons finely chopped onion	2 tablespoons fresh lemon juice

Drain salmon and remove any skin and bones. Flake salmon in medium bowl. Add celery, mayonnaise, onion, pickle relish, pepper sauce, liquid smoke and lemon juice. Mix thoroughly. Cover and refrigerate several hours. Serve with assorted crackers.

Makes about 2 cups   Bev Tillberry, Spring Hill, Florida

Per tablespoon: 26 calories, 2 g fat, 3 g protein, 1 g carbohydrate, 7 mg cholesterol, 87 mg sodium.

Mini Quiches

Pastry:

1 recipe *Cream Cheese Pastry*, or
1 (15-ounce) package refrigerated
pie crusts

Spinach Filling:

½ cup half-and-half or milk
1 teaspoon dried minced onion
1 (12-ounce) package frozen
spinach soufflé
3 eggs, lightly beaten
⅛ teaspoon cayenne pepper
Dash of salt
Dash of ground nutmeg
4 ounces sharp Cheddar or Swiss
cheese, shredded (1 cup)

Bacon-Cheese Filling:

10 tablespoons half-and-half or
milk (½ cup plus 2 tablespoons)
1 teaspoon dried minced onion
2 eggs, lightly beaten
⅛ teaspoon cayenne pepper
¼ teaspoon salt
Dash of ground nutmeg
6 slices bacon, cooked and
crumbled[14]
7 ounces sharp Cheddar or Swiss
cheese, shredded (1¾ cup)
Paprika

Pastry: Prepare *Cream Cheese Pastry* and wrap in plastic. Refrigerate 1 hour or overnight. Divide into 24 pieces and roll into balls. Place balls in sprayed miniature muffin cups. Press into bottom and up sides to form thin pastry shells (a tart tamper[62] works well). Cover and refrigerate or freeze until ready to fill. If frozen, thaw before filling.

If using refrigerated pie crusts, leave in pouches and let stand at room temperature 15 minutes to soften. Remove dough from one pouch, unfold and press out fold line. Cut twelve 2½-inch circles with floured cookie cutter. Press into bottoms and up sides of sprayed miniature muffin cups. Repeat with remaining pie crust. Cover and refrigerate or freeze until ready to fill. If frozen, thaw before filling.

Mini Spinach Quiches: Mix half-and-half and dried onion in small bowl or glass measure. Let stand several minutes to reconstitute onion. Defrost spinach soufflé in microwave according to package directions. Put soufflé, eggs, cayenne pepper, salt and nutmeg in medium bowl. Whisk in onion mixture. Stir in cheese. Fill pastry shells *full*. Bake at 350° for 30 to 32 minutes or until firm. Let stand in tins 5 to 10 minutes. Lift quiches from cups with tip of sharp knife. Transfer to serving plate. Serve warm or at room temperature.

Mini Bacon Cheese Quiches: Mix half-and-half and dried onion as above and let stand. Put eggs, cayenne pepper, salt and nutmeg in medium bowl. Whisk in onion mixture. Stir in bacon and cheese. Fill pastry shells *full* and sprinkle with paprika. Bake and serve as directed above.

Makes 24 mini quiches

Per mini quiche: 127 calories, 10 g fat, 4 g protein, 7 g carbohydrate, 63 mg cholesterol, 180 mg sodium.

Kat's Deviled Eggs

Kat's deviled eggs are famous, always the first to go!

6 hard-cooked eggs[18]	½ teaspoon cider vinegar
¼ teaspoon salt	1 teaspoon mayonnaise
⅛ teaspoon pepper	1 to 2 tablespoons coleslaw dressing
Pinch of sugar	Paprika
½ teaspoon prepared mustard[G]	

Peel eggs and carefully cut in half lengthwise with sharp wet knife. Remove yolks to shallow bowl. Set whites aside. Mash yolks; stir in salt, pepper, sugar, mustard, vinegar, mayonnaise and coleslaw dressing. Mix well. Add more coleslaw dressing or mayonnaise if dry. Fill each white with 1 tablespoon yolk mixture. Refrigerate in covered container. Sprinkle with paprika just before serving. Garnish with parsley.

Makes 12 deviled eggs   Katherine Forsyth, Boulder, Colorado

Per deviled egg: 44 calories, 3 g fat, 3 g protein, 1 g carbohydrate, 108 mg cholesterol, 83 mg sodium.

Mother's Deviled Eggs

6 hard-cooked eggs[18]	½ teaspoon prepared mustard
1 teaspoon butter, softened	2 teaspoons sweet pickle relish
¼ teaspoon salt	1½ to 2 tablespoons mayonnaise
⅛ teaspoon pepper	Paprika
Pinch of sugar	

Peel eggs while still warm. Carefully cut in half lengthwise with sharp wet knife. Remove yolks to shallow bowl. Set whites aside. Mash yolks with butter and stir in salt, pepper, sugar, mustard and pickle relish. Mix in mayonnaise until spreadable. Fill each white with 1 tablespoon yolk mixture. Refrigerate in covered container. Sprinkle with paprika just before serving.

Makes 12 deviled eggs   Willie McCaleb Rabb, Lexington, Mississippi

Per deviled egg: 55 calories, 5 g fat, 3 g protein, 1 g carbohydrate, 109 mg cholesterol, 98 mg sodium.

Cowboy Caviar

¼ cup red wine vinegar
½ teaspoon salt
⅛ teaspoon freshly ground black pepper
Pinch of sugar
⅛ teaspoon hot pepper sauce
½ teaspoon minced garlic
¼ cup canola oil
2 (15-ounce) cans black beans,[19] rinsed and drained

2 (11-ounce) cans Mexican-style corn, drained
1 or 2 jalapeños,[44] seeded and chopped
½ cup sliced green onions
1 tablespoon fresh lime juice
1 large tomato, seeded[53] and chopped (optional)
1 avocado, diced[29] (optional)

Combine vinegar, salt, pepper, sugar, pepper sauce and garlic in small jar with tight-fitting lid. Shake well. Add oil and shake until emulsified.[G] Mix beans, corn, jalapeño and green onion in large bowl. Stir in vinegar mixture and lime juice. Cover and refrigerate at least 3 hours, stirring occasionally. (May prepare to this point a day ahead.) Add 1 teaspoon lime juice for additional zip, if desired. Stir well. Fold in tomato and avocado just before serving. Serve with curved tortilla chips or spoon-shaped corn chips.

Makes 6 cups

Per ¼-cup serving: 65 calories, 3 g fat, 2 g protein, 4 g carbohydrate, 0 mg cholesterol, 191 mg sodium.

Sauerkraut Balls

Sauerkraut balls are usually deep fried; these are baked. Make ahead and bake later.

1 (14½-ounce) can sauerkraut, drained
1 (16-ounce) package pork sausage

½ cup finely chopped onion
1 egg, lightly beaten
Dry breadcrumbs

Snip sauerkraut into small pieces. Mix sauerkraut, sausage, onion and egg in large bowl (I use my hands). Add just enough breadcrumbs to hold mixture together, about 3 tablespoons. Form into walnut-size balls with slightly dampened hands. Roll in breadcrumbs and place on sprayed foil-lined 11x17-inch jelly-roll pan. Cover tightly with foil and refrigerate several hours. Remove 30 minutes before baking. Bake uncovered at 350° for 30 minutes. Set oven to BROIL, leaving pan on middle rack. Brown tops with door ajar, being careful not to burn. Drain on paper towels. Serve hot or warm with Dijon mustard.

Makes 48 sauerkraut balls

Per ball: 49 calories, 4 g fat, 2 g protein, 2 g carbohydrate, 11 mg cholesterol, 131 mg sodium.

Big Batch Bridge Mix

"Using enough garlic powder is the secret," Marcie says.

2	cups (4 sticks) butter		Garlic powder
1	(12-ounce) box corn cereal squares (about 11 cups)	1	or 2 (12-ounce) cans roasted salted peanuts
1	(23½-ounce) box wheat cereal squares (about 13 cups)	1	(12-ounce) can roasted salted Spanish peanuts
1	(17½-ounce) box rice cereal squares (about 20 cups)	1	(15-ounce) bag thin pretzel sticks
	Celery salt	4	cups fish-shaped Cheddar or Parmesan cheese crackers
	Onion powder		

This recipe makes 12 quarts and uses two large roasting pans. If your oven cannot accommodate two pans, divide ingredients and make two batches, or halve recipe.

Melt butter in medium saucepan; set aside. Mix cereals in large plastic bag. Spray two large roasting pans and place thin layer of cereal in each. Drizzle melted butter over cereal. Sprinkle with celery salt, onion powder and garlic powder (heavy on the garlic powder). Repeat layering in both pans until cereal, butter and seasonings are used. Add half the peanuts, pretzels and fish crackers to each pan. Mix with hands, tossing to coat. Bake at 250° for 3 to 4 hours, stirring every hour with large wooden spoon.

Makes 12 quarts   Marcie Mershon, Bella Vista, Arkansas

Per ½-cup serving: 165 calories, 8 g fat, 4 g protein, 20 g carbohydrate, 10 mg cholesterol, 289 mg sodium.

Microwave Salted Pecans

It was hard for me to believe that microwave-toasted pecans could taste this great!

2½	tablespoons butter	Salt
2	cups pecan halves	

Melt butter in shallow microwave-safe dish or 9-inch glass pie plate. Add pecans, stirring to coat. Microwave on HIGH 2 minutes. Stir pecans, coating well. Heat on HIGH 2 more minutes and stir again. Place pecans on paper towels and sprinkle with salt. Let stand until dry.

Makes 6 cups   Mary Lee Skourup, Bella Vista, Arkansas

Per 2 tablespoons: 62 calories, 7 g fat, 1 g protein, 2 g carbohydrate, 6 mg cholesterol, 53 mg sodium.

Note: Whole natural almonds may be substituted for pecans.

Prissy Pecans

1 pound pecan halves	1 teaspoon ground nutmeg
½ cup (1 stick) butter	Dash of salt
¼ cup sugar	

Place single layer of pecans in foil-lined 10x15-inch jelly-roll pan. Bake at 325° for 18 to 20 minutes or until lightly browned, stirring every 5 minutes.

Meanwhile, melt butter in small saucepan and add sugar, nutmeg and salt. Stir over low heat 1 minute. Extend oven rack and pour butter mixture over pecans, tossing to coat. Slide rack back into oven and bake 5 minutes or until pecans absorb most of butter mixture, tossing two or three times. Remove and spread out pecans on wax paper or foil to dry. Do not make on humid day or pecans will be sticky.

Makes about 1 quart   Jane Swanson, Bella Vista, Arkansas

Per 2-tablespoons: 127 calories, 13 g fat, 1 g protein, 4 g carbohydrate, 8 mg cholesterol, 37 mg sodium.

Sherry Pecans variation: Increase sugar to ⅓ cup and stir in 1 tablespoon dry sherry. Bake as directed above.

Black Pepper Almonds

1 tablespoon crushed black peppercorns[21]	2 tablespoons water
1 tablespoon kosher or coarse salt	1 cup packed light brown sugar[1]
¼ cup (½ stick) butter	1 pound whole natural almonds (3 cups)

Mix pepper and salt in small bowl; set aside. Place almonds in single layer in sprayed foil-lined 10x15-inch jelly-roll pan. Bake at 325° for 15 minutes, stirring every 5 minutes. Meanwhile, melt butter in medium nonstick skillet over low heat. Add water, brown sugar and *half* the pepper mixture. Stir over low heat for 3 minutes; sugar will dissolve and mixture will foam.

Extend oven rack and pour syrup mixture over almonds; stir to coat (wooden spatulas work well). Slide rack back into oven. Bake at 325° for 5 minutes. Extend rack and stir almonds. Sprinkle with remaining pepper mixture and stir. Return to oven and bake 5 more minutes or until most of sugar mixture is absorbed. Stir almonds and pour onto sprayed piece of foil about 24 inches long, separating almonds and distributing syrup. Cool completely. Break almonds apart and store at room temperature in airtight containers. Recipe may be halved. Do not make on humid day or almonds will be sticky.

Makes 6 cups

Per ¼ cup: 142 calories, 9 g fat, 4 g protein, 12 g carbohydrate, 5 mg cholesterol, 258 mg sodium.

Vegetable Crescent Squares

1 (8-ounce) can refrigerated original crescent dinner rolls

1 (8-ounce) package regular or reduced-fat cream cheese

¾ cup light mayonnaise

2 tablespoons dry original ranch salad dressing mix

1 to 2 tablespoons butter, softened

10 to 12 tablespoons finely chopped vegetables (choose from red, yellow and green bell peppers, carrots, red and green onions, broccoli and cauliflower)

2 ounces sharp Cheddar cheese (about ½ cup grated)

Unroll crescent roll dough in 10x15-inch jelly-roll pan. Press all seams together and pat out to fit pan. Bake at 350° for 8 to 9 minutes or until lightly browned. Cool. Beat cream cheese in large bowl with mixer until fluffy. Add mayonnaise and salad dressing mix; beat until smooth. Scrape down sides. Spread butter over crust. Spread cream cheese mixture over butter. Sprinkle with mixed chopped vegetables. Finely grate Cheddar cheese over top. Cover with foil and refrigerate several hours or overnight. Cut into bite-size squares and serve. Will keep several days covered in refrigerator.

Makes 96 squares   Joye Miller, Bella Vista, Arkansas

Per piece: 23 calories, 2 g fat, 1 g protein, 2 g carbohydrate, 3 mg cholesterol, 48 mg sodium.

Spicy Artichoke Dip

There are many artichoke dips, but this one is especially good!

1 (8-ounce) package cream cheese, softened

1½ cups regular or light mayonnaise

⅛ teaspoon garlic powder

3 tablespoons fresh lemon juice

1 (13¾-ounce) can artichoke hearts or quarters, well drained and coarsely chopped

3 ounces Parmesan cheese, grated (1 cup)

1 (4-ounce) can chopped green chiles, drained

Fresh tomatoes, seeded[53] and chopped

Chopped green onions, including some tops

Beat cream cheese in large bowl with mixer until fluffy. Beat in mayonnaise, garlic powder and lemon juice until smooth. Scrape down sides. Stir in artichokes, Parmesan cheese and green chiles. Pour mixture into 10-inch pie plate or shallow baking dish. Bake at 350° for 20 to 30 minutes or until hot and bubbly. Make a circle of tomatoes around edge of dip and a circle of green onion inside tomatoes. Serve with spoon-shaped tortilla chips.

Makes 4 cups   Marge Baker, Bella Vista, Arkansas

Per 2 tablespoons: 81 calories, 7 g fat, 2 g protein, 2 g carbohydrate, 14 mg cholesterol, 185 mg sodium.

Festive Tuna Mold

½ cup cold water
2 envelopes unflavored gelatin
1 (7-ounce) and 1 (3-ounce) foil pouch albacore tuna*
1 (10¾-ounce) can tomato soup
1 (8-ounce) package cream cheese, softened and cut into pieces
1 cup mayonnaise

¼ teaspoon salt
⅛ teaspoon white pepper
1 tablespoon fresh lemon juice
½ cup finely chopped celery
½ cup finely chopped green onion, including some tops
½ teaspoon Worcestershire sauce
Dash of hot pepper sauce

Pour water into 1-cup glass measure, sprinkle in gelatin and let stand 2 minutes. Microwave on HIGH 50 seconds; stir thoroughly and let stand at least 2 minutes. Put tuna in shallow bowl and finely flake; set aside. Heat soup and cream cheese in medium saucepan over medium heat and beat with mixer until smooth. Stir in gelatin. Cool. Beat in mayonnaise, salt, pepper and lemon juice until smooth. Stir in celery, green onion, Worcestershire sauce and pepper sauce. Fold in tuna. Pour mixture into sprayed 6-cup fish mold or other 6-cup mold. Cover with plastic wrap and refrigerate until firm or up to two days. Unmold⁵⁴ fish mold onto glass or silver platter and sprinkle with paprika and finely snipped parsley. Surround with lettuce leaves. Serve with assorted crackers.

* Two (6-ounce) cans albacore tuna (5 ounces drained weight) may be substituted for foil pouches.

Makes 12 servings   Betty Mossman, Bella Vista, Arkansas

Per serving: 248 calories, 23 g fat, 9 g protein, 5 g carbohydrate, 34 mg cholesterol, 425 mg sodium.

Almond Cheese Ball

1 (8-ounce) package cream cheese, softened
½ cup mayonnaise
7 slices bacon, cooked and crumbled¹⁴
1 tablespoon chopped green onions

½ teaspoon dried dill weed, crushed
⅛ teaspoon pepper
½ cup coarsely chopped toasted sliced almonds or enough to cover cheese ball

Beat cream cheese in medium bowl with mixer until fluffy; add mayonnaise and beat until smooth. Stir in bacon, green onion, dill and pepper. Cover and refrigerate overnight. Form mixture into ball and roll in chopped almonds. Serve with shredded wheat crackers or thin wheat wafers.

Makes 8 servings   Nancy Rorick, Longmont, Colorado

Per serving: 283 calories, 29 g fat, 6 g protein, 3 g carbohydrate, 41 mg cholesterol, 252 mg sodium.

Hot Crab Dip

2 (8-ounce) packages cream cheese, softened
2 tablespoons milk
5 teaspoons white wine Worcestershire sauce*
   Hot pepper sauce to taste
1 teaspoon crab or shrimp boil seasoning, or use seasoned salt
½ teaspoon lemon pepper
2 (6-ounce) cans crabmeat, drained, or 1 cup pasteurized crabmeat
⅓ cup plus 2 tablespoons grated Parmesan cheese
⅓ cup plus 2 tablespoons chopped green onions
¼ cup chopped walnuts

Beat cream cheese in medium bowl with mixer until fluffy. Beat in milk, Worcestershire sauce, pepper sauce, crab boil seasoning and lemon pepper until smooth. Fold in crabmeat, ⅓ cup Parmesan cheese and ⅓ cup green onion. Spoon dip into shallow baking dish or 10-inch pie plate. Sprinkle with walnuts, remaining 2 tablespoons Parmesan cheese and remaining 2 tablespoons green onion. Bake at 350° for 30 minutes or until hot and bubbly. Serve with melba toast or *Crostini*.

* *If white wine Worcestershire sauce is not readily available, substitute lesser amount of regular Worcestershire sauce to taste.*

Makes 5 cups   Ardith Bradshaw, West Memphis, Arkansas

Per 2 tablespoons: 53 calories, 4 g fat, 3 g protein, 1 g carbohydrate, 21 mg cholesterol, 120 mg sodium.

Art's Favorite Shrimp Dip

2 (4-ounce) cans tiny shrimp
1 (8-ounce) package cream cheese, softened
⅓ cup mayonnaise
½ teaspoon grated onion[55]
3 dashes of hot pepper sauce
½ teaspoon Worcestershire sauce
½ teaspoon fresh lemon juice

Rinse shrimp in cold water; drain and pat dry. Beat cream cheese in medium bowl with mixer until fluffy. Beat in mayonnaise until smooth. Scrape down sides. Blend in onion, pepper sauce, Worcestershire sauce and lemon juice. Beat in shrimp until shredded and combined. Add more mayonnaise, if dry. Adjust seasoning. Cover and refrigerate at least 1 hour. Serve with ridged potato chips.

Note: You may substitute and stir in 2 cups chopped cooked fresh shrimp or 2 cups chopped thawed frozen boiled shrimp in place of beating in canned shrimp. Serve as spread or dip.

Makes 2 cups

Per 2-tablespoons: 94 calories, 9 g fat, 4 g protein, 0 g carbohydrate, 46 mg cholesterol, 233 mg sodium.

Colorado Spinach Dip

1 (10-ounce) package frozen chopped spinach, thawed and well drained[43]	½ teaspoon dried dill weed, crushed
	¼ cup chopped green onions, including some tops
1 (1.8-ounce) package leek soup mix, less 1 tablespoon, or use 1 (1.4-ounce) package vegetable soup mix (use whole package)	½ to 1 teaspoon seasoned salt
	1½ tablespoons fresh lemon juice
	1 (8-ounce) can sliced water chestnuts, rinsed and drained
1 cup sour cream	1 medium-size round loaf of sourdough, French or pumpernickel bread
1 cup mayonnaise	
½ cup snipped flat-leaf parsley	

Mix spinach, soup mix, sour cream, mayonnaise, parsley, dill, green onion, seasoned salt, lemon juice and water chestnuts in large bowl. Transfer to food processor, if possible, and pulse several times to give dip a blended consistency. Cover and refrigerate several hours or overnight.

Slice off upper third of bread loaf and hollow out center, leaving 1-inch thick walls. Cut removed bread into bite-size pieces. (May brush outside of hollowed-out sourdough or French bread loaf with vegetable oil. Place on baking sheet and bake at 375° until crusty outside and golden inside.) Stir dip and pour into bread "bowl." Serve with bread pieces, potato chips and wheat crackers. Also serve with assorted vegetable dippers: carrots and celery sticks, red or green bell pepper strips, jícama[G] slices, cherry tomatoes, whole mushrooms and broccoli florets. When dip diminishes or is finished, eat the bread bowl!

Makes about 3 cups   Eda Mills, Longmont, Colorado

Per 2-tablespoons: 98 calories, 10 g fat, 1 g protein, 71 g carbohydrate, 7 mg cholesterol, 195 mg sodium.

Sweet Onion Dip

2 cups finely chopped sweet onion (Vidalia, Maui, Walla Walla, Colorado #4166 or Texas #1015)	3 ounces Parmesan or Asiago cheese, freshly grated (1 cup)
	2 cups mayonnaise
4 ounces Swiss cheese, shredded (1 cup)	Paprika

Mix onion, cheeses and mayonnaise in medium bowl. Pour into 10-inch quiche dish or large pie plate. Sprinkle with paprika. Bake at 350° for 25 to 30 minutes or until hot. Serve with round buttery crackers or ridged potato chips.

Makes about 4 cups

Per 2 tablespoons: 130 calories, 14 g fat, 3 g protein, 1 g carbohydrate, 11 mg cholesterol, 146 mg sodium.

Green Apple Dip

1 (8-ounce) package cream cheese, softened
¾ cup packed light brown sugar[1]
1 tablespoon vanilla extract

½ cup coarsely chopped dry roasted peanuts[21]
2 tart green apples, cut into wedges[7]

Beat cream cheese in medium bowl with mixer until fluffy. Beat in brown sugar and vanilla until smooth. Stir in peanuts. Cover and refrigerate several hours. Serve with apple wedges as dippers.

Makes about 1½ cups   Katherine Forsyth, Boulder, Colorado

Per serving: 235 calories, 9 g fat, 4 g protein, 36 g carbohydrate, 6 mg cholesterol, 32 mg sodium.

Caramel Almond Dip

1 (18-ounce) container caramel apple dip
1 (6-ounce) container vanilla custard yogurt (thick and creamy)
Dash of ground nutmeg

1 tablespoon almond-flavored liqueur or ½ teaspoon almond extract
⅓ cup finely chopped dry roasted peanuts[21]

Blend caramel dip, yogurt, nutmeg and liqueur in medium bowl with mixer. Cover and refrigerate several hours. Stir in peanuts shortly before serving. Serve with apple and pear wedges, whole strawberries and banana chunks.[7]

Makes 2¼ cups

Per 2-tablespoons: 115 calories, 5 g fat, 2 g protein, 16 g carbohydrate, 3 mg cholesterol, 59 mg sodium.

Blue Cheese and Pineapple Spread

1 (8-ounce) package cream cheese, softened
⅓ cup blue cheese, crumbled
1 tablespoon finely chopped candied or crystallized ginger[G]
1 (8-ounce) can crushed pineapple in juice, well drained

½ cup chopped toasted pecans
1 teaspoon dried minced onion, or 1 tablespoon finely chopped green onions
⅛ teaspoon red pepper flakes
¼ teaspoon Greek seasoning
2 teaspoons sugar

Beat cream cheese and blue cheese in medium bowl with mixer until smooth. Stir in candied ginger, pineapple, pecans, dried onion, pepper flakes, Greek seasoning and sugar. Refrigerate in covered container. Stir and serve with crackers.

Make 1⅓ cups

Per tablespoon: 72 calories, 6 g fat, 2 g protein, 3 g carbohydrate, 14 mg cholesterol, 74 mg sodium.

Apricot Cream Cheese Dip

1 (8-ounce) package cream cheese, softened
¼ teaspoon garlic powder
½ teaspoon dried minced onion
1 tablespoon finely chopped candied or crystallized ginger[G]

1 tablespoon toasted sliced almonds[5]
1 teaspoon finely chopped seeded jalapeño, or to taste
⅓ cup apricot or plum preserves, or ⅓ cup *Hot Pepper Peach Preserves*

Beat cream cheese in medium bowl with mixer until smooth. Blend in garlic powder, dried onion, candied ginger, almonds, jalapeño and apricot preserves. Refrigerate in covered container 3 to 4 hours. Serve in small cheese crock with round buttery crackers or shredded wheat crackers.

Makes 1¼ cup

Per tablespoon: 72 calories, 5 g fat, 1 g protein, 5 g carbohydrate, 16 mg cholesterol, 45 mg sodium.

Cranberry Chutney Dip

1 (8-ounce) package cream cheese, softened
½ teaspoon curry powder, or to taste
Ginger's Blue Ribbon Chutney, or apple-cranberry chutney

6 slices bacon, cooked and crumbled[14]
5 small green onions, sliced, including some tops

Beat cream cheese in medium bowl with mixer until fluffy. Add curry and beat until smooth. Spread over bottom of small quiche dish or other shallow-rimmed dish. Cover and chill. Spread layer of chutney over cream cheese. Sprinkle with crumbled bacon and green onion. Serve with wheat wafers.

Makes about 2 cups   Evie Tate, Bella Vista, Arkansas

Per tablespoon: 50 calories, 3 g fat, 1 g protein, 4 g carbohydrate, 9 mg cholesterol, 47 mg sodium.

Chicken Salad Puffs

2 cups *My Favorite Chicken Salad*   48 *Mini Puffs*

Prepare chicken salad. Cover and refrigerate 2 hours or overnight. Slice off top third of puffs. Remove and discard any webbing inside. Fill bottoms with 1 tablespoon chicken salad and cover with tops. Garnish with fresh parsley.

Makes 48 salad puffs

Per salad puff: 43 calories, 3 g fat, 2 g protein, 2 g carbohydrate, 33 mg cholesterol, 73 mg sodium.

Big Bunch Punch

A refreshing punch, good for large gatherings.

5 quarts cranberry juice
1 (12-ounce) can frozen orange juice, thawed
1 (12-ounce) can frozen grapefruit juice, thawed

1 (12-ounce) can frozen lemonade, thawed
2 (1-liter) bottles ginger ale, chilled
2 (1-liter) bottles soda water, chilled

Mix cranberry juice, concentrated orange juice and concentrated grapefruit juice in large container; add concentrated lemonade and stir well. Refrigerate. Pour half the juice mixture into large punch bowl. Stir in 1 bottle ginger ale and 1 bottle soda water. Add ice ring or stir in ice cubes. Replenish with remaining juice mixture, ginger ale and soda water. Add ice, if needed.

Makes 100 servings   Louise Atteridg, Granby, Colorado

Per ½ cup: 59 calories, 0 g fat, 0 g protein, 15 g carbohydrate, 0 mg cholesterol, 4 mg sodium.

Hot Perked Punch

Bring out that old percolator for this hearty beverage, or use Alternative Directions.

2 cups cranberry juice
2½ cups pineapple juice
1¾ cups water
½ cup brown sugar

1 teaspoon whole allspice
1 teaspoon whole cloves
3 whole cinnamon sticks

Pour cranberry and pineapple juice into 10-cup percolator. Mix water and brown sugar in glass measure; add to percolator. Put allspice, cloves and cinnamon sticks in percolator basket. Perk. Serve hot.

Makes 12 servings   Terry VanderVeen Bright, Lynchburg, Virginia

Per ½ cup: 93 calories, 0 g fat, 0 g protein, 24 g carbohydrate, 0 mg cholesterol, 7 mg sodium.

Alternative Directions: Pour cranberry and pineapple juice into large saucepan. Add water and brown sugar; stir until sugar dissolves. Put spices in brew bag^G or bouquet-garni bag,^G or tie in piece of cheesecloth; add to pan. Bring to boil. Reduce heat and simmer covered 7 to 10 minutes. Remove brew bag and serve.

Lemonade Iced Tea

3	quarts water	½ to ¾ cup sugar
8	regular-size tea bags	1	(1-liter) bottle ginger ale, chilled
1	(12-ounce) can frozen lemonade		

Boil water in large pot. Remove from heat and add tea bags. Cover and steep 10 minutes; remove tea bags. Mix in concentrated lemonade. Stir in sugar until dissolved. Pour into large container; cover and refrigerate. Add ginger ale just before serving.

Makes 18 servings   Eleanor Weathersby, Dawsonville, Georgia

Per 8 ounce serving: 87 calories, 0 g fat, 0 g protein, 23 g carbohydrate, 0 mg cholesterol, 11 mg sodium.

Cranberry Raspberry Iced Tea

3	quarts cold water	1	(11½-ounce) can frozen cranberry-raspberry concentrate, thawed
8	family-size tea bags, or 24 regular-size tea bags		

Pour water into large jar or pitcher.* Add tea bags, cover and let stand 7 hours. Remove and discard tea bags. Stir in concentrate and sweeten, if desired. Serve over ice with sprig of fresh mint.

I use a gallon-size pickle jar with lid. Hang tea bag strings over side of jar; add lid and tighten to keep bags suspended in water.

Makes 3 quarts

Per 8 ounces: 86 calories, 0 g fat, 1 g protein, 21 g carbohydrate, 0 mg cholesterol, 15 mg sodium.

Frozen Margaritas

	Ice to fill 5-cup blender	1	(12-ounce) can frozen limeade
8	ounces tequila		Lime wedge
3	ounces Triple Sec		Coarse salt

Put ice in blender. Pour in tequila and Triple Sec. Add frozen limeade and blend on high until slushy. Moisten rims of margarita glasses with lime wedge. Dip rims into saucer of coarse salt. Fill glasses and serve.

Makes 6 servings

Per serving: 237 calories, 0 g fat, 0 g protein, 32 g carbohydrate, 0 mg cholesterol, 358 mg sodium.

Cranberry Cordial

With advance planning, you can have this pretty, delicious cordial ready for the holidays.

1 (12-ounce) package fresh cranberries	2 cups sugar
	2 cups vodka

Wash and drain cranberries. Coarsely chop in food processor with metal blade or chop with food chopper. Transfer to large bowl and stir in sugar and vodka. Pour into large glass jar and cover. Store in cool dark place. Stir once a day for 21 days. Strain through strainer lined with dampened coffee filter or dampened cheesecloth.[41] Pour into decorative bottles and cork or cap. Makes nice holiday gifts. Serve in cordial glasses, or drizzle over sliced fruit arranged on top of cheesecakes.

Makes 2 pints

Per 2 ounces: 161 calories, 0 g fat, 0 g protein, 25 g carbohydrate, 0 mg cholesterol, 1 mg sodium.

Peach Sangría

2 (750-ml) bottles Soleo white wine or peach chardonay	2 teaspoons grenadine syrup
1 cup orange juice	½ cup *Simple Syrup* (optional)
1 cup peach schnapps	1 (16-ounce) package frozen unsweetened sliced peaches (optional)

Mix wine, orange juice, schnapps and grenadine in large container. For sweeter sangría, stir in simple syrup to taste. Stir in peaches. Refrigerate 2 hours or until chilled. Serve over crushed ice in balloon-shaped wine glasses. Thread wedges of lime, lemon and orange onto wooden skewers and place one across top of each glass.

Makes 8½ to 10½ cups

Per ½ cup: 126 calories, 0 g fat, 0 g protein, 11 g carbohydrate, 0 mg cholesterol, 7 mg sodium.

Simple Syrup

¾ cup sugar	¾ cup water

Mix sugar and water in small saucepan. Cook over medium heat until sugar dissolves. Use in recipes calling for simple syrup.

Makes 1 cup

Per tablespoon: 36 calories, 0 g fat, 0 g protein, 9 g carbohydrate, 0 mg cholesterol, 0 mg sodium.

Breads

Breads

Lemon Bread

Small loaves are nice to have on hand in the freezer.

½ cup (1 stick) butter or margarine,[50] softened
½ cup shortening
2 cups sugar
4 eggs, room temperature
3 cups flour
1 teaspoon baking soda
½ teaspoon salt

1 cup buttermilk[42]
1 tablespoon grated lemon zest
1 cup chopped toasted nuts (optional)

Glaze:
1 cup sugar
⅓ cup fresh lemon juice
1 teaspoon grated lemon zest

Beat butter, shortening and sugar in large bowl with mixer until creamed, about 2 minutes. Add eggs one at a time, beating well after each addition. Scrape down sides. Whisk flour, baking soda and salt in separate bowl.[2] Beat into creamed mixture alternately with buttermilk, beginning and ending with flour mixture. Scrape down sides. Stir in lemon zest and nuts. Spoon batter equally[25] into two sprayed 9x5-inch or five 5x3-inch loaf pans.[4] Bake at 350° for 50 to 60 minutes for large pans, 30 to 35 minutes for small pans, or until wooden pick inserted in centers comes out clean. Meanwhile, prepare glaze.

Punch holes in tops of loaves with meat fork or wooden skewer while loaves are still warm in pans. Spoon glaze equally over loaves and let stand until absorbed. Cool. Remove loaves from pans when thoroughly cooled. Serve with *Chicken and Strawberry Tossed Salad*. Also a good dessert bread. Wrap extra loaves in foil and freeze.

Glaze: Mix sugar, lemon juice and lemon zest in small bowl. Stir well until sugar dissolves (warming lemon juice in microwave will help dissolve sugar). Stir glaze frequently while bread is baking.

Makes 2 large loaves or 5 small loaves   Hazel Woodson, Farmington, New Mexico

Per 1/16 large loaf: 201 calories, 9 g fat, 3 g protein, 27 g carbohydrate, 35 mg cholesterol, 118 mg sodium.

Banana Nut Bread

⅔ cup (10⅔ tablespoons) butter, softened	½ teaspoon baking powder
2 cups sugar	1 (5-ounce) can evaporated milk
2 eggs, room temperature	1 teaspoon butter-flavored flavoring
2¼ cups flour	1 teaspoon vanilla extract
¼ teaspoon salt	3 ripe medium bananas, mashed[7]
1 teaspoon baking soda	¾ cup chopped toasted pecans

Beat butter and sugar in large bowl with mixer until light, fluffy and creamed, about 2 minutes. Beat in eggs one at a time, beating well after each addition until no yellow streaks remain. Scrape down sides. Whisk flour, salt, baking soda and baking powder in medium bowl.[2] Beat into creamed mixture alternately with evaporated milk, beginning and ending with flour mixture (beat in about ¾ cup flour mixture and ½ can evaporated milk alternately each time). Scrape down sides. Beat in butter flavoring and vanilla. Fold in bananas and pecans. Spoon batter equally[25] into two sprayed 8½x4½-inch loaf pans dusted with sugar. Gently bounce pans on counter several times to remove air bubbles. Bake at 350° for 60 minutes[4] or until wooden pick inserted in centers comes out clean. Cool in pans on rack 10 minutes. Remove loaves to rack. Cool completely.[27]

Makes 2 loaves   Terry VanderVeen Bright, Lynchburg, Virginia

Per 1/16 loaf: 151 calories, 6 g fat, 2 g protein, 23 g carbohydrate, 25 mg cholesterol, 109 mg sodium.

Mango Bread

3 eggs, room temperature	1 teaspoon ground cinnamon
1¼ cups sugar	¼ teaspoon salt
1 teaspoon vanilla extract	½ cup chopped toasted nuts
¾ cup vegetable oil	1 cup raisins
2 cups flour	2 cups chopped ripe mangoes[67]
1 teaspoon baking soda	

Beat eggs, sugar, vanilla and oil in large bowl with mixer until combined. Whisk flour, baking soda, cinnamon and salt in medium bowl[2] and blend into egg mixture. Stir in nuts and raisins; fold in mangoes. Pour batter into two sprayed 8½x4½-inch loaf pans. Gently bounce pans on counter to remove air bubbles. Bake at 325° for 1 hour[4] or until wooden pick inserted in centers comes out clean. Cool in pans on rack 10 minutes. Remove loaves to rack. Cool completely.[27]

Makes 2 loaves   Mary Ann Evans, San Jose, California

Per 1/12 loaf: 194 calories, 9 g fat, 3 g protein, 26 g carbohydrate, 27 mg cholesterol, 84 mg sodium.

Banana Date Nut Bread

Very moist. Freezes well.

½ cup (1 stick) butter, cut into
    pieces
1 cup sugar
2 eggs, lightly beaten
1 teaspoon vanilla extract
3 ripe medium bananas, mashed

1¼ cups flour, *divided*
¼ teaspoon salt
1 teaspoon baking soda
½ cup chopped dates
1 cup chopped toasted pecans

Beat butter and sugar in large bowl with mixer until creamed, about 2 minutes. Scrape down sides. Beat in eggs and vanilla on low, about 1 minute. Fold in bananas. Whisk 1 cup flour, salt and baking soda in medium bowl.[2] Mix into creamed mixture until just combined. Dust dates and pecans with remaining ¼ cup flour in small bowl; fold into batter along with dusting flour. Pour batter into sprayed 9x5-inch loaf pan. *Let stand 20 minutes.* Bake at 350° for 1 hour or until wooden pick inserted in center comes out clean.[4] Cool in pan on rack 10 minutes. Remove loaf to rack and cool completely.[27] Cut into slices and cut slices in half. Arrange on serving plate dusted with confectioners' sugar.

Makes 1 loaf

Per 1/16 loaf: 189 calories, 11 g fat, 2 g protein, 23 g carbohydrate, 27 mg cholesterol, 187 mg sodium.

Blueberry Muffins

The recipe card from Jeanne's great aunt read, "Good to take to friends!" Jeanne agrees and adds, " This recipe calls for very little sugar, and if you keep blueberries in the freezer, you will usually have the other ingredients on hand."

1½ cups flour
½ cup sugar
2 teaspoons baking powder
½ teaspoon salt
½ cup milk

½ cup vegetable oil
1 egg, lightly beaten
1 teaspoon vanilla extract (optional)
1 cup fresh blueberries, rinsed and
    drained, or frozen blueberries[32]

Whisk flour, sugar, baking powder and salt in medium bowl.[2] Whisk milk, oil, egg and vanilla in small bowl. Stir into flour mixture until *just* combined (mixture will be thick). Fold in blueberries.[65] Spray muffin cups or paper baking cups in muffin tins and fill two-thirds full (¼-cup dry measure or ice cream scoop works well). Bake at 400° for 22 to 25 minutes.[4]

Makes 12 muffins   Jeanne Rabb, Boulder, Colorado

Per muffin: 150 calories, 10 g fat, 2 g protein, 13 g carbohydrate, 19 mg cholesterol, 161 mg sodium.

Sour Cream Muffins

1½	cups flour	1	cup sour cream
¾	cup sugar	¼	cup milk or orange juice
1½	teaspoons baking powder	6	tablespoons butter, melted and
½	teaspoon baking soda		cooled
½	teaspoon salt	1	teaspoon vanilla
1	egg, lightly beaten	½	cup chopped toasted pecans

Whisk flour, sugar, baking powder, baking soda and salt in large bowl.[2] Whisk egg, sour cream and milk in medium bowl; mix in butter and vanilla. Fold into flour mixture (batter will be slightly thick and lumpy). Do not overmix or muffins will be tough. Stir in nuts.

Spray muffin cups and fill two-thirds full. Bake at 400° for 18 to 20 minutes.[4] Cool in tins 3 minutes. Run knife around muffins and remove to rack. Cool. Frost with *Confectioners' Sugar Glaze* prepared with lemon extract. Sprinkle tops with additional chopped toasted pecans.

Makes 12 muffins

Per muffin: 231 calories, 13 g fat, 3 g protein, 27 g carbohydrate, 25 mg cholesterol, 258 mg sodium.

Herb Pita Toast

Keep pita bread in the freezer. Thaw in microwave and in minutes you can have crisp crunchy pita toast to serve with soups, salads or casseroles.

4	pitas (pocket bread)	Your favorite herb blend, or
	Olive oil, vegetable oil, or	garlic salt mixed with grated
	cooking spray	Parmesan cheese

Cut pitas in half and split pockets apart. Brush insides with olive oil or spray. Sprinkle with herb blend. Place herb-side up on ungreased baking sheets. (May prepare ahead to this point. Cover with foil and set aside.) Bake uncovered in upper third of oven at 425° for 10 minutes or until golden brown and crisp.

Makes 16 pieces

Per serving: 71 calories, 3 g fat, 3 g protein, 9 g carbohydrate, 2 mg cholesterol, 171 mg sodium.

Cinnamon Pita Triangles variation: Cut whole pitas into triangles with kitchen shears. Separate triangles and brush insides with vegetable oil or spray. Mix equal amounts of cinnamon and sugar in small bowl and sprinkle over pita triangles. Bake as directed above.

Herb Roll-ups

Unique bread accompaniment.

18 slices firm, white sandwich bread, crusts removed	1 teaspoon dried basil, crushed
½ cup (1 stick) butter, softened	½ teaspoon dried summer savory, or Italian herb seasoning, crushed
2 tablespoons finely chopped fresh chives	¼ teaspoon salt (optional)
	Butter-flavored cooking spray

Roll bread slices with a rolling pin to flatten. Mix butter, chives, basil, summer savory and salt in small bowl. Spread slices with butter mixture, covering to edge. Roll up from corner to corner and place on foil-lined baking sheet. Spray roll-ups with butter-flavored cooking spray, turn over and spray again. Flash freeze[26] on baking sheet seamside down. Transfer to ziptop bags and store in freezer. Bake frozen roll-ups on ungreased baking sheet at 400° for 15 minutes, or thaw and bake at 350° for 15 minutes. Serve with soups, salads or casseroles.

Makes 18 roll-ups   Dody Martin, Boulder, Colorado

Per roll-up: 110 calories, 6 g fat, 2 g protein, 12 g carbohydrate, 0 mg cholesterol, 189 mg sodium.

Herb Tortillas

4 (8-inch) flour tortillas (soft taco size)	Your favorite herb blend, or coarse sea salt

Spray both sides of tortillas with cooking spray and sprinkle one side with herb blend. Place tortillas herb-side up on large foil-lined baking sheet. Bake at 400° for 8 to 10 minutes or until lightly browned and crisp (like a large cracker). Serve with soups or salads. Store in airtight containers.

Makes 4 servings

Per serving: 160 calories, 3 g fat, 3 g protein, 27 g carbohydrate, 0 mg cholesterol, 430 mg sodium.

Herb Tortilla Strips variation: Cut sprayed unbaked **Herb Tortillas** into ¾-inch strips with kitchen shears. Place on foil-lined baking sheet and bake at 400° for 6 to 8 minutes or until crisp and brown. Serve with soups or salads.

Cinnamon Tortilla Strips variation: Mix ⅓ cup sugar, 1 teaspoon cinnamon and ⅛ teaspoon nutmeg in empty spice jar. Shake well. Sprinkle over one side of sprayed unbaked tortillas. Cut into ¾-inch strips. Place on foil-lined baking sheet and bake at 400° for 6 to 8 minutes or until crisp and brown. Serve with chicken salad or as bread accompaniment for brunch.

Irish Soda Bread

2 cups flour	1 egg, room temperature[88]
½ cup sugar	1 cup sour cream
½ teaspoon baking soda	¾ cup dark or golden raisins
1 teaspoon baking powder	1 teaspoon caraway seeds
¼ teaspoon salt	Butter-flavored cooking spray

Whisk flour, sugar, baking soda, baking powder and salt in large bowl.[2] Stir in egg, sour cream and raisins until just combined. Turn dough out onto lightly floured surface and shape into loaf. Put in well-greased 8½x4½-inch loaf pan. Sprinkle top with caraway seeds and spray with butter-flavored cooking spray. Bake at 325° for 1 hour.[4] Remove from oven and spray again. Serve warm with butter.

Makes 1 loaf

Per 1/16 loaf: 138 calories, 4 g fat, 3 g protein, 24 g carbohydrate, 20 mg cholesterol, 108 mg sodium.

Natchez Bread

A delicious and different accompaniment to any meal.

1 (1-pound) loaf French bread	2 tablespoons snipped flat-leaf parsley (optional)
½ cup (1 stick) butter	4 ounces Monterey Jack cheese, shredded (1 cup)
½ cup regular or light mayonnaise	
¾ cup chopped ripe olives	
1 tablespoon chopped green onions	

Cut loaf in half horizontally. Melt butter in small saucepan over low heat. Cool. Whisk mayonnaise into butter. Stir in olives, green onion, parsley and cheese. Spread on cut sides of bread halves. Center each half on large piece of foil, bring up sides and double or triple fold over top to enclose. Fold in ends to seal packet. Refrigerate overnight. Bake sealed packets at 350° for 15 to 20 minutes. Unwrap and slice diagonally into 2-inch pieces. Serve warm. For crusty bread, unfold foil and crush around sides of bread before baking.

Makes about 20 slices   Sandy Black, Madison, Mississippi

Per slice: 175 calories, 12 g fat, 5 g protein, 13 g carbohydrate, 13 mg cholesterol, 329 mg sodium.

Cornbread

¼	cup vegetable oil	4	teaspoons baking powder
1	cup white cornmeal	2	to 4 tablespoons sugar
1	cup flour	2	eggs
¾	to 1 teaspoon salt	1	cup milk

Preheat oven to 400°. Pour oil into 10-inch iron skillet and heat in oven until very hot, about 5 minutes. Meanwhile, whisk cornmeal, flour, salt, baking powder and sugar in large bowl.[2] Lightly whisk eggs in medium bowl, add milk and whisk until frothy. Pour into cornmeal mixture, mixing until just combined. Remove skillet from oven and pour hot oil into batter. Stir until oil is just incorporated. Pour batter into hot skillet and return to oven. Bake at 400° for 25 minutes or until lightly browned on top. Cut into wedges.

Makes 4 to 6 servings (8 cups crumbled)

Per serving of 6: 316 calories, 13 g fat, 8 g protein, 43 g carbohydrate, 77 mg cholesterol, 559 mg sodium.

Baking Pan variation: Preheat oven. Whisk dry ingredients in large bowl as directed above. Do not heat oil, but mix into milk mixture. Quickly stir into dry ingredients until just combined. Pour mixture into sprayed 8x8-inch baking pan and bake as directed above. Cut into 9 squares.

Cornbread Muffins variation: Mix batter as directed for baking pan. Fill sprayed muffin cups two-thirds full. Bake at 350° for 30 to 35 minutes or until golden brown. Makes 12 muffins.

Cranberry Cornbread Muffins variation: Stir ½ cup dried cranberries into batter just before filling muffin cups two-thirds full. Bake as directed above.

Seasoning Cast Iron Cookware

New cast iron cookware is gray in color; after usage it turns black. Wash new cookware in hot soapy water with stiff brush. Rinse and dry completely. Rub cookware inside and out with solid shortening (not butter-flavored) or use vegetable oil (next best). Place upside-down on top shelf of oven with foil on bottom shelf to catch any drips. Bake at 250° for 1½ hours. Turn off heat. Let cookware cool down in oven. Wipe with paper towels and store in dry place. Frying bacon, hamburgers or other fatty foods will help season cookware.

To reseason an iron skillet: Heat skillet on top of stove until almost smoking. Turn off heat and sprinkle inside with salt. Scrape salt with inverted metal spatula and rub with paper towel. Wipe clean. Dip paper towel in vegetable oil and rub inside of skillet. Reheat on top of stove, wipe out and cool.

Southern Cornbread

1½	tablespoons vegetable oil	1	tablespoon sugar (optional)
1	cup white cornmeal*	1	teaspoon salt
½	cup flour	1	egg
1	teaspoon baking powder	1	to 1¼ cups buttermilk
½	teaspoon baking soda		

Preheat oven to 450°. Pour oil into well-seasoned 9-inch iron skillet; heat in oven until oil is very hot, about 5 minutes. Meanwhile, whisk cornmeal, flour, baking powder, baking soda, sugar and salt in medium bowl.[2] Add egg and 1 cup buttermilk, whisking until just combined. (Mixture should be like pancake batter. If thick, add more buttermilk.) Pour hot oil from skillet into batter; stir until oil is just incorporated. Pour batter into hot skillet. Bake at 450° for 20 minutes. If desired, brown top by broiling[13] in upper third of oven. Let stand in skillet 5 minutes. Remove and cut into wedges. Serve warm with butter.

** If using stoneground cornmeal, which has a good texture for **Cornbread Dressing**, buttermilk may need to be increased to 1½ cups for right consistency.*

Makes 8 servings

Per serving: 145 calories, 4 g fat, 4 g protein, 23 g carbohydrate, 28 mg cholesterol, 439 mg sodium.

Southern Cornbread Cornsticks variation: Pour 1½ tablespoons oil into small bowl. Dip pastry brush or small paintbrush in oil and brush two well-seasoned iron cornstick pans (see **Seasoning Cast Iron Cookware**). *Set remaining oil aside.* Heat pans in preheated 450° oven until very hot. Meanwhile, prepare batter as directed above, but do not heat set-aside oil; whisk unheated oil into batter until just incorporated. Pour batter into hot cornstick pans two-thirds full using ¼-cup dry measure–do not overfill. Bake at 450° for 15 minutes or until cornsticks are brown on bottom and begin to pull away from sides. Broil[13] as directed above to brown tops, if desired. Remove cornsticks from pans and serve warm with butter.

Makes 12 cornsticks

Per cornstick: 97 calories, 3 g fat, 3 g protein, 15 g carbohydrate, 19 mg cholesterol, 293 mg sodium.

Baking Powder Test
Stir ¼ teaspoon baking powder into ¼ cup tap water.
Baking powder will fizz if still active.

Savory Corn Cakes

2 to 3 tablespoons plus ¼ cup vegetable oil
¼ cup chopped green onions
1 tablespoon finely chopped seeded jalapeño[44]
1 garlic clove, minced
1 (11-ounce) can Mexican corn, drained
Freshly ground black pepper
½ cup cornmeal

½ cup flour
1½ teaspoon baking powder
½ teaspoon salt
⅛ teaspoon cayenne pepper
1 egg
⅔ cup milk
1 tablespoon snipped fresh chives, or finely chopped green onion tops

Heat 1 tablespoon oil in medium skillet. Stir in green onion and jalapeño. Sauté until tender, about 1½ minutes. Add garlic and sauté 30 seconds. Stir in corn; add pepper to taste. Set aside.

Whisk cornmeal, flour, baking powder, salt and cayenne pepper in medium bowl.[2] Whisk egg, milk and ¼ cup oil in separate bowl until frothy. Add all at once to cornmeal mixture and stir until just combined. Mix in corn mixture and chives.

Heat 1 tablespoon oil in large nonstick skillet over medium-high heat. Add ¼-cup batter for each corn cake. Cook six at a time about 2 minutes or until golden; turn with wide spatula and cook 2 more minutes. Drain on paper towels. Cook six more, adding more oil if needed. Place in single layer on baking sheet, cover loosely with foil and keep warm up to 30 minutes in 200° oven. Serve as appetizers with *Salsa* and sour cream, as a side dish for grilled meat or serve for breakfast with sausage or ham.

Makes 12 corn cakes

Per corn cake: 156 calories, 9 g fat, 3 g protein, 16 g carbohydrate, 20 mg cholesterol, 427 mg sodium.

Cornbread Dressing

Sheila Thomas and Ardith Bradshaw at Wimmer could not believe that there is no sage in this dressing—there isn't! My family likes dressing without sage. Add sage to taste, if desired.

1	recipe *Cornbread*	¼	cup snipped parsley
6	slices white bread	3	cups plus ¼ cup chicken broth
2	large freshly baked or purchased freezer biscuits, baked (optional) (do not use canned biscuits)	1	teaspoon chicken bouillon granules
¾	cup (1½ sticks) butter	¼	teaspoon celery salt
1	cup finely chopped onion	1	egg, lightly beaten
1	cup finely chopped celery	¼	cup turkey pan drippings (optional)

Make cornbread one day ahead. Break into chunks in large bowl and cover with paper towel. Let stand overnight. Next day place bread slices on rack and dry out several hours, or place slices on baking sheet in 200° oven 10 to 15 minutes, turning after 5 minutes; cool on rack. Coarsely crumble cornbread in bowl. Break or tear bread slices into small pieces and add to cornbread. Crumble in biscuits.

Melt butter in medium saucepan. Sauté onion, celery and parsley until tender, about 5 minutes. Stir in 3 cups chicken broth, bouillon granules and celery salt. Heat until almost boiling. Pour over cornbread mixture and stir to combine. Mix in additional ¼ cup broth if dry. Season with salt and pepper. Stir in egg. Cover and refrigerate at least 1 hour or until ready to bake. Stir pan drippings into dressing if used. Spoon into sprayed 9x13-inch baking dish, making six to eight large mounds. Spoon extra dressing in mounds into sprayed pie plate. Reserve two tablespoons dressing for making *Giblet Gravy*, if desired. Bake at 350° for 35 to 45 minutes or until golden brown and hot. Serve with *Giblet Gravy* or *Turkey Gravy*.

Makes 8 to 10 servings

Per serving of 10: 295 calories, 15 g fat, 7 g protein, 33 g carbohydrate, 69 mg cholesterol, 778 mg sodium.

Blueberry Cornmeal Muffins

½	cup yellow cornmeal	1	egg, lightly beaten
1½	cups flour	⅓	cup (5⅓ tablespoons) butter, melted and cooled
½	or ⅔ cup sugar*		
2	teaspoons baking powder	⅔	cup milk
¼	teaspoon baking soda	1	cup fresh blueberries, rinsed and drained, or frozen blueberries[32]
½	teaspoon salt		

Whisk cornmeal, flour, sugar, baking powder, baking soda and salt in large bowl.[2] Whisk egg, butter and milk in medium bowl and stir into flour mixture until just combined, being careful not to overmix. Fold in blueberries.[65] Spray muffin cups or paper baking cups in muffin tins and fill three-fourths full with batter. Bake at 400° for 12 to 15 minutes. Serve warm.

* *Use ½ cup sugar for muffins served with salads, or ⅔ cup for breakfast muffins.*

Makes 12 muffins

Per muffin: 174 calories, 6 g fat, 3 g protein, 27 g carbohydrate, 33 mg cholesterol, 242 mg sodium.

Freezer Biscuits

2	cups flour	2	tablespoons sugar
4	teaspoons baking powder	½	cup shortening
½	teaspoon cream of tartar	1	egg, room temperature
½	teaspoon salt	⅔	cup milk

Whisk flour, baking powder, cream of tartar, salt and sugar in large bowl.[2] Cut shortening into bits and work into flour mixture with finger tips until crumbly, or cut in with pastry blender. Mix egg and milk in small bowl with fork. Stir into flour mixture until dough just clings together. Form into ball and place on lightly floured surface. Knead dough 1 to 2 minutes,[78] folding and turning about four times. Roll out or pat dough to ½-inch thick on lightly floured surface. Cut dough with biscuit cutter, or pat dough into ½-inch-thick rectangle and cut into squares. Place biscuits on ungreased baking sheets and flash freeze.[26] Transfer to ziptop bags and return to freezer. Place *frozen* biscuits on ungreased baking sheet. Bake at 450° for 10 to 15 minutes or until golden.

Makes 10 large or 24 small biscuits

Per small biscuit: 86 calories, 5 g fat, 2 g protein, 10 g carbohydrate, 9 mg cholesterol, 111 mg sodium.

Shortcake Biscuits variation: Follow above recipe, adding 1 teaspoon vanilla to egg and milk mixture.

Buttermilk Biscuits

2 cups flour	½ cup shortening, cut into pieces
2 teaspoons baking powder	⅔ cup buttermilk[42]
½ teaspoon baking soda	¼ cup (½ stick) butter, melted
½ to ¾ teaspoon salt	

Whisk flour, baking powder, baking soda and salt in large bowl.[2] Cut in shortening with pastry blender or two knives until mixture resembles coarse cornmeal (a few large pieces of shortening are okay–they will make biscuits flakier). Make well in center and add buttermilk all at once. Toss with fork until dough just clings together. Gently press dough against sides and bottom of bowl, turning bowl and pressing dough until loose pieces adhere and dough comes together, about 30 seconds. Do not try to make dough completely smooth, overworking will make biscuits tough. Roll out to ½-inch thick on lightly floured surface. Cut biscuits with biscuit cutter, or pat dough into 6x8-inch rectangle and cut into 2-inch squares with pizza cutter. Bake on lightly-sprayed baking sheet at 400° for 14 minutes or until golden. Brush tops with melted butter while hot. Serve with *Chocolate Gravy*.

Makes 15 to 18 biscuits

Per biscuit: 106 calories, 6 g fat, 2 g protein, 11 g carbohydrate, 0 mg cholesterol, 372 mg sodium.

Asiago Poppy Seed Biscuits variation: After cutting shortening into flour mixture, stir in ½ teaspoon poppy seeds, 1 tablespoon crushed dried parsley flakes, and 1 cup shredded Asiago cheese. Make well in center and add buttermilk all at once. Continue as directed above. Bake at 400° for 16 to 17 minutes.

Toast Points

Firm white sandwich bread slices, crusts removed, many as needed	Butter or margarine, softened, or butter-flavored cooking spray

Spread both sides of bread lightly with butter or spray. Cut into 2 or 4 triangles. Bake in single layer on baking sheet at 350° for 8 to 10 minutes or until lightly browned. Cool. Store in airtight containers overnight. Reheat before serving.

Per toast-point: 32 calories, 2 g fat, 1 g protein, 3 g carbohydrate, 0 mg cholesterol, 34 mg sodium.

Mini Crustades: Cut 2½-inch circles from buttered bread slices. Push into mini muffin cups and bake and store as directed above. Use to hold salmon mousse or other appetizer fillings.

Large Bread Cups: Push prepared bread slices into regular muffin tin cups, allowing points to stick up. Bake and store as directed above. Use for shrimp Newburg, *Chicken à la King* or other creamy fillings that use puff-pastry shells.

Popovers

When making popovers, it is very important that all ingredients be at room temperature.

1	cup bread flour or unbleached flour	2	eggs, lightly beaten
½	teaspoon salt	1¼	cups milk
¼	teaspoon baking powder	1	tablespoon butter, melted
			Canola oil

Whisk flour, salt and baking powder in medium bowl.[2] Set aside. Whisk eggs, milk and butter in separate bowl. Gradually stir into flour mixture until just combined (some small lumps are okay). Dip paper towel in oil and wipe insides of popover pan or muffin tin cups. Dust cups with flour (flour helps batter grip the sides). Pour batter into small pitcher. Fill cups half full. Place in *cold* oven, set oven to 450° and bake 15 minutes. Reduce heat to 350° and bake 20 more minutes. (Do not open oven door during this time or popovers will fall.) Extend rack and stick side of each puff all the way through with wooden skewer to let moisture escape, or make small slit in side of popovers with small sharp knife. Push rack back into oven and bake 5 more minutes or until firm and crusty. Remove and cool in pan on rack. Popovers should release from cups after several minutes. Serve immediately. Serve with seafood, soups and stews, or eat with jam or honey.

Makes 6 popovers

Per popover: 149 calories, 6 g fat, 6 g protein, 19 g carbohydrates, 84 mg cholesterol, 243 mg sodium.

Cheese and Herb Pull-Aparts

1½	ounces Asiago or Parmesan cheese, freshly grated (½ cup)	18	rolls of frozen white roll dough, *divided*
½	teaspoon dried thyme, crushed	3	tablespoons butter or margarine, melted, *divided*
½	teaspoon dried basil, crushed		
2	tablespoons toasted sesame seeds[5]		

Mix cheese, thyme, basil and sesame seeds in small bowl and sprinkle one third into bottom of sprayed 10-inch Bundt pan. Arrange 9 frozen rolls over cheese mixture. Drizzle 1½ tablespoons butter over rolls and sprinkle with another third cheese mixture. Add remaining 9 rolls and drizzle with remaining 1½ tablespoons butter. Sprinkle remaining cheese mixture on top. Cover with sprayed plastic wrap and let rise in warm place[36] about 2 hours or until doubled in size. Bake at 350° for 20 minutes. Loosely tent with foil and bake 10 more minutes. Loosen bread from center and sides and invert onto serving plate. Serve hot.

Makes 16 servings

Per serving: 125 calories, 6 g fat, 4 g protein, 15 g carbohydrate, 9 mg cholesterol, 228 mg sodium.

Petite Rolls

¼	cup warm water (105° to 115°)	½	teaspoon salt
1	(¼-ounce) package dry yeast	2½	cups flour
1	cup milk		
4	tablespoons butter, *divided*		**Glaze:**
1	tablespoon sugar	½	cup confectioners' sugar
		1	tablespoon water

Put warm water in small bowl and sprinkle yeast granules over surface. Let stand about 2 minutes to absorb water, then stir to dissolve. Heat milk, 2 tablespoons butter, sugar and salt in small saucepan to just below boiling. Cool to lukewarm.ᴳ Stir in dissolved yeast.

Put flour in large bowl. Stir in milk mixture with wooden spoon until combined, about 2 minutes (dough will look rough.) Scrape down sides. Cover with sprayed pizza pan or sprayed plastic wrap. Let dough rise in warm place[36] 1 to 1½ hours or until doubled in size.

Tender rolls result from minimal rolling and handling. Toss dough onto lightly floured surface; turn to coat with flour. Roll out from one side of dough to about ⅓-inch thick. Use shot glass or 1½-inch biscuit cutter to cut out rolls. Continue rolling and cutting out rolls from same side until all dough is used. Lightly sprinkle rolling surface with flour if dough sticks. Melt remaining 2 tablespoons butter. Cool. Dip rolls halfway into butter, fold in half and place close together in sprayed 9x13-inch baking pan. Brush tops with any remaining butter. Cover with sprayed plastic wrap and let rise in warm place 30 minutes or until nearly doubled in size. Bake at 450° for 10 minutes being careful not to burn. Brush rolls with glaze and serve.

Glaze: Mix confectioners' sugar and water in small bowl.

Note: If 60 rolls are not needed, divide rolls among three sprayed 8-inch round cake pans. Let rise and bake only as many pans as needed. Cover any remaining pans of unrisen rolls with sprayed plastic wrap and refrigerate up to two days. Remove and let rise until nearly doubled in size (will take longer with refrigeration).

Makes about 60 rolls   Patty Hogan, Boulder, Colorado

Per roll: 34 calories, 1 g fat, 1 g protein, 5 g carbohydrate, 3 mg cholesterol, 30 mg sodium.

About Dissolving Dry Yeast

Run hot water from tap until instant-read thermometer reads between 105° to 115°. Sprinkle yeast granules over ¼-cup warm water in small bowl. Let stand to absorb water, then stir until dissolved. If yeast clumps, let stand a few more minutes and stir again. Yeast will start to foam if active; if not foamy after 5 or 6 minutes, discard.

Joey's Holiday Rolls

Joey uses the wine-and-water combination when she makes these cloverleaf rolls. I tested the recipe that way, and the rolls were light and delicious.

½ cup warm water (105° to 115°)	¾ cup sugar
2 (¼-ounce) packages dry yeast	2 teaspoons salt
¾ cup butter-flavored shortening	1 cup cold water, or ½ cup cold
1 cup boiling water	water and ½ cup cold blush wine
2 eggs, lightly beaten	7½ cups *sifted* flour[24]

Pour warm water in small bowl and sprinkle yeast granules over surface. Let stand about 2 minutes to absorb water, then stir to dissolve. Put shortening in medium bowl, add boiling water and stir until shortening melts. Let mixture cool to lukewarm. Beat eggs, sugar, salt, cold water and melted shortening in large bowl with mixer until combined. Stir in dissolved yeast. Add flour all at once and mix well with strong wooden spoon, about 2 minutes (dough will look rough). Cover bowl with sprayed plastic wrap and refrigerate overnight.

Next morning *gently* punch down dough with fist in 3 or 4 places. Pinch off walnut-size pieces of dough with lightly greased hands. Roll into balls. Group three balls close together on large greased jelly-roll pan (will form cloverleaf rolls when baked). Cover loosely with sprayed plastic wrap and let rise in warm place[36] until doubled in size. Bake at 400° for 15 minutes or until lightly browned. Brush with melted butter for golden finish.

Makes 30 cloverleaf rolls   Joey Danenhauer, Springdale, Arkansas

Per roll: 162 calories, 6 g fat, 3 g protein, 24 g carbohydrate, 14 mg cholesterol, 148 mg sodium.

Muffin Tin Cloverleaf Rolls variation: Place 3 walnut-size balls in each cup of two sprayed 12-cup muffin tins and one sprayed 6-cup muffin tin. Cover with sprayed plastic wrap and let rise until doubled in size. Bake as directed above. If all rolls are not needed, cover and refrigerate one or more tins of unrisen rolls up to two days. Remove from refrigerator and let rise.

Cinnamon Rolls variation: After using one-third dough to make twelve cloverleaf rolls, I refrigerated remaining dough an additional day. Next morning I punched down dough, divided in half, and prepared two recipes of *Old-Fashioned Cinnamon Rolls* (baked at 400° for 20 minutes). The re-refrigerated dough worked fine and the rolls were great.

Overnight Crescent Rolls

Easy, prepare-ahead recipe, especially good for holidays when time and refrigerator space are at a premium.

1 (¼-ounce) package dry yeast	½ cup (1 stick) butter, melted
¼ cup sugar	1 teaspoon salt
1 cup warm water (105° to 115°)	4 cups flour
2 eggs, lightly beaten	

Mix yeast, sugar and water in large bowl. Let stand 30 minutes. Stir in eggs, butter and salt. Add flour, 2 cups at a time; mix with wooden spoon (dough will look lumpy). Cover dough with sprayed plastic wrap and let stand overnight at room temperature. Next day, gather dough and shape into 9-inch loaf on lightly floured surface. Cut into thirds. Form each third into a ball. Roll into 9-inch or 10-inch circle on lightly floured surface. Cut each circle into eight wedges. Roll wedges from wide end to tip and place on sprayed baking sheets, tips underneath. Shape rolls into crescents. Cover with sprayed plastic wrap and let stand at room temperature 1 hour or up to 8 hours. Bake at 375° for 12 to 15 minutes; tent with foil if browning too fast. Brush with melted butter, if desired.

Makes 24 crescent rolls   Judy Whitford, Centerton, Arkansas

Per roll: 133 calories, 4 g fat, 3 g protein, 20 g carbohydrate, 18 mg cholesterol, 139 mg sodium.

Note: When I tested this recipe, I made two portions of dough into crescent rolls and one portion into **Old-Fashioned Cinnamon Rolls.** *We had cinnamon rolls for breakfast and crescent rolls for dinner.*

Baguettes

These are so easy to make, and they are perfect for making Crostini.

1 (1-pound) loaf frozen bread dough

Place frozen dough on lightly floured cutting board, cover with sprayed plastic wrap and let stand until thawed enough to cut with a knife, but still cold (center may still be frozen). Cut lengthwise into two pieces (four pieces for *Crostini*). Replace plastic. Thaw enough to roll into 10- or 12-inch "ropes" with lightly floured hands on lightly floured surface. Place 4 inches apart (2 inches apart for Crostini) on sprayed baking sheet. Cover with sprayed plastic wrap and let rise in warm place until doubled in size.[36] Uncover and bake at 350° for 25 minutes (20 minutes for Crostini) or until golden—should sound hollow when thumped. Spray with butter-flavored spray, if desired. Transfer baguettes to rack and cool.

Makes 2 baguettes or 4 *Crostini* **baguettes**

Per baguette: 62 calories, 1 g fat, 2 g protein, 12 g carbohydrate, 0 mg cholesterol, 124 mg sodium.

Old-Fashioned Cinnamon Rolls

1	portion of *Overnight Crescent Rolls* dough	1½	teaspoons ground cinnamon
2	tablespoons butter, melted	¼	cup raisins (optional)
¼	cup sugar	1	recipe *Confectioners' Sugar Frosting*

Roll out dough to 10x12-inch rectangle on lightly floured surface. Brush with melted butter. Mix sugar and cinnamon in small bowl and sprinkle evenly over dough. Sprinkle with raisins. Roll dough tightly from short side like a jelly roll. Pinch seam to seal. Pat ends to make roll even and round. Cut crosswise[81] into four or eight slices. Place cutside down in sprayed 8x8-inch baking pan. Cover with sprayed plastic wrap and let rise in warm place[36] until doubled in size, 1 to 1½ hours. Uncover and bake at 350° for 15 to 20 minutes. Spray with butter-flavored topping spray for golden color, if desired. Frost with *Confectioners' Sugar Frosting* while warm.

Makes 4 large or 8 smaller rolls

Per large roll: 515 calories, 18 g fat, 6 g protein, 84 g carbohydrate, 44 mg cholesterol, 412 mg sodium.

Crostini

1	*Baguette* or 1 purchased baguette	Olive-oil cooking spray, olive oil or grape seed oil

Cover baguette with paper towel and dry out 24 hours or overnight. Slice diagonally into ¼-inch rounds and lightly spray or brush both sides with oil (small narrow paintbrush works well). Place in single layer on ungreased baking sheets. Bake on middle rack at 350° for 7 to 8 minutes or until crisp and lightly golden. Transfer to racks and cool. Layer crostini in covered container separated by paper towel. Store up to two weeks at room temperature, or freeze.

Makes 36 to 48 crostini

Per crostini: 16 calories, 2 g fat, 0 g protein, 0 g carbohydrate, 0 mg cholesterol, 1 mg sodium.

Basic Crêpes

Crêpes are thin, tender pancakes that can be used to enclose a variety of sweet or savory fillings. They add elegance to a meal.

1 cup cold milk	2 cups flour
1 cup cold water	¼ cup (½ stick) butter, melted and
4 eggs	cooled
½ teaspoon salt	

Put milk, water, eggs, salt, flour and butter in blender. Blend on high about 30 seconds. Scrape down sides and pulse or blend 15 more seconds or until smooth. Alternatively, put ingredients in large bowl and beat with mixer on high until blended and smooth. Cover and refrigerate at least 1 hour or overnight. Remove and whisk batter to recombine. Should have consistency of half-and-half. If thick, add water, a tablespoon at a time. Makes 3⅔ cups.

Heat 6-inch nonstick skillet over medium-high heat. Brush lightly with vegetable oil, if necessary. Lift skillet from heat and pour 2 to 3 tablespoons batter over bottom, tilting and rotating to coat bottom only. Return to heat and cook crepes until almost dry on top and lightly browned around edges, about 1 minute. Loosen edges and flip with spatula or fingers. Cook about 15 seconds or until lightly browned. (Second side will brown unevenly; use this side for fillings. You will inevitably mess up and have to discard the first one or two crepes.) Place crepes in single layer on paper towels to cool.

Crêpes may be made ahead. Stack completely cooled crêpes separated by wax paper. Wrap in foil and refrigerate up to five days or freeze up to two months. Thaw at room temperature if frozen.

Makes 26 to 28 crêpes

Per crêpe: 63 calories, 3 g fat, 2 g protein, 7 g carbohydrate, 36 mg cholesterol, 68 mg sodium.

Quick Crêpes variation: Blend 2 cups buttermilk baking mix, 1½ cups milk and 4 eggs in blender until smooth (mixture will be thin). Cover and refrigerate at least 30 minutes. Continue as directed above.

Makes 26 to 28 crêpes

Per crêpe: 53 calories, 2 g fat, 2 g protein, 6 g carbohydrate, 33 mg cholesterol, 115 mg sodium.

Brunch

Brunch

Basic Omelet

An omelet has been described as an envelope for enclosing any combination of filling ingredients. Several small omelets will be fluffier and easier to handle than one large omelet. Use ¼ to ½ cup filling for each small omelet.

3 eggs, room temperature[88]	Dash of pepper
1 tablespoon water[82]	½ tablespoon butter
⅛ teaspoon salt	

Beat eggs, water, salt and pepper in small bowl with fork until whites and yolks are combined. Heat butter in 8- to 10-inch nonstick skillet (10-inch preferred) over medium-high heat, tilting skillet to coat. When foaming stops, add eggs and let cook several seconds. As eggs begin to set, stir in circular motion with back of fork until omelet is just set, but still moist on surface. Sprinkle cheese or add filling, if using, across middle of omelet perpendicular to handle. Fold nearest third of omelet over filling with heatproof rubber spatula. Slide spatula around and under farthest third and fold over center. Shake skillet to loosen and invert omelet onto plate. (Alternatively, sprinkle cheese or filling on one side of omelet and fold in half. Slide onto plate.)

Makes 1 omelet

Per 2-egg omelet: 182 calories, 14 g fat, 13 g protein, 1 g carbohydrate, 441 mg cholesterol, 431 mg sodium.

Western Omelet: Heat ¼ cup diced cooked ham, 1 tablespoon chopped bell pepper and 1 tablespoon chopped onion in small bowl in microwave or in small skillet. Fill *Basic Omelet* and sprinkle ¼ cup (packed) finely grated Cheddar cheese over filling (optional).

Per 2-egg omelet: 252 calories, 18 g fat, 19 g protein, 4 g carbohydrate, 461 mg cholesterol, 893 mg sodium.

Mushroom Omelet: Sauté ¼ cup sliced fresh mushrooms[3] and 1 tablespoon chopped shallots or green onions in 1 teaspoon butter in small skillet. Add herbs of your choice. Fill *Basic Omelet* and sprinkle ¼ cup (packed) grated cheese over filling.

Per 2-egg omelet: 215 calories, 16 g fat, 14 g protein, 5 g carbohydrate, 446 mg cholesterol, 187 mg sodium.

Pine Nut Omelet: Heat 1 teaspoon olive oil in small skillet. Add 1 tablespoon pine nuts, 1 tablespoon snipped flat-leaf parsley and 1 tablespoon chopped shallots or green onions. Sauté until pine nuts are golden. Fill *Basic Omelet*.

Per 2-egg omelet: 262 calories, 21 g fat, 15 g protein, 5 g carbohydrate, 441 mg cholesterol, 169 mg sodium.

Cheese Omelet: Fill *Basic Omelet* with ¼ to ½ cup (packed) finely grated Cheddar, Swiss or Monterey Jack cheese.

Per 2-egg omelet: 410 calories, 33 g fat, 27 g protein, 2 g carbohydrate, 500 mg cholesterol, 782 mg sodium.

Stuffed Eggs with Country Ham

Nice to serve at a bridal, Easter or Derby Day brunch.

Sauce:
3 tablespoons butter
3 tablespoons flour
1 cup chicken broth[11]
¾ cup milk

8 hard-cooked eggs[18]
¼ cup (½ stick) butter, melted

½ teaspoon Worcestershire sauce
¼ teaspoon prepared mustard
1 teaspoon snipped fresh parsley
1 teaspoon snipped fresh chives
⅓ cup finely chopped country ham
4 ounces Cheddar cheese, shredded (1 cup)

Sauce: Melt butter in small saucepan and whisk in flour. Gradually stir in chicken broth and milk. Cook and stir over medium heat until thickened.

Peel warm eggs[18] and cut in half lengthwise with sharp wet knife. Carefully remove yolks to medium bowl. Set whites aside. Mash yolks with butter and mix in Worcestershire sauce, mustard, parsley, chives and ham (mixture will be stiff). Spoon equally into whites and place in sprayed 7x11-inch baking dish. Pour sauce over eggs. (May prepare to this point early in the day. Cover and refrigerate; remove about 30 minutes before baking.) Sprinkle with cheese and bake at 350° for 25 to 30 minutes or until thoroughly heated. Let stand 5 to 10 minutes before serving. Serve over *Toast Points*, if desired. Serve with *Hot Fruit Casserole*. Recipe may be doubled.

Makes 6 to 8 servings
Laura Leftwich, Lynchburg, Virginia

Per serving of 8: 268 calories, 22 g fat, 13 g protein, 5 g carbohydrate, 264 mg cholesterol, 540 mg sodium.

Poached Eggs

4 eggs
3 to 4 cups water

1 teaspoon vinegar
½ teaspoon salt

Break eggs into separate custard cups and have ready near stovetop. Pour water into 10-inch nonstick skillet, cover, and bring to boil. Add vinegar and salt (vinegar helps eggs hold their shape). Grip lip of cup with thumb and forefinger and gently immerse opposite lip into boiling water; tilt cup and let egg float out into water. Repeat with remaining three eggs. Reduce heat and simmer covered 2½ to 3 minutes (whites should be completely set and firm, and yolks should remain soft but not runny in center). Remove eggs with slotted spoon and hold briefly above skillet to drain off water.

Makes 4 poached eggs

Per egg: 75 calories, 5 g fat, 6 g protein, 1 g carbohydrate, 212 mg cholesterol, 140 mg sodium.

Libba's Christmas Morning Strata

14 to 15 slices white sandwich bread	2 (4-ounce) cans diced green chiles, drained
2 pounds hot pork sausage, or half regular and half hot, *divided*	8 eggs
8 ounces sharp Cheddar cheese, shredded (2 cups), *divided*	3 cups whole milk
	1½ teaspoons dry mustard[9]
4 ounces Monterey Jack cheese, shredded (1 cup)	½ teaspoon salt

Dry out bread slices on racks several hours. (Alternatively, place on baking sheets in 200° oven for 10 minutes, turning once. Cool.) Meanwhile, brown sausage in large skillet; drain well. Remove crusts from bread (kitchen shears work well). Cut slices in half into rectangles. Cover bottom of sprayed 9x13-inch baking dish with half the rectangles, trimming to fit. Layer half the sausage, 1 cup Cheddar cheese, all the Monterey Jack cheese and all the green chiles over bread. Sprinkle remaining sausage on top and cover with remaining rectangles. Whisk eggs, milk, dry mustard and salt together in large bowl and pour over strata. Place plastic wrap on surface of strata and press down gently with spatula, allowing bread to absorb milk mixture. Cover with foil and refrigerate overnight.

Remove strata from refrigerator 30 minutes before baking. Remove foil and plastic wrap. Place strata on jelly-roll pan to prevent overbrowning bottom. Bake uncovered at 325° for 60 to 75 minutes or until sharp knife inserted in center comes out clean. Sprinkle remaining 1 cup Cheddar cheese over top and bake just until cheese melts. Let stand 15 minutes uncovered. Cut into squares. Serve with fresh fruit or *Hot Fruit Casserole* and *Old-fashioned Cinnamon Rolls*.

Makes 10 servings   Libba Letton, Austin, Texas

Per serving: 572 calories, 43 g fat, 23 g protein, 22 g carbohydrate, 223 mg cholesterol, 1058 mg sodium.

Easy Eggs Benedict

2 English muffins, split and toasted	4 *Poached Eggs*
4 slices Canadian bacon or ham, heated, or 8 slices cooked bacon	1 recipe *Microwave Hollandaise Sauce*[51]
4 tomato slices (optional)	Paprika

Put one or two muffin halves on each plate. Add slice of Canadian bacon, tomato slice and poached egg to each muffin half. Spoon warm hollandaise sauce over eggs and sprinkle with paprika. Serve with *Fresh Asparagus*, fresh fruit and a flute of champagne! Recipe may be doubled.

Makes 2 to 4 servings

Per serving of 4: 305 calories, 23 g fat, 11 g protein, 14 g carbohydrate, 361 mg cholesterol, 516 mg sodium.

Hot Chicken Salad Strata

14 slices white sandwich bread	½ cup finely chopped onion
3 to 4 tablespoons butter, softened	8 eggs, lightly beaten
1 (15-ounce) can extra-long asparagus spears	1½ cups half-and-half
	1 cup whole milk
½ cup mayonnaise	¾ teaspoon salt
1 (10¾-ounce) can cream of mushroom soup	¼ teaspoon celery salt
	¼ teaspoon pepper
2 tablespoons fresh lemon juice	Dashes of hot pepper sauce
3 cups bite-size *Easy Cooked Chicken*	6 ounces sharp Cheddar cheese, shredded (1½ cups)
1 cup thinly sliced celery	Paprika
½ cup finely chopped bell pepper	

Dry out bread slices on racks several hours. (Alternatively, place on baking sheets in 200° oven for 10 minutes, turning once. Cool.) Remove crusts from bread (kitchen shears work well). Butter slices on one side. Cut each slice in half into rectangles. Cover bottom of sprayed 9x13-inch baking dish with 14 rectangles, buttered side up, trimming to fit. Meanwhile, drain asparagus spears well on paper towels.

Whisk mayonnaise, soup and lemon juice together in large bowl. Stir in chicken, celery, bell pepper and onion. Spoon over bread pieces. Stagger asparagus spears crosswise down middle of strata with tips toward outside. Cover with remaining rectangles, buttered side up.

Whisk eggs, half-and-half, milk, salt, celery salt, pepper and pepper sauce in separate bowl. Pour over bread. Cover surface of strata with plastic wrap, leaving edges loose. Press down gently with spatula, allowing bread to absorb milk mixture. Place large sheet of foil loosely over plastic wrap. Put 2 pounds dry beans or rice in 2-gallon-size ziptop bag; seal bag and place on foil. Distribute beans in bag evenly over strata (weight will help keep bread immersed). Fold foil over edge of baking dish to seal. Refrigerate several hours or overnight.

Remove strata from refrigerator and remove beans and foil. Let stand 30 minutes. Remove plastic. Place baking dish on jelly-roll pan to prevent overbrowning bottom of strata. Bake at 325° for 60 minutes or until top begins to puff and brown. (Center should be almost firm. Do not overbake or chicken salad will curdle–strata will continue to firm while standing.) Sprinkle cheese and paprika over top and return to oven. Bake just until cheese melts. Let stand 15 minutes uncovered. Cut into squares. Serve with *Raspberry Shimmer* and *Overnight Rolls*.

Makes 10 to 12 servings

Per serving of 12: 415 calories, 26 g fat, 26 g protein, 20 g carbohydrate, 223 mg cholesterol, 805 mg sodium.

Bacon and Cheese Strata

Good lunch for bridge foursome or friends.

8 slices white bread	4 Cheddar cheese slices
½ cup thinly sliced celery	4 eggs, lightly beaten
¼ cup finely chopped bell pepper	1¾ cups whole milk
¼ cup finely chopped onion	1 teaspoon dry mustard[9]
½ pound bacon, cooked and crumbled[14]	¼ teaspoon salt
	⅛ teaspoon pepper

Dry out bread slices on rack about 1 hour. Sauté celery, bell pepper and onion until tender in sprayed nonstick skillet. Mix in bacon. Trim crusts from bread and place four slices in sprayed 8x8-inch baking dish. Sprinkle sautéed vegetable mixture over bread. Cover with cheese and remaining bread slices. Beat eggs, milk, dry mustard, salt and pepper in medium bowl and pour over strata. Gently press bread down with spatula to absorb liquid. Cover and refrigerate 1 hour or overnight; if overnight, let stand 30 minutes. Bake strata uncovered on baking sheet at 325° for 50 to 60 minutes or until puffy and brown. Let stand uncovered 10 to 15 minutes. Cut into squares. Serve with *Strawberry Tossed Salad*.

Makes 4 servings   Ethel Schulte, Boulder, Colorado

Per serving: 686 calories, 44 g fat, 36 g protein, 35 g carbohydrate, 301 mg cholesterol, 2124 mg sodium.

Cheese Grits

6 cups water	2 teaspoons seasoned salt
2 teaspoons salt	10 ounces sharp Cheddar cheese, shredded (2½ cups)
1½ cups regular or quick grits (not instant grits)	3 eggs, room temperature
½ cup (1 stick) butter, cut into pieces	1 (4-ounce) can diced green chiles, drained (optional)
⅛ teaspoon hot pepper sauce	

Bring water to boil in large saucepan; add salt and slowly stir in grits to prevent lumps. Reduce heat to medium-low and cook covered until water is absorbed and mixture thickens, stirring occasionally. Remove from heat and mix in butter, pepper sauce and seasoned salt; stir in cheese. Lightly beat eggs in small bowl. Stir warm grits into eggs 1 tablespoon at a time until you have about ½ cup grits mixed into eggs. Return egg mixture to grits in saucepan and stir. Stir in green chiles. Pour into sprayed 2½-quart deep casserole. Bake uncovered at 350° for 1 hour. For thicker grits, bake about 15 more minutes. Let stand 10 minutes.

Makes 12 servings   Katherine Chandley, Atlanta, Georgia

Per serving: 255 calories, 17 g fat, 9 g protein, 16 g carbohydrate, 99 mg cholesterol, 859 mg sodium.

Turkey and Ham Mornay

Mornay Sauce:
¼ cup (½ stick) butter
4 tablespoons flour
1 cup chicken broth
¾ cup milk
Dash of hot pepper sauce
2 ounces shredded Swiss cheese (½ cup)

8 fresh asparagus spears[34]
4 slices white bread, lightly toasted
½ pound thinly sliced smoked turkey, divided into 4 portions
¼ pound thinly sliced baked ham, divided into 4 portions
Paprika (optional)

Mornay Sauce: Melt butter in small saucepan and whisk in flour. Cook and stir 1 minute (will bubble and foam). Mix in chicken broth, milk and pepper sauce. Cook over medium heat until slightly thickened. Stir in cheese and cook until smooth and thick, whisking constantly. Season with salt and pepper. Set aside.

Cook asparagus until crisp-tender (see *Fresh Asparagus*); drain well. Remove crusts and cut toast diagonally in half. Place two halves in each of four sprayed individual shallow ovenproof dishes. Cover toast with turkey and ham. Spoon Mornay sauce over each serving. Bake at 375° for 8 to 10 minutes. Broil[13] until golden on top. Sprinkle with paprika. Cross two asparagus spears over each sandwich, forming an "X". Serve with *Pickled Peaches*.

Makes 4 servings   Norma Daub, Berkeley Heights, New Jersey

Per serving: 389 calories, 21 g fat, 28 g protein, 22 g carbohydrate, 84 mg cholesterol, 1864 mg sodium.

Hot Swiss Chicken Salad

2 cups bite-size *Easy Cooked Chicken*
2 cups chopped celery
⅓ cup chopped bell pepper
2 tablespoons minced onion
½ cup mayonnaise

2 tablespoons fresh lemon juice
3 tablespoons diced pimiento, drained
½ teaspoon salt
⅓ cup shredded Swiss cheese
3 cups broken potato chips

Mix chicken, celery, bell pepper, onion, mayonnaise, lemon juice, pimiento and salt in large bowl. Spoon into sprayed 7x11-inch baking dish and sprinkle with cheese and potato chips. Bake at 350° for 25 to 30 minutes or until hot and bubbly.

Makes 4 to 6 servings   Mary Lee Skourup, Bella Vista, Arkansas

Per serving of 6: 392 calories, 28 g fat, 22 g protein, 18 g carbohydrate, 64 mg cholesterol, 545 mg sodium.

Chicken Asparagus Enchiladas

Green Taco Enchilada Sauce:
½ cup (1 stick) butter
½ cup flour
2 (14-ounce) cans chicken broth
1 teaspoon chicken bouillon granules
 Dashes of hot pepper sauce
½ cup green taco sauce
1 cup sour cream
24 fresh asparagus spears
¼ teaspoon salt

Pinch of sugar
½ cup finely chopped celery
½ cup chopped green onion
3 cups bite-size *Easy Cooked Chicken*
12 ounces Monterey Jack cheese, shredded (3 cups), *divided*
12 (8-inch) flour tortillas (soft taco size)
1½ ounces Asiago or Parmesan cheese, grated (½ cup)
 Paprika

Green Taco Enchilada Sauce: Melt butter in medium saucepan over low heat and whisk in flour. Raise heat to medium. Cook and stir until flour loses its raw taste, about 2 minutes, being careful not to burn roux.ᴳ Gradually whisk in chicken broth. Mix in bouillon granules and pepper sauce, whisking until mixture begins to simmer. Reduce heat to low. Cook until sauce thickens, 8 to 10 minutes, whisking frequently. Remove from heat and stir in green taco sauce. Cool slightly and fold in sour cream. Add salt and pepper to taste. Set aside.

Snap asparagus where they break; rinse and drain.³⁴ Fill large nonstick skillet three-fourths full of water and bring to boil. Add salt, sugar and asparagus. Blanch,ᴳ boiling covered, about 5 minutes. Drain and plunge asparagus into bowl of ice water to stop cooking. Drain well and set aside.

Mix celery, green onion, chicken and 2 cups Monterey Jack cheese in large bowl. Work with one tortilla at a time, leaving remaining tortillas in package to prevent drying out. Lightly spray tortilla on both sides with cooking spray. Place about ⅓ cup chicken mixture down middle, add 2 asparagus spears with tips in opposite directions and pour 3 tablespoons sauce over filling. Roll up enchilada and place seamside down in lightly-sprayed 9x13-inch baking dish. Repeat with remaining tortillas, packing enchiladas tightly in baking dish. (May prepare ahead to this point and cover. Pour remaining sauce into covered container. Refrigerate enchiladas and sauce overnight. Remove enchiladas 20 to 30 minutes before baking. Reheat sauce without boiling.) Sprinkle remaining 1 cup Monterey Jack cheese over enchiladas. Pour reheated sauce over cheese and sprinkle with Asiago cheese. Sprinkle paprika over casserole just before baking. Bake at 400° for 25 to 30 minutes or until hot and bubbly and lightly golden. Let stand 10 minutes before serving. Serve with additional green taco sauce, if desired. Serve *Daiquiri Cheesecake* for dessert.

Makes 12 servings

Fran Fee, Scottsdale, Arizona

Per serving: 417 calories, 24 g fat, 27 g protein, 25 g carbohydrate, 98 mg cholesterol, 982 mg sodium.

Chicken Florentine Crêpes

Chicken Florentine Filling:
1 tablespoon butter
¼ cup chopped onion
1 to 2 teaspoons anisette, or ¼ teaspoon anise extract
1½ cups bite-size *Easy Cooked Chicken*
1 (10-ounce) package frozen creamed spinach, thawed
1½ ounces Asiago or Parmesan cheese, finely grated (½ cup)

Cheese Sauce:
1½ tablespoons butter

2 tablespoons flour
½ cup chicken broth[11]
1 cup half-and-half
1½ ounces Asiago or Parmesan cheese, finely grated (½ cup)
2 tablespoons dry vermouth or other dry white wine
Dash of hot pepper sauce

Assembly:
8 *Quick Crêpes* or *Crêpes* Paprika
1 recipe *Plain Fluffy White Rice*

Chicken Florentine Filling: Melt butter in medium skillet. Sauté onion about 1½ minutes. Stir in anisette. Remove from heat and stir in chicken, spinach and Asiago cheese. Set aside.

Cheese Sauce: Melt butter in medium saucepan and whisk in flour. Cook and stir over medium heat about 1 minute. Gradually add chicken broth and half-and-half. Cook until thickened, stirring frequently. Stir in Asiago cheese, vermouth and pepper sauce. Add salt and pepper to taste. Cook and stir until smooth.

Assembly: Spread ¼ cup filling down center of each crêpe. Roll up and place seamside down in sprayed 7x11-inch or oblong baking dish. Thin Cheese Sauce with additional broth if thick and pour over crêpes. Sprinkle with paprika. Bake covered at 375° for 18 to 20 minutes or until thoroughly heated.

Prepare individual servings by placing a bed of rice on each plate. Top with two filled crêpes and spoon Cheese Sauce over each serving. Serve *Banana Nut Bread* with *Strawberry or Raspberry Butter* on the side.

Makes 4 servings

Adapted from recipe by Chef Scott McCarty,
Food and Beverage Operations Manager,
Bella Vista Village, Bella Vista, Arkansas

Per serving: 499 calories, 27 g fat, 39 g protein, 22 g carbohydrate, 185 mg cholesterol, 935 mg sodium.

Ham and Eggs au Gratin

Cream Sauce:

6	tablespoons butter
6	tablespoons flour
1	cup half-and-half
2	cups milk
½	teaspoon salt
	Dash of pepper
½	teaspoon paprika
12	hard-cooked eggs[18]
¼	cup finely minced green onions
½	cup (1 stick) butter, melted

¼	cup mayonnaise
1	tablespoon Dijon mustard
1	tablespoon Worcestershire sauce
½	teaspoon salt
⅛	teaspoon pepper
1	tablespoon finely snipped parsley
12	thin slices baked ham, any rind removed and slices cut in half lengthwise*
4	ounces Swiss or mild Cheddar cheese, shredded (1 cup)
½	cup buttered soft breadcrumbs[45]

Cream Sauce: Melt butter in medium saucepan and whisk in flour. Cook about 1 minute. Stir in half-and-half and milk. Cook and stir until thickened. Stir in salt, pepper and paprika. Set aside.

Peel eggs[18] and cut in half lengthwise with sharp wet knife. Carefully remove yolks to pie plate or large shallow dish; set whites aside. Mash yolks and stir in green onion and butter. Mix in mayonnaise, mustard, Worcestershire sauce, salt, pepper, and parsley. Spoon equally into whites. Wrap ham strip around each egg with overlap underneath and place in sprayed 9x13-inch baking dish. Cover with Cream Sauce. (May prepare to this point early in the day. Cover and refrigerate. Remove 15 minutes before baking.) Sprinkle shredded cheese and breadcrumbs over casserole. Bake at 325° for 25 minutes or until hot and bubbly.

* I cut large ham slices into thirds, making 2-inch wide strips 5 to 6 inches long.

Makes 12 servings   Sandy Brodie, Boulder, Colorado

Per serving: 412 calories, 33 g fat, 17 g protein, 14 g carbohydrate, 283 mg cholesterol, 787 mg sodium.

To prevent stringy cheese in sauces and casseroles, especially when using Swiss, mozzarella and Cheddar cheese, squeeze about 1 teaspoon fresh lemon juice over each cup of shredded cheese or sprinkle with white wine; fluff with fork.

Barbara's Quiche

I frequently make this quiche for an easy supper or quick lunch for friends.

½ pound bacon, cooked and crumbled[14]

6 ounces Swiss or Cheddar cheese, grated (1½ cups)

1 (9-inch) *Partially Baked Pie Crust*

3 eggs, room temperature

¾ teaspoon salt

Dash of ground nutmeg

Dash of cayenne pepper

1½ cups heavy cream or half-and-half*

Paprika

Sprinkle bacon and cheese over pie crust. Lightly whisk eggs in medium bowl. Whisk in salt, nutmeg, cayenne pepper and cream until well combined. Pour over bacon and cheese. Sprinkle with paprika. Bake at 375° for 35 to 40 minutes or until golden and firm.[37] Cover edge with foil if browning too fast.[17] Cool on rack 10 minutes before serving.

Makes 6 servings   Barbara Ringkjob, Boulder, Colorado

Per serving: 574 calories, 44 g fat, 26 g protein, 18 g carbohydrate, 188 mg cholesterol, 1016 mg sodium.

* Recipe was also tested using reduced-fat milk; it was great.

Asparagus Chicken Quiche

An attractive quiche–asparagus pieces float to surface and paprika adds rich color.

1 (9-inch) *Prebaked Pie Crust*

6 ounces Cheddar or Swiss cheese, shredded (1½ cups), *divided*

⅔ cup chopped *Easy Cooked Chicken*

4 slices bacon, cooked and crumbled[14] (about ⅓ cup)

8 to 10 fresh asparagus spears,[34] cut diagonally into 1-inch pieces

¼ cup sliced green onions, including some tops

1 to 2 teaspoons vegetable oil

4 eggs, room temperature

½ teaspoon salt

Dash of cayenne pepper

1½ cups half-and-half

Paprika

Prebake pie crust; let cool slightly. Sprinkle 1 cup cheese over crust. Sprinkle chicken and bacon over cheese. Sauté asparagus and green onion in oil in small skillet over medium-low heat until tender, about 3 minutes. Spoon over bacon. Lightly whisk eggs in medium bowl. Whisk in salt, cayenne pepper and half-and-half until just combined. Carefully pour over asparagus. Sprinkle remaining ½ cup cheese on top. Sprinkle with paprika. Bake at 325° for 45 minutes or just until sharp knife inserted near center comes out clean.[37] Cover edges with foil after 30 minutes if browning too fast.[17] Let stand 15 minutes before serving.

Makes 6 servings

Per serving: 412 calories, 30 g fat, 29 g protein, 20 g carbohydrate, 207 mg cholesterol, 634 mg sodium.

Bacon and Green Chile Quiche

½ pound bacon, cooked and crumbled[14]	6 ounces Colby-Jack cheese, shredded (1½ cups)
1 (9-inch) *Partially Baked Pie Crust*	3 eggs, room temperature
1 (4-ounce) can diced green chiles, drained	¼ to ½ teaspoon salt
	Dash of cayenne pepper
¼ cup chopped sweet or green onion	1½ cups half-and-half or heavy cream

Sprinkle bacon over crust. Layer green chiles, onion and cheese over bacon. Beat eggs, salt, cayenne pepper and half-and-half in medium bowl until combined. Pour over cheese. Bake at 375° for 35 to 40 minutes or until golden and firm.[37] Cover crust if browning too fast.[17] Let stand 10 minutes before serving.

Makes 6 servings

Per serving: 586 calories, 44 g fat, 26 g protein, 19 g carbohydrate, 188 mg cholesterol, 1057 mg sodium.

Crustless Ham Quiche

Perfect for using leftovers. Add a little steamed broccoli or asparagus and leave out the ham. Experiment!

1 tablespoon butter	1 cup sour cream
2 tablespoons chopped red or green bell pepper (optional)	½ teaspoon dried dill weed, crushed
½ cup chopped onion	½ teaspoon dry mustard[9]
1 (8-ounce) package sliced fresh mushrooms,[3] or 1 (4-ounce) can sliced mushrooms, drained	1½ ounces Asiago or Parmesan cheese, grated (½ cup)
1 cup chopped cooked ham	¼ cup flour
	Dash of hot pepper sauce
1 (2¼-ounce) can sliced ripe olives, drained (optional)	4 ounces Cheddar cheese, shredded (1 cup), or combination of Cheddar, Swiss, mozzarella or other leftover pieces of cheese
4 eggs	
1 cup small-curd cottage cheese	Paprika

Melt butter in medium skillet. Sauté bell pepper, onion and mushrooms until most liquid evaporates. Stir in ham. Spread into sprayed 9-inch deep-dish pie plate. Sprinkle with olives. Beat eggs, cottage cheese, sour cream, dill, dry mustard, grated cheese, flour and pepper sauce in medium bowl with mixer until combined. Stir in Cheddar cheese. Pour over ham mixture and sprinkle with paprika. Bake at 350° for 35 to 40 minutes or until golden and firm.[37] Let stand 10 minutes. Serve with salsa and tortilla chips, or serve with *Cranberry Salad* and rolls.

Makes 6 servings

Per serving: 417 calories, 30 g fat, 25 g protein, 12 g carbohydrate, 220 mg cholesterol, 837 mg sodium.

Hot Fruit Casserole

*Jackie's **Hot Fruit Casserole** is the best!*

½ cup golden raisins	3 tablespoons butter
½ cup boiling water	3 tablespoons flour
1 (15½-ounce) can peach halves	¾ cup sugar
1 (16-ounce) can pear halves	Dash of salt
1 (15¼-ounce) can pineapple chunks in juice	½ cup dry or cream sherry (not cooking sherry)
1 (30-ounce) can fruit cocktail	

Put raisins in small bowl and cover with boiling water. Let plump 5 minutes. Drain and set aside. Place colander over large bowl and pour in peaches, pears, pineapple and fruit cocktail. Drain well. Reserve 1 cup juice. Melt butter in small saucepan over medium-low heat. Stir in flour and cook until bubbly. Add reserved juice, sugar and salt. Cook and stir over medium heat until sauce is thick and smooth. Remove from heat and cool. Stir in sherry.

Arrange peach and pear halves cutside down in 9x13-inch baking dish. Sprinkle pineapple chunks, fruit cocktail and raisins around fruit halves. Pour sauce over fruit. Cover and refrigerate overnight. Remove about an hour before baking. Bake at 350° for 30 to 40 minutes or until hot and bubbly. Let stand 10 minutes.

Makes 10 servings   Jackie Andrishok, Destin, Florida

Per serving: 187 calories, 4 g fat, 2 g protein, 37 g carbohydrate, 0 mg cholesterol, 49 mg sodium.

Pineapple Casserole

1 cup sugar	1 (8-ounce) package cream cheese, cubed
2 tablespoons flour	
1 (20-ounce) can crushed pineapple in juice, drained, reserve juice	2 cups miniature marshmallows
2 eggs, lightly beaten	8 ounces Cheddar cheese, shredded (2 cups)

Mix sugar and flour in medium saucepan. Add enough water to reserved pineapple juice to make 1 cup; stir into saucepan. Whisk in eggs and cook over low heat until thickened, whisking frequently. Set aside. Distribute cream cheese over bottom of sprayed 7x11-inch baking dish. Cover with pineapple and sprinkle with marshmallows. Pour egg mixture over marshmallows. (Casserole may be prepared ahead. Refrigerate covered several hours or overnight; remove 30 minutes before baking.) Bake uncovered at 350° for 25 minutes. Sprinkle cheese over top. Bake 5 more minutes or until cheese melts. Let stand 10 minutes.

Makes 6 servings   Gwin Cumo, Hilton Head Island, South Carolina

Per serving: 548 calories, 27 g fat, 15 g protein, 62 g carbohydrate, 153 mg cholesterol, 426 mg sodium.

Cinnamon Gems

24	slices white sandwich bread	1	cup sugar
1	(8-ounce) package cream cheese, softened	1	teaspoon ground cinnamon
		½	cup (1 stick) butter, melted

Remove crusts from bread slices and cut each slice into two rectangles. Stir cream cheese in bowl until spreadable and spread thin layer on each rectangle. Roll up jelly-roll fashion from short side. Mix sugar and cinnamon in shallow bowl. Brush entire surface of each roll with butter (small paintbrush works well) and roll in sugar mixture. Place seamside down on foil-lined baking sheet. (May prepare ahead to this point; refrigerate or flash-freeze.[26] Bring to room temperature before baking.) Bake at 350° for 10 minutes or until golden.

Makes 48 rolls   Mona Bell, Lawrence, Kansas

Per roll: 83 calories, 4 g fat, 1 g protein, 11 g carbohydrate, 10 mg cholesterol, 101 mg sodium.

Bundt Coffee Cake

Quick, easy and always a hit!

1	(18¼-ounce) package yellow cake mix	1	teaspoon imitation butter flavoring
1	(4-serving size) package vanilla instant pudding mix	1	teaspoon vanilla extract
¾	cup vegetable oil	½	cup chopped toasted pecans
¾	cup cold water	2	teaspoons ground cinnamon
4	eggs, room temperature	¼	cup sugar
		1	recipe *Confectioners' Sugar Glaze*

Beat cake mix, pudding mix, oil, water, eggs, butter flavoring and vanilla in large bowl with mixer on low until combined, about 1 minute. Scrape down sides and beat on medium 2 minutes. Pour half the batter into lightly sprayed 10-inch Bundt pan. Mix pecans, cinnamon and sugar in small bowl and sprinkle half over batter. Add remaining batter and sprinkle remaining pecan mixture on top. Bake at 350° for 45 to 50 minutes[4] or until wooden pick inserted in center comes out clean. Cool in pan 10 minutes.[8] Invert onto serving plate and cool completely. Drizzle *Confectioners' Sugar Glaze* over cake.

Makes 16 servings   Velma Goettel, Bella Vista, Arkansas

Per serving: 352 calories, 19 g fat, 4 g protein, 42 g carbohydrate, 57 mg cholesterol, 250 mg sodium.

Lite variation: Use ⅓ cup vegetable oil and 1 cup water in batter. Omit glaze; dust cake with confectioners' sugar.

Per serving: 250 calories, 12 g fat, 4 g protein, 32 g carbohydrate, 54 mg cholesterol, 239 mg sodium.

Apple Breakfast Cake

Lorraine finely chops the apples in a food processor, giving the cake a different texture from most apple cakes.

Butter Sauce:
1 cup (2 sticks) butter, cut into pieces
1 cup sugar
1 cup packed brown sugar[1]
½ to ¾ cup milk or cream
2 tablespoons flour
2 teaspoons vanilla extract
½ cup shortening

2 cups sugar
2 eggs, room temperature
2 teaspoons vanilla extract
2¼ cups flour
½ teaspoon salt
1 teaspoon ground cinnamon
1 teaspoon ground nutmeg
4 cups peeled and finely chopped tart green apples

Butter Sauce: Put butter in sprayed medium saucepan[38] and add sugars, milk and flour. Heat on low, stirring until butter melts and mixture is smooth. Bring to boil (bubbles all over top). Boil 1½ minutes without stirring, lifting and swirling pan frequently. Remove from heat and whisk in vanilla. Pour into pitcher and serve warm. Makes 2⅔ cups. Recipe may be halved. (Sauce may be prepared ahead. Reheat in microwave or in small saucepan.)

Beat shortening and sugar in large bowl with mixer until creamed, about 2 minutes. Beat in eggs and vanilla, mixing well. Whisk flour, salt, cinnamon and nutmeg in medium bowl.[2] Beat into creamed mixture (mixture will be thick). Stir in apples with strong wooden spoon. Pour into sprayed 9x13-inch baking pan or baking dish, spreading out evenly. Bake at 350° for 40 minutes[4] or until wooden pick inserted in center comes out clean. Cut into squares and serve with warm Butter Sauce.

Makes 12 servings   Lorraine Newberry, Bella Vista, Arkansas

Per serving: 608 calories, 25 g fat, 4 g protein, 94 g carbohydrate, 78 mg cholesterol, 267 mg sodium.

Sour Cream Coffee Cake

½ cup (1 stick) butter, cut into pieces
1⅓ cups sugar, *divided*
2 eggs, room temperature
1 teaspoon vanilla extract
2 cups flour
1½ teaspoons baking powder
1 teaspoon baking soda
½ teaspoon salt
1 cup sour cream
1 teaspoon ground cinnamon
½ cup coarsely chopped toasted pecans
1 recipe *Confectioners' Sugar Glaze*, or use confectioners' sugar

Beat butter and 1 cup sugar in large bowl with mixer until light and fluffy, about 2 minutes; scrape down sides. Beat in eggs and vanilla, about 1 minute. Whisk flour, baking powder, baking soda and salt in medium bowl.[2] Beat into creamed mixture alternately with sour cream, beginning and ending with flour mixture. (Add flour mixture in three additions and sour cream in two additions. Beat about 30 seconds and scrape down sides after each addition.)

Mix remaining ⅓ cup sugar and cinnamon in small bowl. Set aside. Pour slightly more than half the batter into sprayed and floured 10-inch tube or Bundt pan. Make wide, shallow trench in middle of batter with back of tablespoon, pushing some batter up sides of pan. Sprinkle sugar mixture into and up sides of trench. Sprinkle pecans into trench. Cover with remaining batter. Draw table knife lightly though batter to swirl, being careful not to touch bottom or sides (cake will stick to pan). Smooth out top. Bake at 350° for 45 to 50 minutes[4] or until wooden pick inserted in center comes out clean. Cool in pan 10 minutes.[8] Invert onto serving plate. Drizzle glaze over cake. Sprinkle with chopped nuts, if desired, or sprinkle cake with confectioners' sugar.

Makes 12 servings   **Adapted from recipe by Barbara Stewart, Annandale, Virginia**

Per serving: 315 calories, 16 g fat, 4 g protein, 40 g carbohydrate, 44 mg cholesterol, 334 mg sodium.

Danish Puff Coffee Cake

Pastry:
½ cup (1 stick) butter
1 cup flour
1 to 2 tablespoons cold water

Cream Puff Mixture:
½ cup (1 stick) butter, cut into pieces
1 cup water
1 teaspoon almond extract

1 cup bread flour[63] (may substitute unbleached all-purpose flour)
¼ teaspoon salt
3 eggs, room temperature

Frosting:
1½ cups confectioners' sugar
2 tablespoons water
½ teaspoon almond extract
½ cup toasted sliced almonds

Pastry: Cut butter into flour in medium bowl with pastry blender until crumbly. Sprinkle in water, 1 tablespoon at a time (one may be enough), tossing with fork until moist enough to shape into ball. Wrap in plastic and chill. Divide in half and roll each portion into a 12-inch cylinder. Place cylinders 6 inches apart on ungreased baking sheet; pat each into 3-inch wide strip and turn up edges slightly, leaving center portion of strip quite thin. Refrigerate while preparing Cream Puff Mixture.

Cream Puff Mixture: Put butter in medium saucepan. Add water and bring to boil. Add almond extract, flour and salt. Stir vigorously with wooden spoon until smooth ball forms and pulls away from sides of pan. Remove from heat and cool slightly, about 3 minutes. Add eggs, one at a time, beating well with wooden spoon after each addition until smooth and glossy. (See *Cream Puffs*.)

Frosting: Stir confectioners' sugar, water and almond extract together in medium bowl until smooth.

Assembly: Remove pastry from refrigerator and spread half the Cream Puff Mixture evenly over each pastry strip. Bake at 350° for 1 hour. Cool 10 minutes. Cut each pastry strip down middle, then cut crosswise into twelve pieces. Frost tops and sprinkle with almonds.

Makes 24 pieces   Jean Koppernolle, Bella Vista, Arkansas

Per piece: 149 calories, 9 g fat, 2 g protein, 150 g carbohydrate, 49 mg cholesterol, 93 mg sodium.

Cakes & Frostings

Cakes

Frostings, Glazes, Fillings and Toppings

Kay's Carrot Cake

1	cup sugar
¾	cup packed light brown sugar[1]
1¼	cups vegetable oil
4	eggs, room temperature
1	cup flour
1	cup whole wheat flour
2	teaspoons ground cinnamon
1½	teaspoons baking soda
1	teaspoon baking powder
½	teaspoon salt
3	cups grated peeled carrots

Cream Cheese Frosting:

1	(8-ounce) package cream cheese, softened
½	cup (1 stick) butter, softened
2	cups confectioners' sugar
2	teaspoons clear imitation vanilla extract[22]
	Dash of salt
1	cup chopped toasted pecans (optional)

Beat sugars and oil in large bowl with mixer until combined, about 1 minute. Add eggs, one at a time, beating well after each addition until no yellow streaks remain. Whisk flours, cinnamon, baking soda, baking powder and salt in separate bowl.[2] Beat into sugar mixture on low until combined. Stir in carrots. Spoon batter equally[25] into three 8-inch round cake pans lined with sprayed wax paper.[79] Tap pans on counter to remove air bubbles. Bake at 350° for 25 to 30 minutes[4] or until wooden pick inserted in centers comes out clean. Cool in pans on racks 10 minutes. Remove layers to racks and cool completely.[27] If time permits, chill or freeze layers for easier handling and to reduce crumbling. Meanwhile, prepare Cream Cheese Frosting.

Peel wax paper from layers as cake is assembled. Place first layer topside down on plate. Spread layer with frosting. Position second layer topside down over first, aligning thick and thin parts to make cake level, if necessary. Frost layer. Add third layer topside up. Frost sides and top of cake.[23] Pat chopped pecans into sides and top, if used. Refrigerate until ready to serve. Cake freezes well.

Cream Cheese Frosting: Beat cream cheese and butter in large bowl with mixer until smooth. Gradually beat in confectioners' sugar 1 cup at a time. Add vanilla and salt. Beat until light and fluffy.

Makes 12 servings   Kay Sonnesyn, Longmont, Colorado

Per serving: 640 calories, 39 g fat, 6 g protein, 69 g carbohydrate, 113 mg cholesterol, 447 mg sodium.

Mandarin Layer Cake

Ruthie Warnall gave me permission to adapt this recipe from her "3 Ingredient Cookbook, Volume III." She encouraged me to write my cookbook, saying, "Just go for it!"

1 (18¼-ounce) package yellow cake mix

2 (11-ounce) cans Mandarin oranges, snipped and drained,* reserve juice

Pineapple Frosting:
1 (20-ounce) can crushed pineapple in juice or in syrup

1 (6-serving size) package vanilla instant pudding mix

1 teaspoon lemon juice (optional)

1 (8-ounce) container whipped topping, thawed

Prepare cake mix according to package directions, except mix reserved Mandarin orange juice with enough water to make amount of water called for in cake-mix directions. Stir orange pieces into batter. Spray two 9-inch round cake pans. Line with wax paper.[79] Spoon batter equally[25] into pans. Tap pans on counter to remove air bubbles. Bake at 350° for 20 to 30 minutes[4] or until wooden pick inserted in center comes out clean. Cool in pans on rack 10 minutes. Remove layers to racks and cool completely.[27] If time permits, chill or freeze layers for easier handling and to reduce crumbling. Meanwhile, prepare Pineapple Frosting.

Peel wax paper from layers as cake is assembled. Place first layer topside down on plate. Spread layer with frosting. Add second layer topside up, aligning thick and thin areas to make cake level if necessary. Frost sides and top.[23] Refrigerate until ready to serve.

Pineapple Frosting: Drain pineapple, reserving ½ cup juice. Stir pineapple and pudding mix together in large bowl. Stir in reserved juice and lemon juice. Fold in whipped topping. Refrigerate until ready to use.

* Mandarin oranges will be easy to cut if you snip them with kitchen shears while draining in strainer. You will get extra juice that way, too.

Makes 12 servings   Ruthie Warnall, Overland Park, Kansas

Per serving: 370 calories, 10 g fat, 3 g protein, 68 g carbohydrate, 1 mg cholesterol, 420 mg sodium.

Bundt pan variation: Pour batter into greased and floured 10-inch Bundt pan. Run knife through batter and bounce pan on counter to remove air bubbles. Bake at 350° for 45 to 50 minutes[4] or until wooden pick inserted in center comes out clean. Cool in pan 25 minutes.[8] Loosen cake around stem with plastic knife and gently shake up and down to release cake from pan. Invert onto serving plate and cool completely. Frost[23] with Pineapple Frosting and refrigerate.

Cream Cheese Pound Cake

Martha and I became good friends when we lived in Scottsdale, Arizona. This recipe is from her aunt, Inez Rheney of White Rock, South Carolina, a retired home-economics teacher and serious cake maker. She lived to be 103 in 2001.

1½	cups (3 sticks) butter, softened	6	eggs
1	(8-ounce) package cream cheese, softened	3	cups cake flour
			Dash of salt
3	cups sugar	1½	tablespoons vanilla extract

All ingredients should be at room temperature. Beat butter and cream cheese in large bowl with mixer until smooth. Gradually add sugar and beat until light and fluffy, about 2 minutes. Scrape down sides. Add eggs, one at a time, beating well after each addition until no yellow streaks remain. Whisk flour and salt in medium bowl. Gradually beat into creamed mixture on low until just combined. Mix in vanilla. Pour batter into greased and floured 10-inch tube or Bundt pan. Bake at 300° for 1½ hours[4] or until wooden pick inserted in center comes out clean. Cool in pan on rack 15 minutes.[8] Invert cake onto serving plate and cool completely. Dust with confectioners' sugar, if desired.

Makes 20 servings   Martha Tompkins, Greenville, South Carolina

Per serving: 360 calories, 19 g fat, 4 g protein, 44 g carbohydrate, 77 mg cholesterol, 226 mg sodium.

Pound Cake Tips

Generously grease Bundt or tube pans with shortening, spreading evenly with small brush; dust pan with flour and tap out excess.

If many extracts and flavorings are called for in recipe, put them in a line on one side of mixing bowl in order listed and transfer to other side as they are added. That way you will know they have all been included.

Be careful not to overbeat butter-sugar mixture, especially on warm days. Overbeating could break down air cells, causing batter to be heavy.

Rather than adding and beating in one whole egg at a time into creamed mixture, lightly beat all the eggs in glass measure and slowly pour into creamed mixture in thin stream while beating. Will help prevent curdling appearance in mixture and will produce a light and tender cake.

Pound cakes will begin to pull away from sides of pan when done; however, also check for doneness with wooden pick inserted in center.

Proper cooling of cake is important. Removing from pan before 10 minutes, while cake is still quite warm and tender, may cause cake to break; after 20 minutes shortening begins to harden and can "glue" cake to pan.

Macadamia Pineapple Apricot Pound Cake

1	cup (2 sticks) butter, cut into pieces	½	teaspoon imitation rum extract
2½	cups sugar	½	cup apricot brandy
6	eggs	½	cup coarsely chopped macadamia nuts
3	cups flour, *divided*	½	cup dried pineapple chunks, cut in half
¼	teaspoon baking soda		
½	teaspoon salt	½	cup dried apricots, cut into fourths
1	cup sour cream		
1	teaspoon orange extract		Apricot Sauce:
½	teaspoon lemon extract	1	(18-ounce) jar apricot preserves
½	teaspoon almond extract	¼	cup apricot brandy
1	teaspoon clear imitation vanilla extract[22]	1	tablespoon fresh lemon juice

Review *Pound Cake Tips* before starting this recipe.

Beat butter in large bowl with mixer until fluffy. Add sugar gradually and beat until creamed, about 2 minutes. Scrape down sides. Lightly beat eggs in 2-cup glass measure with fork. Slowly pour into creamed mixture in thin stream while beating, 4 to 5 minutes. Scrape down sides.

Whisk 2¾ cups flour, baking soda and salt in medium bowl.[2] Mix sour cream, extracts (orange, lemon, almond, vanilla and rum) and brandy in separate bowl. Beat flour mixture into creamed mixture on low, alternately with sour cream mixture, beginning and ending with flour mixture. (Sprinkle in flour mixture in three additions and add sour cream mixture in two additions. Beat about 30 seconds and scrape down sides after each addition.) Put nuts and dried fruit in medium bowl and dust with remaining ¼ cup flour. Fold into batter.

Pour batter into well-greased and floured 10-inch tube or Bundt pan and spread out evenly with spoon-shaped rubber spatula. Run knife through batter and gently bounce pan on counter to remove air bubbles. Bake at 325° for 1 hour 15 minutes[4] or until wooden pick inserted in center comes out clean. Cool in pan on rack 15 minutes.[8] Run plastic knife around sides and center to loosen cake. Gently, but firmly, shake pan up and down to release cake. Invert onto serving plate. Cool completely. Spoon half the sauce over cake.[23] Pour remaining sauce into small pitcher to serve over cake slices, if desired. Top with whipped cream.

Apricot Sauce: Mix preserves, brandy and lemon juice in small saucepan. Bring to boil. Cook and stir until mixture liquefies. Cool.

Makes 16 servings

Per serving: 601 calories, 22 g fat, 7 g protein, 91 g carbohydrate, 116 mg cholesterol, 344 mg sodium.

continues

Macadamia Pineapple Apricot Pound Cake (continued)

Apricot Brandy Pound Cake variation: Whisk all 3 cups flour, baking soda and salt in medium bowl; set aside. Continue as directed in *Macadamia Pineapple Apricot Pound Cake*, omitting nuts and dried fruit. Serve with Apricot Sauce.

Almond Pound Cake variation: Substitute almond-flavored liqueur for brandy. Increase almond extract to 1 teaspoon in cake batter. Omit nuts and dried fruit. Bake as directed in *Macadamia Pineapple Apricot Pound Cake*. Substitute almond-flavored liqueur for apricot brandy in Apricot Sauce. Spoon over cooled cake. Sprinkle ⅓ cup toasted sliced almonds on top of cake to form a crown. Dab almonds with sauce.

Grandma's Imperial Pound Cake

Butter was rationed during World War II. Some cooks found that half or all the butter in a pound cake recipe could successfully be replaced with quality margarine; hence the name.

1 pound butter, or ½ pound butter and ½ pound margarine,[50] cut into pieces	3½ cups *sifted* cake flour[24]
	½ teaspoon almond extract or lemon extract
6 eggs	½ teaspoon vanilla extract
1 (16-ounce) box confectioners' sugar (3¾ cups)	¼ cup crushed toasted pecans, walnuts or sliced almonds[21]

All ingredients should be at room temperature. Cream butter in large bowl with mixer, about 1 minute. Beat in eggs, one at a time, alternately with confectioners' sugar (about ½ cup at a time) until eggs and sugar are used. Scrape down sides occasionally. Add flour, a cup at a time, and continue beating. (Kathy says, "The more you beat this cake, the lighter it gets.") Mix in almond and vanilla extracts.

Grease and flour 10-inch tube or Bundt pan. Sprinkle nuts over pan bottom. Spoon in batter and smooth out with spoon-shaped rubber spatula. Bake at 325° for 60 to 65 minutes,[4] testing with wooden pick at 60 minutes. Do not overbake. Remove and cool in pan on rack 10 minutes.[8] Loosen sides and center of cake with plastic knife. Invert onto serving plate. Cool completely. Sprinkle with confectioners' sugar, if desired.

Makes 16 servings Kathy Beckett, Aurora, Colorado

Per serving: 439 calories, 26 g fat, 5 g protein, 47 g carbohydrate, 112 mg cholesterol, 276 mg sodium.

Red Velvet Cake

½	cup shortening	1	teaspoon baking soda
1½	cups sugar	1	tablespoon white vinegar
2	eggs, room temperature		
2	heaping tablespoons unsweetened cocoa powder		Velvet Frosting:
		1	cup whole milk
2	(1-ounce) bottles red food coloring (4 tablespoons)	¼	cup flour
		¼	teaspoon salt
2¼	cups *sifted* cake flour[24]	½	cup shortening
½	teaspoon salt	½	cup (1 stick) margarine
1	cup buttermilk[42]	1	cup sugar
1	teaspoon vanilla extract	1	teaspoon clear imitation vanilla extract[22]

Beat shortening, sugar and eggs in large bowl with mixer until creamed, about 2 minutes. Stir cocoa and food coloring together in small bowl to make paste. Mix into creamed mixture. Whisk flour and salt in separate bowl. Beat into creamed mixture alternately with buttermilk, beginning and ending with flour mixture. (Add flour mixture in three additions and buttermilk in two additions. Beat about 30 seconds and scrape down sides after each addition.) Mix in vanilla. Combine baking soda and vinegar in small bowl, holding over batter as it foams. *Fold* into batter. Spray two 9-inch round cake pans. Line with wax paper.[79] Spoon batter equally[25] into pans. Tap pans on counter to remove air bubbles. Bake at 350° for 25 to 30 minutes[4] or until wooden pick inserted in centers comes out clean. Cool in pans on racks 15 minutes. Remove cake layers to racks and cool completely.[27] If time permits, chill or freeze layers for easier handling and to reduce crumbling. Peel wax paper from layers as cake is assembled. Place first layer topside down on plate. Spread layer with frosting. Add second layer topside up, aligning thick and thin parts to make cake level if necessary. Frost sides and top.[23] Refrigerate until ready to serve.

Velvet Frosting: Put milk in small saucepan and whisk in flour and salt. Cook over medium-low heat, whisking frequently at first, then constantly until very thick paste forms (lift pan to prevent burning if necessary). Remove from heat and run spatula around sides. Place plastic wrap on surface to prevent skin from forming. Cool completely (refrigerate, if desired). Beat shortening and margarine in large bowl until combined. Beat in ⅓ cup sugar at a time until fluffy and creamed, about 4 minutes. Scrape down sides. Mix in vanilla. Gradually beat in cooled flour mixture on medium, then beat on high until sugar is dissolved and frosting is smooth, 5 to 6 minutes (frosting should look like whipped cream). Makes about 3 cups. (Note: Cream Cheese Frosting from **Kay's Carrot Cake** may be substituted for Velvet Frosting.)

Makes 16 servings

Per serving: 376 calories, 20 g fat, 3 g protein, 47 g carbohydrate, 29 mg cholesterol, 261 mg sodium.

Easy Red Velvet Cake

Red Velvet Cake batter   *Red Velvet Cake* Velvet Frosting

Bake cake batter as directed in *Easy Layer Cake* for 2-layer cake. Frost sides and top with Velvet Frosting or Cream Cheese Frosting (see *Kay's Carrot Cake*).

Makes 16 servings

Per serving: 376 calories, 20 g fat, 3 g protein, 47 g carbohydrate, 29 mg cholesterol, 261 mg sodium.

Easy Layer Cake

Use one 10x15-inch jelly-roll pan to make this easy layer cake.

1   (18¼-ounce) package cake mix,   Filling (optional)
    or cake batter from recipe for   Frosting or Glaze
    2-layer cake

Prepare cake mix according to package directions, or prepare cake batter according to recipe directions (batter should not exceed 5½ cups).

Spread batter evenly into well-sprayed foil-lined 10x15-inch jelly-roll pan.[6] Run knife through batter and tap pan gently on counter to remove air bubbles. Bake at 325° for 15 to 30 minutes (wide range of baking time covers type and content of batter) or until wooden pick inserted in center comes out clean (top of cake should feel firm). Cool in pan on rack 10 minutes. Lift and slide liner onto large cutting board. Carefully peel down foil from sides of cake. Cool 15 minutes. Cut cake crosswise in half for 2-layer cake or into thirds for 3-layer cake or torte (long piece of dental floss works well). Cut through foil with scissors and separate sections. Place sections on baking sheets and put in freezer 20 minutes.[39]

Remove foil from layers as cake is assembled. Sprinkle confectioners' sugar over rectangular serving plate or platter. For 2-layer cake, place first section topside down on prepared serving plate and spread section with filling or frosting.[23] Add second section topside up, aligning thick part over thin part of first section to make cake level. If time permits, refrigerate assembled cake 10 minutes to set layers and filling. Finish frosting sides and top or glaze as directed in recipe. Refrigerate if required.

For 3-layer cake or torte, place one end section on plate topside up. Spread section with filling or frosting. Place other end section topside down with thick part over thin part of first section to make cake level if necessary. Spread with filling or frosting. Add middle section topside up. If time permits, refrigerate assembled cake 10 minutes to set layers and filling. Finish frosting sides and top or glaze cake as directed in recipe. Refrigerate if required.

Makes 16 servings

Per serving: 376 calories, 20 g fat, 3 g protein, 47 g carbohydrate, 29 mg cholesterol, 261 mg sodium.

Carrot Pineapple Cake

Simple and easy; no grating or shredding carrots. I saw a recipe that called for pureed carrots, so I decided to use baby food carrots.

2	(6-ounce) jars junior baby food carrots	1	cup chopped toasted pecans or walnuts, *divided*
2	cups sugar	½	cup golden raisins
¾	cup vegetable oil		Cream Cheese Frosting:
2	teaspoons vanilla extract	1	(8-ounce) package cream cheese, softened
3	eggs, room temperature		
2¼	cups flour, *divided*	½	cup (1 stick) butter, softened
1	teaspoon salt	2	cups confectioners' sugar
2	teaspoons baking soda	2	teaspoons clear imitation vanilla extract[22]
2	teaspoons ground cinnamon		
¼	teaspoon ground nutmeg		Dash of salt
2	(8-ounce) cans crushed pineapple in juice, undrained		

Beat carrots, sugar, oil and vanilla in large bowl with mixer, about 1 minute. Add eggs, one at a time, beating about 30 seconds on low after each addition. Reserve 1 tablespoon flour in small bowl and set aside. Whisk remaining flour, salt, baking soda, cinnamon and nutmeg in separate bowl.[2] Sprinkle 1 cup flour mixture at a time into carrot mixture and beat on low until combined. Scrape down sides. Fold in pineapple with juice. Dust ½ cup nuts and raisins with reserved tablespoon flour and fold into batter. Pour into sprayed 9x13-inch baking pan. Tap pan on counter to remove air bubbles. Bake at 350° for 45 to 50 minutes[4] or until wooden pick inserted in center comes out clean. Transfer cake in pan to rack and cool completely.

Frost top of cake. Sprinkle with remaining ½ cup nuts. Cover and refrigerate. To serve, bring to room temperature and cut into squares. Cake freezes well.

Cream Cheese Frosting: Beat cream cheese and butter in large bowl with mixer until creamed. Gradually beat in confectioners' sugar 1 cup at a time. Add vanilla and salt; beat until light and fluffy.

Makes 16 servings

Per serving: 512 calories, 27 g fat, 5 g protein, 65 g carbohydrate, 71mg cholesterol, 425 mg sodium.

Chocolate Black Raspberry Torte

½ cup (1 stick) butter, cut into
   pieces
1 cup sugar
4 eggs, room temperature
1½ cups *Chocolate Syrup*, or
   1 (16-ounce) can chocolate syrup
1 teaspoon vanilla extract
2 tablespoons black raspberry
   liqueur
1 cup flour

½ teaspoon salt
1 teaspoon baking powder

Black Raspberry Cream:
3 tablespoons black raspberry
   liqueur
2 tablespoons confectioners' sugar
1 (8-ounce) container whipped
   topping, thawed

1 recipe *Chocolate Glaze*

Beat butter and sugar in large bowl with mixer until creamed, about 2 minutes. Scrape down sides. Lightly beat eggs in 2-cup glass measure. Slowly pour into creamed mixture in thin stream while beating, about 3 minutes. Scrape down sides. Blend in *Chocolate Syrup*, vanilla and liqueur until combined.

Whisk flour, salt and baking powder in medium bowl.[2] Sprinkle half the flour mixture into chocolate mixture, blending in with mixer on low. Sprinkle in remaining flour mixture and blend about 1 more minute. Pour batter into well-sprayed foil-lined 10x15-inch jelly-roll pan.[6] Spread out evenly with rubber spatula and bounce pan on counter to remove air bubbles. Bake at 325° for 30 to 33 minutes or until wooden pick inserted in center comes out clean. Cool in pan 10 minutes.

Lift and slide liner onto large cutting board. Carefully peel down foil from sides of cake. Cool 15 minutes. Cut cake crosswise into three 5-inch sections. Cut through foil and separate sections. Place sections on baking sheets and put in freezer 30 to 60 minutes.[39] Meanwhile, prepare filling and glaze.

Remove foil from layers as cake is assembled. Place one end section on rectangular serving plate topside up. Spread with half the Black Raspberry Cream (not too close to edge–weight of layers will push filling toward edge). Place other end section topside down with thick part over thin part of first section to make cake level, if necessary. Spread top with remaining cream filling. Add middle section topside up. If time permits, refrigerate assembled cake 10 minutes to set layers and filling.

Drizzle thickened *Chocolate Glaze* over layers without covering entire torte. Let dry. Drizzle additional glaze over torte, if desired, and let dry. Place fresh raspberries on top. Refrigerate. Slice several minutes before serving for best flavor.

Black Raspberry Cream: Fold[G] liqueur and confectioners' sugar into container of whipped topping; refrigerate until ready to assemble cake.

Makes 8 to 10 servings

Per serving: 571 calories, 22 g fat, 6 g protein, 88 g carbohydrate, 111 mg cholesterol, 339 mg sodium.

Lemon Chiffon Cake

6 eggs, separated[12]
½ teaspoon cream of tartar
1¼ cups sugar, *divided*
2¼ cups cake flour
5 teaspoons finely grated lemon zest
2 teaspoons baking powder
½ teaspoon baking soda
¼ teaspoon salt
½ cup water

½ cup fresh lemon juice
⅓ cup vegetable oil
1 teaspoon lemon extract

Lemon Frosting:
5 cups confectioners' sugar
½ cup shortening
¼ cup fresh lemon juice
1 teaspoon lemon extract

Beat egg whites and cream of tartar in large, deep, metal or glass bowl with mixer on medium until cream of tartar dissolves and egg whites are foamy throughout, about 2 minutes. Beat on high until soft peaks just begin to form. Gradually beat in ¼ cup sugar until stiff peaks form; set aside.

Whisk flour, remaining 1 cup sugar, lemon zest, baking powder, baking soda and salt in large bowl.[2] Make well in center and add egg yolks, water, lemon juice, oil and lemon extract. With same beaters, beat mixture on medium until smooth batter forms. Fold[G] one-third beaten egg whites into yolk mixture with large rubber spatula. Gently fold in remaining egg whites until no white streaks remain.

Pour batter into *ungreased* 10-inch tube pan and spread out evenly. Bake at 325° for 60 to 65 minutes or until wooden pick inserted in center comes out clean (test at 60 minutes). Transfer immediately to inverted level position over narrow-necked bottle, large funnel or over a colander to prevent cake from sinking. Cool cake completely, 1 to 1½ hours. Run plastic knife around tube and sides. For 2-piece pan, lift tube with cake out of pan, loosen cake from bottom with plastic knife and invert onto serving plate. For 1-piece pan, bounce on counter several times and invert onto serving plate. Frost cake with Lemon Frosting.[23]

Lemon Frosting: Beat confectioners' sugar, shortening, lemon juice and lemon extract in large bowl with mixer on low to combine; increase speed to medium and beat until smooth, scraping down sides occasionally. If thick, add 1 teaspoon lemon juice at a time until spreading consistency.

Makes 12 servings   Judy Coats, Longmont, Colorado

Per serving: 529 calories, 17 g fat, 6 g protein, 89 g carbohydrate, 108 mg cholesterol, 190 mg sodium.

Pudding Cakes

Pudding cakes are similar, yet different. They all use cake mix and instant pudding mix, but the number of eggs, amount of water, milk, juice, flavorings, oil and possibly liqueur, differ for each recipe.

If using dark or treated cake pans, adjust baking temperature and baking time.[4] Beat dry cake mix and dry pudding mix together in large bowl with mixer to break up large lumps. I have found that these cakes will have better texture if eggs and liquids are mixed together before adding to dry ingredients. If cakes containing liqueur, rum, sherry or whiskey are prepared a day before serving, their flavor will improve. I have also found that even though cake mix may contain pudding, use package of pudding mix as well and add another egg; however, cakes should not contain more than four eggs.

A "universal" pudding cake recipe with so many variations would be hard to follow; therefore, full recipes are given for these, my favorites.

Sherry Cake

1 (18¼-ounce) package yellow cake mix	¾ cup cream sherry
	⅓ cup vegetable oil
1 (4-serving size) package vanilla instant pudding mix	
	Sherry Glaze:
1 teaspoon ground nutmeg	1½ tablespoons butter, softened
3 eggs, room temperature	1 cup confectioners' sugar
¼ cup water	Dash of salt
1 teaspoon vanilla extract	3 tablespoons cream sherry

Beat cake mix, pudding mix and nutmeg in large bowl with mixer on low to break up large lumps (pea-size lumps are okay). Blend eggs, water, vanilla, sherry and oil in medium bowl with same beaters until combined. Add to dry mixture and beat on low until moistened, about 30 seconds. Scrape down sides and beat 2 more minutes on medium. Pour batter into lightly-sprayed 10-inch Bundt or tube pan. Run knife through batter and bounce pan on counter to remove air bubbles. Bake at 350° for 45 to 50 minutes[4] or until wooden pick inserted in center comes out clean. Remove to rack and cool in pan 10 minutes.[8] Loosen center with plastic knife; cake should pull away from sides as it cools. Gently shake pan up and down to release bottom. Invert cake onto serving plate. Drizzle glaze over cake when completely cool.

Sherry Glaze: Whisk butter, confectioners' sugar and salt in medium bowl. Whisk in 1 tablespoon sherry at a time until drizzling consistency.

Makes 16 servings

Per serving: 272 calories, 10 g fat, 3 g protein, 42 g carbohydrate, 43 mg cholesterol, 291 mg sodium.

Lemon Poppy Seed Cake

1 (18¼-ounce) package
    yellow cake mix
1 (4-serving size) package lemon
    instant pudding mix
¼ cup poppy seeds
4 eggs, room temperature
1 cup water

1 teaspoon vanilla extract
½ cup vegetable oil

Lemon Glaze:
1 cup confectioners' sugar
1 teaspoon lemon extract, or
    1 tablespoon fresh lemon juice
1 tablespoon milk

Beat cake mix, pudding mix and poppy seeds in large bowl with mixer on low to break up large lumps (pea-size lumps are okay). Blend eggs, water, vanilla and oil in medium bowl with same beaters until combined. Add to dry mixture and beat on low until moistened, about 30 seconds. Scrape down sides and beat 2 more minutes on medium. Pour batter into lightly-sprayed 10-inch Bundt or tube pan. Run knife through batter and bounce pan on counter to remove air bubbles. Bake at 350° for 45 to 50 minutes[4] or until wooden pick inserted in center comes out clean. Remove to rack and cool in pan 10 minutes.[8] Loosen center with plastic knife; cake should pull away from sides as it cools. Gently shake pan up and down to release bottom. Invert cake onto serving plate. When completely cool, drizzle glaze over cake. Sprinkle with additional poppy seeds.

Lemon Glaze: Mix confectioners' sugar, lemon extract and milk in medium bowl, adjusting amount of milk until drizzling consistency.

Makes 16 servings   Nancy Paurus, Boulder, Colorado

Per serving: 281 calories, 12 g fat, 4 g protein, 41 g carbohydrate, 34 mg cholesterol, 268 mg sodium.

Cake Mix Cake Tip

Add a teaspoon vanilla extract, a teaspoon softened butter and a teaspoon sugar to yellow and chocolate cake mixes to give cake a "homemade flavor."

Chocolate Rum Cake

1 (18¼-ounce) package devil's food or dark chocolate cake mix
1 (4-serving size) package chocolate instant pudding mix
4 eggs, room temperature
½ cup water
1 teaspoon vanilla extract
½ cup dark rum
½ cup vegetable oil

Rum Butter Glaze:
¼ cup (½ stick) butter
1 cup sugar
¼ cup water
Dash of salt
¼ cup dark rum

Chocolate Frosting (optional):
1 cup semisweet chocolate chips
1 tablespoon shortening

½ cup chopped toasted pecans

Beat cake mix and pudding mix in large bowl with mixer on low to break up large lumps (pea-size lumps are okay). Blend eggs, water, vanilla, rum and oil in medium bowl with same beaters until combined. Add to dry mixture and beat on low until moistened, about 30 seconds. Scrape down sides and beat 2 more minutes on medium. Pour batter into lightly-sprayed 10-inch Bundt or tube pan. Run knife through batter and gently bounce pan on counter to remove air bubbles. Bake at 350° for 45 to 50 minutes[4] or until wooden pick inserted in center comes out clean. Remove to rack. While still warm in pan, make holes in cake with wooden skewer or meat fork and pour warm glaze over cake. Cool in pan 25 minutes.[8] Loosen center with plastic knife; cake should pull away from sides as it cools. Gently shake pan up and down to release bottom. Invert cake onto serving plate. When completely cool, drizzle frosting over cake. Sprinkle with ½ cup chopped toasted pecans.

Rum Butter Glaze: Spray medium saucepan. Add butter, sugar, water and salt. Stir over low heat until butter melts and sugar dissolves. Bring to boil. Boil 3 minutes over medium heat without stirring, lifting and swirling pan occasionally. Cool slightly. Gradually stir in rum.

Chocolate Frosting: Melt chocolate chips and shortening over very low heat in small heavy saucepan. Stir until combined. (See *Chocolate Covered Strawberries* to melt in microwave.)

Makes 16 servings   Theresa Nuzum, Grand Lake, Colorado

Per serving: 402 calories, 22 g fat, 4 g protein, 43 g carbohydrate, 103 mg cholesterol, 413 mg sodium.

Vanilla Rum or Irish Whiskey Cake

1 (18¼-ounce) package yellow cake mix

1 (4-serving size) package vanilla instant pudding mix

4 eggs, room temperature

½ cup water

1 teaspoon vanilla extract

½ cup dark rum or Irish whiskey

½ cup vegetable oil

Rum Butter Glaze:

¼ cup (½ stick) butter

1 cup sugar

¼ cup water

Dash of salt

¼ cup dark rum or Irish whiskey

Beat cake mix and pudding mix in large bowl with mixer on low to break up large lumps (pea-size lumps are okay). Blend eggs, water, vanilla, rum and oil in medium bowl with same beaters until combined. Add to dry mixture and beat on low until moistened, about 30 seconds. Scrape down sides and beat 2 more minutes on medium. Pour batter into lightly-sprayed 10-inch Bundt or tube pan. Run knife through batter and bounce pan on counter to remove air bubbles. Bake at 350° for 45 to 50 minutes[4] or until wooden pick inserted in center comes out clean. Remove to rack. While still warm in pan, make holes in cake with wooden skewer or meat fork and pour warm glaze over cake. Cool in pan 25 minutes.[8] Loosen center with plastic knife; cake should pull away from sides as it cools. Gently shake pan up and down to release bottom. Invert cake onto serving plate. Serve with lightly sweetened whipped cream.

Rum Butter Glaze: Spray medium saucepan and add butter, sugar, water and salt. Stir over low heat until butter melts and sugar dissolves. Bring to boil. Boil 3 minutes over medium heat without stirring, lifting and swirling pan occasionally. Remove from heat and gradually stir in rum or Irish whiskey.

Makes 16 servings   Theresa Nuzum, Grand Lake, Colorado

Per serving: 336 calories, 14 g fat, 3 g protein, 46 g carbohydrate, 62 mg cholesterol, 313 mg sodium.

Note: When my friend Joye Miller serves her rum cake, she warms additional rum and spoons about 1 tablespoonful over each slice of cake; she also adds vanilla extract (to taste) to her thawed whipped topping to spoon over each serving.

Very, Very Chocolate Cake

A moist, delicious cake with little pockets of melted chocolate.

1   (18¼-ounce) package devil's food cake mix

1   (4-serving size) package white chocolate or vanilla instant pudding mix

2   eggs

¼   cup water

⅓   cup plus 3 tablespoons coffee-flavored or almond-flavored liqueur

1   teaspoon vanilla extract

¼   cup vegetable oil

1   cup sour cream

1½ cups milk chocolate chips

1   recipe *Chocolate Glaze*

¼   cup chopped toasted pecans or toasted sliced almonds, or 2 (2-ounce) bars white bakers chocolate, melted according to package directions[87]

Beat cake mix and pudding mix in large bowl with mixer on low to break up large lumps (pea-size lumps are okay). Blend eggs, water, ⅓ cup liqueur, vanilla, oil and sour cream in medium bowl on low with same beaters until combined. Add to dry mixture and beat on low until moistened, about 30 seconds, then beat on medium 1½ minutes. Fold in chocolate chips.

Spoon batter evenly as possible into lightly sprayed 10-inch tube pan (batter will be thick). Bake at 350° for 55 to 60 minutes[4] or until wooden pick inserted in center comes out clean (if you hit a pocket of chocolate, test again). Meanwhile, prepare *Chocolate Glaze.*

Cool cake in pan on rack 25 minutes.[8] Run plastic knife around center and sides of pan and invert onto serving plate. Cool completely. Brush top and sides with 3 tablespoons liqueur. Let dry. Frost with *Chocolate Glaze.*[23] Sprinkle with chopped toasted pecans or toasted sliced almonds. For nice contrast, omit nuts and drizzle white chocolate over dry glazed cake.

Makes 16 servings

Per serving: 383 calories, 18 g fat, 4 g protein, 53 g carbohydrate, 40 mg cholesterol, 330 mg sodium.

Note: It is easier to cut pecans or walnuts, if you cut them from the round, ridged side.

Fresh Coconut

When I was growing up, fresh coconut cake and ambrosia were as much a part of Christmas dinner as pecan pie and pumpkin pie were for Thanksgiving. My mother would bake a coconut cake and make ambrosia with fresh coconut. I can remember the large, special nail she used to pierce the "eyes" of the coconut—I kept that nail in my utensil drawer for years.

1   **fresh medium coconut**

Select coconut, heavy for its size—one that sounds full of liquid when shaken. The "eyes" should be dry, not wet or moldy.

Line kitchen sink drain with dish towel and set coconut in drain. Hammer a large strong nail or screwdriver into "eyes". Turn coconut upside down over 2-cup glass measure or wide-mouth jar to drain. Taste liquid, making sure coconut is not rancid.* (Strain sweet liquid and reserve for other uses, if desired). Put drained whole coconut in shallow pan and bake at 350° for 30 minutes to dry. Remove promptly to keep coconut meat from cooking.

Today, most coconuts have a groove cut around the middle to make the shell easier to crack. Place coconut on newspapers on hard solid surface (like concrete floor) and strike groove around middle with hammer. Tap and crack shell all over. Break open, leaving coconut pieces as large as possible. Pry meat from shell, using clean screwdriver or small knife, if necessary. Peel brown skin from coconut pieces with vegetable peeler or sharp knife. Wipe pieces with paper towel to remove any shell fragments.

I have found that using a food processor is one of the easiest ways to shred or grate coconut meat. First shred coconut pieces using shredder disc. Remove disc and coconut. For "grated" coconut, install steel blade and return shredded coconut to work bowl. Pulse to desired "grated" consistency. Remove coconut to plate. Fluff with fork and pack lightly to measure amount needed. (May prepare ahead and refrigerate or freeze. If frozen, thaw and fluff before measuring.) Use in *Fresh Coconut Cake* and *Ambrosia* or in other recipes calling for fresh coconut.

* Coconuts are very high in saturated fat and can easily turn rancid. If the liquid tastes oily rather than sweet, the coconut is rancid and should be thrown away.

Makes 3 to 4 cups grated coconut

Per cup: 283 calories, 27 g fat, 3 g protein, 12 g carbohydrate, 0 mg cholesterol, 16 mg sodium.

Fresh Coconut Cake

1 (18¼-ounce) package moist deluxe yellow cake mix
1 teaspoon imitation coconut extract
1 teaspoon clear imitation vanilla extract[22]

1½ to 2 cups *Easy Seven-Minute Frosting* or Velvet Frosting from *Red Velvet Cake* recipe
2 cups freshly grated or shredded coconut, or frozen unsweetened shredded coconut, thawed, or sweetened flaked coconut, *divided*

Prepare cake mix according to package directions through blending about 30 seconds. Add extracts. Continue as directed on package.

Spray two 9-inch round cake pans and line with wax paper.[79] Spoon batter equally[25] into pans and tap on counter to remove air bubbles. Bake at 350° for 28 to 30 minutes[4] or until wooden pick inserted in center comes out clean. Cool in pans 15 minutes. Remove from pans to racks and cool completely.[27] If time permits, chill or freeze layers for easier handling and to reduce crumbling.

Prepare *Easy Seven-Minute Frosting* or Velvet Frosting. Add 1 teaspoon imitation coconut extract, if desired, along with the clear imitation vanilla extract called for in frosting recipe.

Remove wax paper from layers as cake is assembled. Place first layer topside down on plate. Spread layer with frosting and sprinkle with ½ cup coconut. Position second layer topside up over first layer, aligning thick and thin areas to make cake level, if necessary. Frost sides and top of cake.[23] (Do not worry about appearance, coconut will hide any flaws.) Sprinkle remaining 1½ cups coconut on sides and top. Lightly pat into frosting. Refrigerate until ready to serve. Serve with *Ambrosia*.

Makes 12 servings

Per serving: 467 calories, 28 g fat, 5 g protein, 52 g carbohydrate, 105 mg cholesterol, 438 mg sodium.

Mother's Nut Cake

My brother's favorite cake. Mother made Nut Cake for his December birthday every year.

2 cups flour	1½ cups raisins
¼ rounded teaspoon salt	¾ cup (1½ sticks) butter, cut
1 teaspoon ground cinnamon	into pieces
¼ teaspoon ground cloves	1 cup sugar
¼ teaspoon ground nutmeg	3 eggs, lightly beaten
¼ teaspoon ground allspice	¼ cup bourbon
1 pound pecans, toasted and	¼ cup unsulphured molasses[16]
coarsely chopped (4 cups)	½ teaspoon baking soda

Whisk flour, salt, cinnamon, cloves, nutmeg and allspice in medium bowl.[2] Dust[G] pecans and raisins with 2 tablespoons flour mixture and set aside. Beat butter and sugar in large bowl with mixer until creamed, about 2 minutes. Scrape down sides. Beat in eggs about 1 minute. Scrape down sides. Mix bourbon and molasses in glass measure and stir in baking soda. Beat into creamed mixture. Add flour mixture and beat on low until caramel colored and combined, about 1 minute. Stir in pecans and raisins with spoon-shaped rubber spatula, lifting and folding as you stir.

Spoon batter into sprayed parchment- or wax-paper-lined *9-inch* tube pan. Press and pack batter evenly to remove air bubbles. Place shallow pan (like cake pan) or ovenproof bowl of water in back of oven on bottom rack. Bake cake at 300° for 1 hour 10 minutes[4] or until wooden pick inserted in center comes out clean. (Check with pick after 1 hour; tent with foil to prevent overbrowning if necessary.) Remove to rack and cool in pan 20 minutes.[8] Run plastic knife around sides and center. Invert onto rack;[27] remove wax paper. Cool completely.

Turn cake rightside up and place on large piece of extra-fine cheesecloth. Season cake with 3 to 4 tablespoons bourbon, brushing top and sides (nut cakes, like fruitcakes needs to be "seasoned" to be good). Place unpeeled apple wedge in center. Wrap cheesecloth around cake, then wrap in foil. Store in cool place (do not refrigerate). After a week, unwrap and brush cake with 3 to 4 more tablespoons bourbon. Wrap and store one more week.

Makes 16 servings   Willie McCaleb Rabb, Lexington, Mississippi

Per serving: 447 calories, 30 g fat, 5 g protein, 41 g carbohydrate, 40 mg cholesterol, 88 mg sodium.

Applesauce Fruitcake

A delicious alternative to the traditional fruitcake. Prepare right after Thanksgiving so loaves will have time to "season" for the holidays.

1	cup shortening	1	pound pecans, toasted and coarsely chopped
3	cups thick applesauce		
2	cups *sugar*	4½	cups *sifted* flour[24]
1	pound chopped dates	1	teaspoon salt
1	pound golden raisins	4	teaspoons baking soda
¼	pound candied cherries, quartered	1	teaspoon ground nutmeg
¼	pound candied pineapple, chopped into small pieces	2½	teaspoons ground cinnamon
		½	teaspoon ground cloves
¼	pound citron,ᴳ finely chopped	9	tablespoons bourbon, *divided*

Melt shortening in large saucepan. Add applesauce and sugar. Boil 5 minutes, stirring occasionally. Remove from heat and cool.

Combine dates, raisins, cherries, pineapple, citron and pecans in large bowl. Whisk flour, salt, baking soda, nutmeg, cinnamon and cloves in separate bowl.[2] Sift flour mixture through coarse-mesh strainer over fruit and nuts. Toss to coat. Stir applesauce mixture into fruit and nut mixture with wooden spoon, digging deeply from bottom until well combined. Spoon batter equally into three sprayed wax-paper-lined 8½x4½-inch loaf pans.[25] Press batter evenly into pans to remove air bubbles. Place shallow pan (like cake pan) of water in back of oven on bottom rack. Bake loaves on middle rack at 275° for 1½ to 2 hours or until wooden pick inserted in center comes out clean. Cool in pans on racks 15 minutes. Transfer loaves to racks[27] and remove wax paper. Cool completely.

Place each loaf on large piece of extra-fine cheesecloth. Brush tops and sides with 3 tablespoons bourbon. Wrap in cheesecloth, then in foil. Store loaves in cool place (do not refrigerate). After a week, unwrap and brush each loaf with 3 more tablespoons bourbon. Wrap and store another week. Loaves should now be well seasoned.

Makes 3 loaves

Per slice of 24: 492 calories, 20 g fat, 6 g protein, 790 g carbohydrate, 0 mg cholesterol, 309 mg sodium.

A friend tells the story about her mother who kept a pint of whiskey in her closet for "seasoning" her Christmas fruitcake. My friend's brother discovered the whiskey during a visit and imbibed a little. Before leaving, he filled the bottle with tea. When the "seasoned" fruitcake was unwrapped at Christmas, it was moldy! Good to "test" seasonings occasionally.

Apple Cake

1¼	cups vegetable oil	1	cup chopped toasted pecans
2	cups sugar	3	cups peeled and finely chopped
3	eggs, room temperature		Jonathan or other firm apples
2	teaspoons vanilla extract		
3	cups flour		Caramel Sauce:
1	teaspoon baking soda	½	cup (1 stick) butter
1	teaspoon salt	2	tablespoons milk
½	teaspoon apple pie spice	½	cup packed light brown sugar[1]
		1	teaspoon vanilla extract

Beat oil, sugar and eggs in large bowl with mixer about 3 minutes. Mix in vanilla. Whisk flour, baking soda, salt and apple pie spice in medium bowl[2] and gradually beat into egg mixture. Mix in pecans and apples with wooden spoon. Spoon batter into sprayed and floured 10-inch tube pan and spread out evenly. Bake at 325° for 1 hour 20 minutes or until wooden pick inserted in center comes out clean. Cool in pan on rack 20 minutes.[8] Pour sauce over warm cake in pan. Let stand to absorb sauce. Invert cake onto serving plate.

Caramel Sauce: Combine butter, milk and brown sugar in sprayed medium saucepan.[38] Stir over low heat until butter melts. Bring to boil over medium heat. Boil 5 minutes without stirring, swirling pan occasionally. (If boiling too fast, reduce heat, but keep mixture at a boil.) Remove from heat. Stir in vanilla.

Makes 12 servings   Doris Brasfield, Dunwoody, Georgia

Per serving: 468 calories, 29 g fat, 4 g protein, 52 g carbohydrate, 56 mg cholesterol, 286 mg sodium.

Easy Seven-Minute Frosting

2	egg whites[12]	¼	teaspoon fresh lemon juice
1	cup sugar	1	teaspoon clear imitation vanilla
¼	teaspoon cream of tartar		extract[22] or other flavoring
⅓	cup water		

Put egg whites in medium, deep, metal or glass bowl. Set aside and let whites come to room temperature. Rinse medium saucepan with water, leaving pan wet.[38] Add sugar, cream of tartar, ⅓ cup water and lemon juice to pan. Stir over low heat until sugar dissolves. Cover and bring to full boil over medium-high heat. Uncover and boil 2 minutes without stirring, swirling pan once or twice. Start timing as you begin beating egg whites and pouring in hot syrup in thin stream. Beat 7 minutes or until frosting is thick and fluffy. Beat in vanilla. Makes enough frosting for 9-inch two-layer cake or 9x13-inch cake.

Makes 1½ to 2 cups

Per recipe: 915 calories, 0 g fat, 7 g protein, 224 g carbohydrate, 0 mg cholesterol, 399 mg sodium.

Fluffy Cream Cheese Frosting

Change the flavor of this frosting by changing extracts. Use almond extract and stir in toffee bits, or use lemon extract and decorate frosted cake with grated lemon zest.

1   (8-ounce) package cream cheese, softened
1   cup confectioners' sugar
¼   cup half-and-half or milk
    Dash of salt

1   teaspoon clear imitation vanilla extract,[22] or ½ teaspoon almond, lemon or orange extracts
1   (16-ounce) container whipped topping, thawed

Beat cream cheese and confectioners' sugar in large bowl with mixer until combined. Beat in half-and-half, salt and vanilla until creamy. Fold in whipped topping. Cakes using this frosting must be refrigerated. Use to frost an *Easy Layer Cake*, or cut recipe in half to frost smaller cakes or cupcakes.

Makes about 7 cups

Per ¼ cup: 146 calories, 10 g fat, 1 g protein, 14 g carbohydrate, 12 mg cholesterol, 39 mg sodium.

Caramel Frosting

Keeping Caramel Frosting from becoming grainy can be a little tricky–follow directions closely.

2   cups sugar
½   cup packed brown sugar[1]
    Dash of salt
1   (5-ounce) can evaporated milk

¾   cup (1½ sticks) butter (not margarine), cut into pieces
1   teaspoon vanilla extract

Spray medium saucepan.[38] Add sugars, salt, evaporated milk and butter. Cook and stir over low heat until butter melts and sugars dissolve. Bring to full boil (bubbles all over top). Boil without stirring, lifting and swirling pan occasionally until mixture reaches soft ball stage,[15] 1 to 1½ minutes. Remove pan from heat and place on cooling rack. Add vanilla and beat with mixer on medium-high until frosting loses its gloss, about 15 minutes. Cool 1 to 2 minutes. Makes enough frosting for 9-inch two-layer cake, 9x13-inch cake or 24 to 32 cupcakes.

Makes 2 cups   Lauren Rabb Wells, Meridian, Mississippi

Per 2 tablespoons: 211 calories, 9 g fat, 1 g protein, 33 g carbohydrate, 26 mg cholesterol, 99 mg sodium.

Confectioners' Sugar Frosting

2 tablespoons butter, softened	Dash of salt
2 cups confectioners' sugar	½ teaspoon clear imitation vanilla
4 tablespoons milk	extract[22] or almond extract

Beat butter and confectioners' sugar in medium bowl with mixer. Beat in milk, salt and vanilla until combined, then beat on high until creamy. For thicker frosting add more confectioners' sugar or use less milk.

Makes 1 cup

Per 2 tablespoons: 147 calories, 3 g fat, 0 g protein, 30 g carbohydrate, 9 mg cholesterol, 66 mg sodium.

Confectioners' Sugar Glaze

1 tablespoon butter or margarine	1 teaspoon vanilla extract,
2 tablespoons milk	clear imitation vanilla extract[22]
1 cup confectioners' sugar	or lemon extract
Dash of salt	

Heat butter and milk in small saucepan over low heat until butter melts, or heat in microwave-safe bowl on MEDIUM 1 to 2 minutes. Whisk in confectioners' sugar, salt, and vanilla until smooth. Add 1 to 2 teaspoons milk if thick.

Makes ½ cup   Velma Goettel, Bella Vista, Arkansas

Per ½ cup: 593 calories, 13 g fat, 1 g protein, 122 g carbohydrate, 35 mg cholesterol, 132 g sodium.

Chocolate Glaze

⅔ cup sugar	1¼ cups milk chocolate, semisweet
⅛ teaspoon salt	chocolate or white chocolate chips
¼ cup light corn syrup	1 teaspoon vanilla extract
¼ cup water	

Lightly spray small saucepan.[38] Add sugar and salt. Mix corn syrup and water in glass measure and pour into saucepan. Heat over low heat, stirring until sugar dissolves. Increase heat and bring to full boil without stirring (bubbles all over top including middle). Remove from heat. Add chocolate chips and swirl pan to coat chips with syrup. Let stand 2 minutes without stirring. Add vanilla and whisk until smooth, heating slightly if needed. Let stand 15 to 20 minutes. Glaze will thicken as it stands. If too thick, reheat slightly over low heat.

Makes about 1¼ cups

Per tablespoon: 118 calories, 5 g fat, 1 g protein, 21 g carbohydrate, 0 mg cholesterol, 18 mg sodium.

Strawberry Glaze

1	(16-ounce) package frozen sweetened sliced strawberries	¼	cup water
			Sugar to taste
1½	teaspoons cornstarch	3	to 5 dashes of red food coloring
	Dash of salt		(optional)

Thaw strawberries. Mix cornstarch and salt in small saucepan. Add water and stir until cornstarch dissolves. Add strawberries and bring to boil. Cook and stir over medium heat until thick and clear (cook only 2 to 3 minutes; overcooked glaze will be lumpy). Stir in sugar if needed and food coloring if desired. Cool thoroughly. Spread Strawberry Glaze over cheesecakes or cream cheese pies.

Makes 2 cups

Per 2 tablespoons: 30 calories, 0 g fat, 0 g protein, 7 g carbohydrate, 0 mg cholesterol, 17 mg sodium.

Caramelized Sugar

Caramelized sugar is often called for in cake toppings, desserts and salads.

Sugar (amount specified in recipe)   Dash of salt

Sprinkle sugar and salt evenly into sprayed small or medium iron or other heavy skillet, depending on amount. Place over medium-low heat. Stir with wooden spoon, frequently at first, then constantly as sugar begins to melt into syrup. Continue to cook and stir until amber in color. Be careful not to burn–be patient. Remove from heat. Use as directed in recipe. (Soak skillet in hot water.) *Caution! Caramelized sugar can reach temperatures of 320° to 350° during cooking!*

Makes about 1⅔ cups

Per ½ cup: 467 calories, 19 g fat, 7 g protein, 74 g carbohydrate, 0 mg cholesterol, 93 mg sodium.

Praline Topping

1	cup sugar	¾	cup toasted whole natural almonds
	Dash of salt		

Caramelize sugar and salt following directions for *Caramelized Sugar* in medium skillet. Remove from heat and stir in almonds. Coat well. Pour mixture into sprayed foil-lined jelly-roll pan. Cool. Break caramel into pieces and put in ziptop bag. Coarsely crush with meat mallet or rolling pin. May store in covered container at room temperature several days or freeze for later use.

Makes 1⅔ cups

Per ½ cup: 467 calories, 19 g fat, 7 g protein, 74 g carbohydrate, 0 mg cholesterol, 93 mg sodium.

Joye's Lemon Filling

1 tablespoon grated lemon zest	1 cup (2 sticks) butter cut into
½ cup fresh lemon juice	pieces (do not use margarine)
2 cups sugar	4 eggs, well beaten

Put water in bottom of double boiler to a level that will not touch top boiler and bring to moderate boil. Combine lemon zest, lemon juice, sugar and butter in top boiler.* Heat and stir until butter melts. Stir in eggs and continue cooking over moderately boiling water, stirring occasionally at first, then frequently. Cook 15 to 20 minutes or until thick enough to "pile slightly." Cool. Filling may be frozen (will not freeze solid and may be used directly from freezer). Use to fill hard-meringue shells or tarts, cream puffs, or pastry tarts.

* If you do not have a double boiler, place a stainless-steel or heatproof glass bowl over a slightly smaller saucepan. Add water to saucepan without letting it touch bowl.

Makes 3⅓ cups   Joye Miller, Bella Vista, Arkansas

Per tablespoon: 66 calories, 4 g fat, 1 g protein, 8 g carbohydrate, 26 mg cholesterol, 40 mg sodium.

Quick Lemon Curd

Good filling for cream puffs and tarts.

1 teaspoon grated lemon zest[61]	1 teaspoon cornstarch
½ cup fresh lemon juice	Dash of salt
5 eggs, lightly beaten	½ cup (1 stick) butter, melted
1 cup sugar	and slightly cooled

Put lemon zest, lemon juice and eggs in blender. Whisk sugar, cornstarch and salt in small bowl and add to blender. Blend on low until combined. Add butter through top and blend until smooth. Pour mixture into medium saucepan. Cook over medium-low heat, stirring constantly with wooden spoon until thick enough for finger to leave path down back of coated spoon, 4 to 6 minutes. (Do not boil or mixture will curdle.) Cool. Refrigerate up to 2 weeks in tightly covered glass container. Serve with scones, lemon bread, toast, pound cake or gingerbread.

Makes about 2 cups

Per tablespoon: 62 calories, 4 g fat, 1 g protein, 7 g carbohydrate, 41 mg cholesterol, 47 mg sodium.

Filling for Cream Puffs and Tarts: Mix 1 cup lemon curd with ½ cup whipped cream or ½ cup thawed whipped topping.

Cookies, Bars & Candies

Cookies

Bars

Candies

Oatmeal Raisin Cookies

1 cup raisins	½ cup butter-flavored shortening
¼ cup rum or water	1⅓ cups sugar
3 cups quick or old-fashioned oats (not instant)	⅔ cups packed light brown sugar[1]
	2 eggs, room temperature
2 cups flour	1 tablespoon vanilla extract
1 teaspoon baking soda	1 cup coarsely chopped toasted pecans
1 teaspoon salt	
½ cup (1 stick) butter, softened	

Mix raisins and rum in small bowl. Set aside 20 minutes or longer, stirring occasionally. Fluff oats with scoop. Measure and put in large bowl. Beat oats with mixer 1 to 2 minutes to slightly break up flakes. Whisk in flour, baking soda and salt.[2] Set aside. Beat butter and shortening in separate large bowl with same beaters until fluffy. Add sugars and beat until creamed, about 2 minutes. Scrape down sides. Add eggs and vanilla; beat 1 more minute and scrape down sides. Gradually beat in oat mixture 1½ to 2 cups at a time, beating until you can add more oats; beat in last addition until just combined. Stir in undrained raisins and pecans with wooden spoon. Cover dough and refrigerate at least 1 hour. If dough is very cold or stiff, let stand about 20 minutes before making cookies.

Drop walnut-size balls of dough about 2 inches apart on cool, clean, lightly sprayed or parchment-lined baking sheets (2-teaspoon cookie scoop works well).[103] Do not flatten dough. Bake one sheet of cookies at a time at 375° for 9 to 10 minutes or until golden. Cookies should look slightly underbaked. Cool on baking sheets 2 minutes. Transfer to racks and cool completely. Store in airtight containers. Cookies freeze well.

Makes 6 dozen

Per cookie: 90 calories, 4 g fat, 1 g protein, 13 g carbohydrate, 9 mg cholesterol, 63 mg sodium.

Tip for Softening Hard Raisins

Place damp paper towel in bottom of microwave-safe bowl. Add 1 cup raisins. Cover with another damp paper towel and cover bowl loosely with plastic wrap. Microwave on HIGH 15 seconds. Uncover and fluff with fork. Cover raisins again and microwave on HIGH 15 more seconds. Fluff again.

Nutty Chocolate Chip Cookies

1	cup (2 sticks) unsalted butter, cut into pieces	2	eggs, room temperature
¾	cup sugar	2½	cups flour
¾	cup packed light brown sugar[1]	1	teaspoon baking soda
		½	teaspoon salt
1	tablespoon vanilla extract	2	(11½-ounce) packages milk-chocolate chips
1	tablespoon coffee-flavored liqueur	1	cup coarsely chopped walnuts
1	tablespoon hazelnut-flavored liqueur	½	cup coarsely chopped pecans
		½	cup coarsely chopped macadamia nuts

Beat butter, sugars, vanilla and liqueurs in large bowl with mixer until light and fluffy. Scrape down sides. Beat in eggs until well combined. Whisk flour, baking soda and salt in medium bowl.[2] Stir into butter mixture with wooden spoon. Stir in chocolate chips and nuts. Drop ¼-cupfuls dough about 3 inches apart onto ungreased baking sheets. Bake at 325° for 16 minutes or until golden. Cool on baking sheets 2 minutes. Transfer to racks and cool completely.

Makes 36 cookies   Bev Lehmann, Bella Vista, Arkansas

Per cookie: 255 calories, 15 g fat, 4 g protein, 28 g carbohydrate, 29 mg cholesterol, 137 mg sodium.

Peanut Butter Cookies

1	cup (2 sticks) butter	1	teaspoon vanilla extract
1	cup sugar	1½	cups flour
1	cup packed light brown sugar[1]	1	teaspoon baking soda
1	cup creamy peanut butter	¼	teaspoon salt
2	eggs, lightly beaten		

Beat butter and sugars in large bowl with mixer until creamed, about 2 minutes. Blend in peanut butter, eggs and vanilla in that order. Whisk flour, baking soda and salt in medium bowl[2] and beat into creamed mixture until just combined. Drop rounded teaspoonfuls of dough 2 inches apart onto ungreased baking sheets. Make crisscross patterns with wet fork on top. Bake at 350° for 12 minutes or until light brown. Cool on baking sheets 2 minutes. Transfer to racks and cool completely. Store in airtight containers.

Makes 72 cookies   Gertie Howell, Northport, Alabama

Per cookie: 77 calories, 5 g fat, 1 g protein, 9 g carbohydrate, 13 mg cholesterol, 71 mg sodium.

Earth Cookies

Jackie keeps batches of these cookies ready in the freezer for her husband, Earl, to share with golf buddies. They always hope he will bring a bag when he comes to play.

1	cup (2 sticks) margarine[50]	1	teaspoon baking powder
1	cup sugar	½	teaspoon salt
1	cup packed brown sugar[1]	2	cups cornflakes, slightly crushed
2	eggs, room temperature	2	cups old-fashioned oats
1	teaspoon vanilla extract	1	cup flaked coconut
2	cups flour	1	cup chopped toasted nuts
2	teaspoons baking soda	1	pound chopped dates (2 cups)

Use mixer on stand, if possible. Cut margarine into pieces and beat until fluffy. Add sugars and beat until creamed, about 2 minutes. Add eggs one at a time, beating well after each addition. Mix in vanilla. Sift flour, baking soda, baking powder and salt in medium bowl (coarse-mesh strainer works well). Beat into creamed mixture until well combined. Toss cornflakes, oats, coconut, nuts and dates together in separate bowl and beat into dough. Cover and refrigerate 2 hours or overnight (if refrigerated overnight, let dough stand 30 minutes before making cookies). Drop rounded teaspoonfuls of dough 2 inches apart onto lightly-sprayed baking sheets. Bake at 325° for 12 minutes or until lightly browned. Do not overbake–these are soft cookies. Cool on baking sheets for 2 minutes. Carefully transfer to racks and cool completely.

Makes 100 cookies   Jackie Berdine, Bella Vista, Arkansas

Per cookie: 70 calories, 3 g fat, 1 g protein, 11 g carbohydrate, 4 mg cholesterol, 69 mg sodium.

Oatmeal Lace Cookies

Crisp and delicious. Easy to make.

2½	cups quick or old-fashioned oats (not instant)	1	egg, lightly beaten
2	teaspoons baking powder	½	teaspoon vanilla extract
¼	teaspoon salt	½	cup (1 stick) butter, melted and cooled
1	cup packed dark brown sugar[1]		

Mix oats, baking powder, salt and brown sugar in medium bowl. Stir in egg, vanilla and butter. Drop teaspoonfuls of dough 1½ inches apart onto sprayed baking sheets. Bake at 350° for 10 minutes. Cool on baking sheets 2 minutes. Remove to racks and cool completely. Store in airtight containers.

Makes 48 cookies

Per cookie: 58 calories, 2 g fat, 1 g protein, 9 g carbohydrate, 10 mg cholesterol, 47 mg sodium.

Emma's Sugar Cookies

I took a batch of these cookies and copies of the recipe to a church social in Granby, Colorado. We were new members and for a while several women called me Emma.

1 cup (2 sticks) butter, softened	2 eggs, room temperature
1 cup (2 sticks) plus 2 tablespoons margarine[50]	4 cups flour
	1 teaspoon cream of tartar
1 cup plus 2 tablespoons sugar	1 teaspoon baking soda
1 cup confectioners' sugar	1 teaspoon vanilla extract

Beat butter, 1 cup margarine, 1 cup sugar and confectioners' sugar in large bowl with mixer until creamed, about 2 minutes. Beat in eggs until light and fluffy. Whisk flour, cream of tartar and baking soda in separate large bowl.[2] Gradually beat into creamed mixture until combined. Beat in vanilla. Refrigerate 30 minutes. Roll dough into 1-inch balls. Melt 2 tablespoons margarine in small bowl in microwave; cool. Put 2 tablespoons sugar in another small bowl. Dip top of each ball into melted margarine, then dip into sugar. Place sugar side up 3 inches apart on ungreased baking sheets (12 to a sheet). Flatten slightly with bottom of glass or metal dry measure dipped in sugar. Bake at 350° for 10 minutes. Cool on baking sheets 2 minutes. Transfer to racks and cool completely. Store in airtight containers. These cookies freeze well.

Makes about 90 cookies   Emma Campbell, Boulder, Colorado

Per cookie: 60 calories, 4 g fat, 1 g protein, 7 g carbohydrate, 9 mg cholesterol, 50 mg sodium.

Coconut Shortbread

1 cup (2 sticks) butter, softened (not margarine)	1 teaspoon vanilla extract
	1 cup flaked coconut, snipped
½ cup sugar	
2 cups flour	Confectioners' sugar

Beat butter and sugar in large bowl with mixer until creamed, about 2 minutes. Scrape down sides. Add flour, vanilla and coconut and beat until creamy, about 2 minutes. Gather dough into ball. Divide in half and roll each portion into 1½-inch-diameter log 10 inches long. Wrap in wax paper and put in freezer 2 hours. Unwrap and slice logs ¼-inch-thick with sharp knife. Place 2 inches apart on ungreased baking sheets. Bake at 350° for 14 to 15 minutes or until edges are lightly browned. Cool on baking sheets 2 minutes. Transfer to racks and cool completely. Dust with confectioners' sugar. Store in airtight containers.

Makes 65 cookies   Fran Fee, Scottsdale, Arizona

Per cookie: 83 calories, 5 g fat, 1 g protein, 8 g carbohydrate, 0 mg cholesterol, 61 mg sodium.

Sugar Cookies

Sally's cookies are so good, everybody asks for her recipe!

1 cup (2 sticks) butter, softened	4 cups plus 4 heaping tablespoons flour
1 cup vegetable oil	
1 cup sugar	1 teaspoon baking soda
1 cup confectioners' sugar	1 teaspoon cream of tartar
2 eggs, room temperature	1 teaspoon salt
1 teaspoon vanilla or almond extract, or ½ teaspoon of each	

Beat butter, oil and sugars in large bowl with mixer until creamed, about 2 minutes. Beat in eggs and vanilla. Whisk flour, baking soda, cream of tartar and salt in another large bowl.[2] Beat into creamed mixture until combined. Roll dough into 1-inch balls and place 2 inches apart on ungreased baking sheets. Flatten slightly with bottom of glass dipped in sugar. (Sally has a glass with a fancy bottom, which makes a nice imprint on the cookie.) Bake at 375° for 8 to 10 minutes or until lightly browned around edges. Cool on baking sheets 2 minutes. Transfer to racks and cool completely. Cookies freeze well.

Makes about 90 cookies   Sally Peterson, Bella Vista, Arkansas

Per cookie: 115 calories, 7 g fat, 1 g protein, 12 g carbohydrate, 15 mg cholesterol, 90 mg sodium.

Rolls Royce Cookies

1 cup (2 sticks) margarine[50]	2 teaspoons ground cinnamon
1 cup butter-flavored shortening	½ teaspoon salt
2 cups sugar	2 teaspoons baking soda
1 cup packed light brown sugar[1]	3 cups quick or old-fashioned oats (not instant)
2 eggs, lightly beaten	
4 teaspoons vanilla extract	½ cup chopped toasted nuts
3 cups flour	

Beat margarine, shortening and sugars in large bowl with mixer until creamed, about 2 minutes. Mix in eggs and vanilla. Whisk flour, cinnamon, salt and baking soda in separate bowl[2] and gradually beat into creamed mixture. Stir in oats and nuts. Refrigerate 1 hour. Drop walnut-size spoonfuls of dough 2 inches apart onto ungreased baking sheets and flatten slightly with fork. Bake at 350° for 10 minutes (may look slightly underbaked). Cool on baking sheets 2 minutes. Transfer to racks and cool completely. Recipe may be halved.

Makes 116 cookies   Nancy Sherbondy, Bella Vista, Arkansas

Per cookie: 75 calories, 4 g fat, 1 g protein, 9 g carbohydrate, 4 mg cholesterol, 51 mg sodium.

Chocolate Chip Cookies

1 cup (2 sticks) butter, cut into pieces	3 cups flour
¾ cup sugar	¾ teaspoon salt
1 cup packed light brown sugar[1]	¾ teaspoon baking soda
2 eggs	3 cups semisweet chocolate chips
1 tablespoon vanilla extract	1 cup chopped toasted walnuts or pecans (optional)

Beat butter and sugars in large bowl with mixer until creamed, about 2 minutes. Scrape down sides. Beat in eggs and vanilla until well blended, about 1 minute. Whisk flour, salt and baking soda in separate bowl.[2] Stir into creamed mixture with wooden spoon until combined (mixture will be thick). Stir in chocolate chips and nuts.

For jumbo cookies, drop level ¼-cupfuls of dough about 2 inches apart onto ungreased baking sheets.* Bake at 350° for 14 to 16 minutes (cookies should look slightly underbaked). For crispier cookie, bake at 375° for 14 minutes. Cool on baking sheets 3 minutes.

For regular-size cookies, drop rounded tablespoonfuls of dough about 2 inches apart on ungreased baking sheets.* Bake at 350° for 10 to 12 minutes or until edges are light brown. For crispier cookie, bake at 375° for 10 minutes. Cool on baking sheets 2 minutes.

Transfer cookies to racks and cool completely. Store in airtight containers. Recipe may be doubled–use 3 eggs. Cookies are best when freshly baked; if doubled, bake only amount needed. Cover and refrigerate remaining dough (dough will just get better as sugar dissolves, enhancing flavor). Bake within a few days.

* Cookies remove easily when baked and cooled on parchment paper (parchment may be wiped off, turned over and used again).

Makes 25 jumbo or 50 regular cookies   Terry VanderVeen Bright, Lynchburg, Virginia

Per regular cookie: 146 calories, 7 g fat, 2 g protein, 20 g carbohydrate, 17 mg cholesterol, 97 mg sodium.

White Chocolate Macadamia Nut Cookies variation: Substitute white chocolate chips for semisweet chocolate chips and ¾ cup coarsely chopped macadamia nuts for 1 cup chopped toasted nuts. Bake as directed above.

Pauline's Praline Cookies

Beth's mother's favorite cookie recipe.

¾	cup (1½ sticks) butter or margarine[50]	1⅓	cups plus 1 heaping tablespoon flour
1½	cups packed light brown sugar[1]	¼	teaspoon baking powder
1	egg, room temperature	¼	teaspoon salt
1	teaspoon vanilla extract	1	cup chopped toasted pecans

Beat butter and brown sugar in large bowl with mixer until creamed, about 2 minutes. Mix in egg and vanilla. Whisk flour, baking powder and salt in another bowl.[2] Beat into creamed mixture until just combined. Stir in pecans. Drop rounded teaspoonfuls of dough onto sprayed baking sheets. Flatten lightly with bottom of damp glass dipped in sugar. Bake at 350° for 10 to 12 minutes or until lightly browned around edges. Let cool on baking sheets 2 minutes. Transfer to racks and cool completely. Store in airtight containers.

Makes about 36 cookies   Beth Huffman, Longmont, Colorado

Per cookie: 109 calories, 6 g fat, 1 g protein, 14 g carbohydrate, 16 mg cholesterol, 61 mg sodium.

Kringla

Shirley's husband, Dave, says Shirley makes kringla better than his Norwegian grandmother did. "Kringla" means "eight" in Norwegian, the shape of these cookies; they are made for special occasions, usually reserved for Christmas.

½	cup (1 stick) butter, softened	3	cups flour
1	cup sugar	1	scant teaspoon baking soda
1	cup sour cream	1	tablespoon baking powder
1	egg, room temperature	½	teaspoon salt

Beat butter and sugar in large bowl with mixer until creamed, about 2 minutes; scrape down sides. Beat in sour cream, then beat in egg. Whisk flour, baking soda, baking powder and salt in separate bowl[2] and add to creamed mixture. Beat until well combined, about 1 minute. Refrigerate several hours or overnight.

Roll scant tablespoonfuls of dough into pencil-thin "ropes" about 6 inches long on lightly floured surface with floured hands (dough will be very soft and sticky); place on ungreased baking sheets and shape into figure 8's with ends joined in the middle. Bake at 450° for 5 to 7 minutes or until bottoms are lightly browned and seams show tinge of brown on top. Cookies should be soft–do not overbake. Remove from oven. Transfer to racks and cool.

Makes about 48 cookies   Shirley Haraldson, Bella Vista, Arkansas

Per cookie: 73 calories, 3 g fat, 1 g protein, 10 g carbohydrate, 12 mg cholesterol, 91 mg sodium.

Benne Wafers

Benne wafers and Charleston, South Carolina just seem to go together. Here is my version of this very Southern cookie.

½ cup (1 stick) butter, cut into pieces	½ teaspoon lemon juice
½ cup sugar	1 cup flour
½ cup packed light brown sugar[1]	1 teaspoon baking powder
1 egg, lightly beaten	¼ teaspoon baking soda
½ teaspoon sesame oil	½ scant teaspoon salt
½ teaspoon vanilla extract	¼ cup toasted sesame seeds[5] (benne seeds[G])

Beat butter and sugars in large bowl with mixer until creamed, about 2 minutes. Add egg, sesame oil, vanilla and lemon juice and beat about 1 minute. Scrape down sides. Whisk flour, baking powder, baking soda and salt in separate bowl.[2] Gradually beat into creamed mixture on low until dough just comes together. Stir in sesame seeds. Gather dough together and wrap in plastic wrap. Refrigerate 1 hour or put in freezer 30 minutes.

Roll pinches of dough into ½-inch balls and place about 2½ inches apart on parchment-lined baking sheets. Dampen heel of hand frequently and flatten balls (new, thoroughly-rinsed, wet sponge placed in bowl works well). Press and rock heel of hand on each ball to make very thin wafer. Bake at 350° for 9½ to 10 minutes or until lightly browned. Slide parchment with wafers onto rack; when cool, wafers will easily release from parchment. Transfer to racks and cool completely. Benne wafers should be crunchy and slightly brittle, not chewy. Store in airtight containers.

Makes about 200 benne wafers

Per benne wafer: 12 calories, 1 g fat, 0 g protein, 2 g carbohydrate, 2 mg cholesterol, 11 mg sodium.

Fudgy Liqueur Brownies

½	cup (1 stick) butter	1½	cups flour
2	tablespoons vegetable oil	1½	cups sugar
½	cup unsweetened cocoa powder	½	teaspoon baking powder
⅓	cup plus 2 tablespoons coffee-flavored liqueur	½	scant teaspoon salt
1	teaspoon vanilla extract	½	cup chopped toasted pecans or walnuts
2	eggs, lightly beaten		

Melt butter in small saucepan over low heat. Stir in oil and cocoa powder; mix well. Set aside and cool 10 minutes. Whisk in ⅓ cup liqueur, vanilla and eggs until combined. Whisk flour, sugar, baking powder and salt in large bowl.[2] Add to cocoa mixture and mix with wooden spoon until just combined. Stir in nuts. Spoon mixture into sprayed foil-lined 7x11-inch brownie pan or 8x8-inch baking pan.[6] Smooth out batter with wet knife as much as possible (mixture will be thick). Bake at 350° for 25 minutes. Center will be soft, but will firm when cool; do not overbake. Remove to rack and cool in pan completely. Lift and slide liner onto cutting board; peel down sides. Brush top and sides with 2 tablespoons liqueur; let stand until absorbed. Cut into 1½- to 2-inch brownies using wet knife or wet dough scraper. Dust brownies with confectioners' sugar.

Makes about 24 brownies

Per brownie: 154 calories, 7 g fat, 2 g protein, 20 g carbohydrate, 37 mg cholesterol, 99 mg sodium.

Fudgy Brownies variation: Mix ¼ cup strong black coffee with 1 teaspoon sugar in glass measure and substitute for ⅓ cup liqueur; whisk into cocoa mixture with vanilla and eggs. Continue with "Whisk flour, sugar, baking powder and salt . . ." as directed above, but omit brushing top and sides with liqueur.

Toffee Bars

2 (1.4-ounce) milk chocolate English toffee bars	½ cup packed light brown sugar[1]
11 graham cracker sheets	½ cup finely chopped toasted pecans
1 cup (2 sticks) butter	2 cups milk chocolate chips

Freeze toffee bars 30 minutes. Unwrap and put in ziptop bag. Crush into small pieces with meat mallet. Return to freezer. Place whole graham cracker sheets in sprayed foil-lined 10x15-inch jelly-roll pan, adding single crackers to fill any spaces. Spray medium saucepan. Add butter and brown sugar. Cook and stir over low heat until butter melts and sugar dissolves. Bring to full boil (bubbles all over top). Boil 3 minutes without stirring, lifting and swirling pan occasionally. Pour mixture over crackers and spread out evenly. Sprinkle with pecans. Bake at 350° for 10 minutes. Remove and sprinkle chocolate chips over pecans. As chips melt, spread with narrow spatula to cover top. Sprinkle toffee pieces over chocolate. Gently press pieces into chocolate with wide spatula. Cool 10 minutes. Put in freezer 1 hour. Lift and slide liner onto cutting board. Peel off foil and cut toffee into bars or triangles. Store in airtight containers. Refrigerate or freeze.

Makes 120 bars   Mona Bell, Lawrence, Kansas

Per toffee bar: 52 calories, 3 g fat, 1 g protein, 6 g carbohydrate, 5 mg cholesterol, 40 mg sodium.

Cinnamon Pecan Squares

1 cup (2 sticks) butter, cut into pieces	1½ to 2 *tablespoons* ground cinnamon
1 cup sugar	1 cup flour
1 egg, separated[12]	⅛ teaspoon salt
½ teaspoon vanilla	1 cup finely chopped toasted pecans

Beat butter and sugar in large bowl with mixer until creamed, about 2 minutes. Scrape down sides. Beat in egg yolk and mix in vanilla. Whisk cinnamon, flour and salt in medium bowl[2] and beat into creamed mixture until well combined, about 2 minutes. Transfer dough to sprayed foil-lined 10x15-inch jelly-roll pan;[6] pat evenly into liner with slightly dampened hands. Lightly beat egg white in small bowl with fork and brush over dough to coat completely (all egg white may not be needed). Sprinkle pecans on top and gently press into dough. Bake at 325° for 25 minutes. Cool in pan 5 minutes. Lift and slide liner onto large cutting board and peel down sides. Cut into squares. Transfer to paper-towel covered racks. Cool completely. Store in airtight containers.

Makes about 70 squares

Per square: 52 calories, 4 g fat, 1 g protein, 5 g carbohydrate, 10 mg cholesterol, 31 mg sodium.

Sherry Bars

First Layer:

1 cup (2 sticks) butter
2 (2-ounce) unsweetened baking chocolate bars, or 4 (1-ounce) packets premelted unsweetened chocolate
2 cups sugar
4 eggs, room temperature
1 teaspoon vanilla extract
1 cup flour
½ teaspoon salt

Second Layer:

½ cup (1 stick) butter, softened
4 cups confectioners' sugar
¼ cup half-and-half
¼ cup sherry (not cooking sherry)
Dash of salt
1 cup chopped toasted pecans

Top Layer:

1½ cups semisweet chocolate chips
4½ tablespoons water
6 tablespoons butter

First Layer: Melt butter and chocolate in medium saucepan over low heat, stirring until combined; cool. Beat in sugar, eggs and vanilla with mixer. Combine flour and salt in medium bowl and beat into chocolate mixture on low. Pour into sprayed foil-lined 11x17-inch jelly-roll pan[6] and spread out evenly in pan. Bake at 350° for 15 minutes. Set aside to cool.

Second Layer: Beat butter, confectioners' sugar, half-and-half, sherry and salt in medium bowl with mixer until smooth. Spread evenly over first layer. Sprinkle with pecans. Refrigerate until thoroughly chilled.

Top Layer: Combine chocolate chips, water and butter in small saucepan over medium heat, stirring until smooth. Cool. Spread mixture over second layer. Refrigerate.

Lift and slide liner onto large cutting board. Peel down sides and cut into 1x2-inch bars. Store in airtight containers, separating layers with foil or wax paper. Refrigerate or freeze.

Makes 108 bars   Mona Bell, Lawrence, Kansas

Per bar: 97 calories, 6 g fat, 1 g protein, 12 g carbohydrate, 12 mg cholesterol, 48 mg sodium.

Fresh Apple Squares

1	medium tart apple	1	teaspoon baking soda
½	cup (1 stick) margarine[50]	1	teaspoon vanilla
1	cup sugar	½	cup chopped toasted pecans
½	cup raisins		Frosting:
1¾	cups flour	1	cup sifted confectioners' sugar
¼	teaspoon ground cloves	1	to 1½ tablespoons water
1	teaspoon ground cinnamon	½	teaspoon vanilla extract
¼	teaspoon ground nutmeg	1	to 2 teaspoons fresh lemon juice
¼	teaspoon salt		

Core and cut apple into wedges (apple wedger works well). Peel and coarsely chop (about 1 cup).[7] Set aside.

Melt margarine in medium saucepan and stir in sugar. Add apples and raisins and bring to boil. Stir and cook over medium heat 5 minutes; cool. Whisk flour, cloves, cinnamon, nutmeg, salt and baking soda in medium bowl.[2] Mix into apple mixture with wooden spoon. Stir in vanilla and pecans (mixture will be thick). Spoon into sprayed foil-lined 8x8-inch baking pan[6] and spread out evenly with wet knife. Bake at 350° for 25 minutes. Squares will firm as they cool–do not overbake. Cool in pan 10 minutes. Lift and slide liner onto cutting board. Cool completely. Peel down sides and cut into squares. Drizzle with frosting or sprinkle with confectioners' sugar.

Frosting: Stir confectioners' sugar, water, vanilla and lemon juice together in medium bowl with fork until smooth.

Makes 16 squares

Per square: 224 calories, 8 g fat, 2 g protein, 36 g carbohydrate, 0 mg cholesterol, 180 mg sodium.

Pecan Pie Squares

Instead of baking several pecan pies for large holiday gatherings, try these Pecan Pie Squares.

Crust:
10 tablespoons butter, chilled and cut into pieces
1 cup packed light brown sugar[1]
¼ teaspoon salt
2 cups flour

Filling:
4 eggs, lightly beaten
1 cup sugar
1 teaspoon vanilla extract
1 teaspoon bourbon (optional)
⅛ teaspoon salt
3 tablespoons butter, melted and cooled
1 teaspoon grated lemon zest
1 teaspoon fresh lemon juice
1 teaspoon flour
1 tablespoon water
1 cup dark corn syrup[16]
1¼ cups coarsely chopped toasted pecans

Crust: Beat butter, brown sugar, salt and flour in larger bowl with mixer until crumbly. Sprinkle evenly into well-sprayed foil-lined 9x13-inch baking pan.[6] Place plastic wrap over mixture and press firmly to form crust. Remove plastic. Bake at 350° for 10 minutes. Cool. Set oven to 300°.

Filling: Beat eggs, sugar, vanilla, bourbon, salt, butter, lemon zest and lemon juice in medium bowl with mixer until just combined or mix in medium saucepan for easier pouring. Mix flour and water in small bowl and beat into egg mixture. Beat in corn syrup until smooth. Stir in pecans.

Pour filling evenly over baked crust. Bake at 300° for 50 to 60 minutes or until surface is set and lightly browned. Cool completely on rack. Lift and slide liner onto cutting board. Peel down sides and cut into 2-inch squares.

Makes 24 squares

Per square: 233 calories, 10 g fat, 3 g protein, 34 g carbohydrate, 60 mg cholesterol, 118 mg sodium.

Poor Man's Raisin Bars

1	cup dark or golden raisins	1	teaspoon baking soda
2	cups water	¼	teaspoon salt
½	cup regular or butter-flavored shortening	1	teaspoon ground cinnamon
		1	teaspoon vanilla extract
2	cups flour, *divided*	1	egg, room temperature
1	cup sugar	1	recipe *Confectioners' Sugar Glaze*

Combine raisins and water in large saucepan and bring to boil. Reduce heat and simmer covered about 10 minutes or until water reduces to just cover raisins. Remove from heat and stir in shortening until melted. Let cool to lukewarm[6] (pan bottom may be placed in cold water to hasten cooling).

Whisk 1 cup flour, sugar, baking soda, salt and cinnamon in medium bowl.[2] Beat into raisin mixture with mixer until combined. Beat in vanilla and remaining 1 cup flour, then beat in egg. Pour into sprayed foil-lined 9x13-inch jelly-roll pan.[6] Bake at 400° for 10 to 13 minutes or until wooden pick inserted in center comes out clean. Cool in pan 10 minutes. Meanwhile, prepare *Confectioners' Sugar Glaze*. Lift and slide liner onto cutting board. Peel down sides and glaze. Cut into 1x2-inch bars.

Makes 54 bars   Donna Gaedtke, Bella Vista, Arkansas

Per bar: 58 calories, 2 g fat, 1 g protein, 9 g carbohydrate, 4 mg cholesterol, 35 mg sodium.

Microwave Peanut Brittle

1	cup sugar	1	teaspoon butter
½	cup light corn syrup[16]	1	teaspoon vanilla extract
1	cup salted dry-roasted peanuts	1	teaspoon baking soda

Mix sugar and syrup in 1½-quart microwave-safe bowl or 8-cup glass measure and microwave 4 minutes on HIGH. Stir in peanuts and microwave 3 to 5 minutes on HIGH until syrup becomes light brown. Stir in butter and vanilla. Microwave 1 to 2 minutes on HIGH. Do not let mixture get very dark. Remove and stir in baking soda. Pour mixture into sprayed 10x15-inch jelly-roll pan, spreading out evenly in pan.* Let cool. Break into pieces and store in airtight containers.

Makes about 1 pound   Marge Baker, Bella Vista, Arkansas

Per 2 ounces: 267 calories, 10 g fat, 4 g protein, 45 g carbohydrate, 1 mg cholesterol, 336 mg sodium.

** I poured mixture into center of pan and cooled slightly. Then, with two inverted forks, I pulled peanut brittle into thin layer as directed in **Norma's Peanut Brittle**.*

Norma's Peanut Brittle

Norma safeguarded this recipe for many years, thinking she would market her special peanut brittle one day. We became good friends, and several years before she died, she shared her recipe with me and showed me how to make it.

½ cup (1 stick) plus 1½ tablespoons butter

1 cup light corn syrup[16]

1½ cups sugar

1 teaspoon salt

¼ cup water

1½ cups raw peanuts

1½ teaspoons vanilla extract

1½ teaspoons baking soda

Cut two pieces of heavy duty foil about 2½ feet long. Overlap long sides to make a large rectangle and tape edges securely to countertop. Use stick of butter to grease foil well; bunch last 2 tablespoons in center.

Spray large saucepan and add corn syrup, sugar, salt and water. Cover and bring to boil over medium-high heat. Carefully swirl covered pan until sugar dissolves. When steam rises around lid, uncover and reduce heat to medium. Cook uncovered without stirring until syrup reaches hard crack stage,[15] swirling pan as mixture cooks. Stir in 1½ tablespoons butter. Add peanuts, a few at a time so syrup does not cool down. Cook over medium heat, stirring frequently, until mixture smells like peanut butter and begins to turn brown, 20 to 30 minutes. Remove from heat. Stir in vanilla and baking soda (mixture will foam).

Begin pouring peanut mixture over butter in middle of prepared surface and continue pouring in expanding circles without leaving gaps. Smooth out with wooden spatula. Starting at edge, lift and pull mixture out as far as possible with two inverted forks. As mixture cools you will be able to pull faster using your well-greased (buttered) hands—just break off pieces and push aside while pulling. Ends of brittle will form thin feathery strands. Keep lifting and pulling. Butter in center will help keep middle area soft. Cool on foil. Store in airtight containers.

Makes 1¾ pounds   Norma Carpenter, Boulder, Colorado

Per 2-ounce serving: 109 calories, 4 g fat, 2 g protein, 18 g carbohydrate, 1 mg cholesterol, 144 mg sodium.

Peanut Butter Fudge

1 (11-ounce) package peanut butter chips	Dash of salt
1 cup creamy peanut butter	1 cup evaporated milk
1 (7-ounce) jar marshmallow cream[75]	½ cup (1 stick) butter, cut into pieces
1 tablespoon vanilla extract	1 cup chopped toasted pecans (optional)
4 cups sugar	

Put peanut butter chips in large bowl. Place peanut butter, marshmallow cream and vanilla on top. Set aside. Spray 4-quart saucepan or Dutch oven. Add sugar, salt and evaporated milk; stir until combined. Add butter. Stir over medium heat with wooden spoon until butter melts and sugar dissolves. Raise heat to medium-high and bring to full boil. Carefully lift and swirl pan without stirring, using hot pad if necessary. Reduce heat but continue to boil, lifting and swirling pan occasionally. Boil 8 minutes or until mixture reaches soft ball stage.[15] Pour over peanut butter and marshmallow cream. Quickly stir with wooden spoon until combined. Then beat with mixer until smooth. Stir in pecans.

Pour fudge into sprayed foil-lined 10x15-inch jelly-roll pan,[6] spreading into corners with spatula. As fudge sets up, run flat side of table knife over top in serpentine manner to swirl surface. Cool pan on rack to room temperature. Refrigerate or place in freezer until firm. Lift and slide liner onto large cutting board. Peel down sides and cut fudge into 1-inch squares (a dough scraper cuts well). Store in covered containers, separating layers with wax paper or foil. Refrigerate or freeze.

Makes 3¾ pounds

Per square: 54 calories, 2 g fat, 1 g protein, 8 g carbohydrate, 2 mg cholesterol, 24 mg sodium.

Holiday Fudge

2¼ cups milk chocolate chips	Dash of salt
2 cups semisweet chocolate chips	1 (12-ounce) can evaporated milk
2 (7-ounce) jars marshmallow cream[75]	1 cup (2 sticks) butter, cut into pieces
1 tablespoon vanilla extract	2 cups chopped toasted pecans or walnuts
4½ cups sugar	

Put all chocolate chips in large bowl. Place marshmallow cream and vanilla on top. Set aside. Spray 4½- to 5-quart saucepan or Dutch oven. Add sugar, salt and evaporated milk; stir until combined. Add butter. Stir over medium heat with wooden spoon until butter melts and sugar dissolves. Raise heat to medium-high and bring to full boil. Carefully lift and swirl pan without stirring, using hot pads, if necessary. Reduce heat but continue to boil, lifting and swirling pan occasionally. Boil 8 minutes or until mixture reaches soft ball stage.[15] Pour over chocolate chips and marshmallow cream. Quickly stir with wooden spoon until combined. Then beat with mixer until smooth. Stir in nuts.

Pour fudge into sprayed foil-lined 11x17-inch jelly-roll pan,[6] spreading into corners with spatula. As fudge sets up, run flat side of table knife over top in serpentine manner to swirl surface. Cool pan on rack to room temperature. Refrigerate or place in freezer until firm. Lift and slide liner onto large cutting board. Peel down sides and cut fudge into 1-inch squares (a dough scraper cuts well). Store in covered containers, separating layers with wax paper or foil. Refrigerate or freeze. (I have kept this fudge in the freezer from Christmas until Easter and it was still wonderful!)

Makes about 4 pounds

Per square: 62 calories, 3 g fat, 1 g protein, 9 g carbohydrate, 3 mg cholesterol, 15 mg sodium.

Miss Maude's Fudge

Maude Thompson made the best fudge in Lexington, Mississippi! She said it was easy and gave me the recipe.

2 cups sugar	1 (2-ounce) bar unsweetened
¼ teaspoon salt	chocolate, cut into pieces, or
¼ cup light corn syrup[16]	2 (1-ounce) packets premelted
½ cup whole milk	unsweetened chocolate
½ cup (1 stick) margarine,[50] cut into pieces	1 teaspoon vanilla extract
	½ cup chopped toasted pecans

Put sugar, salt, corn syrup, milk, margarine and chocolate in medium saucepan. Stir over low heat until margarine and chocolate melt. Bring rapidly to full boil, stirring constantly. Cook without stirring 1½ minutes or until syrup reaches soft ball stage,[15] swirling pan as it cooks. Remove from heat and beat with mixer until lukewarm. Add vanilla and beat until mixture loses its gloss. Stir in pecans. Working quickly, drop teaspoonfuls of fudge onto wax paper, twirling to make a peak. Place a pecan half on top of each piece.

Note: Do not try to make this fudge on humid or rainy day—it will not set up.

Makes about 50 pieces   Maude Thompson, Lexington, Mississippi

Per piece: 60 calories, 3 g fat, 0 g protein, 10 g carbohydrate, 0 mg cholesterol, 35 mg sodium.

Chocolate Fudge Frosting variation: Bring mixture in saucepan rapidly to boil, stirring constantly. Cook 1 minute. Remove from heat and beat with mixer until mixture loses its gloss and has consistency for spreading.

Microwave Pralines

2⅓ cups packed light brown sugar[1]	1 cup toasted pecan halves or
Dash of salt	large pecan pieces
1 cup heavy cream	1 teaspoon vanilla extract
2 tablespoons butter	

Mix brown sugar, salt and cream in large microwave-safe bowl (8-cup glass measure works well). Microwave on HIGH 13 minutes. Remove and stir in butter, pecans and vanilla.

Wait 30 seconds so first praline will set up, then drop by tablespoonfuls onto foil. Cool. Remove from foil and store in airtight containers, separating layers with foil or wax paper.

Makes 24 pralines

Per praline: 154 calories, 8 g fat, 1 g protein, 22 g carbohydrate, 16 mg cholesterol, 33 mg sodium.

Colorado Toffee

Do not make toffee on a humid day—it will not set up.

1	cup (2 sticks) butter	Dash of salt
1	cup sugar	¾ (7-ounce) milk chocolate bar
3	tablespoons water	½ cup chopped toasted pecans
1	teaspoon vanilla extract	

Put butter, sugar, water, vanilla and salt in large electric skillet. Set control to low and stir until butter melts and sugar dissolves. Increase temperature to 380° (medium-high) and bring to boil. Stir frequently with wooden spatula in smooth serpentine manner—not too vigorously or toffee will separate. Let mixture bubble and foam. After 8 minutes reduce heat to 360° (medium). Boil and stir 2 more minutes or until mixture is dark *golden* brown, being careful not to burn toffee.

Working quickly, pour toffee into ungreased 10x15-inch jelly-roll pan and spread out as thinly as possible with spatula (toffee will be irregularly shaped and will not fill pan). Cool 1 minute. Break chocolate bar into 2-section pieces and place on toffee. As chocolate melts, move pieces around with fork to coat toffee. Sprinkle with nuts and gently pat into chocolate. Let stand in cool place 1 hour (I set pan outside in winter). When hard, break toffee into pieces by twisting pan.

Makes 1½ pounds   Nelle Pollard, Boulder, Colorado

Per 2-ounces: 300 calories, 22 g fat, 2 g protein, 25 g carbohydrate, 44 mg cholesterol, 165 mg sodium.

Date Roll Candy

3	cups sugar	8 ounces chopped dates (1 cup)
1	cup milk	¼ cup (½ stick) butter, softened
¼	cup plus 2 tablespoons light corn syrup[16]	1 teaspoon vanilla extract
		1 cup chopped toasted pecans

Spray large saucepan. Add sugar, milk and syrup. Stir over medium-low heat until sugar dissolves and mixture is smooth. Bring to full boil without stirring. Continue boiling over medium-high heat, lifting and swirling pan to prevent sticking, until mixture reaches soft ball stage.[15] Stir in dates. Reduce heat and cook slowly, stirring frequently, until dates are soft and mixture leaves sides of pan, about 15 minutes. Remove from heat and add butter and vanilla. Beat with mixer until thickened. Stir in pecans. Roll mixture into 1½-inch diameter log. Wrap in plastic and refrigerate several hours or until cold. Unwrap and cut into ¼-inch slices. Layer between wax paper in airtight container. Refrigerate.

Makes 32 pieces   Nancy Blackwell, Annandale, Virginia

Per piece: 143 calories, 4 g fat, 1 g protein, 28 g carbohydrate, 5 mg cholesterol, 21 mg sodium.

Divinity

Making divinity at Christmastime with a friend or with your spouse can get you in the holiday spirit. It is also helpful to have an extra pair of hands.

2	egg whites, room temperature[12]	1	teaspoon clear imitation vanilla extract[22]
2	tablespoons plus 2½ cups sugar		
¼	teaspoon salt	½	cup chopped toasted pecans
½	cup light corn syrup[16]	48	toasted pecan halves* (approximate)
½	cup boiling water		

Beat egg whites in large, deep, grease-free, copper, stainless steel or glass bowl with mixer on medium until soft peaks form. Gradually add 2 tablespoons sugar, beating on high until stiff peaks form. Set aside.

Rinse large heavy saucepan with water, leaving pan wet.[38] Add remaining 2½ cups sugar, salt, corn syrup and *boiling* water. Stir with wooden spoon until sugar dissolves. Bring to rolling boil (bubbles all over top). Reduce heat but continue boiling without stirring until mixture reaches hard ball stage, 4 to 5 minutes.[15] Carefully lift and swirl pan from time to time to prevent sticking.

Pour hot syrup in thin stream into beaten egg whites, beating constantly while pouring. (Here is where a second person can really be of help—one to beat while the other pours. Alternatively, use mixer on stand.) Halfway through pouring in syrup reheat remaining syrup over medium heat while continuing to beat candy in saucepan. Gradually pour and beat in remaining hot syrup. Continue beating 6 to 8 minutes or until mixture loses its gloss and holds its shape when dropped from spoon. Stir in vanilla and chopped pecans.

Working quickly (second person is also helpful here), drop teaspoonfuls of candy onto wax paper using two teaspoons—one to scoop candy from bowl and other to push candy from spoon onto wax paper. Scoop from bottom of bowl and work to top because candy hardens first at bottom of bowl. Give a twirl to top of candy with a twisting motion. Press pecan half on top of each piece. Place in single layer in covered containers and store at room temperature.

* Mother would sometimes place well-drained maraschino cherry halves cutside down on top of divinity in place of pecan halves.

Makes about 48 pieces

Per piece: 79 calories, 3 g fat, 1 g protein, 14 g carbohydrate, 0 mg cholesterol, 21 mg sodium.

Applets or Apricotlets

2	cups sugar	1	cup thick applesauce
2	envelopes unflavored gelatin	1	teaspoon fresh lemon juice
1	(4-serving size) package lemon-flavored gelatin	1	teaspoon vanilla extract
3½	tablespoons cornstarch, *divided*	½	cup finely chopped toasted nuts
	Dash of salt	½	cup confectioners' sugar

Applets: Put sugar, unflavored gelatin, lemon gelatin, 1½ tablespoons cornstarch and salt in medium saucepan. Stir in applesauce with wooden spoon. Bring to boil over medium-high heat, stirring constantly; then reduce to very low heat and cook 10 minutes, stirring occasionally. Add lemon juice. Cook 3 more minutes. Remove from heat. Stir in vanilla and nuts. Pour mixture into sprayed 8x8-inch baking dish and cool. Cover loosely with paper towels and let stand overnight at room temperature.

Mix confectioners' sugar and remaining 2 tablespoons cornstarch in small bowl.* Sprinkle about 1 tablespoon over jellied mixture, patting in with your fingers. Generously cover cutting board with remaining confectioners' sugar mixture. Run knife around edge of baking dish and cut jellied mixture into 1-inch-wide strips. Carefully remove one strip at a time to cutting board. Roll to coat all sides. Cut into 1½-inch pieces (kitchen shears work well) and coat ends of pieces as well. Place each piece in paper or foil candy cup. Store in airtight containers.

Apricotlets variation: Drain one 15½-ounce can of apricots, reserving juice. Puree apricots in blender or in saucepan with handheld blender until smooth. Add enough reserved juice, about 1 tablespoon, to make 1 cup puree. Substitute apricot puree for applesauce and stir into gelatin mixture in saucepan. Continue as directed above, omitting vanilla.

* Confectioners' sugar is a combination of sugar and cornstarch; additional cornstarch helps keep the sugar dry.

Makes 40 pieces   Ruth Riach, Bella Vista, Arkansas

Per piece: 94 calories, 1 g fat, 3 g protein, 20 g carbohydrate, 0 mg cholesterol, 15 mg sodium.

Tiger Butter

3 (6-ounce) boxes white chocolate baking bars, or 2½ cups white chocolate chips

1 cup extra crunchy peanut butter

1 cup semisweet or milk chocolate chips

½ tablespoon regular or butter-flavored shortening[69]

Break white chocolate into sections in 2-quart glass measure or microwave-safe bowl. Microwave on MEDIUM-HIGH 3 minutes; stir well. Continue microwaving on MEDIUM-HIGH at 15 second intervals and stirring well after each interval until chocolate is almost smooth (chips may take fewer intervals of heating than baking chocolate). Stir well each time, because chocolate keeps its shape, even when melted internally. Stir peanut butter into melted chocolate. Microwave on MEDIUM-HIGH 1 minute. Stir until creamy and spread into sprayed foil-lined 10x15-inch jelly-roll pan.[6]

Put semisweet chocolate chips in 2-cup glass measure. Place shortening in center of chips. Microwave on HIGH 1½ minutes; stir well. If not smooth, heat 30 more seconds and stir well. If still not smooth, heat an additional 10 seconds and stir until smooth. Pour chocolate in thin stream up and down and across peanut butter mixture. Using a sharp knife, swirl tip *lightly* across surface in circular pattern for a marbled effect.

Chill until set or freeze 20 to 30 minutes. Peel foil off back of candy, place candy on cutting board and cut into 2-inch wide strips with sharp knife. Cut strips into squares, then cut diagonally into triangles. Store in airtight containers. Refrigerate or freeze.

Makes about 2½ pounds

Per ounce: 170 calories, 13 g fat, 4 g protein, 14 g carbohydrate, 0 mg cholesterol, 79 mg sodium.

Dessserts & Dessert Sauces

Desserts

Dessert Sauces

Crustless Cheesecake

3 (8-ounce) packages cream cheese, softened	½ teaspoon almond extract
5 eggs, room temperature	1 (16-ounce) container sour cream
1 cup plus 2 tablespoons sugar	½ teaspoon vanilla extract
¼ teaspoon salt	⅛ teaspoon fresh lemon juice (optional)

Beat cream cheese in medium bowl with mixer until smooth. Add eggs, one at time, beating well after each addition. Add 1 cup sugar, salt and almond extract. Beat until creamy, about 1 minute. Pour batter into sprayed 9x13-inch baking dish. Gently slide dish back and forth to settle batter. Bake at 325° for 30 minutes or until center is almost set. Remove from oven. Carefully run tip of sharp knife around upper edge of cheesecake to allow surface to pull away from sides freely as it cools. *Cool 20 minutes.*

Mix sour cream, 2 tablespoons sugar, vanilla and lemon juice in medium bowl. Spread over cheesecake. Return to oven and bake at 325° for 10 minutes. Cool completely on rack. Refrigerate uncovered 8 hours or overnight.

Makes 16 servings   Marion and Russ Krapf, Forest, Virginia

Per serving: 267 calories, 23 g fat, 6 g protein, 22 g carbohydrate, 208 mg cholesterol, 395 mg sodium.

Strawberry Glaze Cheesecake variation: Prepare recipe of *Strawberry Glaze*. Rinse 1 pint of small whole fresh strawberries and remove caps. Drain on paper towels. Dip strawberries in glaze and place points up on Crustless Cheesecake (if strawberries are large cut in half and arrange halves outside down. Pour remaining glaze over strawberries and cheesecake. Refrigerate until ready to serve.

Cheesecake Tips

Immediately after baking, carefully run tip of sharp knife around upper edge of cheesecake to allow surface to pull away from sides freely as it cools.

Let cheesecakes cool completely before refrigerating—a hot or warm cheesecake placed in refrigerator will definitely crack; an overbaked cheesecake will also crack.

Cheesecakes should be refrigerated uncovered 8 hours or overnight; however, freezing cheesecakes is not recommended.

Cheesecakes may be prepared up to two days ahead of serving.

Almond Praline Cheesecake

Crust:
½ cup (1 stick) butter
1½ cups graham cracker crumbs
½ cup ground whole natural almonds*
3 tablespoons sugar

Filling:
2½ (8-ounce) packages cream cheese, softened
¾ cup sugar
3 eggs, room temperature
½ cup ground whole natural almonds
½ teaspoon almond extract
⅛ teaspoon salt

1½ cups sour cream
3 tablespoons sugar
1 teaspoon vanilla extract
1 recipe *Praline Topping*

Crust: Melt butter in small saucepan. Stir in graham cracker crumbs, almonds and sugar. Press crumb mixture into sprayed 9-inch springform pan to form crust with ½-inch side.[92] Chill in freezer while preparing filling.

Filling: Beat cream cheese in large bowl with mixer until fluffy. Gradually beat in sugar. Add eggs, one at a time, beating well after each addition until no yellow streaks remain. Beat until smooth. Stir in almonds, almond extract and salt.

Pour filling evenly into crust. Gently rotate pan back and forth to settle batter. Bake at 350° for 45 to 50 minutes or until center is almost set. Remove from oven. Carefully run tip of sharp knife around upper edge of cheesecake to allow surface to pull away from sides freely as it cools. Do not remove ring. Let stand on rack 20 minutes. Combine sour cream, sugar and vanilla in bowl. Spread over cheesecake. Return cake to oven and bake at 350° for 15 more minutes. Remove to rack and cool completely. Refrigerate uncovered 8 hours or overnight. Meanwhile, prepare *Praline Topping*.

Carefully run knife around cheesecake to loosen from sides of pan. Sprinkle *Praline Topping* over top. Remove ring, leaving cake on pan bottom. Place on serving plate. Loosely cover with foil and refrigerate until ready to serve.

* Grind almonds in small food processor or blender, or use handheld blender. Some handheld blenders have chopper attachments.

Makes 8 to 10 servings   Marianne Goga, Bentonville, Arkansas

Per serving of 8: 917 calories, 64 g fat, 18 g protein, 75 g carbohydrate, 208 mg cholesterol, 537 mg sodium.

Amaretto Chocolate Cheesecake

Crust:
6 tablespoons butter
30 thin chocolate wafers, finely crushed (about 1½ cups)*
1 tablespoon sugar

Filling:
3 (2-ounce) semisweet baking chocolate bars

4 ounces almond paste (not almond filling)
½ cup amaretto liqueur
3 (8-ounce) packages cream cheese, cubed and softened
½ cup sugar
4 eggs, room temperature
½ cup heavy cream

Crust: Melt butter in small saucepan. Stir in wafer crumbs and sugar. Press crumb mixture into sprayed 9-inch springform pan, forming crust with ½-inch side.[92] Refrigerate 30 to 40 minutes.

Filling: Melt chocolate according to package directions. Cool slightly. Shred almond paste into medium bowl and gradually add amaretto, beating with mixer on low until thoroughly blended. Set aside. Beat cream cheese in large bowl until smooth, scraping down sides occasionally. Blend in sugar. Add eggs, one at a time, beating until just combined. Blend in almond mixture and melted chocolate. Add heavy cream and beat until smooth.

Carefully pour filling into crust. Gently rotate pan back and forth to settle batter. Bake at 350° for 45 to 50 minutes (do not overbake–it will have a soft center about the size of a saucer but will solidify as cake cools). Remove to rack. Carefully run tip of knife around top edge of cheesecake to allow surface to pull away from sides freely as it cools. Do not remove ring. Cool completely at room temperature. Refrigerate uncovered 8 hours or overnight. Just before slicing, remove ring, leaving cake on pan bottom. Place on serving plate and dust with unsweetened cocoa powder, if desired.

Chocolate graham crackers or chocolate vanilla wafers may be substituted.

Makes 12 servings

Per serving: 344 calories, 21 g fat, 5 g protein, 32 g carbohydrate, 110 mg cholesterol, 171 mg sodium.

Daiquiri Cheesecake

Crust:
- 6 tablespoons butter
- 1¼ cups *cinnamon* graham cracker crumbs
- ¼ cup sugar

Filling:
- 1 envelope unflavored gelatin
- 1 cup sugar, *divided*
- ½ cup light rum
- 2 teaspoons grated lemon zest
- 1 teaspoon grated lime zest
- ½ cup fresh lime juice
- 4 egg yolks, beaten
- 2 (8-ounce) packages cream cheese, cubed and softened
- 3 egg whites*
- 1 cup heavy cream

Crust: Melt butter in medium saucepan. Stir in crumbs and sugar. Reserve 2 tablespoons crumb mixture. Press remainder into bottom of sprayed 9-inch springform pan. Refrigerate 45 minutes.

Filling: Combine gelatin and ½ cup sugar in medium saucepan. Stir in rum, lemon zest, lime zest, lime juice and egg yolks. Cook over medium heat 8 to 10 minutes or until slightly thickened, stirring constantly. Remove from heat and beat in cream cheese with mixer. Cool. Beat egg whites in medium bowl with mixer on high until soft peaks form. Gradually add remaining ½ cup sugar, beating until stiff peaks form, about 5 minutes. Fold into cream cheese mixture. Whip heavy cream in separate bowl to soft peaks and fold into cream cheese and egg white mixture.

Pour filling into crust and sprinkle with reserved crumb mixture. Refrigerate uncovered several hours until firm or overnight. Run knife around sides and remove ring, leaving cake on pan bottom. Place on serving plate. Decorate by twisting and standing thin half-slices of lime into top of cake.

Makes 12 to 16 servings   Dody Martin, Boulder, Colorado

Per serving of 16: 320 calories, 22 g fat, 6 g protein, 23 g carbohydrate, 115 mg cholesterol, 189 mg sodium.

* You may substitute 6 teaspoons meringue powder and 6 tablespoons water for the 3 uncooked egg whites. Beat on high 5 minutes, gradually add remaining ½ cup sugar, and beat 5 more minutes. Fold into cream cheese mixture and continue as directed above. (I tested this cheesecake using meringue powder and the cheesecake was delicious.)

Cherry Ladyfinger Dessert

Tie a red or lacy ribbon around dessert for a beautiful presentation.

2 (3-ounce) packages *soft* ladyfingers	½ to ⅔ cup sugar
¼ cup rum or brandy	1 teaspoon clear imitation vanilla extract[22]
2 cups heavy cream	1 (16-ounce) can cherry pie filling
1 (8-ounce) package cream cheese, softened	¼ teaspoon almond extract
	⅛ teaspoon ground cinnamon

Before starting, read **About Whipped Cream** below. Separate and place ladyfinger halves split-side up on piece of foil. Brush with rum (small narrow paintbrush works well). Set aside. Whip cream in large, deep glass or metal bowl with mixer. Beat cream cheese in separate large bowl with same beaters until smooth. Add sugar and vanilla. Beat until light and fluffy. Add whipped cream to cream-cheese mixture and beat in slowly with mixer until beginning to combine. Stop. Start *folding*ᴳ in whipped cream with rubber spatula (you do not want to deflate whipped cream). Continue, alternately beating slowly and folding in with spatula, until mixture is fluffy and combined.

Line sides of sprayed 9-inch springform pan with as many ladyfinger halves as needed, standing on end with rounded side against pan. Line bottom with *half* the remaining ladyfingers rounded side up, breaking if necessary. Spread with half the whipped cream mixture. Add remaining ladyfinger halves and spread with remaining whipped cream mixture. Cover with foil and refrigerate overnight. Stir cherry pie filling, almond extract and cinnamon together in medium bowl. Cover and refrigerate overnight for flavors to blend.

Several hours before serving spread cherry mixture over dessert. Carefully release clamp and remove sides, leaving dessert on pan bottom for stability. Place on serving plate. Refrigerate uncovered until ready to serve. Slice between ladyfingers.

Makes 10 servings

Per serving: 271 calories, 17 g fat, 3 g protein, 26 g carbohydrate, 64 mg cholesterol, 83 mg sodium.

About Whipped Cream

Use a deep, glass or metal (copper preferred) bowl, one large enough to hold twice the unwhipped volume of cream. Put bowl and beaters in freezer 10 minutes before whipping. Pour no more than two cups cream into bowl. Begin beating on low for less spattering; increase speed to high. When soft peaks just begin to form, add sugar (confectioners' sugar dissolves easier), extracts and flavorings. Continue beating; medium peaks will form (soft peaks that droop slightly). Beat until stiff peaks form (peaks will stand straight up). Do not overbeat or cream will turn to butter; if this happens, *stir in* 1 tablespoon cream at a time until desired consistency–do not beat in or cream will return to butter.

Hummel Fritters

Fritter:
1   cup sugar
1   tablespoon baking powder
2   tablespoons flour
⅛   teaspoon salt
2   eggs, lightly beaten
½   teaspoon vanilla extract
½   cup chopped dates

½   cup chopped toasted pecans

Fruit Mixture:
6   oranges
2   bananas
1   to 2 tablespoons sugar, or to taste

Whipped cream
6   maraschino cherries

Fritter: Line 10x15-inch jelly-roll pan with foil liner,[6] extending foil slightly over each end for lifting. Grease liner well with shortening; dust with flour and tap out excess. Whisk sugar, baking powder, flour and salt in medium bowl.[2] Beat in eggs and vanilla with mixer about 1 minute. Fold in dates and pecans. Spread batter evenly into prepared pan. Bake at 375° until puffed and brown, about 17 minutes (surface will begin to crisp). Cool in pan 10 minutes.

Fruit Mixture: Segment oranges,[47] squeezing and reserving juice from membranes. Peel and slice bananas. Combine bananas, orange segments and juice in medium bowl; stir in sugar. Cover and refrigerate until ready to serve.

Lift and slide liner onto rack. Peel down sides and cool completely. Place jelly-roll pan over fritter and invert into pan. Peel foil away from fritter, using knife to free any part that sticks. Let stand bottom-side up about 20 minutes to evaporate moisture. Break fritter into bite-size pieces and turn rightside up in pan. Let stand several minutes. Store fritter pieces in airtight container. (May be prepared a day ahead.)

To serve, divide fritter pieces among six sherbets or other stemmed glasses and cover with servings of Fruit Mixture. Top each with whipped cream and a maraschino cherry.

Makes 6 servings   Margie Broome, Midlothian, Virginia

Per serving: 427 Calories, 14 g fat, 7 g protein, 78 g carbohydrate, 72 mg cholesterol, 213 mg sodium.

Lemon Spoom

*In the 1970's we were members of a gourmet dinner group. **Lemon Spoom** was served as the grand finale to an elegant dinner.*

1	recipe *Easy Seven-Minute Frosting*	6	large whole strawberries
1	pint lemon or pineapple sherbet, softened	1	or 2 kiwi fruit, peeled and sliced[76]
1	tablespoon fresh lemon juice		Asti spumante or champagne, chilled

Prepare frosting. Beat sherbet and lemon juice into frosting with mixer on low until combined. Fill champagne glasses three-fourths full. Cover with plastic wrap and freeze. Remove plastic and serve each dessert garnished with a strawberry and 1 or 2 slices of kiwi. Pass asti spumante for lacing spoom. Serve with *Coconut Shortbread* or *Emma's Sugar Cookies*. Drink any remaining bubbly.

Makes 6 servings

Per serving: 172 calories, 1 g fat, 2 g protein, 41 g carbohydrate, 20 mg cholesterol, 53 mg sodium.

Peach Melba

3	large fresh freestone peaches		Melba Sauce:
½	cup water	¾	cup seedless raspberry jam
¾	cup sugar	¼	cup raspberry-flavored liqueur or raspberry syrup
½	teaspoon vanilla extract		
	Dash of salt		Whipped cream (optional)
	Vanilla ice cream		

Remove skins[35] and cut peaches in half. Carefully remove pits, keeping peach halves intact, and set aside. Mix water, sugar, vanilla and salt in large saucepan and boil 2 minutes without stirring. Add peach halves, cutside up, reduce heat to low, and simmer 2½ minutes. Turn peaches over and simmer 2½ more minutes or until tender but still firm. Transfer peaches with syrup to medium bowl and cool. Cover and refrigerate until chilled, turning peaches occasionally.

Place serving of ice cream in each of six dessert dishes and cover with peach half, rounded side up. Spoon warm Melba Sauce over each serving and top with whipped cream. Garnish with fresh raspberries and sprigs of mint. Serve with chocolate mint cookies.

Melba Sauce: Heat jam and liqueur in 2-cup glass measure in microwave on HIGH about 1 minute, or in small saucepan on stove until jam melts. Stir to combine. Reheat before serving.

Makes 6 servings

Per serving: 416 calories, 7 g fat, 3 g protein, 84 g carbohydrate, 29 mg cholesterol, 114 mg sodium.

Pots de Crème

⅓ cup *superfine* sugar[116]	2 tablespoons orange-flavored
1½ cups half-and-half	liqueur, or 2 teaspoons dark rum
1 cup semisweet chocolate chips	Whipped cream
4 egg yolks, lightly beaten	Shaved bittersweet chocolate
1 teaspoon vanilla extract	Fresh raspberries

Preheat oven to 350°. Combine sugar and half-and-half in medium saucepan. Heat to just before boiling, stirring occasionally. Remove from heat and add chocolate chips. Let stand 1 minute. Whisk until chocolate is thoroughly melted. Whisk in beaten egg yolks, vanilla and liqueur. Spoon custard equally into six 4-ounce custard cups or ramekins;[G] place on folded kitchen towel in 9x13-inch baking pan. Set pan on extended oven rack. Add hot water to pan until halfway up sides of cups. *Carefully* slide rack back into oven. Bake at 350° for 25 minutes or until centers are almost set–do not overbake. Remove cups to cooling rack. Cool slightly. Serve warm with whipped cream, shaved chocolate and fresh raspberries. (Alternatively, place plastic wrap directly on surface of each custard. Refrigerate up to 3 days–do not freeze. Let stand 30 minutes before serving.)

Makes 6 servings

Per serving: 363 calories, 24 g fat, 5 g protein, 33 g carbohydrate, 174 mg cholesterol, 81 mg sodium.

Frozen Raspberry Dessert

½ cup (1 stick) butter	2 tablespoons fresh lemon juice
1 cup flour	1 cup sugar
½ cup finely chopped toasted nuts	2 egg whites or meringue powder[95]
1 (10-ounce) package frozen sweetened raspberries or strawberries, thawed	1 (8-ounce) container whipped topping, thawed

Cut butter into flour in medium bowl with pastry blender until mixture resembles coarse cornmeal. Stir in nuts. Sprinkle mixture evenly into 9x13-inch baking pan and cover with plastic wrap. Press crumbs firmly into pan with flat-bottom glass. Remove plastic. Bake at 325° for 15 minutes or until light brown. Cool. Crumble mixture into medium bowl and sprinkle *two-thirds* over bottom of 9x13-inch baking dish. Put raspberries, lemon juice and sugar in large bowl. Add egg whites and beat with mixer 10 minutes (I used meringue powder.) Fold in whipped topping. Spread raspberry mixture over crumbs. Sprinkle remaining crumb mixture on top. Freeze until firm. Cut into squares and serve.

Makes 12 servings   Katie Henkel, Bella Vista, Arkansas

Per serving: 244 calories, 12 g fat, 3 g protein, 32 g carbohydrate, 0 mg cholesterol, 100 mg sodium.

Crème Caramel

Caramel:
½ cup sugar
3 tablespoons water

Custard:
1½ cups heavy cream

1½ cups whole milk
½ cup sugar
2 eggs
3 egg yolks
Pinch of salt
1 teaspoon vanilla

Caramel: Rinse small saucepan with water and leave wet.[38] Put sugar in pan and add water. Stir to dissolve. Bring to rolling boil over high heat (bubbles all over top). Continue boiling without stirring, lifting and swirling until water evaporates and sugar begins to caramelize.[G] Lift and swirl pan above heat–heat of pan will continue to brown sugar. Return to stove and continue heating, lifting and swirling until caramel becomes a deep honey color. Watch carefully–caramel can burn in just seconds. Working quickly (but carefully–caramel is very hot), pour thin layer into each of six 6-ounce ramekins;[G] lift and swirl ramekins to cover bottom with caramel.

Custard: Heat cream and milk in medium saucepan over medium heat until scalded (small bubbles around edge of pan), stirring occasionally. Meanwhile, slowly whisk sugar into eggs and egg yolks in large bowl until just combined. Scrape down sides. Remove milk mixture from heat and slowly drizzle about ½-cup, 1 tablespoon at a time, into egg mixture to warm eggs, whisking all the while. Add remaining milk mixture, whisking until just combined. Strain mixture through fine-mesh strainer into large glass measure or pitcher. Stir in salt and vanilla.

Preheat oven to 325°. Meanwhile, bring 2 quarts water to boil in large saucepan. Place folded kitchen towel in bottom of 11x17-inch roasting pan. Make a mark halfway up outside of one ramekin. Fill ramekins equally with custard and place on towel in pan without touching sides. Extend middle oven rack and place pan on rack. Pour heated water into pan up to mark on ramekin. Cover pan loosely with foil. *Carefully* push rack into oven. Bake just until set. (Could take anywhere from 35 to 50 minutes depending on oven, ramekins, etc. After 30 minutes, test for doneness by gently shaking ramekin–should be like gelatin. Some softness in center is okay–just make sure custard is not soupy; custard will continue to cook in foil-covered water bath.) Remove from oven and cool covered 1½ to 2 hours in water bath to room temperature. Remove ramekins from water bath and cover each with plastic wrap. Refrigerate several hours or up to 2 days.

To unmold ramekins, run sharp knife around edge of custard. Place dessert plate on top and invert. Gently shake to release custard, allowing caramel to flow over and around custard.

Makes 6 servings

Per serving: 429 calories, 28 g fat, 7 g protein, 38 g carbohydrate, 268 mg cholesterol, 100 mg sodium.

Apple Crisp

Our daughter, Terry, makes Apple Crisp when she needs a dessert in a hurry. Guests love it!

6 to 8 medium tart green apples	¾ cup flour
1 cup quick or old-fashioned oats	1¼ teaspoons ground cinnamon
1 cup packed brown sugar[1]	⅔ cup (10⅔ tablespoons) butter, chilled
Dash of salt	

Core, peel and thinly slice apples. Cut slices in half and put in bowl of cold lemon water.[7] Pat apples dry and spread out in sprayed 9x13-inch baking dish. Mix oats, brown sugar, salt, flour and cinnamon in large bowl. Cut in butter with pastry blender or use mixer on low to form coarse crumb topping. Sprinkle over apples. Bake at 350° for 45 minutes. Cut into squares and serve warm—with ice cream, of course.

Makes 12 servings   Nancy Paurus, Boulder, Colorado

Per serving: 244 calories, 11 g fat, 2 g protein, 37 g carbohydrate, 27 mg cholesterol, 180 mg sodium.

Apple Dumplings

2 medium tart green apples	Streusel Topping:
2 (8-ounce) cans refrigerated original crescent dough	1 cup sugar
Flour	1 teaspoon cinnamon
10 ounces orange-flavored, dew-like carbonated beverage	Dash of ground nutmeg
	⅓ cup butter, cut into pieces

Core, peel and cut apples into eight wedges. Put wedges in bowl of cold lemon water[7] while preparing crescent dough. Drain wedges and pat dry.

Working with one can at a time, separate crescent dough into triangles. Lightly dust each triangle in flour and pat or roll widest part slightly larger. Place an apple wedge across wide end of each triangle and roll toward point. Pinch sides together to seal. Place dumplings, tips underneath, on sprayed foil-lined 9x13-inch jelly-roll pan. Sprinkle with Streusel Topping. Pour carbonated beverage around dumplings. Bake at 350° for 25 minutes or until golden. Remove and spoon pan liquid over dumplings—I use a bulb baster. (May make ahead and bake. Cool. Cover loosely with foil. Reheat, if desired.) Serve with ice cream.

Streusel Topping: Whisk sugar, cinnamon and nutmeg in medium bowl. Add butter and cut in with pastry blender, or rub between fingertips until crumbly. (May prepare topping ahead. Refrigerate.)

Makes 16 dumplings (8 servings)

Per serving: 376 calories, 21 g fat, 4 g protein, 50 g carbohydrate, 20 mg cholesterol, 525 mg sodium.

Death By Chocolate Brownie Dessert

There are many "Death By Chocolate" desserts—I think this one is a keeper! The many visible layers of the Trifle Bowl variation make an impressive presentation.

1	recipe *Fudgy Liqueur Brownies**	2	teaspoons vanilla extract, *divided*
6	(1.45-ounce) milk-chocolate bars with almonds	2	dashes of salt, *divided*
2	(2.8-ounce) packages milk-chocolate mousse mix	2	(8-ounce) containers whipped topping, thawed

Prepare brownies; cool and set aside. Freeze chocolate bars 15 minutes. Meanwhile, prepare each mousse mix according to package directions in *separate* bowls for fluffier mousse. Add 1 teaspoon vanilla and dash of salt to each mousse; do not chill. Unwrap frozen chocolate bars, place in ziptop bag and pound into small pieces with meat mallet. Return to freezer until ready to use.

Spray 9x13-inch baking dish. Break brownies into medium-size pieces. Cover bottom of dish, using all the pieces, and press down gently. Spread one bowl prepared mousse over brownie layer, cover with 1 container whipped topping and sprinkle with half the milk-chocolate pieces. Repeat layering with remaining mousse, whipped topping and chocolate pieces. Cover and refrigerate overnight. Cut into small squares (very rich) and serve.

Trifle Bowl variation: Place *half* the brownie pieces in bottom of unsprayed trifle bowl or other large clear-glass bowl and press down gently to fill spaces. Cover with one bowl prepared mousse followed by 1 container whipped topping. Sprinkle with half the milk-chocolate pieces. Repeat layers. Refrigerate. Scoop through all layers with large spoon and serve in short sherbets or glass dessert dishes.

** In a pinch for time, prepare family-size brownie mix and substitute for **Fudgy Liqueur Brownies**. When baked and still warm, punch holes all over top of brownies and drizzle with ⅓ cup coffee-flavored liqueur. Continue as directed above.*

Makes 24 servings

Per serving: 294 calories, 15 g fat, 3 g protein, 34 g carbohydrate, 39 mg cholesterol, 118 mg sodium.

Chocolate Mocha Ice Cream Dessert

A rich, decadent, frozen dessert that can be made ahead. Great for a party!

Crust:
¼ cup (½ stick) butter
1¼ cups *chocolate* graham cracker crumbs (about 10 sheets crushed)
2 tablespoons sugar

6 (1.4-ounce) milk chocolate English toffee bars
1 quart coffee ice cream
½ gallon chocolate ice cream
¼ cup coffee-flavored liqueur

Crust: Melt butter in medium saucepan. Stir in graham cracker crumbs and sugar. Spread crumb mixture in sprayed 9x13-inch baking dish. Cover crumbs with plastic wrap and press crumbs firmly into place with flat-bottom glass. Remove plastic. Spray crust with nonstick spray. Freeze 30 minutes.

Unwrap toffee bars and place in ziptop bag. Freeze 30 minutes. Meanwhile, put ice cream in separate large bowls and let soften. Mash coffee ice cream with potato masher to slushy consistency. Put in freezer. Mash chocolate ice cream until slushy and mix in liqueur. Put in freezer. Crush frozen toffee bars in bag into small pieces with meat mallet (makes about 1½ cups).

Stir coffee ice cream and spread over crust. Sprinkle with half the toffee pieces. Cover with chocolate ice cream mixture and sprinkle with remaining toffee. Freeze until firm. Cut into squares and serve with *Hot Fudge Sauce.*

Makes 24 servings

Per serving: 246 calories, 14 g fat, 3 g protein, 26 g carbohydrate, 55 mg cholesterol, 134 mg sodium.

Frozen Grasshoppers

An easy, refreshing summer dessert.

½ gallon French vanilla ice cream, softened

½ cup green créme de menthe
⅓ cup white créme de cacao

Blend ice cream and liqueurs in blender or in large bowl with mixer. Pour into parfait glasses or wine glasses. Freeze.

Remove 5 minutes before serving. Garnish each with two chocolate twig cookies stuck in top and a sprig of fresh mint or sprinkle each with grated unsweetened chocolate and serve with a chocolate cookie.

Makes 8 to 10   Ruth Grosshuesch, Bella Vista, Arkansas

Per serving of 10: 373 calories, 18 g fat, 6 g protein, 40 g carbohydrate, 125 mg cholesterol, 85 mg sodium.

Chocolate Covered Strawberries

2	pints medium, fresh strawberries with caps (about 24)	½ cup white chocolate chips
1	cup semisweet chocolate chips	1½ tablespoons butter-flavored or regular shortening,[69] *divided*

Rinse strawberries and pat dry with paper towels. Berries must be *completely* dry before dipping. Put semisweet chocolate chips in microwave-safe bowl. Place 1 tablespoon shortening in middle of chips and heat on HIGH 2 minutes. Stir. If not smooth, heat 30 seconds and stir again. Hold strawberries by the cap and dip three-fourths the way into melted chocolate. Gently shake off any excess and place on wax-paper-lined jelly-roll pan to dry. For two-tone strawberries, melt ½-cup white chocolate chips and remaining ½ tablespoon shortening in microwave-safe bowl on HIGH 1 minute. Stir. If not smooth, heat 15 seconds and stir. Dip chocolate-covered strawberries *halfway* into melted white chocolate and return to jelly-roll pan to dry. Let dry unrefrigerated in cool place. (Strawberries are 75% water. Refrigeration will cause humidity to condense on chocolate, making semisweet chocolate white; berries will become soggy.) Chocolate covered strawberries are best if served within 24 hours.

Makes 24 strawberries

Per strawberry: 46 calories, 3 g fat, 1 g protein, 6 g carbohydrate, 0 mg cholesterol, 1 mg sodium.

Brownie Pie

Ruth LaMontagne and I made Brownie Pie often for impromptu bridge get-togethers with our husbands. We were neighbors in Burlington, North Carolina in the 1960's. Recently we got together and reminisced about the time Ruth forgot to put in the sugar!

½	cup (1 stick) butter or margarine[50]	¼ cup flour
1	cup sugar	2 eggs, lightly beaten
	Dash of salt	1 teaspoon vanilla extract
3	tablespoons unsweetened cocoa powder	½ cup toasted chopped pecans

Melt butter in medium saucepan. Cool slightly. Stir in sugar, salt, cocoa and flour. Mix in eggs and vanilla; stir in pecans. Pour into well-sprayed 8- or 9-inch pie plate. Bake at 350° for 25 to 30 minutes or until almost firm in center (will be soft–almost like pudding). Allow to stand 30 minutes if time permits. Cut into four pieces. Serve with vanilla ice cream.

Makes 4 servings   Ruth LaMontagne, Cary, North Carolina

Per serving: 584 calories, 36 g fat, 8 g protein, 63 g carbohydrate, 108 mg cholesterol, 301 mg sodium.

Baked Fudge

4	eggs, room temperature	½	cup unsweetened cocoa powder
2	cups sugar	1	cup (2 sticks) butter, melted
½	cup flour	2	teaspoons vanilla extract
¼	teaspoon salt	1	cup chopped toasted nuts

Beat eggs in large bowl with mixer until lemon colored. Whisk sugar, flour, salt and cocoa in separate bowl.[2] Beat into eggs until well combined. Blend in butter and vanilla. Stir in nuts. Pour mixture into sprayed 9x9-inch baking pan or 7x11-inch brownie pan.

Fold kitchen towel and place in separate pan about 2 inches larger than fudge pan. Place fudge pan on towel. Extend middle rack of oven; place pans on rack and pour very hot water into outer pan to about 1 inch up sides of fudge pan.[64] Carefully push rack into oven. Bake at 325° for 45 to 50 minutes or until set like custard. Fudge should be crusty on top and knife should come out clean when inserted about one-half inch from edge; fudge will continue to firm as it stands.

Carefully remove pan from hot water bath and cool completely on rack (will need time for bottom to set up; do not refrigerate). When set, cut into squares and serve with ice cream or whipped cream.

Makes 16 squares

Per square: 293 calories, 18 g fat, 4 g protein, 32 g carbohydrate, 85 mg cholesterol, 167 mg sodium.

Chocolate Cobbler Bread Pudding

6	slices white sandwich bread	1	cup milk
1	(14-ounce) can sweetened condensed milk	2	eggs, lightly beaten
		1	teaspoon vanilla extract
⅓	cup purchased chocolate syrup, or *Chocolate Syrup*	¼	teaspoon salt
		2	tablespoons butter

Place bread slices on racks to dry out for about 1 hour or place in 325° oven 3 to 4 minutes. Leaving crusts on, cut each slice into four strips, then cut strips into four pieces (about 4 cups). Set aside. Whisk condensed milk, chocolate syrup and milk in large bowl. Whisk in eggs, vanilla and salt. Gently fold bread pieces into milk mixture and submerge with spatula, saturating bread. Pour mixture into sprayed 9x9-inch baking pan. Let stand 10 minutes. Dot with butter and bake at 325° for 55 to 60 minutes or until set. Remove pudding from oven. While still hot, stir with fork to break up lumps and even out consistency. Cool on rack. Serve with vanilla ice cream, or refrigerate to serve later.

Makes 6 servings

Per serving: 405 calories, 13 g fat, 11 g protein, 63 g carbohydrate, 104 mg cholesterol, 378 mg sodium.

Mobile Bread Pudding

I am always looking for a good bread pudding recipe. When my nephew, Willie Rabb, married Sara Lamb, this dessert was served at their rehearsal dinner. Chef Cortlanst Inge graciously dictated it to me as I wrote it on paper napkins. Roberta's Butter Sauce makes it extra special!

4	eggs, room temperature	3	cups whole milk
1¾	cups packed light brown sugar,[1] *divided*	½	cup heavy cream
		1	(1-pound) loaf Italian or French bread
2	teaspoons vanilla extract		
1	teaspoon ground cinnamon	2	recipes *Roberta's Butter Sauce*
1	teaspoon ground nutmeg	½	cup chopped toasted pecans
¾	teaspoon salt		Whipped cream

Beat eggs in large bowl with mixer on high until extremely frothy and most bubbles are size of pinheads, about 4 minutes. Add 1½ cups brown sugar, vanilla, cinnamon, nutmeg and salt. Beat on high until combined, about 1 minute, then beat in milk and heavy cream on medium.

Preheat oven to 350°. Tear bread, including crusts, into chunks. Dip handfuls of bread into milk mixture, lift and gently squeeze out most milk. Dip in again, allowing bread to absorb milk mixture. Lift out handfuls of bread without squeezing, letting excess milk drip back into bowl. Place in sprayed 9x13-inch baking dish. Repeat procedure until all bread is used. Pour any remaining milk over bread pieces in dish. Place pudding in oven. Lower heat immediately to 300°. Bake 40 to 45 minutes or until sharp knife inserted in center comes out clean. Meanwhile, prepare *Roberta's Butter Sauce*.

Remove pudding from oven. Sprinkle with remaining ¼ cup brown sugar and pecans. Set oven to BROIL[13] and place oven rack about 6 inches below heating element. Broil pudding for 1 minute or until top is golden brown. Serve warm or at room temperature with warm *Roberta's Butter Sauce*. Top with whipped cream.

Makes 12 servings   Cortlanst Inge, Chef, Bakery Café, Mobile, Alabama

Per serving: 266 calories, 5 g fat, 7 g protein, 49 g carbohydrate, 78 mg cholesterol, 408 mg sodium.

Malva Pudding

Similar to a soufflé, Malva Pudding is traditionally served upside down and hot. The Boschendal Winery Restaurant outside of Capetown, South Africa served this delicious dessert when Frank and Patsy Minter were there. The restaurant gave Patsy the recipe and she prepared it for us in Destin.

1 cup sugar	1 tablespoon butter, melted
1 egg, room temperature	1 teaspoon white vinegar
1 tablespoon apricot jam*	**Butter Sauce:**
1 cup flour	¾ cup (1½ sticks) butter
1 teaspoon baking soda	1 cup heavy cream
¼ teaspoon salt	1 cup sugar
1 cup milk	½ cup hot water

Beat sugar, egg and jam in medium bowl with mixer on high 15 minutes. Whisk flour, baking soda and salt in separate bowl[2] and beat into egg mixture, alternately with milk. Stir butter and vinegar together in small bowl and mix into batter. Pour into sprayed 9x9-inch baking dish. Cover with foil and bake at 350° for 45 to 60 minutes or until entire top becomes a rich brown color. Meanwhile, make Butter Sauce.

Remove pudding from oven. Immediately pour Butter Sauce over top. Allow to stand until sauce is absorbed. Cut pudding into 3-inch squares and turn squares upside down. Pour half-and-half over each serving or serve with whipped cream. Sprinkle with nutmeg. (If you reheat pudding, keep it moist by pouring small amount of boiling water over top after removing from oven.)

Butter Sauce: Melt butter in saucepan and mix in cream, sugar and hot water. Cook over low heat 5 to 10 minutes or until sugar dissolves and sauce thickens slightly.

* If apricot jam is not available, apricot preserves may be substituted—finely snip fruit pieces (preserves contain pieces of fruit while jam is a thick puree).

Makes 9 servings   Patsy Minter, Destin, Florida

Per serving: 431 calories, 21 g fat, 4 g protein, 58 g carbohydrate, 82 mg cholesterol, 401 mg sodium.

Sticky Date Pudding

8	ounces chopped dates (1 cup)	1½	teaspoons baking powder
1	cup boiling water	¼	teaspoon salt
½	teaspoon baking soda		Caramel Sauce:
½	cup (1 stick) butter, cut into pieces	½	cup (1 stick) butter, cut into pieces
¾	cup packed light brown sugar[1]	1	cup packed light brown sugar[1]
2	eggs, room temperature		Dash of salt
½	teaspoon vanilla extract	1	cup heavy cream
1¼	cups flour	1	teaspoon vanilla extract

Put dates and boiling water in medium bowl. Stir in baking soda and set aside until cool, about 15 minutes, stirring occasionally. Beat butter and brown sugar in large bowl with mixer until creamed, about 2 minutes. Beat in eggs, one at a time, mixing well after each addition. Stir in vanilla, then stir in date mixture. Whisk flour, baking powder and salt in separate bowl[2] and fold into date mixture until combined. Pour into sprayed 9x9-inch baking dish and bake at 350° for 35 minutes. Meanwhile, prepare Caramel Sauce.

Remove pudding from oven. Spoon about 4 tablespoons Caramel Sauce over pudding and return to oven. Bake 5 more minutes. Remove to rack and let stand 15 minutes. Cut into 3-inch squares. Serve with warmed remaining Caramel Sauce and ice cream or half-and-half. Refrigerate any leftover sauce.

Caramel Sauce: Put butter into sprayed[38] medium saucepan. Add brown sugar and salt. Carefully pour in cream and stir over low heat until butter melts and sugar dissolves. Bring to full boil. Reduce heat to moderate boil. Boil 3 minutes without stirring. Remove from heat and whisk in vanilla (sauce will be thin).

Makes 9 servings

Per serving: 573 calories, 31 g fat, 4 g protein, 72 g carbohydrate, 139 mg cholesterol, 408 mg sodium.

Cranberry Ice

1 (12-ounce) package fresh or frozen cranberries, rinsed	2 cups sugar
4 cups water, *divided*	¼ cup lemon juice
	1 teaspoon grated orange zest[61]

Put cranberries in medium saucepan. Add 2 cups water and bring to boil over high heat. Reduce heat and cook uncovered until most berries pop, stirring occasionally. Cool 5 minutes. Blend with handheld blender in saucepan or puree in blender. Press through strainer or food mill into medium bowl. Discard seeds and skins. Wash saucepan, leaving pan wet. Add sugar and remaining 2 cups water. Cook over medium heat until sugar dissolves. Bring to full boil over high heat and boil 5 minutes without stirring. Reduce heat, but continue boiling without stirring until mixture becomes thin syrup, about 3 minutes. Remove from heat. Stir in lemon juice, orange zest and cranberry puree. Pour into 8x8-inch glass baking dish. Cover surface with plastic and freeze until firm around edges, about 2 hours. Remove plastic and whisk or blend with handheld blender. Cover surface and return to freezer 1 more hour. Remove from freezer and whisk or blend again. Spoon into sherbets or wine glasses and cover surfaces with plastic. Return to freezer until firm. Remove plastic and let stand to soften slightly. Top desserts with toasted coconut or finely chopped toasted pecans. May also serve ice without coconut or pecans in short-stemmed glasses as a palate refresher.

Makes 10 servings

Per ½ cup: 173 calories, 1 g fat, 1 g protein, 45 g carbohydrate, 0 mg cholesterol, 4 mg sodium.

Ambrosia

10 large navel oranges	1 cup freshly grated or shredded coconut, or frozen unsweetened shredded coconut, thawed, or sweetened flaked coconut
2 (8-ounce) cans pineapple snack wedges, drained, reserve juice	
6 tablespoons sugar, *divided*	

Segment[47] oranges into strainer or colander over large bowl. Reserve juice. Mix orange segments and pineapple in bowl. Set aside. Combine ½ cup reserved orange juice with ¼ cup reserved pineapple juice in glass measure. Set aside. Combine and refrigerate remaining orange and pineapple juices in covered container. Layer one-third combined fruit in glass bowl and sprinkle with 2 tablespoons sugar and ⅓ cup coconut. Repeat layers two more times, ending with coconut. Pour reserved juice in glass measure over ambrosia. Cover with plastic wrap. Chill. (May prepare a day ahead and refrigerate.) Stir in desired amount of refrigerated juice before serving if dry. Serve in crystal goblets.

Makes 8 to 10 servings

Per serving of 10: 1223 calories, 3 g fat, 2 g protein, 283 g carbohydrate, 0 mg cholesterol, 10 mg sodium.

Roberta's Butter Sauce

Best butter sauce I ever tasted! Serve over bread puddings and fresh apple cakes, or just steal a spoonful and smile.

½ cup (1 stick) butter, cut into pieces	2 teaspoons vanilla extract
¼ cup sugar	1 tablespoon bourbon whiskey, or traditional Southern liqueur (optional)
½ cup packed light brown sugar[1]	
½ cup heavy cream	

Spray medium saucepan.[38] Add butter, sugars and cream. Cook and stir over medium-low heat until butter melts and sugars dissolve. Increase heat to medium-high. Boil 5 minutes without stirring, lifting and swirling pan occasionally. Swirl more frequently toward end of boiling time. Remove from heat. Whisk in vanilla and bourbon until smooth. (May prepare ahead. Place in covered container and refrigerate. Reheat over low heat or in microwave.)

Makes 1⅓ cups.   Roberta McKay, Bella Vista, Arkansas

Per tablespoon: 91 calories, 6 g fat, 0 g protein, 8 g carbohydrate, 19 mg cholesterol, 61 mg sodium.

Orange-Flavored Butter Sauce: Substitute 1 or 2 tablespoons orange-flavored liqueur for 1 tablespoon bourbon.

Hot Fudge Sauce

2 cups (12 ounces) semisweet chocolate chips	¼ teaspoon salt
1 (14-ounce) can sweetened condensed milk	2 tablespoons butter
½ cup water	1 tablespoon vanilla extract
	½ tablespoon crème de cacao (optional)

Combine chocolate chips, condensed milk, water, salt and butter in heavy saucepan. Stir over medium heat until chocolate melts and mixture is smooth. Cook 5 to 7 more minutes or until thickened, stirring occasionally. Remove from heat. Stir in vanilla and crème de cacao. Refrigerate covered in microwave-safe jar. To reheat, uncover and microwave on MEDIUM. Stir until smooth. Serve warm.

Makes about 2 cups

Per tablespoon serving: 114 calories, 6 g fat, 2 g protein, 16 g carbohydrate, 5 mg cholesterol, 38 mg sodium.

Chocolate Syrup

¾ cup unsweetened cocoa powder
¾ cup sugar
¼ teaspoon salt

2 tablespoons corn syrup
1 cup cold water
1 teaspoon vanilla extract

Whisk cocoa powder, sugar and salt in medium heavy saucepan. Stir corn syrup into water in 1-cup glass measure. Add to saucepan. Stir until thoroughly combined. Bring to full boil (bubbles all over top). Reduce heat to moderate boil and boil about 3 minutes, whisking constantly (lift pan from heat to prevent burning, if necessary). Remove from heat, continuing to whisk, and cool slightly. Stir in vanilla. Use whenever chocolate syrup is called for in a recipe or serve over ice cream. Store in jar with lid in refrigerator.

Makes about 1½ cups

Per tablespoon: 36 calories, 1 g fat, 1 g protein, 9 g carbohydrate, 0 mg cholesterol, 24 mg sodium.

Chocolate Gravy

Yes, Chocolate Gravy! A real Southern treat.

1 cup sugar
1 tablespoon unsweetened cocoa powder

3 tablespoons flour
Dash of salt
2 cups milk (reduced-fat is okay)

Whisk sugar, cocoa powder, flour and salt together in medium iron skillet or heavy saucepan. Gradually whisk in milk until well blended and smooth. Cook over medium-low heat until "gravy" thickens, about 6 minutes, whisking frequently to prevent lumps. Remove from heat. If not serving right away, pour gravy into 2-cup glass measure and cover surface of liquid with plastic wrap. Remove plastic and reheat in microwave when ready to serve.

Spoon gravy over hot, buttered ***Buttermilk Biscuits*** served with a hearty breakfast of scrambled eggs and sausage or bacon. A bowl of fresh whole strawberries or pineapple chunks for dipping in "gravy" would be nice on the side. Refrigerate leftover gravy. Makes about 2 cups.

Makes 8 to 10 servings   Marge O'Dell, Bella Vista, Arkansas

Per ¼ cup: 139 calories, 1 g fat, 3 g protein, 31 g carbohydrate, 5 mg cholesterol, 64 mg sodium.

Fish & Shellfish

Fish

Shellfish

Sole en Papillote

You will have fun preparing this recipe, and your guests will enjoy opening the papillotes to a colorful, tasteful, aromatic, healthy and delightful entrée!

4 (6-ounce) fillets of sole, orange roughy, flounder or other white fish fillets	4 (12-inch) squares of parchment paper or aluminum foil
½ cup water	4 tablespoons dry white wine
1 teaspoon chicken bouillon granules	2 tablespoons fresh lemon juice
	1 cup sliced fresh mushrooms[3]
¾ cup julienned carrots[72]	4 tablespoons butter, melted
¾ cup julienned leeks (white and pale-green parts only) or green onions	2 tablespoons fresh basil chiffonade[70]
½ yellow or red bell pepper, julienned	1 egg white, lightly beaten

Rinse fillets and pat dry. Set aside. Bring water to boil in medium skillet and stir in bouillon granules. Add carrots, cover, and simmer 3 minutes. Add leeks and bell pepper; cook covered until vegetables are crisp-tender, about 2 more minutes. Drain and set aside.

For each papillote, fold parchment in half diagonally. Open parchment and place fillet in middle of bottom half. Season with salt and freshly ground black pepper. Sprinkle with 1 tablespoon wine and ½ teaspoon lemon juice. Layer one-fourth mushrooms and one-fourth cooked vegetables over fillet. Drizzle 1 tablespoon melted butter over vegetables and sprinkle with ½ tablespoon basil chiffonade. Brush bottom edge of parchment with egg white (not necessary if using foil). Fold top half over fillet and vegetables; press along edge to seal. Brush edge with egg white again. Start at one end of sealed edge and make a series of creased folds around edge (like pleating). Finish with a twist of the parchment at opposite end. (Practice with piece of parchment before making papillote.) Repeat for remaining papillotes. Place in jelly-roll pan and refrigerate until 15 minutes before baking. (May assemble up to 4 hours ahead.)

Bake papillotes on baking sheet at 450° for 6 to 8 minutes, depending on thickness of fish, or until parchment is puffy and brown. Serve on individual plates. Allow guests to slit open their papillotes to receive full advantage of the aromatic steam. (Caution guests to avert being burned by hot steam.) Serve with *Aïoli*, *Fluffy Buttered Rice Timbales*, green salad, rolls and *Lemon Spoom* for dessert.

Makes 4 servings   Ann Letton, Houston, Texas

Per serving: 255 calories, 8 g fat, 33 g protein, 8 g carbohydrate, 15 mg cholesterol, 344 mg sodium.

Redfish Alfredo

Alfredo Sauce:
1 cup half-and-half
¼ cup (½ stick) butter, cut into pieces
4 ounces cream cheese, cut into pieces
Dash of nutmeg
Dash of white pepper
3 ounces Parmesan cheese, freshly grated (1 cup)
⅛ teaspoon lemon juice

4 (6- to 8-ounce) redfish or orange roughy fillets
Creole seasoning or Cajun seasoning
2 tablespoons flour
2 tablespoons cornmeal
2 tablespoons dry breadcrumbs
2 tablespoons vegetable oil, *divided*
Fresh lemon juice
8 ounces angel hair pasta
Paprika

Alfredo sauce: Combine half-and-half, butter and cream cheese in medium saucepan. Cook and stir over medium heat until smooth. Stir in nutmeg and white pepper. Add grated cheese and lemon juice. Stir until cheese melts and sauce is creamy–do not boil. Remove from heat and blend with handheld blender until very smooth, if desired. Leave in saucepan and set aside; sauce will continue to thicken. (May prepare ahead. Reheat without boiling.) Makes 2 cups.

Preheat oven to 350°. Rinse fillets and pat dry. Sprinkle lightly with Creole seasoning. Mix flour, cornmeal and breadcrumbs in shallow dish and dust[G] fillets with flour mixture. Pour 1 tablespoon oil into each of two 9-inch iron or other heavy ovenproof skillets, or put 2 tablespoons oil in ovenproof skillet large enough to accommodate all four fillets. Heat oil over high heat until very hot. Sauté fillets *without turning* until crisp on bottom. Squeeze lemon juice over fillets and place skillets in upper third of oven. Bake 8 to 10 minutes or just until fillets can be flaked with fork (tops will not brown). Meanwhile, cook pasta according to package directions. Drain, but do not rinse.

Place serving of pasta on each plate. Cover with fillet, *crusty* side up, and spoon warm Alfredo Sauce over fillet. Sprinkle with paprika. Garnish with fresh chives and parsley. Top each serving with two boiled shrimp, if desired.

Makes 4 servings   **Willie Rabb, Mobile, Alabama**

Per serving: 563 calories, 27 g fat, 31 g protein, 46 g carbohydrate, 84 mg cholesterol, 465 mg sodium.

Note: As an experiment, substitute 1 cup freshly grated aged Asiago cheese (3 ounces) for grated Parmesan cheese–Asiago cheese has a wonderful nutty taste. (Of course, it won't really be Alfredo Sauce if you use Asiago, but I think you will like it.)

Chilean Sea Bass with Tomato Olive Sauce

Tomato Olive Sauce:
- 1 tablespoon olive oil
- ½ cup chopped onion
- 1½ teaspoons minced garlic, or to taste
- 2 cups diced seeded plum tomatoes[53]
- 3 tablespoons fresh basil chiffonade[70]
- 2 teaspoons small capers, rinsed and drained

Pinch of sugar
- ¼ to ½ cup chopped, pitted kalamata olives
- 4 (6- to 8-ounce) Chilean sea bass fillets*
- 2 tablespoons fresh lemon juice
- Salt and pepper
- Flour
- Paprika
- 2 tablespoons olive oil

Tomato Olive Sauce: Heat oil in medium skillet and sauté onion until clear. Add garlic and cook 30 seconds. Stir in tomatoes, basil, capers and sugar. Season with salt and pepper to taste. Cook over medium heat 10 to 12 minutes or until tomatoes wilt. Add olives during last minute. (May prepare ahead; cover and refrigerate. Reheat before serving.)

Rinse fillets and pat dry. Brush with lemon juice; sprinkle with salt and pepper. Dust[G] fillets in flour and sprinkle with paprika. Heat oil in large nonstick skillet over medium-high heat. Lightly brown fillets about 2 minutes on each side. Place fillets in sprayed shallow baking dish. Bake in upper third of oven at 350° for 7 to 8 minutes depending on thickness, or until fillets can just be flaked with fork. Transfer to serving plate or individual plates. Spoon warm Tomato Olive Sauce over servings. Serve with *Roasted Sweet Potato Rounds* and green salad.

* *You may want to substitute halibut because sea bass is so overfished.*

Makes 4 servings   Ann Letton, Houston, Texas

Per serving: 287 calories, 17 g fat, 25 g protein, 9 g carbohydrate, 53 mg cholesterol, 412 mg sodium.

Herb Broiled Orange Roughy

A wonderfully delicate flavor, enhanced by the dill and tarragon–exceptional with fresh French tarragon! Other white fish may be substituted for orange roughy.

2   pounds orange roughy fillets
3   tablespoons butter, softened
2   tablespoons fresh lemon juice
¼   teaspoon freshly ground black pepper
½   teaspoon dried dill weed, crushed
1   teaspoon snipped fresh French tarragon leaves, or ½ teaspoon dried tarragon, crushed

1½   ounces Asiago cheese, freshly grated (½ cup)
¼   cup regular or light mayonnaise
¼   cup thinly sliced green onions, including some tops
¼   teaspoon salt
    Dash of hot pepper sauce
    Paprika

Rinse fillets and pat dry. Spread top of each fillet with butter and place in sprayed shallow flameproof baking dish[58] without overlapping. Sprinkle each fillet with lemon juice, pepper, dill and tarragon. Let stand 10 minutes. Meanwhile, mix grated cheese, mayonnaise, green onion, salt and pepper sauce in small bowl; set aside.

Broil fillets about 4 inches below heating element for 5 minutes. Spread cheese mixture on each fillet and sprinkle with paprika. Broil 2 to 3 more minutes until hot and bubbly. Serve with *Fluffy Buttered Rice Timbales, Orange Glazed Carrots* and *Fairhope Spinach Salad.*

Makes 4 to 6 servings

Per serving of 6: 298 calories, 20 g fat, 26 g protein; 2 g Carbohydrate; 76 mg Cholesterol; 529 mg Sodium.

Herb Broiled Salmon variation: Substitute four 6-ounce rectangular salmon portions for orange roughy. Reduce butter to 2 tablespoons and spread on rounded side of salmon portions. Sprinkle each portion with lemon juice, pepper, dill and tarragon. Let stand 10 minutes. Broil 3 minutes, *rounded side down*; turn and broil 3 minutes. Spread cheese mixture generously over rounded side of each portion. Sprinkle with paprika. Broil 2 more minutes.

Makes 4 servings

Per serving: 535 calories, 38 g fat, 47 g protein, 3 g carbohydrate, 97 mg cholesterol, 716 mg sodium.

Orange Roughy Florentine

1 recipe *Mornay Sauce*	2 cups chopped fresh mushrooms[3]
2 (10-ounce) packages frozen spinach	1 tablespoon dry Madeira or Sherry
Dash of nutmeg	6 (6 ounce) orange roughy fillets
¼ cup (½ stick) butter	3 ounces Asiago or Parmesan cheese, grated (1 cup)
½ cup finely chopped onion	Paprika

Prepare *Mornay Sauce* using 1 cup milk and 1 cup chicken broth. Set aside. Cook spinach according to package directions; add nutmeg and season with salt and pepper. Spread spinach over bottom of sprayed 9x13-inch baking dish.

Melt butter in large skillet; sauté onion and mushrooms over medium heat until liquid evaporates. Stir in Madeira and season with salt and pepper.

Rinse fillets, pat dry and sprinkle lightly with salt and pepper. Spread mushroom mixture evenly over half of each fillet; fold in half and place fillets on spinach. Spoon *Mornay Sauce* over fish and sprinkle with grated cheese and paprika. Bake at 350° for 25 minutes or just until fish can be flaked with fork. Serve with *Fluffy Buttered Rice Timbales*.

Makes 6 servings

Per serving: 522 calories, 36 g fat, 39 g protein, 9 g carbohydrate, 138 mg cholesterol, 787 mg sodium.

Baked Roughy Portuguesa

1½ pounds orange roughy fillets	1 garlic clove, minced
Seasoned salt or Cajun seasoning	2 cups chopped seeded tomatoes
2 tablespoons butter	2 tablespoons fresh lemon juice
½ cup chopped onion	1 bay leaf
½ cup chopped celery	1½ ounces Asiago cheese, grated
¼ cup snipped flat-leaf parsley	(½ cup) (optional)

Rinse fillets, pat dry and cut into serving-size pieces (large chunks). Place in sprayed 10-inch quiche dish or pie plate and sprinkle lightly with seasoned salt; set aside. Melt butter in large skillet; sauté onion, celery and parsley until tender, 3 to 4 minutes. Add garlic and sauté 30 seconds. Add tomatoes, lemon juice and bay leaf. Cook over medium-high heat 3 minutes. Spoon sauce over fish. Bake at 350° for 20 to 25 minutes or just until fish can be flaked with fork. Sprinkle with grated cheese during last 5 minutes of baking. Remove bay leaf. Serve roughy with cooking liquids over *Rice Cooked in Broth*. Sprinkle with parsley.

Makes 4 servings

Per serving: 262 calories, 11 g fat, 2 g protein, 8 g carbohydrate, 59 mg cholesterol, 426 mg sodium.

Sautéed Fish Fillets

2	pounds orange roughy fillets (⅜- to ½-inch thick)
¼	cup flour
¼	teaspoon salt
⅛	teaspoon pepper
1	tablespoon butter
½	teaspoon minced garlic

¼	cup dry white wine
1½	teaspoons lime juice or lemon juice
½	cup water
1	tablespoon olive or vegetable oil
4	green onions, chopped, including some tops

Rinse fillets and pat dry. Whisk flour, salt and pepper together in shallow dish or pie plate. Dust^G fillets and shake off any excess. Transfer to plate in single layer. Set aside. Microwave butter in glass measure until melted. Stir in garlic, wine, lime juice and water. Set aside.

Heat oil in 12-inch skillet over medium-high heat. Sauté fillets without overlapping. (If you have thick and thin fillets, sauté thick ones about 1 minute before adding thin ones). Cook until golden on bottom, about 3 minutes. Turn and cook until opaque^G throughout, 1 to 2 minutes. Transfer to warm platter.

Add butter mixture to hot skillet and boil until thickened, scraping up bits on bottom. Stir in green onion and cook about 30 seconds. Pour over fillets and serve with *Oven-Baked Fries* and coleslaw.

Makes 4 servings

Per serving: 254 calories, 8 g fat, 34 g protein, 7 g carbohydrate, 53 mg cholesterol, 307 mg sodium.

Salmon à l'Orange

4	(6- to 8-ounce) salmon fillets
1	cup orange juice
½	teaspoon salt
1	teaspoon olive oil

1	teaspoon finely chopped fresh French tarragon leaves or dill weed, or ½ teaspoon dried tarragon or dried dill weed, crushed

Rinse fillets and pat dry. Mix orange juice, salt, oil and tarragon in ziptop bag and add salmon. Turn to coat and refrigerate 1 hour. Remove fillets from marinade and transfer to plate; let stand 10 to 15 minutes. Discard marinade. Preheat oven to 500°. Place fillets in sprayed shallow flameproof baking dish.[58] Bake on middle rack 5 to 10 minutes, depending on thickness, or until salmon can just be flaked with fork. Serve with *Brown Sugar Carrots* and *Roasted New Potatoes*.

Makes 4 servings   Pat Johnson, Naples, Florida

Per serving: 294 calories, 8 g fat, 46 g protein, 7 g carbohydrate, 117 mg cholesterol, 219 mg sodium.

Grilled Salmon Steaks with Jalapeño Sauce

4 (¾-inch-thick) salmon steaks, or
   4 (6-ounce) rectangular salmon
   portions about 2 inches wide
2 tablespoons fresh lime juice
1 tablespoon butter, melted
   Sprigs of dill weed (optional)

   Jalapeño Sauce:
1 tablespoon butter

4 jalapeños, seeded and julienned
⅔ cup sour cream
2 teaspoons fresh lime juice

   Lime wedges
   Snipped fresh chives

Rinse salmon steaks and pat dry. Place in 9x13-inch glass baking dish and sprinkle with salt and pepper. Mix lime juice with melted butter in small bowl and brush on both sides of salmon. Cover with plastic and let stand about 15 minutes. Meanwhile, preheat grill to MEDIUM-HOT (see *Grill Tips*). Prepare Jalapeño Sauce and leave in pan. Set aside.

Just before grilling spray grill rack or wire grill basket (place a few sprigs of wet dill in grill basket, if desired). Spray salmon and place on rack. Grill 4 minutes on each side or just until opaque.ᴳ Transfer salmon to serving plate and surround with lime wedges. Spoon warm Jalapeño Sauce over salmon and sprinkle generously with chives. Serve with *Roasted New Potatoes* and *Orange Glazed Carrots*.

Jalapeño Sauce: Melt butter in heavy saucepan over medium-low heat and add jalapeños. Stir and cook until tender, about 3 minutes. Add sour cream. Cook and stir without boiling until thoroughly heated. Stir in lime juice. Season with salt and freshly ground black pepper.

Makes 4 servings

Per serving: 459 calories, 30 g fat, 37 g protein, 10 g carbohydrate, 147 mg cholesterol, 408 mg sodium.

About Salmon Cuts

Salmon is either cut into fillets or steaks. Fillets result when the meat is separated from the backbone from head to tail on each side and usually skin removed; individual fillets are then cut from the large slabs of fish. Some are cut into 6-ounce, 2-inch wide portions. Salmon steaks result from cutting the gutted fish crosswise into portions of desired width; the familiar horseshoe-shaped portions are usually baked, grilled or pan fried with the backbone and skin intact to hold the flesh together.

Lite Salmon Fillets

1 (2 pound) salmon fillet	Lemon pepper
3 lemons, thinly sliced, *divided*	Butter, or butter-flavored granules
1 teaspoon minced garlic	

Rinse salmon and pat dry. Cut into four pieces and set aside. Make 9x13-inch foil pan, like a drip pan.[48] Spray pan and place on cutting board or baking sheet for carrying to grill. Cover bottom of pan with half the lemon slices and place salmon pieces on top. Spread each salmon piece with garlic. Sprinkle generously with lemon pepper and dot with butter or sprinkle with butter-flavored granules. Cover with remaining lemon slices. Slide foil pan onto preheated MEDIUM-HOT grill. Close lid and cook 20 minutes or until fillets can just be flaked with fork.

Makes 4 servings   Karen and Joel Kragt, Bella Vista, Arkansas

Per serving: 264 calories, 8 g fat, 46 g protein, 0 g carbohydrate, 117 mg cholesterol, 152 mg sodium.

Salmon Oscar with Béarnaise

2 (6-ounce) rectangular salmon portions (about 2 inches wide)	1 recipe *Béarnaise Sauce* or *Microwave Béarnaise Sauce*
Salt and pepper	2 ounces pasteurized jumbo lump crabmeat (about ½ cup) (optional)
Flour	
1 tablespoon corn oil	

Sprinkle salmon with salt and pepper and lightly dust[G] with flour. Heat oil in medium ovenproof skillet over medium-high heat until hot; sauté salmon rounded side down until golden brown, about 3 minutes. Turn portions over. Place skillet on middle rack in 450° oven. Bake about 5 minutes or just until portions can be flaked with fork. Transfer to warmed plates. Spoon *Béarnaise Sauce* over each serving, top with ¼ cup crabmeat, and garnish with two long pieces of chives crossed on top. Serve with *Fresh Asparagus* and *Autumn Pear and Pomegranate Salad*. Recipe may be doubled–use two medium or one large ovenproof skillet.

Makes 2 servings

Per serving: 216 calories, 13 g fat, 23 g protein, 1 g carbohydrate, 116 mg cholesterol, 163 mg sodium.

Salmon Loaf with Cream Sauce

1 (14¾-ounce) can pink or red salmon, undrained	Cream Sauce:
2 cups soft breadcrumbs[45]	3 tablespoons butter or margarine
2 eggs, lightly beaten	3 tablespoons flour
½ cup milk	1½ cups milk
2 tablespoons chopped onion	1 teaspoon chicken bouillon granules
2 tablespoons snipped parsley	Dash of hot pepper sauce
½ teaspoon salt	⅓ cup frozen baby green peas, thawed (optional)
⅛ teaspoon pepper	2 hard-cooked eggs, chopped
Dash of paprika	

Remove any dark skin[56] and mash salmon in large bowl. Add breadcrumbs, eggs, milk, onion, parsley, salt and pepper. Mix well. Pour salmon mixture into well-sprayed foil-lined 8½x4½-inch loaf pan[6] (liner provides easy removal and cleanup). Sprinkle with paprika. Bake at 350° for 1 hour or until firm. Remove pan from oven. Lift liner onto cutting board and peel down sides. Let stand 5 minutes. Cut into thick slices and transfer to serving platter. Garnish with parsley. Serve with Cream Sauce.

Cream Sauce: Melt butter in small saucepan. Stir in flour; cook about 1 minute, stirring constantly. Gradually stir in milk. Add bouillon granules and pepper sauce; cook and stir over medium heat until thickened. Stir in peas. Season with salt and pepper. Fold in eggs.

Makes 4 to 6 servings   Pat Carneal, Annandale, Virginia

Per serving of 6: 303 calories, 17 g fat, 22 g protein, 15 g carbohydrate, 191 mg cholesterol, 783 mg sodium.

Salmon Croquettes

1 (14¾-ounce) can pink salmon, drained	½ cup instant potato flakes*
3 eggs, *divided*	½ teaspoon salt
½ cup finely chopped onion	¼ teaspoon pepper
½ cup finely chopped bell pepper	2 dashes of Worcestershire sauce
1 tablespoon snipped parsley	1 cup finely crushed saltine crackers
	3 tablespoons vegetable oil

Remove any dark skin[56] and flake salmon in large bowl. Lightly beat 2 eggs in small bowl and add to salmon along with onion, bell pepper, parsley, potato flakes, salt, pepper and Worcestershire sauce. Mix well with fork. (Croquette mixture should be moist–add 1 tablespoon or more of water if dry.) Shape mixture into four oval-shaped croquettes with dampened hands. Beat remaining egg in pie plate or shallow-rimmed dish. Put cracker crumbs in another dish. Roll each croquette in egg, then in crumbs and transfer to plate.[33] Let dry about 5 minutes.

Heat oil in 9-inch iron or nonstick skillet over medium heat. Add croquettes and cook until golden, turning as they brown, about 4 minutes. Drain on paper towels. Serve with *Tartar Sauce,* ½ cup ketchup mixed with 1 to 2 teaspoons Worcestershire sauce, or serve with Cream Sauce from *Salmon Loaf with Cream Sauce*.

* *When my mother made these croquettes, she would boil, peel and mash a small potato. Potato flakes work well.*

Makes 4 croquettes   Willie McCaleb Rabb, Lexington, Mississippi

Per serving: 344 calories, 16 g fat, 30 g protein, 19 g carbohydrate, 223 mg cholesterol, 1160 mg sodium.

About Scallops

Scallops should have a sweet smell and a fresh, moist sheen. Bay scallops, generally found only on the East Coast, are very tiny, averaging about 100 per pound; their meat is sweeter and more succulent than sea scallops (also more expensive, because they are less plentiful). Sea scallops average about 1½ inches in diameter, yielding about 30 per pound, and are slightly chewy, but still sweet and moist. Their color ranges from pale beige to creamy pink; if white, they have probably been soaked in water to increase weight. (Adapted from *Food Lover's Companion*, by Sharon Tyler Herbst)

Smoked Salmon Fettuccine

¼ cup (½ stick) butter
½ cup thinly sliced green onions
1 garlic clove, minced
2 cups half-and-half, *divided*
1 tablespoon Dijon mustard
4½ ounces Asiago or Parmesan cheese, grated (1½ cups)
¼ cup dry white wine or dry vermouth

Dash of ground nutmeg
8 ounces sliced smoked salmon, cut into strips
2 tablespoons small capers, rinsed and drained (optional)
2 (9-ounce) packages fresh spinach fettuccine or 1 (12-ounce) package dry spinach fettuccine, cooked according to package directions

Melt butter in medium saucepan and sauté green onion 1 to 2 minutes. Add garlic and cook 30 seconds, stirring occasionally. Whisk in ½ cup half-and-half. Add mustard and grated cheese, whisking until cheese melts. Add remaining 1½ cups half-and-half, wine and nutmeg, stirring over medium heat until hot. Add salmon and capers and toss well, being careful not to break up salmon. Spoon over individual servings of cooked fettuccine and garnish with snipped flat-leaf parsley. Serve with *Fresh Asparagus*, *Mandarin Orange Salad* and sourdough rolls.

Makes 4 to 6 servings   Matt Bright, Lynchburg, Virginia

Per serving of 6: 557 calories, 29 g fat, 25 g protein, 48 g carbohydrate, 84 mg cholesterol, 853 mg sodium.

Sautéed Scallops

1½ pounds bay or sea scallops
⅓ cup flour
½ teaspoon salt
½ teaspoon pepper

½ teaspoon paprika
1 tablespoon butter
2 tablespoons olive oil
2 to 3 tablespoons minced shallots

Rinse scallops and pat dry. Combine flour, salt, pepper and paprika in large ziptop bag. Add scallops and shake to coat. Heat butter and oil in large nonstick skillet over medium-high heat. Add scallops and sauté about 30 seconds on each side or until opaque[G] and golden. Remove from heat and transfer to plate with slotted spoon. Tent with foil. Heat drippings in skillet over medium heat, adding more oil if needed. Add shallots and cook until tender, 2 to 3 minutes. Return scallops with any juice to skillet and heat, stirring gently. Unmold *Fluffy Buttered Rice Timbales* centered on individual plates; sprinkle with lemon zest. Add servings of scallops and *Brown Sugar Carrots* around rice. Garnish with parsley.

Makes 4 servings   Charlotte Luer, Denville, New Jersey

Per serving: 278 calories, 11 g fat, 30 g protein, 13 g carbohydrate, 64 mg cholesterol, 571 mg sodium.

Oysters Rockefeller Casserole

A perfect buffet offering. Serve with ham, turkey, **Sweet Potato Casserole** *and sweet and savory salads.*

3 (10-ounce) packages frozen chopped spinach	1 to 2 pints fresh oysters, drained
½ cup (1 stick) butter	¼ cup fresh lemon juice
½ cup chopped celery	Dash of hot pepper sauce
¾ cup chopped onion	½ cup dry breadcrumbs
½ cup snipped parsley	¼ cup Herbsaint, or other anise-flavored liqueur
3 garlic cloves, finely chopped	

Cook spinach according to package directions. Drain and set aside. Melt butter in large heavy skillet and sauté celery, onion, parsley and garlic until tender. Add oysters and cook over medium heat until edges curl, about 3 minutes. Remove from heat and stir in lemon juice, pepper sauce, breadcrumbs, liqueur and spinach; season with salt and pepper. Pour into buttered 2-quart casserole. Bake uncovered at 350° for 35 to 40 minutes.

Makes 8 servings   Clo Ann Rabb, Meridian, Mississippi

Per serving: 251 calories, 14 g fat, 11 g protein, 20 g carbohydrate, 64 mg cholesterol, 496 mg sodium.

Spinach Casserole variation: Omit oysters. Put spinach mixture in sprayed 1½-quart casserole. Bake, uncovered, at 350° for 35 to 45 minutes or until hot and bubbly.

Spinach Dip variation: Omit oysters and dry breadcrumbs. Stir 2 to 3 ounces cubed softened cream cheese into spinach mixture until combined and pour into sprayed 1½- to 2-quart casserole. Bake uncovered at 350° for 25 to 35 minutes or until hot and bubbly. Serve as hot dip with crackers or melba toast. Clo Ann sometimes halves the recipe when making dip.

Boiled Shrimp

2 to 3 pounds medium or large unpeeled raw shrimp	½ teaspoon lemon pepper
3 quarts water	1 lemon, cut in half or quartered
¼ to ½ teaspoon red pepper flakes	1 rib of celery with leaves, broken into thirds
2 tablespoons crab-and-shrimp-boil seasoning	½ onion, quartered
	1 or 2 bay leaves (optional)

Rinse and drain shrimp. Set aside. Bring water to boil in large pot or Dutch oven. Add pepper flakes, crab-and-shrimp-boil seasoning and lemon pepper. Squeeze juice from lemons into pot and throw in lemon pieces. Add celery, onion, bay leaves and shrimp. Return to boil. Cover and cook until shrimp float and turn pink, about 2 minutes–do not overcook. Drain. Transfer shrimp to foil-lined jelly-roll pan and spread out in single layer. Cool to room temperature.

Place shrimp in covered container and refrigerate until ready to serve. Peel and devein, if desired. Serve with *Spicy Cocktail Sauce* or use in dishes calling for boiled shrimp (2 pounds medium unpeeled raw shrimp produces about 1 pound peeled cooked shrimp, about 2⅔ cups).

Makes 4 to 6 servings

Per serving of 6: 116 calories, 1 g fat, 25 g protein, 0 g carbohydrate, 228 mg cholesterol, 262 mg sodium.

Jackie's Quick Crawfish Étouffée

½ cup (1 stick) butter	1 (10¾-ounce) can cream of mushroom soup
1 cup chopped bell pepper	1 (16-ounce) package frozen cooked, peeled and deveined crawfish tailmeat, thawed
1 cup chopped onion	
1 (10-ounce) can diced tomatoes and green chilies (mild or hot), undrained	

Melt butter in heavy skillet and sauté bell pepper and onion until tender, about 5 minutes. Stir in tomatoes and green chilies. Stir in soup, adding water if thick. Simmer over low heat until thoroughly heated. Add crawfish and simmer 3 to 5 more minutes (do not overcook or crawfish will be tough). Serve over hot cooked rice.

Makes 4 to 6 servings   Jackie Andrishok, Destin, Florida

Per serving of 6: 264 calories, 21 g fat, 13 g protein, 10 g carbohydrate, 96 mg cholesterol, 758 mg sodium.

Curry and Cream Shrimp

2 to 3 pounds medium raw shrimp	1 (14-ounce) can chicken broth
⅓ cup (5⅓ tablespoons) butter	1½ cups heavy cream or half-and-half
½ cup finely chopped onion	1½ teaspoons sugar
1 green or red bell pepper, or half green and half red, chopped	½ teaspoon salt
	¼ to ½ teaspoon cayenne pepper
⅓ cup flour	½ teaspoon white pepper
1½ tablespoons curry powder*	

Peel shrimp and set aside. Heat butter in large saucepan and sauté onion and bell pepper until tender, 3 to 5 minutes. Reduce heat. Add flour and curry powder, stirring constantly about 1 minute. Gradually stir in chicken broth and cream, cooking and stirring until thickened. Stir in sugar, salt, cayenne pepper and white pepper. Add shrimp and cook just until pink. Immediately remove from heat. Serve over rice with sliced green onion, toasted coconut, *Mango Chutney*, chopped crystallized ginger[G] or other condiments. Serve with *Fresh Asparagus*, tossed salad and rolls.

* If you love curry, go with 1½ tablespoons curry powder; otherwise, start with 1 teaspoon. You can always add more.

Makes 6 servings   Sara Lamb Rabb, Mobile, Alabama

Per serving: 341 calories, 19 g fat, 30 g protein, 12 g carbohydrate, 283 mg cholesterol, 891 mg sodium.

Pasta with Blush Sauce and Crab

8 ounces radiatore (ruffled pasta)	1 cup (2 sticks) butter
8 ounces pasteurized lump crabmeat	7 pasteurized, spreadable cheese wedges (comes in 8¾-ounce round box containing 8 wedges)
Blush Sauce:	
1 cup heavy cream or half-and-half	2 (14½-ounce) cans tomatoes with garlic and spices, undrained

Cook pasta according to package directions. Meanwhile, prepare Blush Sauce. Drain pasta, but do not rinse.[57] Spoon Blush Sauce over servings of pasta and top with crabmeat. Serve immediately with tossed green salad and French bread.

Blush Sauce: Heat cream, butter and cheese over low heat in double boiler* until smooth. Stir in tomatoes and simmer without boiling until hot.

* If you do not have a double boiler, place a stainless-steel or heatproof glass bowl over a slightly smaller saucepan. Add water to saucepan without letting it touch bowl.

Makes 6 servings   Melissa Shaw O'Connor, Round Hill, Virginia

Per serving: 589 calories, 41 g fat, 16 g protein, 40 g carbohydrate, 144 mg cholesterol, 1228 mg sodium.

Meats

Meats

Beef

Pork

Lamb

Andy's London Broil

This marinade has become our favorite! Thanks, Andy.

Marinade:
- ½ cup soy sauce
- ½ cup red wine vinegar
- 1 teaspoon ground ginger
- 1 teaspoon minced garlic
- 2 tablespoons brown sugar
- ½ cup vegetable oil
- 1 (1½- to 2-pound) top round, top sirloin or chuck shoulder steak (about 1¼ inches thick)

Prepare marinade. Rinse meat. Put in ziptop bag and add marinade. Refrigerate 8 hours or overnight, turning occasionally. Let stand unrefrigerated in marinade about 20 minutes before grilling.

Preheat grill to MEDIUM-HOT. Remove meat from marinade and pat dry. Discard marinade. Spray grill and meat just before placing meat on grill. Grill 7 to 8 minutes on each side, turning once with tongs. Test by feeling resistance of meat with tongs. Meat should be slightly firm—not stiff. Remove to cutting board and tent with foil. Let stand 10 minutes. Thinly slice meat across grain on diagonal. Transfer slices to warm platter. Pour any accumulated juices over meat. Serve with ***Baked Red Potatoes*** and tossed salad.

Marinade: Mix soy sauce, vinegar, ginger, garlic and brown sugar in jar with tight-fitting lid and shake well. Add oil and shake until emulsified.[G]

Makes 6 servings   Andy Flowers, Lynchburg, Virginia

Per serving: 279 calories, 23 g fat, 17 g protein, 0 g carbohydrate, 66 g cholesterol, 87 mg sodium.

About London Broil

London Broil is actually the name of a recipe, not a cut of beef. The original recipe was used for grilling or broiling inexpensive flank steak in the early 1930's, but flank steak's popularity and rising prices has caused a shift to other cuts of beef. London broil is now mostly associated with using top round, top sirloin or chuck shoulder steak.

Select steak about 1¼ inches thick—one that has fine lines of fat. Steak that is completely red in color tends to be tougher. Choose a good marinade, like the one Andy Flowers uses and marinate 8 hours or overnight. The steak should be cooked to medium-rare, usually about 7 or 8 minutes on each side over medium-high heat, turning once with tongs—it will continue to cook as it rests. Tent with foil 10 minutes on cutting board to set juices. Thinly slice from one end across the grain on the diagonal.

Good ol' Southern Hamburgers

Homemade hamburger patties shrink in size and "bulge up" in the middle when grilled. Edges are overdone while centers are undercooked. Willie says, "I mash down the middle with my thumb so patties won't bulge. They cook evenly."

1 pound ground beef or ground sirloin	¼ cup snipped fresh chives, or snipped green onion tops
1 tablespoon black peppercorns, crushed	1 tablespoon fresh lemon juice
2 to 4 garlic cloves, finely chopped[20]	1 tablespoon olive oil

Mix ground beef, crushed peppercorns, garlic (unless you really love garlic, two cloves should be enough), chives, lemon juice and olive oil in large bowl, mixing with your hands.[59] Form into patties and make a depression in middle of each with your thumb. Cook on HOT grill (see *Grill Tips*) 2½ to 3 minutes on each side, or as desired. Sprinkle with salt after turning. Serve on toasted hamburger buns with your favorite condiments.

Makes 4 hamburgers   Willie Rabb, Mobile, Alabama

Per serving: 392 calories, 34 g fat, 19 g protein, 3 g carbohydrate, 96 mg cholesterol, 79 mg sodium.

Poor Man's T-Bone

1 (4-pound) arm-cut chuck roast, (2 to 3 inches thick)	1 teaspoon celery salt
	1 teaspoon dry mustard[9]
Marinade:	1 tablespoon ground ginger
1 tablespoon Worcestershire sauce	¼ cup packed brown sugar[1]
1 tablespoon liquid smoke	1 tablespoon vinegar
½ cup soy sauce	¼ cup vegetable oil
2 garlic cloves, minced	Unseasoned meat tenderizer

Rinse roast and put in ziptop bag. Add marinade and refrigerate 2½ hours or overnight, turning occasionally. Let roast stand in marinade unrefrigerated while preheating grill to LOW. Remove roast from marinade and pat dry; discard marinade. Sprinkle both sides with meat tenderizer.

Grill over LOW heat 35 minutes, turning once after 15 minutes. Remove and tent with foil. Let stand 10 minutes. Thinly slice across grain.

Marinade: Mix Worcestershire sauce, liquid smoke, soy sauce, garlic, celery salt, dry mustard, ginger, brown sugar and vinegar in jar with tight-fitting lid and shake well. Add oil and shake until emulsified.

Makes 8 to 10 servings   Kathy Stephens, Bella Vista, Arkansas

Per serving of 10: 378 calories, 28 g fat, 29 g protein, 0 g carbohydrate, 103 mg cholesterol, 91 mg sodium.

Shish Kebabs

Marinade:

1 tablespoon soy sauce

1 teaspoon Worcestershire sauce

2 garlic cloves, minced or pressed

½ teaspoon freshly ground black pepper[90]

½ teaspoon salt

1 teaspoon dry mustard[9]

⅓ cup extra-virgin olive oil

2 pounds boneless top blade steak (chuck) or top sirloin steak, cut 1-inch thick

2 medium red or sweet onions, cut into 1-inch wedges and halved

2 medium green, red or yellow bell peppers (or combination), cut into 1-inch pieces

12 to 15 *large* red or yellow cherry tomatoes*

Prepare marinade. Set aside. Rinse meat and pat dry. Remove all fat and gristle.[89] Cut meat into 1-inch cubes. Put in large ziptop bag and add marinade. Refrigerate 8 hours or overnight, turning occasionally. Let stand unrefrigerated in marinade about 20 minutes before grilling.

Kebabs cooked directly on grill rack may burn before they cook. For better control of doneness elevate kebabs by placing common bricks at either end of grill rack and rest ends of skewers on bricks. Position grill rack close to heat if using bricks; otherwise, set rack 4 to 5 inches above heat source. Preheat grill to HOT (see *Grill Tips*).

Remove beef cubes from marinade and pat dry; discard marinade. Spray all vegetables with olive-oil cooking spray and sprinkle with favorite herb seasoning or salt and pepper before threading on skewers. Make *each* kebab using 12- to 14-inch *double* metal skewers or *two single* skewers for easier turning and stability. Thread pieces of onion, beef and bell pepper, repeating 3 or 4 times for each. Thread tomatoes separately on two single skewers (they cook faster than meat).

Place kebabs, except tomatoes, across bricks and close grill. Grill about 8 minutes for medium-rare or 10 minutes for medium, turning every 2 minutes. Add tomatoes after turning kebabs once or twice. Transfer grilled kebabs to serving platters. Serve with lime wedges (gives zip to meat and vegetables). Also serve with baked potatoes, tossed salad and French bread. Serve *Lattice-Top Apple Pie* for dessert.

Marinade: Combine soy sauce, Worcestershire sauce, garlic, pepper, salt, dry mustard and olive oil in 2-cup glass measure or small bowl. Blend with handheld blender until emulsified. Or put ingredients in jar with tight-fitting lid and shake until emulsified. Makes about ⅓ cup, enough to marinate 2 pounds beef.

* *Fresh pineapple chunks may be substituted for cherry tomatoes; spray, season and place on skewers with onion, beef and bell pepper.*

Makes 6 servings .

Per serving: 358 Calories, 20 g Fat, 34 g Protein, 11 g Carbohydrate, 92 mg Cholesterol, 454 mg Sodium.

Steak au Poivre

Our son, Arthur, and his friend Kevin Billingsley prepared this elegant entrée for us during a ski vacation in 1983. It was great!

3 tablespoons cracked black peppercorns[21]	3 tablespoons vegetable oil
4 strip, ribeye or beef tenderloin steaks[71] (¾ to 1 inch thick)	¼ cup plus 1 teaspoon brandy
	1 cup heavy cream or half-and-half

Press cracked peppercorns firmly into both sides of steaks. (Do not worry about too much pepper. Oil fries pepper and takes much of the hot flavor out.) Heat oil in large iron skillet or other large heavy skillet over medium-high heat. Cook steaks, close together in skillet, 2 to 3 minutes on each side for medium-rare, turning once. Sprinkle with salt after turning. Drain off fat and return skillet to heat. Heat ¼ cup brandy in glass measure in microwave on HIGH 15 seconds. (If you prefer not to flambé, do not heat brandy, but save for deglazing skillet later.) Pour heated brandy over steaks and ignite. *Be careful—flames will flare up but will die quickly.* Let steaks cook until flames die, then remove to warm serving platter and tent with foil. Add cream to pan drippings and deglaze,[c] scraping up brown bits on bottom. (If you did not flambé, add the brandy instead of cream and stir in cream after deglazing.) Cook over medium-high heat, stirring constantly until thickened. Stir in remaining 1 teaspoon brandy. Spoon sauce over steaks and serve with **Smashed Red Potatoes**, **Green Bean Bundles** and tossed salad.

Makes 4 servings

Per serving: 728 calories, 61 g fat, 33 g protein, 2 g carbohydrate, 168 mg cholesterol, 102 mg sodium.

Beef Tenderloin

Beef tenderloin was always served at First Friday Bridge Group Christmas parties in Colorado.

1 (4-pound) well-trimmed center-cut beef tenderloin roast	2 slices bacon

Remove silver skin and any excess fat from tenderloin.[31] Tie roast with butcher's twine at 2-inch intervals to help roast keep its shape. Refrigerate until about 30 minutes before roasting. Preheat oven to 450°. Place roast on sprayed rack in shallow roasting pan or broiler pan; place bacon slices lengthwise on top. Reduce heat to 375°. Roast tenderloin uncovered 30 to 40 minutes or until instant-read thermometer inserted in thickest part registers 140° to 150° (medium-rare to medium). Remove from oven and tent with foil. Let stand 10 minutes. Cut into ½-inch-thick slices. Serve with **Madeira Sauce**, if desired.

Makes 8 servings   Beth Huffman, Longmont, Colorado

Per serving: 614 calories, 40 g fat, 59 g protein, 0 g carbohydrate, 197 mg cholesterol, 236 mg sodium

Steak Diane

Brown Sauce:
1 tablespoon butter
½ cup finely chopped onion
¼ cup finely chopped carrot
¼ cup finely chopped celery
2 (14-ounce) cans beef broth
1 (1.2-ounce) package classic brown gravy mix, prepared according to package directions

2 (15-ounce) ¾-inch rib eye steaks
1 tablespoon canola oil
2 tablespoons butter, *divided*
2 tablespoons finely chopped shallots
½ cup sliced mushrooms[3]
2 tablespoons brandy
1 teaspoon Dijon mustard
½ cup sour cream

Brown Sauce: Make a mirepoix:[G] Melt butter in large nonstick skillet over medium-low heat and add onion, carrot and celery, cooking slowly and stirring frequently until onion begins to brown and carrot and celery are softened, about 10 minutes. Add beef broth and bring to boil. Boil uncovered until liquid is reduced[G] by half, 15 to 20 minutes. Stir in prepared gravy mix, continuing to boil and reduce until thickened. Strain through fine-mesh strainer into large bowl, pressing juice from vegetables. Pour into 2-cup glass measure. Place plastic wrap on surface and refrigerate until fat solidfies.[77] Makes 1½ cups.

Trim steaks of all fat and cut in half (6- to 7-ounce portions). Gently pound each steak from center to edge between wax paper to ⅜ to ½ inch. Heat oil and 1 tablespoon butter in large heavy skillet over moderately-high heat until foam subsides. Sauté steaks 45 seconds on first side. Turn and sprinkle lightly with salt and pepper; sauté 45 seconds. Remove to warm platter and tent with foil to keep warm. Melt remaining 1 tablespoon butter in same skillet over low heat. Add shallots and cook 2 minutes or until soft. Stir in mushrooms and cook 3 to 4 minutes. (If electing not to flambé steaks, proceed to adding Brown Sauce.)

To flambé: Return steaks to skillet with mushrooms and shallots. Warm brandy in glass measure in microwave on HIGH about 10 seconds. Tilt skillet slightly and pour brandy into front edge of pan. Turn up heat and let flame ignite brandy vapors, swirling pan slightly (use match if stove is electric). Turn off heat and let flames die out. Transfer steaks to serving platter or plates, leaving mushrooms and shallots in skillet.

Add ¾ cup Brown Sauce, mustard and sour cream to skillet. Simmer until thickened, stirring occasionally–do not boil or sour cream will curdle. Spoon mixture over steaks. Serve with *Green Beans*, *Scalloped Potatoes*, green salad and a nice glass of Merlot or Cabernet Sauvignon.

Makes 4 servings   Arthur VanderVeen, Jr., Austin, Texas

Per serving: 524 calories, 43 g fat, 22 g protein, 10 g carbohydrate, 116 mg cholesterol, 1109 mg sodium.

Oven Barbecue Brisket

Brisket should be cooked slowly at low temperature to be tender.

1	(4- to 5-pound) beef brisket		¼	teaspoon garlic salt
	Marinade:		⅓	cup Worcestershire sauce
2	tablespoons liquid smoke			Freshly ground black pepper
½	teaspoon onion salt		1	(18-ounce) bottle of your favorite
½	teaspoon celery salt			barbecue sauce

Trim fat layer from brisket,[89] keeping brisket whole. Rinse. Put brisket in large ziptop bag and add marinade. Place bag in 9x13-inch baking dish and refrigerate 8 hours or overnight, turning occasionally.

Remove from bag and place brisket in baking dish. Sprinkle both sides with pepper. Add marinade. Cover with foil and bake at 275° for 3½ to 4 hours. Test for doneness–should easily be pierced with meat fork. Remove from oven and let stand covered at least 30 minutes in juice, turning once or twice. Transfer brisket to cutting board. Cut across grain into 2-inch wide slabs. Shred meat, pulling apart with two forks along the grain.

Skim off any fat from surface of liquid in baking dish.[77] Stir barbecue sauce into liquid. Return shredded meat to baking dish, stirring to coat. Bake uncovered at 325° for 45 to 60 minutes or until thick as desired, stirring occasionally. Serve brisket on buns with coleslaw on top–a Southern tradition–or alongside. Serve brisket on small buns for buffet.

Marinade: Combine liquid smoke, onion salt, celery salt, garlic salt and Worcestershire sauce in jar with tight-fitting lid. Shake well.

Makes 10 servings

Per serving: 408 calories, 18 g fat, 40 g protein, 18 g carbohydrate, 125 mg cholesterol, 1029 mg sodium.

Grill Tips

The hand test is still a very reliable way to test grill heat. Hold palm just above rack and count number of seconds you can hold it there:

HOT (500° F) – 2 to 3 seconds, MEDIUM-HOT (400° F) – 4 to 5 seconds, MEDIUM (350° F) – 6 to 7 seconds, MEDIUM-LOW (325° F) – 10 seconds, LOW (300° F) – 12 seconds.

Test meat for doneness before grilling time is up. Slice into thickest part of meat. If juices are red, meat is rare; if pink, medium; if juices are clear, meat is well done and overcooked.

Steamed Corned Beef and Cabbage

The usual way of preparing corned beef is to slowly boil the life out of it, leaving it with no flavor. Steaming produces meat that is moist, tender and full of flavor. My husband, Art, said, "I never liked corned beef, but this is really good!"

1 (3½-pound) flat-cut corned beef brisket (this is a lean cut)	2 medium onions
1 small head of cabbage with outer green leaves	1 bunch small fresh carrots, or half carrots and half parsnips
	Cajun seasoning or seasoned salt

Rinse corned beef; do not remove fat. Discard any spice packet. Place an adjustable steamer basket in large Dutch oven or large pot with lid. Add water to just below bottom of basket. Place four rinsed outer cabbage leaves in basket and add corned beef, fat side up, pressing brisket down on stem of basket if necessary. Simmer covered 2 hours. Add water to keep just below steamer basket, if needed. Meanwhile, prepare vegetables.

Cut cabbage into large wedges. Peel and quarter onions. Peel carrots and cut into 2-inch pieces. Peel parsnips and cut into 3-inch lengths; quarter large ends lengthwise and cut out any hard woody core. About 30 minutes before end of cooking time, place vegetables on top of corned beef and sprinkle with Cajun seasoning. Cover and steam until vegetables are *just tender* and corned beef can easily be pierced with meat fork.

Remove vegetables to serving dish. Cover with foil and place in warm oven. Transfer corned beef to cutting board and tent with foil. Let stand 10 minutes. Meanwhile, remove steamer basket from Dutch oven. Reduce^G liquid by boiling uncovered 5 to 10 minutes. Spoon desired amount of liquid over vegetables.

Thinly slice corned beef across grain, slanting knife to make wide slices. Place on serving platter and serve with steamed vegetables and, optionally, cabbage leaves that lined basket (Leaves will be limp, but will have wonderful flavor from absorbing corned beef juices.) Serve with *Creamy Horseradish Sauce* and *Roasted New Potatoes*.

Makes 6 servings

Per serving: 465 calories, 31 g fat, 42 g protein, 9 g carbohydrate, 128 mg cholesterol, 1713 mg sodium.

Favorite Pot Roast

2	tablespoons vegetable oil	½	teaspoon salt
1	(3-pound) chuck roast	¼	teaspoon garlic salt
¾	cup water, *divided*	⅛	teaspoon pepper
1	medium onion, sliced		Dash of ground allspice
1	(10¾-ounce) can beef consommé	½	teaspoon beef bouillon granules
½	teaspoon Worcestershire sauce		

Heat oil in Dutch oven and brown roast on all sides. Transfer to plate. Pour off excess fat from pot and add ¼ cup water. Heat, stirring to loosen brown bits. Return roast to pot and place onion slices on top. Mix consommé, Worcestershire sauce, remaining ½ cup water, salt, garlic salt, pepper and allspice in bowl and pour over roast. Cover and cook at 325° for 2 to 2½ hours or until tender, testing with meat fork after 2 hours. Transfer roast to cutting board and tent with foil 10 minutes. Slice across grain. Strain gravy and return to pot. Stir in bouillon granules and heat. To thicken, stir 1 tablespoon flour into ¼ cup water in small bowl and whisk into gravy; simmer, whisking until thickened.

Makes 6 servings

Per serving: 534 g calories, 40 g fat, 38 g protein, 3 g carbohydrate, 131 mg cholesterol, 450 mg sodium.

Jennifer's Casserole

1	pound ground beef	½	cup burgundy
1	(14½-ounce) can diced tomatoes, undrained	1	(8-ounce) package cream cheese
1	(8-ounce) can tomato sauce	1	cup sour cream
½	cup chopped bell pepper	½	cup chopped green onions
4	medium mushrooms, sliced[3]	1	(8-ounce) package wide egg noodles, cooked according to package directions.
1	garlic clove, minced		
1	to 2 teaspoons sugar	4	ounces mozzarella cheese, shredded (1 cup)
1	teaspoon salt		

Brown ground beef in large skillet. Drain off fat; stir in tomatoes, tomato sauce, bell pepper, mushrooms, garlic, sugar, salt and burgundy. Simmer uncovered 15 to 20 minutes, stirring occasionally. Beat cream cheese in large bowl with mixer until smooth. Blend in sour cream. Stir in green onion and cooked noodles. Spread one-third of meat mixture over bottom of sprayed 9x13-inch baking dish; cover with half the noodle mixture. Cover with another third meat mixture and remaining noodle mixture. Spread remaining meat mixture on top and sprinkle with mozzarella cheese. Bake at 350° for 30 minutes or until hot.

Makes 8 servings   **Ruth Ann Vavrinek, Bentonville, Arkansas**

Per serving: 461 calories, 33 g fat, 19 g protein, 22 g carbohydrate, 116 mg cholesterol, 725 mg sodium.

Stuffed Bell Peppers

Our grandchildren love these stuffed bell peppers. I usually make them when we go to visit.

4½	large bell peppers*	1	teaspoon Worcestershire sauce
1½	pounds ground chuck	1	teaspoon salt
¾	cup chopped onion	¼	teaspoon pepper
¼	cup (½ stick) butter, cut into pieces, plus 3 tablespoons	¼	teaspoon garlic salt
		¼	cup reserved cooking water
½	cup ketchup	30	saltine crackers, *divided*
1	(14½-ounce) can diced tomatoes, undrained		Paprika

Cut bell peppers in half lengthwise; seed and rinse. Fill large pot half full with salted water and bring to boil. Add peppers and cook 3 to 5 minutes or until just tender (water need not come back to boil). Reserve ¼ cup cooking water and drain peppers. Run cold water over peppers to stop cooking. Drain well.

Chop one blanched pepper half and put in large saucepan. Add ground chuck, onion, ¼ cup butter, ketchup, tomatoes, Worcestershire sauce, salt, pepper, garlic salt and reserved cooking water. Cook and stir over medium heat until butter melts and meat is no longer pink, about 4 minutes. Coarsely crush 20 crackers in ziptop bag. Stir into meat mixture and cook 2 to 3 more minutes to incorporate crackers. Mixture should be almost soupy.

Place pepper halves in sprayed 9x13-inch baking dish. Fill with meat mixture, spooning any excess meat mixture around peppers. Crush remaining 10 crackers and sprinkle over stuffed peppers. Dot with 3 tablespoons butter and sprinkle with paprika. Bake at 350° for 40 to 45 minutes or until hot and bubbly and beginning to brown. We always served stuffed peppers with **Candied Sweet Potatoes**, turnip greens and **Southern Cornbread**.

* Buy bell peppers that have four rounded sections on bottom rather than three. They will lie flat when halved.

Makes 6 to 8 servings   **Willie McCaleb Rabb, Lexington, Mississippi**

Per serving of 8: 406 calories, 29 g fat, 17 g protein, 18 g carbohydrate, 91 mg cholesterol, 919 mg sodium.

Our Family's Favorite Spaghetti Sauce

1½ pounds ground chuck or ground round

1 tablespoon vegetable oil

1 cup chopped onion

½ cup chopped celery

½ cup chopped bell pepper

2 tablespoons chopped fresh flat-leaf parsley or 1½ teaspoons dried parsley flakes, crushed

1 teaspoon dried oregano, crushed

1 teaspoon dried basil, crushed

¼ teaspoon red pepper flakes

1 garlic clove,[20] minced

1 bay leaf

1 (28-ounce) can crushed tomatoes, undrained

1 (8-ounce) can tomato sauce

1 (6-ounce) can tomato paste

1 (14-ounce) can beef broth[11]

1 teaspoon sugar

1 teaspoon salt

1 teaspoon Worcestershire sauce

1 teaspoon soy sauce

1 (4-ounce) can sliced mushrooms, drained (optional)

1 (16-ounce) package thin spaghetti, cooked according to package directions

Brown beef in large skillet until no longer pink. Drain in colander and set aside. Heat oil in Dutch oven or large pot and sauté onion, celery, bell pepper and parsley until tender, about 3 minutes. Remove from heat and stir in oregano, basil, pepper flakes, garlic and bay leaf. Return to heat and cook, stirring constantly, 1 minute. Add tomatoes, tomato sauce and tomato paste. Rinse cans with beef broth and add broth to pot. Mix in sugar, salt, Worcestershire sauce, soy sauce, mushrooms and beef. Bring to boil. Reduce heat and simmer covered 30 minutes, stirring occasionally, or simmer uncovered for thicker sauce. Remove bay leaf. Serve over spaghetti with freshly grated Asiago or Parmesan cheese. Serve with sourdough rolls and tossed salad.

Makes 6 servings

Per serving: 666 calories, 32 g fat, 31 g protein, 62 g carbohydrate, 90 mg cholesterol, 1673 mg sodium.

Fix-It-Fast Spaghetti

1½	pounds ground round or ground chuck	½	teaspoon salt
2	tablespoons dried minced onion	¼	teaspoon pepper
2	teaspoons dried oregano, crushed	1	(28-ounce) jar spaghetti sauce, (meat flavored preferred)
1	teaspoon dried basil, crushed	1	(8-ounce) can tomato sauce
¼	teaspoon ground thyme	1	tomato-sauce can of water
¼	teaspoon garlic powder		Pinch of sugar
1	teaspoon beef bouillon granules	1	(8-ounce) package thin spaghetti

Brown beef with dried onion in Dutch oven or large skillet. Drain if necessary. Add oregano, basil, thyme, garlic powder, bouillon granules, salt, pepper, spaghetti sauce and tomato sauce. Rinse jar and can with the water and add to pot. Sprinkle in sugar. Bring mixture to boil. Reduce heat and simmer covered 30 minutes.

Prepare spaghetti according to package directions. Do not rinse.[57] Divide spaghetti among four pasta dishes or shallow-rimmed soup bowls; ladle sauce over spaghetti. Serve with French bread, tossed green salad and a nice glass of red wine.

Makes 4 to 6 servings

Per serving (6): 561 calories, 25 g fat, 29 g protein, 53 g carbohydrate, 83 mg cholesterol, 1109 mg sodium.

Best Ever Beef Loaf

Betty's children say, "It's the best!" Friends ask for it when she offers to bring a dish.

2	eggs	½	cup shredded carrots
⅔	cup milk	4	ounces Cheddar cheese, shredded (1 cup)
2	teaspoons salt		
¼	teaspoon pepper	1½	pounds ground beef
1	teaspoon prepared horseradish	¼	cup packed brown sugar[1]
3	slices white bread, torn into small pieces	¼	cup ketchup
½	cup finely chopped onion	1	tablespoon prepared mustard

Lightly beat eggs, milk, salt, pepper, horseradish and bread pieces in large bowl with mixer until bread is incorporated. Mix in onion, carrots, cheese and ground beef with your hands.[59] Pack mixture into sprayed 9x5-inch loaf pan. Combine brown sugar, ketchup and mustard in small bowl and spread over loaf. Bake at 350° for 1 hour 15 minutes. Let stand in pan 10 minutes. Remove to serving plate and slice. Serve with ***Baked Red Potatoes*** and ***Spicy Creamed Spinach***.

Makes 8 servings   Betty Davis, Bella Vista, Arkansas

Per serving: 356 calories, 22 g fat, 20 g protein, 17 g carbohydrate, 127 mg cholesterol, 872 mg sodium.

Our Favorite Meat Loaf

A "good old standby" when our children were young. Now I make it and reheat the leftovers.

2	pounds ground chuck	2	tablespoons ketchup, *divided*
1	cup soft breadcrumbs[45]	1	teaspoon Worcestershire sauce
1	egg, lightly beaten	1½	teaspoons salt
½	cup finely chopped onion		Freshly ground black pepper
½	cup finely chopped bell pepper	¼	cup milk, or more if needed
½	cup finely chopped celery	2	slices bacon (optional)

Mix meat, breadcrumbs, egg, onion, bell pepper, celery, 1 tablespoon ketchup, Worcestershire sauce, salt and pepper in large bowl (I mix it with my hands). Add milk gradually, mixing until mixture just holds together—do not overmix or meat loaf will be mushy. Pat into large oval shape.

Put small rack in foil-lined 9x9-inch baking pan and set meat loaf on rack (having meat loaf raised will let it brown on all sides). Spread remaining tablespoon ketchup on top and place bacon slices lengthwise over meat loaf. Bake at 350° for 60 to 70 minutes. Tent with foil and let stand 10 minutes. Transfer to cutting board and cut into thick slices. Serve with *Baked Red Potatoes* and *Green Beans*. To heat leftovers, put meat loaf in casserole dish, add ¼ cup chicken broth,[11] and heat covered at 300° for 30 to 45 minutes, depending on amount. Serve with *Mushroom Sauce* and *Perfect Mashed Potatoes*.

Makes 6 servings

Per serving: 462 calories, 34 g fat, 30 g protein, 7 g carbohydrate, 152 mg cholesterol, 497 mg sodium.

About Pork

Many earlier cookbooks recommended that pork be cooked to internal temperatures of at least 160°. Pork no longer needs to be cooked to that extent. Today's American pork producers raise hogs in a controlled environment resulting in less exposure to parasites. Internal temperature in the range of 150° to 155° is now considered safe and meat will be juicy and tender. Cooking pork to medium-rare is not recommended. Pork should be cooked medium to medium-well (a little pink is okay). Recommended internal cooking-temperature guidelines for pork are: 145°-150° for pork roast and 155° for ground pork. Stuffed pork needs to be cooked to 165°. Buy grayish-pink pork with a small amount of marbling[G] and with a thin layer of fat over outside.

Elegant and Easy Pork Tenderloin

Julia Rutland, guest chef and coauthor of **Discover Dinnertime**, *gave a cooking demonstration as part of a Wimmer Companies' Community Cookbook Seminar. Her pork tenderloin, part of the refreshments, became the basis for my buffet variation.*

2 (1-pound) pork tenderloins	1 cup Italian dressing
Seasoned salt	(8-ounce bottle)
Lemon pepper	

Rinse tenderloins and pat dry. Remove silver skin and any excess fat.[31] Sprinkle each tenderloin generously with seasoned salt and lemon pepper. Put in ziptop bag and add well-shaken Italian dressing. Refrigerate 8 hours or overnight, turning occasionally. Remove 15 minutes before grilling and pat dry. Discard marinade. Tuck a few inches of thinnest end under to even out thickness of roast. Tie with butcher's twine at 2-inch intervals. Set aside.

Set grill rack 3 to 4 inches above heat source and preheat grill to MEDIUM-HOT (see *Grill Tips*). Just before grilling spray tenderloins and grill rack. Place meat on grill and close cover. Grill 6 to 8 minutes on each side or until instant-read thermometer registers 150°, turning once. Remove to cutting board and tent with foil. Let stand 10 minutes. Meat will continue to cook while standing.

Slice tenderloins ⅜-inch thick. Overlap slices on serving plate and pour any accumulated juices over slices. Serve with *Madeira Sauce, Twice Baked Potatoes* and *Green Beans with Toasted Pecans.*

Makes 6 servings

Per serving: 173 calories, 5 g fat, 31 g protein, 0 g carbohydrate, 80 mg cholesterol, 59 mg sodium.

Buffet Pork Tenderloin: Prepare and cook tenderloins as directed above–do not slice. Cool. Place tenderloins on separate pieces of foil with any accumulated juice divided. Wrap tightly and refrigerate overnight. Unwrap and transfer tenderloins and juice to baking dish. Cover with foil and bake at 350° for 10 to 15 minutes or until thoroughly heated. Remove tenderloins to cutting board. Let cool slightly and cut into thin slices. Overlap slices attractively on platter and garnish with parsley. Serve with party-size pumpernickel or rye bread, mayonnaise and Dijon mustard. Tenderloins may also be served without reheating. Slice and arrange on platter about 10 minutes before serving.

Makes 36 to 48 servings

Per serving: 87 calories, 3 g fat, 15 g protein, 0 g carbohydrate, 35 mg cholesterol, 34 mg sodium.

Pan-Grilled Boneless Pork Chops

4   center cut loin pork chops   White-wine Worcestershire sauce*
    (1 to 1¼ inches thick)   Steak seasoning crystals

Have chops slightly frozen or freeze 30 minutes. Completely cut away *all* fat from rim of each chop with sharp knife. Rinse chops and pat dry. Lightly sprinkle both sides with white wine Worcestershire sauce and seasoning crystals. Place chops on plate and cover with plastic wrap. Let stand 30 minutes, longer if still frozen.

Heat grill skillet over medium-high heat until very hot. Spray hot skillet and both sides of chops. Add chops to skillet and cook uncovered 3½ minutes (watch sides of chops–you can actually see heat cooking the chops). Turn and cook other side 3½ minutes. Remove chops to shallow ovenproof dish, stacking one on top of the other. Cover loosely with foil. Put in 250° oven and keep warm 10 minutes. Transfer chops to serving plate. Serve with *Madeira Sauce, Green Bean Bundles* and *Scalloped Potatoes.*

* If white wine Worcestershire sauce is not readily available, substitute lesser amount of regular Worcestershire sauce.

Makes 4 servings

Per serving: 306 calories, 19 g fat, 31 g protein, 1 g carbohydrate, 101 mg cholesterol, 298 mg sodium.

Caraway Pork Chops

4   pork rib chops   ¼   cup water
2   teaspoons caraway seeds, or   1   (10¾-ounce) can cream of
    as desired   mushroom soup
    Pepper   1   (4-ounce) can sliced mushrooms,
1   tablespoon vegetable oil   undrained

Rinse chops and pat dry.[71] Press caraway seeds into both sides of chops. Sprinkle with pepper. Heat oil in heavy ovenproof skillet and brown chops about 3 minutes on each side. Transfer chops to plate (or to 8x8-inch baking dish if skillet is not ovenproof). Set aside. Pour off any excess fat from skillet and add water. Heat and loosen any brown bits on bottom with wooden spatula. Add soup and mushrooms. Whisk and cook over medium heat until smooth. Add water if thick. Return chops and any accumulated juice to skillet (or pour sauce over chops in baking dish). Cover and bake at 325° for 60 minutes or until tender. Serve with *Perfect Mashed Potatoes*, noodles or rice and steamed broccoli.

Makes 4 servings   Terry VanderVeen Bright, Lynchburg, Virginia

Per serving: 449 calories, 319 g fat, 33 g protein, 7 g carbohydrate, 96 mg cholesterol, 685 mg sodium.

Pork Shoulder Roast

1 (4-pound) pork shoulder roast, bone in	2 tablespoons vegetable oil
1 large garlic clove, minced	1 cup chopped onion
2 teaspoons salt	¾ cup chicken broth
½ teaspoon pepper	**Gravy:**
1 teaspoon chopped fresh rosemary leaves, or ½ teaspoon dried rosemary, crushed	Strained liquid from pot
	¾ cup chicken broth[11]
1 tablespoon fresh thyme leaves, chopped, or 1 teaspoon dried thyme, crushed	2 tablespoons flour
	¼ cup water
	½ teaspoon chicken bouillon granules

Remove any excess fat from roast; rinse roast and pat dry. Make paste of garlic, salt, pepper, rosemary and thyme with mortar and pestle (or back of spoon in small bowl). Make six ½-inch slits on top of roast and six underneath with point of sharp knife. Push paste into slits and pat remaining paste over roast.

Heat oil in Dutch oven over medium heat and brown roast on all sides. Transfer to plate. Add onion to pot and sauté until tender. Stir in chicken broth with wooden spatula and loosen any browned bits on bottom. Return roast and bake covered in *lower third* of oven at 325° for 2 to 2½ hours or until fork tender. Transfer roast to cutting board and tent with foil. Let rest 10 minutes. Meanwhile, make gravy. Cut roast into thick slices. Serve over split *Cornbread* wedges and spoon gravy over pork, if desired. Serve with *Jalapeño Black-Eyed Peas* and *Candied Sweet Potatoes* for a great New Years Day meal!

Gravy: Strain liquid from Dutch oven into medium saucepan. Remove any fat from surface.[77] Add chicken broth and heat. Mix flour, water and bouillon granules in small bowl until flour dissolves. Whisk into gravy. Cook and whisk until thickened. Season with salt and pepper.

Makes 8 servings

Per serving: 426 calories, 31 g fat, 31 g protein, 4 g carbohydrate, 122 mg cholesterol, 818 mg sodium.

Spicy Pork Shoulder Roast variation: Add 1 tablespoon chopped, seeded fresh jalapeño to paste mixture. After adding and sautéing onions, substitute ¾ cup orange juice for ¾ cup chicken broth and bake as directed above. Transfer roast to cutting board and tent with foil; let rest 10 minutes. Cut into chunks and shred. Strain liquid into medium bowl and remove any fat from surface.[77] Return pork to Dutch oven and pour liquid over meat. Cook uncovered until mixture is hot and thick as desired, stirring occasionally. Use shredded pork in burritos and enchiladas, or serve on toasted buns with mayonnaise, Dijon mustard and coleslaw.

Slow-Cooked Pork

Slow-cooked pork makes great barbecue!

1	(4 to 5 pound) pork shoulder roast, bone-in or boneless	⅓	cup Worcestershire sauce*
1	(14-ounce) can beef broth	⅓	cup hot pepper sauce*
1	(12-ounce) can of beer	1	teaspoon beef bouillon granules
		½	teaspoon salt

Trim roast of excess fat; rinse roast and pat dry. Put in sprayed 4-quart slow-cooker. Combine beef broth, beer, Worcestershire sauce, pepper sauce, bouillon granules and salt in bowl and pour over roast. Cover and cook on high 5 hours[86] (8 to 10 hours on low) or until very tender. Remove to cutting board. When cool enough to handle, remove meat from bone (if bone in) and pull meat apart into large pieces. Discard any internal fat. Cut meat pieces into 2 to 2½-inch chunks and shred into ½-inch-wide strips along the grain. Use for making *Pork Barbecue* (reserve about 1 cup liquid from slow-cooker for barbecue). Cut strips across grain into bite-size pieces for use in *White Bean Chili* or *Pork and Sour Cream Enchiladas*. Makes 6 to 7 cups bite-size pork.

* The heat and spiciness of these sauces dissipate after cooking a long time—do not be alarmed at the amounts; however, those of faint heart may reduce amounts as desired.

Pork Barbecue: Prepare 2 recipes of *Phyllis's Barbecue Sauce*, or use your favorite barbecue sauce. Put shredded pork in large saucepan or Dutch oven and add ½ cup reserved cooking liquid, 1 cup barbecue sauce and, optionally, 1 teaspoon cider vinegar. Stir to coat, adding more reserved liquid if thick. Simmer uncovered over low heat until mixture is hot and thick as desired (longer slow cooking will give flavors time to blend as liquids reduce). Serve on toasted buns, passing remaining barbecue sauce for those who like extra sauce. Serve with *Mother's Potato Salad*, *Smoky Baked Beans* and coleslaw.

Makes 6 to 8 servings of pork barbecue

Per serving of 8: 537 calories, 36 g fat, 45 g protein, 4 g carbohydrate, 127 mg cholesterol, 690 mg sodium.

Italian Sausage Spaghetti Sauce

1	tablespoon olive oil	1	teaspoon dried basil, crushed
2	pounds sweet Italian sausage, or 1 pound sweet and 1 pound hot (about 8 sausages), casings removed	¼	teaspoon fennel seeds
		3	ounces Asiago or Parmesan cheese, grated (1 cup)
2	garlic cloves, minced	1	whole medium onion
1	(6-ounce) can tomato paste[19]	½	bell pepper, seeds removed
2	(28-ounce) cans crushed tomatoes, undrained	½	cup snipped flat-leaf parsley
		1	(8-ounce) package fresh mushrooms, sliced[3]
2	(8-ounce) cans tomato sauce[19]		
½	cup water	1½	(16-ounce) packages thin spaghetti, cooked according to package directions
1	teaspoon sugar		
1	teaspoon dried oregano, crushed		

Heat oil in Dutch oven. Crumble in sausage and add garlic. Sauté, separating and stirring sausage until no longer pink. Drain off fat, reserving 1 tablespoon. Transfer sausage to medium bowl and set aside. Return reserved fat to pot. Whisk in tomato paste and cook over medium heat 1 minute, whisking constantly. Stir in tomatoes and tomato sauce. Rinse cans with the ½-cup water and add to pot. Stir in sugar, oregano, basil, fennel seeds and grated cheese. Mix in sausage. Add onion and bell pepper. Bring to boil. Reduce heat and simmer covered 1½ hours. During last 5 minutes of cooking stir in parsley and mushrooms. Before serving, remove and discard onion and bell pepper or set aside for snacks. Add salt if needed. Serve over spaghetti and garnish with additional grated cheese. Serve with *Mock Caesar Salad* and garlic bread.

Note: You may substitute 2 pounds ground beef for Italian sausage. Season with salt and pepper to taste.

Makes 8 to 10 servings

Per serving (10): 442 calories, 34 g fat, 21 g protein, 16 g carbohydrate, 77 mg cholesterol, 1549 mg sodium.

Sausages and Peppers

3 pounds sweet Italian sausages,
or half sweet and half hot
(about 12 sausages)

1 cup water, *divided*

4 medium bell peppers, sliced
lengthwise into ¾-inch strips

2 large onions, halved vertically and
cut crosswise into ½-inch slices

1 (45-ounce) jar traditional
spaghetti sauce

½ teaspoon beef bouillon granules

¼ teaspoon dried basil, crushed

½ teaspoon dried oregano, crushed

Hoagie buns or sub rolls, cut in
half and toasted

Place half the sausages and ¼ cup water in large nonstick skillet. Do not prick
sausages. Cook over medium heat, turning with tongs, until water evaporates
and sausages are lightly browned on all sides. Drain on paper towels. Add ¼ cup
more water to skillet and repeat with browning remaining sausages.

Alternate layers of bell peppers and onions (slices separated) with sausages in
Dutch oven, making several layers. Pour spaghetti sauce over layers. Pour
remaining ½ cup water into spaghetti-sauce jar, add bouillon granules, shake to
dissolve, and add to pot. Sprinkle with basil and oregano. Cook covered in 350°
oven 1 hour. Lift and turn sausages, peppers and onions to change positions.
Cook 1 more hour. Remove from oven and let stand 30 minutes. (Best if made
a day ahead and refrigerated. Reheat.) Freezes well. Serve open-face on buns.

Slow cooker method: Brown sausages as directed above and alternate layers of
bell peppers and onions with sausages in sprayed 6-quart slow cooker. Pour
spaghetti sauce over layers, rinsing jar with remaining ½ cup water; add to cooker.
(Do not add bouillon granules, basil or oregano at this time; set these aside near
slow cooker as reminder to add later.) Cook 7½ to 8 hours on LOW or 4 hours on
HIGH. Stir every 2 or 3 hours to change positions of sausages and peppers. Stir in
bouillon granules, basil and oregano during last 30 minutes of cooking.

Makes 10 to 12 servings

Per serving of 12: 466 calories, 38 fat, 18 g protein, 11 g carbohydrate, 86 mg cholesterol, 1540 mg sodium.

Brats with Sauerkraut

Arlene got this recipe from her son John. One day her son Mark was going through her recipes and came across "John's Brats, 1/5/92." Mark wrote on recipe, "stolen from Mark in 1982." Arlene is not taking sides, but says this is a great way to serve brats.

1 tablespoon vegetable oil	½ cup chicken broth
6 to 8 large uncooked brats	¼ cup packed brown sugar
1 cup chopped onion	1 (32-ounce) jar or refrigerated
1 cup chopped bell pepper	package sauerkraut, undrained

Heat oil in large skillet. Lightly brown brats on all sides, turning frequently. Transfer to 9x13-inch baking dish. Sauté onion and bell pepper in pan drippings until tender. Stir in chicken broth and brown sugar; mix in sauerkraut. Spoon over brats and bake covered at 325° for 1½ to 2 hours. Place each brat on bed of sauerkraut and serve with French bread; or serve brats on buns with sauerkraut.

Makes 6 to 8 servings   Arlene Steege, Bella Vista, Arkansas

Per serving of 8: 244 calories, 14 g fat, 13 g protein, 13 g carbohydrate, 56 mg cholesterol, 912 mg sodium.

Ham Casserole

Wondering what to do with that leftover ham? This casserole may be the answer.

2 tablespoons butter, *divided*	⅛ teaspoon celery salt
½ cup chopped onion	¼ teaspoon pepper
½ cup chopped bell pepper	Dash of hot pepper sauce
½ cup chopped celery	(optional)
1 (10¾-ounce) can cream of	16 saltine crackers, *divided*
mushroom, chicken or celery	1½ cups bite-size cooked ham
soup (98% fat free is good)	2 hard-cooked eggs,[18] sliced
½ soup can of milk	Paprika
⅛ teaspoon seasoned salt	

Melt 1 tablespoon butter in medium skillet and sauté onion, bell pepper and celery until tender, 2 to 3 minutes. Whisk soup, milk, seasoned salt, celery salt, pepper and pepper sauce in medium bowl and add to skillet. Cook, stirring frequently, until hot, about 3 minutes. Coarsely crumble 10 crackers into sprayed 8x8-inch baking dish. Layer ham and egg slices over crackers. Spoon soup mixture evenly over egg slices. Crumble remaining 6 crackers on top and dot with remaining 1 tablespoon butter. Sprinkle with paprika. Bake uncovered at 350° for 30 minutes or until hot and bubbly. Let stand 5 minutes before serving.

Makes 4 servings   Willie McCaleb Rabb, Lexington, Mississippi

Per serving: 318 calories, 19 g fat, 16 g protein, 21 g carbohydrate, 161 mg cholesterol, 1641 mg sodium.

Grilled Butterflied Leg of Lamb

½ cup snipped flat-leaf parsley
1 tablespoon fresh rosemary leaves
2 tablespoons fresh thyme leaves
1 teaspoon grated lemon zest
4 garlic cloves, minced
1½ teaspoons coarse or kosher salt

½ teaspoon freshly ground black pepper
1 tablespoon olive oil
1 (4- to 5-pound) boneless, butterflied leg of lamb

Put parsley, rosemary and thyme leaves, lemon zest, garlic, salt, pepper and oil in small food processor and process to a paste. (Alternatively, finely chop parsley, rosemary and thyme leaves and mix thoroughly with lemon zest, garlic, salt, pepper and oil in small bowl with back of spoon to form paste.)

Remove any silver skin and any remaining pockets of fat from lamb.[31] Rinse thoroughly and pat dry. If meat is thicker than 2 inches in thickest part, pound to 2 inches with meat mallet. Cut small slits in thicker parts of meat with point of sharp knife. Push paste into slits and rub remaining paste over lamb. Let stand 30 to 40 minutes. (May also put lamb in ziptop bag and refrigerate several hours or overnight. Let stand unrefrigerated 30 minutes before grilling. Remove from bag and pat dry.)

Insert medium-length metal skewers through spread out meat, two lengthwise and two crosswise, to secure loose flaps, bunching meat together on skewers to form a more uniform shape, if desired. Set grill rack 5 or 6 inches above heat and preheat to MEDIUM-HOT (see *Grill Tips*).

Spray grill rack and lamb *just before grilling*. Grill 8 to 10 minutes on each side or until instant-read thermometer inserted into thickest part reads 135° for medium-rare.* Temperature will continue to rise while standing. Transfer lamb to cutting board and tent with foil. Let stand 10 minutes. Remove skewers and thinly slice meat across the grain if possible; otherwise, slice pieces on an angle. Serve with any accumulated juices.

* *Butterflied leg of lamb is usually uneven in thickness. When grilled, there will be rare, medium-rare and medium-well sections to satisfy every palate.*

Makes 8 servings

Per serving: 334 calories, 21 g fat, 33 g protein, 0 g carbohydrate, 120 mg cholesterol, 217 mg sodium.

Rotisserie Roasted Leg of Lamb

A rotisserie lets you relax while lamb self-bastes and browns evenly!

1 (5-pound) boneless leg of lamb	1½ tablespoons fresh rosemary leaves or 1½ teaspoons dried rosemary, crushed
1 tablespoon olive oil	
1 carrot, finely chopped	1 tablespoon Dijon mustard
2 green onions, finely chopped	2 cups soft breadcrumbs[45]
2 to 3 garlic cloves, minced	2 tablespoons flour
2 tablespoons finely snipped flat-leaf parsley	

Unroll lamb and trim off *all* fat and any silver skin.[31] Rinse well and pat dry. Heat oil in medium skillet and sauté carrot, green onion, garlic, parsley and rosemary over medium heat, 2 to 3 minutes or until tender. Remove from heat. Mix in mustard and breadcrumbs, making a paste. Sprinkle flour over inside of lamb and spread paste down middle. Form meat back into roll and truss with butcher's twine.[74] Sprinkle with salt and pepper.

Remove grill racks from gas grill and install rotisserie motor. Preheat grill to MEDIUM (see *Grill Tips*). Insert rotisserie spit through ends of rolled lamb, centering meat for balance. Secure forks in place. Position foil drip pan[48] under lamb on lava rocks. Close grill cover and reduce heat to LOW. Cook 1 hour or until instant-read thermometer inserted near center registers 130° for rare or 140° for medium. When temperature *approaches* desired doneness, turn off gas and prop open lid about 1 inch. Allow meat to turn on spit about 10 more minutes to set juices. (Temperature will continue to rise while meat turns so do not overcook.) Transfer lamb to cutting board and remove spit. Tent with foil and let stand 10 minutes. Remove twine and slice across roll into ⅜- to ½-inch slices. Serve with *Fresh Asparagus* and *Twice Baked Potatoes*.

Makes 10 servings   Ben and Carolyn McCall, Charleston, South Carolina

Per serving: 383 calories, 23 g fat, 34 g protein, 7 g carbohydrate, 120 mg cholesterol, 152 mg sodium.

About Parsley

There is actually more flavor in the stems of parsley than in the leaves, so be sure to include some stems when snipping parsley. Flat-leaf (Italian) parsley has a more distinctive taste than curly-leaf parsley. Rinsing parsley in hot water brings out more flavor.

Stuffed Leg of Lamb

1	(5-pound) boneless leg of lamb
	Juice of 1 lemon
2	garlic cloves, minced
½	cup snipped flat-leaf parsley
1	teaspoon coarse salt, *divided*
½	teaspoon freshly ground black pepper, *divided*
1½	tablespoons fresh rosemary leaves or 1½ teaspoons dried rosemary, crushed, *divided*

1	teaspoon balsamic vinegar
2	tablespoons plus 1 teaspoon extra-virgin olive oil
3	tablespoons dry breadcrumbs
1	carrot, cut into 1-inch pieces
1	medium onion, cut into wedges
1	rib celery, cut into 1-inch pieces
1	(10½-ounce) can chicken broth
1	(10½-ounce) can beef broth
½	cup dry white wine

Unroll lamb and trim off *all* fat and any silver skin.[31] Rinse and pat dry. Squeeze lemon juice over inside of lamb. Put garlic, parsley, ½ teaspoon salt, ¼ teaspoon pepper, 1 teaspoon rosemary, vinegar and 2 tablespoons oil in small bowl; mix well. Stir in breadcrumbs until combined. Spread herb mixture over inside of lamb and into pockets left by boning. Form back into roll and truss with butcher's twine.[74] Cover and refrigerate 4 to 5 hours or overnight. Let stand unrefrigerated 30 minutes before roasting.

Preheat oven to 475°. Rub rolled meat with 1 teaspoon oil and sprinkle with remaining ½ teaspoon salt and ¼ teaspoon pepper. Place meat on shallow rack in roasting pan and surround with carrot, onion and celery. Sprinkle remaining ½ teaspoon rosemary over vegetables. Place pan in oven and immediately reduce temperature to 375°.

Mix chicken broth, beef broth and wine in bowl. Use about 1 cup for basting and reserve remainder for making gravy. After roasting lamb 15 minutes, baste every 10 minutes until instant-read thermometer reaches 130° for rare or 140° for medium. (Meat will continue to cook while standing.) Remove lamb to cutting board and tent with foil. Let stand 10 minutes.

Meanwhile, strain liquid from pan to make gravy, discarding vegetables. Pour into small saucepan and add reserved broth mixture. Heat. To thicken gravy, stir 1 tablespoon flour with ¼ cup water in small bowl until flour dissolves. Quickly whisk into gravy and cook and whisk until thickened.

Remove twine and slice lamb across roll into ⅜- to ½-inch slices. Spoon gravy over lamb slices. Serve with *Fresh Asparagus* and *Twice Baked Potatoes*.

Makes 10 servings   Adapted from recipe by Ben and Carolyn McCall,
                                                        Charleston, South Carolina

Per serving: 387 calories, 24 g fat, 35 g protein, 5 g carbohydrate, 120 mg cholesterol, 539 mg sodium.

Mexican

Mexican

Salsa

1 (28-ounce) can whole tomatoes, drained, reserve juice	2 tablespoons chopped jalapeño with seeds
1 (8-ounce) can tomato sauce	1 teaspoon red pepper flakes
2 tablespoons lime juice	¼ cup snipped cilantro
1 tablespoon red wine vinegar	1 teaspoon kosher salt
3 green onions, cut into 1-inch pieces	⅛ teaspoon sugar
	⅛ to ¼ teaspoon chili powder

Put tomatoes, tomato sauce, lime juice, vinegar, green onion, jalapeño, pepper flakes, cilantro, kosher salt, sugar and chili powder in food processor and pulse until coarsely chopped. Gradually process in enough reserved juice from tomatoes until desired consistency is reached. Serve with tortilla chips.

Makes 2½ cups

Per ¼ cup: 39 calories, 0 g fat, 2 g protein, 8 g carbohydrate, 0 mg cholesterol, 480 mg sodium.

Mango Salsa

1 mango, peeled and diced[67]	1 medium tomato, chopped
¼ cup chopped red onion	1 jalapeño, seeded and chopped[44]
¼ cup chopped cilantro	2 tablespoons fresh lime juice

Put mango, onion, cilantro, tomato, jalapeño and lime juice in medium bowl in that order. Mix well. Season with salt and pepper. Serve on grilled chicken or fish, or serve with tortilla chips.

Makes about 2 cups   Mary Ann Evans, San Jose, California

Per ¼-cup serving: 28 calories, 0 g fat, 1 g protein, 7 g carbohydrate, 0 mg cholesterol, 5 mg sodium.

Mango and Black Bean Salsa variation: Prepare *Mango Salsa* and add 2 teaspoons olive oil, 1 teaspoon freshly grated lime zest and 1 (15-ounce) can of black beans, rinsed and drained.[19] Mix well. Let stand 20 minutes or refrigerate up to 1 hour. Serve with tortilla chips.

Makes about 4 cups

Per ¼-cup serving: 43 calories, 1 g fat, 2 g protein, 4 g carbohydrate, 0 mg cholesterol, 24 mg sodium.

Guacamole

2 or 3 large dark pebble-textured ripe avocados, diced[29]
2 tablespoons fresh lime juice
1 (4-ounce) can diced green chiles, undrained
¼ to ½ cup chopped green onions

1 small tomato, seeded and chopped[53]
½ teaspoon salt
Dash of garlic salt
Freshly ground black pepper

Mash diced avocados in medium bowl, leaving some larger pieces. Mix in lime juice, green chiles, green onion, tomato, salt, garlic salt and pepper with fork. Serve immediately or place plastic wrap on surface and refrigerate 1 to 2 hours. Serve with tortilla chips or use as topping for tacos, burritos, enchiladas and soups.

Makes about 3 cups   Nancy Paurus, Boulder, Colorado

Per tablespoon: 22 calories, 2 g fat, 1 g protein, 1 g carbohydrate, 0 mg cholesterol, 34 mg sodium.

Guacamole with Olives

2 large ripe avocados
½ cup sliced pimiento-stuffed olives
1 cup finely chopped firm ripe tomatoes
¼ cup sliced green onions

¼ cup finely chopped bell pepper
1 to 2 tablespoons cider vinegar
¼ to ½ teaspoon salt
Freshly ground black pepper
2 tablespoons olive oil

Dice avocados[29] into medium bowl. Add olives, tomato, green onion and bell pepper. Put vinegar, salt and pepper in small bowl; stir in oil and mix well. Combine with avocado mixture. Serve immediately or place plastic wrap on surface and refrigerate 1 to 2 hours. Serve with spoon-shaped corn chips or tortilla chips.

Makes 2 cups   Diane Womack, Bella Vista, Arkansas

Per 2 tablespoons: 65 calories, 6 g fat, 1 g protein, 3 g carbohydrate, 0 mg cholesterol, 120 mg sodium.

Note: Chef Annie, who has recipes on the internet website, www.texmextogo.com, recommends adding ⅓ cup water to guacamole to help hold its green color. I was afraid to add ⅓ cup water for fear guacamole would be runny. For 3 avocados I added 2 tablespoons cold water and it really did work.

Mexican Seven Layer Dip

2 (16-ounce) cans refried beans	1½ cups sour cream
2 (4-ounce) cans diced green chiles, drained, or 1 fresh jalapeño, seeded and chopped	1 (1.25-ounce) package taco seasoning mix
3 ripe avocados, peeled and diced[29]	1 large bunch green onions
2 tablespoons fresh lemon juice	3 medium tomatoes
½ teaspoon salt	1 (6-ounce) can pitted ripe olives
Freshly ground black pepper	8 ounces Cheddar cheese, shredded (2 cups)
½ cup mayonnaise	

Stir refried beans and green chiles together in medium bowl. Mash avocados in separate bowl and mix in lemon juice, salt, pepper and mayonnaise. Stir sour cream and taco seasoning mix together in another bowl. Layer dip in large shallow-rimmed dish, 10- or 11-inch quiche dish or 9x13-inch baking dish as follows:

(1) Spread refried bean mixture over bottom. (2) Cover with avocado mixture. (3) Spread sour cream mixture on top. Cover and refrigerate overnight, if possible; otherwise chill at least 2 hours.

Next day chop green onions including some tops (about 1 cup). Seed tomatoes,[53] chop and drain well. Drain olives well and coarsely chop. Finish layers:

(4) Sprinkle green onion over sour cream mixture. (5) Cover with layer of tomatoes. (6) Sprinkle chopped olives over tomatoes. (7) Cover top with cheese. Cover and refrigerate until ready to serve. Spoon dip onto small plates and serve with tortilla chips.

Makes 16 servings   Martha Tompkins, Greenville, South Carolina

Per serving: 289 calories, 24 g fat, 8 g protein, 15 g carbohydrate, 27 mg cholesterol, 685 mg sodium.

Southwest Seasoning

4 teaspoons ground black pepper	2 teaspoons chili powder
¼ cup (scant) ground cumin	¼ teaspoon cayenne pepper
2 tablespoons dried Mexican oregano, crushed	1 tablespoon salt
1 teaspoon paprika	¼ teaspoon garlic powder

Mix black pepper, cumin, oregano, paprika, chili powder, cayenne pepper, salt and garlic powder in small bowl. Store in a jar at room temperature. Seasoning will keep indefinitely. Stir well before using.

Makes ½ cup

Per teaspoon: 6 calories, 1 g fat, 1 g protein, 1 g carbohydrate, 0 mg cholesterol, 232 mg sodium.

Stuffed Jalapeños

16 fresh jalapeños, 2 to 3 inches long
1 (8-ounce) package cream cheese, softened
1 (8-ounce) package shredded Mexican four cheese, or 1 cup shredded Cheddar cheese and 1 cup shredded Monterey Jack cheese
¼ teaspoon chili powder
¼ teaspoon garlic powder
½ teaspoon salt
    Dash of Worcestershire sauce
½ teaspoon fresh lemon juice
8 slices lean bacon, cooked and crumbled[14]
½ cup dry breadcrumbs
    Paprika

Cut jalapeños in half lengthwise, leaving stems intact. Remove seeds and veins.[44] Rinse halves and drain on paper towels. Set aside.

Beat cream cheese in medium bowl with mixer until smooth. Blend in shredded cheese. Add chili powder, garlic powder, salt, Worcestershire sauce and lemon juice. Mix well. Stir in bacon. Spoon filling into each pepper half, mounding slightly. Cover with plastic wrap and refrigerate 2 hours.

Put breadcrumbs in small shallow bowl. Coat each filled pepper half by rolling in breadcrumbs. Place filled side up on foil-lined baking sheets. Sprinkle with paprika. Bake at 300° for 15 to 20 minutes or until thoroughly heated. Remove and let stand 5 minutes. Serve with ranch dressing, *Guacamole* or sour cream.

Makes 32 stuffed peppers   Janet VanderVeen, Winfield, Illinois

Per stuffed pepper: 74 calories, 5 g fat, 3 g protein, 4 g carbohydrate, 15 mg cholesterol, 125 mg sodium.

Jalapeño Poppers

15 fresh jalapeños
1 (8-ounce) package cream cheese
15 slices lean bacon, cut in half

Cut jalapeños in half lengthwise, leaving stems intact. Remove seeds and veins.[44] Rinse halves and drain on paper towels. Fill pepper halves with cream cheese. Wrap bacon piece around each, overlapping on top. Secure bacon with toothpick. Place on sprayed foil-lined baking sheets. Bake at 350° for 30 minutes or until bacon is crisp.

Makes 30 poppers   Cindy VanderVeen Ippel, Zeeland, Michigan

Per popper: 123 calories, 10 g fat, 6 g protein, 2 g carbohydrate, 21 mg cholesterol, 265 mg sodium.

Nachos Grande

Years ago our son-in-law, Matt, and his family went to lunch and had nachos as an appetizer. His mother CharLee, who had never had nachos before, enjoyed them so much that she decided to try to reproduce them. This recipe was the result; recipe makes mucho nachos.

1 pound ground beef	1 (8-ounce) jar hot taco sauce
1 (1.25-ounce) packet taco seasoning mix	½ cup water
2 (16-ounce) cans refried beans	1 (16-ounce) bag cheese-flavored tortilla chips
1 (8-ounce) jar mild taco sauce	Condiments of choice

Brown beef in Dutch oven or electric skillet. Drain, if necessary. Sprinkle in taco seasoning mix and follow package directions for adding water and cooking to make taco filling. Add refried beans and taco sauces. Rinse out jars with ½ cup water and add to meat mixture. Cook and stir until thoroughly heated.

Put servings of tortilla chips on microwave-safe plates and ladle desired amount of beef mixture over chips. Cover with desired amounts of pickled jalapeño slices, chopped onion, sliced ripe olives and shredded Cheddar cheese. Microwave each serving on HIGH 1 to 1½ minutes or until cheese melts. Serve with salsa, guacamole, sour cream and chopped green onions.

Makes 16 servings　　　　　　　　CharLee Bright Hollinger, Westminster, Maryland

Per serving: 496 calories, 30 g fat, 18 g protein, 40 g carbohydrate, 54 mg cholesterol, 1240 mg sodium.

Slow Cooker Taco Soup

Good for Super Bowl parties or a group of hungry skiers!

2 pounds ground beef	2 (14½-ounce) cans sliced stewed tomatoes, undrained
1 cup chopped onion	1 (10-ounce) can diced tomatoes and green chilies, undrained
1 (15-ounce) can chili, no beans	
2 (15-ounce) cans pinto beans, rinsed and drained	1 pound regular or light pasteurized prepared cheese product, cubed
2 cups sour cream	

Brown ground beef and onion in large skillet or Dutch oven. Drain. Transfer to sprayed 6-quart slow cooker. Add chili, beans, sour cream, stewed tomatoes, diced tomatoes and green chilies and cheese. Stir to blend. Cover and cook on LOW 4 hours.[86] Recipe may be halved; cook in sprayed 3- or 4-quart slow cooker on LOW about 3 hours.

Makes 16 servings　　　　　　　　Mary Lee Skourup, Bella Vista, Arkansas

Per serving: 428 calories, 29 g fat, 21 g protein, 18 g carbohydrate, 92 mg cholesterol, 975 mg sodium.

Sloppy Josés

1	pound ground beef	1	(4-ounce) can diced green chiles, undrained
1	teaspoon salt		
½	teaspoon ground cumin	½	cup chopped onion
½	teaspoon dried oregano, crushed	½	cup beer
	Pinch of sugar	1	garlic clove, minced
1	teaspoon beef bouillon granules	1	teaspoon chili powder
1	(16-ounce) can refried beans[19]	8	(8-inch) flour tortillas (soft taco size), or 8 hamburger buns
¾	cup salsa		

Brown ground beef in large skillet. Drain. Mix in salt, cumin, oregano, sugar and bouillon granules. Stir in refried beans, salsa, green chiles, onion, beer, garlic and chili powder. Bring to boil. Reduce heat and simmer uncovered 15 minutes—longer for thicker mixture. Spoon mixture onto warmed tortillas in a line just below center. Fold in sides to partially enclose filling, fold bottom up over part of filling and roll to form tight cylinder. Serve with Spanish Rice, shredded lettuce, salsa and grated cheese, or serve on toasted split buns.

Makes 8 servings   Kaylene Miller, Granby, Colorado

Per serving: 341 calories, 18 g fat, 16 g protein, 30 g carbohydrate, 48 mg cholesterol, 976 mg sodium.

Chicken and Sour Cream Enchiladas

12	corn tortillas	16	ounces Monterey Jack or Cheddar cheese, shredded (4 cups)
1	recipe (4 cups) *Green Chile Sauce, divided,*		
		¼	cup finely chopped onion
3	cups chopped *Easy Cooked Chicken*	2	cups sour cream
			Paprika

Warm tortillas according to package directions. Mix 1 cup *Green Chile Sauce* with chicken in medium bowl. Place ⅓ cup chicken mixture down middle of each tortilla. Roll up and place tortillas seamside down in sprayed 9x13-inch baking dish. Sprinkle with cheese. Mix onion into remaining 3 cups *Green Chile Sauce*. Pour over enchiladas. Bake at 350° for 20 minutes or until hot and bubbly. Remove from oven and spread sour cream over enchiladas. Sprinkle with paprika. Return to oven and bake 10 more minutes. Remove and let stand 5 minutes. Serve with shredded lettuce, salsa, sour cream, *Spanish Rice* and *Refried Beans*.

Makes 6 servings

Per enchilada: 386 calories, 25 g fat, 26 g protein, 17 g carbohydrate, 89 mg cholesterol, 456 mg sodium.

Pork and Sour Cream Enchiladas variation: Substitute 3 cups shredded *Slow-Cooked Pork* for chicken. Continue as directed above.

Fumi's Fajitas Marinade

Fumi Roach is Mary Ann's mother.

½   cup lime juice
1   (12-ounce) can of beer
1   teaspoon garlic powder

¼   cup red wine vinegar
¼   cup vegetable oil

Combine lime juice, beer, garlic powder and vinegar in jar with tight-fitting lid and shake well. Add oil and shake until emulsified. Makes enough marinade for 4 pounds of skirt steak or flank steak. Recipe may be halved.

Makes 2½ cups   **Mary Ann Evans, San Jose, California**

Per ½ cup: 136 calories, 11 g fat, 1 g protein, 6 g carbohydrate, 0 mg cholesterol, 4 mg sodium.

Steak Fajitas

The secret to tender fajitas is a hot fire and short cooking time.

½   recipe *Fumi's Fajitas Marinade*
2   pounds skirt steak or flank steak
2   tablespoons canola oil
2   medium onions, sliced

1   green, ½ yellow and ½ red bell pepper, cut into strips
12   (7-inch) flour tortillas (fajita size) or corn tortillas

Prepare marinade and set aside. Rinse steak and pat dry. Using sharp knife, remove fatty membrane from both sides of steak–very important, or meat will be tough.[31] Place steak in ziptop bag. Add marinade and turn to coat. Marinate skirt steak 20 minutes at room temperature or refrigerate up to 3 hours. Remove 20 minutes before grilling. (Flank steak may be marinated somewhat longer than skirt steak, but marinating overnight may cause flank steak to lose much of its delicious flavor.) Drain on paper towels. Discard marinade.

Set racks close to heat and preheat grill to HOT (see *Grill Tips*). Grill steak 2 to 3 minutes on each side, allowing crust to form. Transfer to cutting board and tent with foil. Let stand 5 to 10 minutes. Thinly slice meat across grain.

Meanwhile, heat oil in large nonstick skillet. Sauté onions and bell peppers over medium heat about 8 minutes or until crisp-tender. Sprinkle with salt and pepper. Warm tortillas, following package directions.

Fill warm tortillas with meat, onions and bell peppers. If desired, add any or all of the following: shredded lettuce, guacamole, shredded Cheddar cheese, salsa, chopped tomato and sour cream. *(Tip: Fold bottom up and sides in over filling; eat from open end–will help prevent dripping.)*

Makes 4 to 6 servings

Per serving of 6: 520 calories, 22 g fat, 36 g protein, 45 g carbohydrate, 77 mg cholesterol, 442 mg sodium.

Green Chile

1	(3-pound) bone in pork shoulder roast		Mexican Seasoning:
1	(14-ounce) can chicken broth	1½	teaspoons garlic salt
1	(14-ounce) can beef broth	1½	teaspoons onion salt
5	cups water, *divided*	1	tablespoon Mexican oregano
4	(4-ounce) cans diced green chiles, undrained	1	tablespoon ground cumin
		¼	cup dried minced onion
½	to 1 (4-ounce) can chopped jalapeños, drained (1 can is hot!)	2	teaspoons beef bouillon granules
		½	cup flour

Remove excess fat from pork. Rinse and put in Dutch oven or large pot with lid. Add broths and bring to boil. Reduce heat and simmer covered 1½ hours or until meat is tender and pulls away from bone. Remove roast to cutting board and cool. Leave liquid in pot. When meat is cool enough to handle, cut into large chunks and pull into ½-inch-wide strips. Cut strips crosswise into 1-inch pieces with kitchen shears. Discard any fat.

Add 2 cups water to liquid in pot. Stir in green chiles, jalapeños and Mexican Seasoning. Return meat and bring mixture to boil. Reduce heat and simmer uncovered 45 minutes, stirring occasionally. Stir in 2 more cups water. Whisk flour and remaining 1 cup water in medium bowl until smooth. Stir into chile. Cook uncovered over low heat 30 minutes, stirring occasionally. Add more water if thick. Season with salt if needed. Serve in bowls with warm flour tortillas or serve over burritos, enchiladas or *Potato Huevos*. Freezes well.

Mexican Seasoning: Blend garlic salt, onion salt, oregano, cumin, dried onion and bouillon granules in small food processor or blender; otherwise, mix in small bowl. Makes about ½ cup.

Makes about 3 quarts

Per cup: 166 calories, 9 g fat, 10 g protein, 11 g carbohydrate, 29 mg cholesterol, 1187 mg sodium.

Potato Huevos

1	recipe *Baked Potato Fries*	8	ounces Cheddar cheese, shredded
4	cups *Green Chile*	8	eggs

Put serving of *Baked Potato Fries* on each of four oblong ovenproof plates. Cover each with 1 cup *Green Chile* and sprinkle with ½ cup Cheddar cheese. Bake at 375° for 7 to 10 minutes or until bubbly and cheese melts. Top each serving with two fried eggs. Serve with warm rolled flour tortillas and salsa.

Makes 4 servings

Per serving: 700 calories, 45 g fat, 39 g protein, 35 g carbohydrate, 526 mg cholesterol, 1779 mg sodium.

Pork and Green Chiles

½ cup flour	3 (4-ounce) cans chopped green chiles, undrained
1 teaspoon chili powder	
1¾ pounds pork shoulder roast, cut into ½-inch cubes	2 to 3 teaspoons ground cumin
	2 teaspoons dried Mexican oregano, crushed
2 tablespoons vegetable oil	
1 cup chopped onion	1 jalapeño, seeded and chopped
2 garlic cloves, minced	1 teaspoon chicken bouillon granules
1 (14-ounce) can chicken broth	
1 (14-ounce) can beef broth	1 teaspoon salt
1 (14½-ounce) can sliced stewed tomatoes, undrained, snipped[73]	⅛ teaspoon pepper
	1 to 2 tablespoons fresh lime juice
½ teaspoon sugar	

Mix flour and chili powder in ziptop bag. Add pork cubes, several at a time, and shake to coat. Transfer to plate without stacking. Set aside. Heat oil in Dutch oven and brown pork in small batches,[84] adding more oil as needed. Drain on paper towels. Pour off any excess fat from pot. Add onion, cook 3 minutes, scraping up brown bits on bottom with spatula (moisture released by onions will help loosen brown bits). Add garlic and cook 30 seconds. Stir in broths and scrape up any remaining bits. Add tomatoes, sugar, green chiles, cumin, oregano, jalapeño, bouillon granules, salt and pepper to pot. Cook over medium heat, stirring until combined. Return pork and bring mixture to boil. Reduce heat and simmer covered 45 minutes or until pork is tender and mixture is thickened, stirring occasionally. Stir in fresh lime juice–very important, gives the "stew" zip. Serve in bowls with warm flour tortillas or *Herb Tortillas*.

Makes 6 to 8 servings

Per serving of 8: 332 calories, 22 g fat, 18 g protein, 12 g carbohydrate, 62 mg cholesterol, 1278 mg sodium.

Chile versus Chili

Chile is the authentic Spanish spelling of the word, and its plural is *chiles*; however, Anglos have changed the word to chili and chilies. Chili is mostly associated with chili con carne, Spanish for "chili with meat." Since most of the cans of chile peppers we researched were spelled *chiles*, except for certain *tomatoes and green chilies*, we have chosen to use the Spanish spelling to avoid confusion.

Chile peppers, whether jalapeños, habaneros, serranos, poblanos, Anaheims, bell peppers or pimientos are all peppers–some are pungent and some are sweet–and they grow green on the plant. They proceed through various stages of yellow, orange, flame red, dark red and brown-red as they ripen.

Posole

A thick, hearty soup traditionally served at Christmastime in Mexico's coastal region.

2	teaspoons vegetable oil	2	teaspoons chili powder
3	cups cubed boneless pork shoulder or Boston butt (¾-inch cubes)	3	(14-ounce) cans chicken broth
		2	teaspoons fresh lime juice
1½	cups chopped onion	1	to 2 teaspoons chicken bouillon granules
2	garlic cloves, minced[20]	3	(14½-ounce) cans white hominy, rinsed and drained
1	teaspoon ground cumin		
1	teaspoon dried Mexican oregano, crushed	1	bay leaf

Heat oil in Dutch oven or soup kettle. Add pork and onion. Cook over medium heat until most moisture evaporates, 10 to 15 minutes. Add garlic, cumin, oregano and chili powder. Cook and stir about 5 minutes, being careful not to burn. Stir in chicken broth, lime juice, bouillon granules, hominy and bay leaf. Bring to boil. Reduce heat and simmer covered 30 to 40 minutes or until tender. Remove bay leaf. If thicker, stew-like consistency is desired, stir 1 tablespoon flour into ¼ cup water in small bowl until flour dissolves. Stir into posole and cook until thickened. Season with salt and pepper. Add additional lime juice, cumin and oregano, if needed. Serve with warm flour tortillas or *Cornbread Muffins*.

Makes 6 to 8 servings

Per serving of 8: 304 calories, 10 g fat, 21 g protein, 33 g carbohydrate, 43 mg cholesterol, 909 mg sodium.

Quick Posole variation: Sauté onion in 2 teaspoons oil 3 minutes over medium heat. Add garlic, cumin, oregano and chili powder. Cook 1 more minute. Add 3 cups leftover pork, turkey or chicken, stirring until coated. Stir in chicken broth, lime juice, bouillon granules, hominy and bay leaf. Bring to boil. Simmer covered about 15 minutes. Remove bay leaf and check seasoning. Thicken, if desired. Serve as directed above.

Green Chile Casserole

2 (4-ounce) cans whole green chiles	3 eggs
2 tablespoons butter, melted	½ teaspoon salt
8 ounces Mexican-style four cheese, or shredded Monterey Jack and Cheddar cheese (2 cups)	2 cups milk
	1 cup buttermilk baking mix

Cut green chiles open. Rinse, removing any seeds. Drain on paper towels. Coat 7x11-inch baking dish with melted butter. Place chiles in baking dish, covering bottom as evenly as possible. Sprinkle with cheese. Whisk eggs, salt, milk and baking mix in medium bowl until just combined. Pour over cheese. Bake at 350° for 45 to 50 minutes or until sharp knife inserted in center comes out clean. Let stand 10 minutes before serving. Cut into squares and serve with salsa.

Makes 6 servings   Sandra Travis, Bella Vista, Arkansas

Per serving: 319 calories, 20 g fat, 15 g protein, 20 g carbohydrate, 154 mg cholesterol, 982 mg sodium.

Green Chile and Chicken Casserole variation: Place chiles in prepared dish. Sprinkle with half the cheese and cover with 2 cups bite-size *Easy Cooked Chicken*. Sprinkle 3 tablespoons chopped green onion and one 2¼-ounce can ripe olives, drained, over chicken. Sprinkle with remaining cheese and pour milk mixture over cheese. Bake as directed above. Serve with salsa.

Makes 6 servings

Per serving: 411 calories, 23 g fat, 29 g protein, 22 g carbohydrate, 197 mg cholesterol, 1255 mg sodium.

Huevos Rancheros

2 cups *Easy Red Chile Sauce*	4 corn tortillas
4 eggs	½ cup shredded Cheddar cheese

Preheat oven to 375°. Bring chile sauce to simmer in 12-inch nonstick skillet. Break one egg at a time into custard cup or saucer and slide into sauce without breaking yolk. Simmer covered over very low heat 5 to 7 minutes or until whites are set and yolks begin to thicken, spooning sauce over yolks occasionally. Wrap tortillas in foil and warm along with two ovenproof serving plates 5 minutes. Remove and set oven to BROIL.[13] Spoon 2 tablespoons sauce onto each plate and cover with two warm tortillas. Top each tortilla with a poached egg. Cover with additional sauce and sprinkle with shredded cheese. Broil in upper third of oven until cheese melts. Serve with *Fried Potatoes* and *Refried Beans*.

Makes 2 servings

Per serving: 413 calories, 25 g fat, 23 g protein, 24 g carbohydrate, 461 mg cholesterol, 585 mg sodium.

Red Chile Sauce

A spicy hot sauce, especially if you use the larger amounts of spices.

2 tablespoons vegetable or olive oil	½ teaspoon dried Mexican oregano, crushed
½ cup finely chopped celery	1 teaspoon salt
½ cup finely chopped bell pepper	¼ to ½ teaspoon black pepper
1 cup finely chopped onion	2½ cups water, *divided*
1 garlic clove, minced	2 teaspoons chicken bouillon granules
½ to 1 tablespoon chili powder	1 teaspoon beef bouillon granules
1 tablespoon paprika	2 plum tomatoes, seeded[53] and diced
⅛ to ¼ teaspoon cayenne pepper	Pinch of sugar
½ teaspoon ground cumin, or ¼ teaspoon ground cumin and ¼ teaspoon whole cumin seeds, crushed[21]	1 tablespoon flour

Heat oil in medium saucepan and sauté celery, bell pepper and onion over medium heat until tender, about 3 minutes. Remove from heat. Stir in garlic, chili powder, paprika, cayenne pepper, cumin, oregano, salt and black pepper. Return to heat and cook 30 seconds, stirring constantly to blend flavors.

Boil 2 cups water in small saucepan or microwave in 2-cup glass measure. Stir in chicken and beef bouillon granules. Stir into sautéed vegetables along with tomatoes and sugar. Simmer covered about 25 minutes. Mix remaining ½ cup water with flour in small bowl and stir into sauce. Cook over medium heat 8 to 10 minutes or until thickened, stirring frequently. May refrigerate for later use; reheat before serving. Serve over burritos or use in ***Huevos Rancheros***.

Makes 4 cups

Per ¼ cup: 26 calories, 2 g fat, 1 g protein, 2 g carbohydrate, 0 mg cholesterol, 234 mg sodium.

Easy Red Chile Sauce

¼ cup finely chopped onion
¼ cup finely chopped celery
2 tablespoons vegetable oil
3 tablespoons flour
1 teaspoon dried Mexican
   oregano, crushed
1 teaspoon chili powder
1 teaspoon ground cumin

Dash of cayenne pepper
½ teaspoon garlic salt
2½ cups water, *divided*
1 teaspoon beef bouillon granules
   Pinch of sugar
1 (8-ounce) can tomato sauce
½ teaspoon vinegar

Sauté onion and celery in oil in medium saucepan until tender, about 3 minutes. Mix flour, oregano, chili powder, cumin, cayenne pepper and garlic salt in small bowl. Add and stir into sautéed vegetables. Stir in 2 cups water. Add bouillon granules, sugar and tomato sauce. Rinse can with remaining ½ cup water and add to pan. Mix well. Bring to boil. Reduce heat and simmer covered 15 to 20 minutes or until thickened. Stir in vinegar. Serve over beef or pork burritos and enchiladas, or use in *Huevos Rancheros*. Sauce may be made ahead. Refrigerate.

*Note: You may substitute 3 teaspoons **Southwest Seasoning** for the oregano, chili powder, cumin, cayenne pepper and garlic salt.*

Makes 2½ cups

Per 2 tablespoons: 20 calories, 1 g fat,1 g protein, 2 g carbohydrate, 0 mg cholesterol, 86 mg sodium.

Green Chile Sauce

2 cups water
3 to 4 teaspoons chicken
   bouillon granules
¼ cup vegetable oil
1 cup finely chopped onion
2 garlic cloves, minced
¼ teaspoon ground cumin

¼ teaspoon pepper
¼ teaspoon dried Mexican
   oregano, crushed
½ teaspoon salt
3 tablespoons flour
3 (4-ounce) cans diced green chiles,
   undrained

Bring water to boil in small saucepan, or microwave in 2-cup glass measure. Stir in bouillon granules and set aside. Heat oil in medium saucepan and sauté onion over medium heat about 5 minutes. Add garlic and cook about 2 more minutes. Stir in cumin, pepper, oregano, salt and flour. Cook and stir 1 minute (mixture will ball up). Pour in bouillon mixture. Cook and whisk until thick. Stir in green chiles and bring to boil. Reduce heat and simmer uncovered 7 to 10 minutes or until thickened, stirring frequently. Recipe may be halved.

Makes 4 cups

Per cup: 172 calories, 14 g fat, 1 g protein, 10 g carbohydrate, 0 mg cholesterol, 577 mg sodium.

Summer Squash Enchiladas

Cheese Sauce:
2 tablespoons butter
2 tablespoons flour
1¼ cups milk
1 teaspoon chicken bouillon granules
2 teaspoons chili powder
¼ teaspoon salt
⅛ teaspoon pepper
4 ounces Pepper Jack or Monterey Jack cheese, shredded (1 cup)
½ (4-ounce) can diced green chiles, undrained

Filling:
1 tablespoon vegetable oil

¾ cup chopped onion
2 garlic cloves, minced
3 cups chopped yellow summer squash
¼ teaspoon salt
Pinch of sugar
½ (4-ounce) can diced green chiles, undrained
8 (8-inch) flour tortillas (soft taco size)
1 cup chopped fresh tomatoes
2 tablespoons snipped flat-leaf parsley leaves

Cheese Sauce: Melt butter in small saucepan over medium heat. Sprinkle in flour. Cook and stir about 1 minute. Add milk, bouillon granules, chili powder, salt and pepper. Cook until thickened, stirring occasionally. Stir in cheese and green chiles until cheese melts. (Makes 1½ cups.)

Filling: Heat oil in large nonstick skillet over medium heat and sauté onion until clear, about 3 minutes. Add garlic and cook 30 seconds. Stir in squash. Sprinkle with salt and sugar. Cover and cook 5 minutes, stirring occasionally. Drain. Stir in green chiles and ½ cup Cheese Sauce. Adjust seasoning if needed.

Spoon ½ cup filling down middle of each tortilla. Roll up and place tortillas seamside down in sprayed 7x11-inch baking dish. Spoon remaining 1 cup Cheese Sauce over enchiladas. Bake covered at 400° for 25 minutes. Remove from oven and sprinkle tomatoes across middle of enchiladas. Sprinkle parsley over tomatoes. Return to oven and bake uncovered 5 more minutes. Let stand 10 minutes before serving. Serve with *Savory Grilled Chicken* and *Almond Citrus Salad*.

Makes 6 to 8 servings   Wendy Hatcher, Bella Vista, Arkansas

Per serving of 8: 246 calories, 12 g fat, 9 g protein, 26 g carbohydrate, 25 mg cholesterol, 443 mg sodium.

Use of Flour Tortillas in Enchiladas

When making enchiladas with flour tortillas, use the thinner 8-inch soft-taco-size tortilla instead of the thicker 7-inch fajita-size. The thicker 7-inch tortillas may leave the enchiladas with a doughy taste.

Spanish Rice

3 tablespoons canola oil, *divided*
1 cup long-grain white rice
½ cup chopped onion
½ cup chopped bell pepper
1 garlic clove, minced
2 cups water
1 teaspoon chili powder

3 teaspoons chicken bouillon granules
1 (14½-ounce) can stewed tomatoes, undrained, snipped[73]
½ teaspoon salt
¼ teaspoon pepper

Heat 2 tablespoons oil in medium saucepan. Add rice and cook over medium heat 3 to 4 minutes or until lightly browned, stirring to prevent sticking. Mix in remaining 1 tablespoon oil, onion and bell pepper. Cook 2 to 3 more minutes or until vegetables are tender. Stir in garlic, water, chili powder, bouillon granules, tomatoes, salt and pepper. Bring to boil. Reduce heat and simmer covered 20 to 30 minutes or until rice is tender and liquid is absorbed.

Makes 4 to 6 servings

Per serving of 6: 208 calories, 7 g fat, 3 g protein, 28 g carbohydrate, 0 mg cholesterol, 716 mg sodium.

Refried Beans

1 tablespoon bacon drippings or vegetable oil
½ cup chopped onion
1 garlic clove, minced

1 (16-ounce) can refried beans[19]
2 ounces Cheddar cheese, shredded (½ cup)

Heat bacon drippings in medium iron skillet or other heavy skillet. Sauté onion until lightly browned, about 3 minutes. Add garlic and cook 30 seconds. Stir beans well in can, then stir into onion and garlic. Season with salt and pepper and sprinkle with shredded cheese. Bake in 375° oven until cheese melts.

Makes about 2 cups

Per ½ cup: 183 calories, 10 g fat, 9 g protein, 18 g carbohydrate, 18 mg cholesterol, 544 mg sodium.

Note: If using refried beans in burritos or enchiladas, prepare through seasoning with salt and pepper, omit cheese and heat on top of stove.

Jalapeño Cornbread

¼	cup vegetable oil	2	eggs, lightly beaten	
1	cup yellow cornmeal	1	cup sour cream* or buttermilk[42]	
1	cup flour	1	(8¼-ounce) can cream-style corn	
¼	teaspoon garlic powder	1	tablespoon chopped fresh	
1	tablespoon baking powder		jalapeño,[44] seeded for less heat	
1	teaspoon baking soda*	2	ounces sharp Cheddar cheese,	
1	teaspoon salt		shredded (½ cup)	
2	tablespoons sugar			

Pour oil into 10-inch well-seasoned iron skillet and heat in 425° oven until oil is very hot, about 5 minutes.

Whisk cornmeal, flour, garlic powder, baking powder, baking soda, salt and sugar in large bowl. Whisk eggs and sour cream together in separate bowl and mix in corn, jalapeño and cheese. Stir into cornmeal mixture until just combined—do not overmix.

Remove skillet from oven and pour hot oil into batter. Mix until oil is just incorporated. Pour batter into skillet. Return to oven and bake at 425° for 30 to 35 minutes or until golden. Let stand in skillet 5 to 10 minutes. Remove and cut into wedges. Serve with *Easy Beans and Ham* or *Posole*.

* Milk may be substituted for sour cream or buttermilk—omit baking soda.

Makes 8 servings

Per serving: 283 calories, 12 g fat, 8 g protein, 36 g carbohydrate, 65 mg cholesterol, 494 mg sodium.

Jalapeño Cornbread Muffins variation: Do not heat oil; mix into eggs and sour cream with corn, jalapeño and cheese. Continue as directed above for combining cornbread mixture. Fill sprayed muffin cups ⅔ full. Bake at 425° for 15 to 20 minutes. Alternatively, fill sprayed miniature muffin cups three-fourths full and bake at 400° for 15 to 20 minutes or until golden. (Fill any empty muffin cups half-full with water before baking.) Serve warm.

Makes 16 regular or 42 mini muffins

Per regular muffin: 142 calories, 6 g fat, 4 g protein, 18 g carbohydrate, 33 mg cholesterol, 247 mg sodium.

Chipotle Cranberry Compote

1½ cups water	1 tablespoon finely chopped shallots or green onions
1 (6-ounce) package dried cranberries (about 1½ cups)	¼ teaspoon minced ginger root, or ¼ teaspoon ground fresh ginger*
1 small or medium chipotle^G pepper in adobo sauce, or to taste, finely chopped	½ teaspoon dried thyme, crushed
⅓ cup brandy	2 tablespoons butter
½ cup packed brown sugar¹	¼ cup chopped toasted pecans (optional)
⅓ cup fresh lemon juice	

Bring water to boil in medium saucepan. Add cranberries. Remove from heat and allow cranberries to reconstitute 10 minutes, stirring occasionally. Add chipotle pepper, brandy, brown sugar, lemon juice, shallots, ginger and thyme. Simmer uncovered about 20 minutes. Remove from heat and stir in butter and pecans. Add salt if needed. Let stand 10 minutes. Refrigerate or freeze in covered container. Serve with turkey, ham or lamb.

Jars of fresh ground ginger can be found in produce section of supermarket.

Makes 2 cups

Per 2 tablespoons: 58 calories, 1 g fat, 0 g protein, 9 g carbohydrate, 4 mg cholesterol, 18 mg sodium.

Chipotle Cranberry Sauce variation: Pour *Chipotle Cranberry Compote* without pecans into food processor or blender. Pulse to desired consistency. Stir in pecans, if desired. Refrigerate in covered container. For appetizer, warm and serve over cream cheese with crackers.

About Chipotle Peppers

Chipotle peppers are dried jalapeño peppers that have been smoked. They are available dried whole, powdered and pickled.

Chipotle peppers are also available canned in adobo sauce. Adobo sauce is a combination of tomato sauce or puree, vinegar and spices. Sometimes ground ancho peppers (dried pablanos) are added. You may use the canned peppers, the sauce, or both in recipes. Peppers are quite hot, so start with a small amount and add more, if desired. You may prefer to rinse peppers before chopping and adding to recipes. Remaining peppers and sauce may be frozen in covered containers.

Flan de Coco

2 tablespoons water	Dash of salt
1 cup sugar, *divided*	1 cup frozen shredded
1 cup heavy cream	unsweetened coconut*
1¼ cups milk	3 eggs plus 3 egg yolks

Heat water in small saucepan and add ½ cup sugar. Stir over low heat until sugar dissolves. Increase heat and cook without stirring until syrup turns a caramel color, swirling pan occasionally, being careful not to burn. Pour syrup quickly into sprayed 9-inch metal ring mold and tilt to coat sides (use oven mitts). Cool.

Combine cream, milk, salt and coconut in saucepan. Bring to boil. Remove from heat and let stand 30 minutes. Pour mixture through strainer into large bowl, pressing coconut against sides of strainer. Discard coconut. Return liquid to saucepan and heat until almost scalded.ᴳ Beat eggs and egg yolks in medium bowl with mixer and add remaining ½ cup sugar. Beat until light and fluffy. Gradually add coconut liquid, stirring constantly to prevent curdling. Pour mixture through strainer into mold.

Fold a kitchen towel and place in 9x13-inch baking pan. Place ring mold on towel, extend middle oven rack and put pan on rack. Pour very hot water into baking pan to about 1 inch up sides of mold. Bake at 325° for 40 minutes or until knife inserted in center of flan comes out clean–do not overbake (flan will continue to set up as it cools). Cool completely on rack. Place plastic wrap directly on surface of flan and refrigerate overnight.

Run spatula around edge of mold. Place serving plate over mold and invert, shaking gently to release flan. Remove mold, allowing caramel syrup to run down sides of flan. Spoon servings into dessert dishes and serve with lightly whipped cream. Garnish with fresh mint.

* *Frozen shredded coconut can be found in freezer section of supermarket.*

Makes 10 servings   Miriam Chiarello, Bella Vista, Arkansas

Per serving: 220 calories, 13 g fat, 4 g protein, 23 g carbohydrate, 165 mg cholesterol, 45 mg sodium.

Pies & Pastries

Pies and Cobblers

Meringues for Pies and Desserts

Pie Crusts

Pastries

Lattice-Top Apple Pie

The nutmeg adds wonderful flavor.

3	pounds Golden Delicious apples	⅛	teaspoon ground nutmeg
⅔	cup plus 1 tablespoon sugar	⅛	teaspoon salt
¼	cup packed light brown sugar[1]	1	tablespoon fresh lemon juice*
2	tablespoons flour	2	(9-inch) unbaked pie crusts
1	teaspoon grated lemon zest*	1	to 2 tablespoons butter
⅛	teaspoon ground cinnamon		Egg wash[30] or milk

Core, peel and cut apples lengthwise into ¼-inch-thick slices (about 8 cups). Put in large bowl of cold lemon water.[7] Mix ⅔ cup sugar, brown sugar, flour, lemon zest, cinnamon, nutmeg and salt in separate large bowl. Drain apples and pat dry. Stir into sugar mixture. Mix in lemon juice. Let stand 30 minutes.

Line 9-inch pie plate with one crust, allowing ½- to ¾-inch overhang. Mound apples in center and dot with butter. Moisten edges of crust with egg wash or water. Cut remaining crust into twelve 1-inch-wide strips. Arrange six strips across pie and place six strips diagonally across first strips to form a lattice. Trim *strips* even with rim of pie plate and gently press ends into bottom crust. Fold extended bottom crust up and over ends of lattice strips. Flute rim, making raised crust to help contain bubbling juices. Brush lattice top with egg wash or milk and sprinkle with 1 tablespoon sugar.[30]

Place pie in lower third of 400° oven and bake 10 minutes. Reduce heat to 375° and bake 1 hour 20 minutes or until crust is golden and thick juices bubble through lattice. Cover edges with foil[17] or tent whole pie if browning too fast. Remove to rack. Cool uncovered at least 1 hour.

* Grate zest from whole lemon. Squeeze 1 tablespoon juice for the pie and squeeze remaining juice for lemon water.

Makes 8 servings

Per serving: 533 calories, 28 g fat, 5 g protein, 66 g carbohydrate, 6 mg cholesterol, 461 mg sodium.

Sour Cream Apple Pie

2	medium Golden Delicious, Jonathan or MacIntosh apples
¾	cup sugar
2	tablespoons flour
⅛	teaspoon salt
1	cup sour cream (light is okay)
1	egg, lightly beaten
1	teaspoon grated lemon zest

½	teaspoon vanilla extract
1	(9-inch) unbaked pie crust

Crumb Topping:

⅓	cup sugar
⅓	cup flour
½	to 1 teaspoon ground cinnamon
¼	cup (½ stick) cold butter, cubed

Peel, core and cut apples into wedges (apple wedger works well). Put in bowl of lemon water.[7] Whisk sugar, flour and salt in large bowl. Beat in sour cream, egg, lemon zest and vanilla with mixer until smooth. Drain apple wedges and pat dry; cut crosswise into ½-inch pieces (about 2½ cups). Stir into sour cream mixture. Pour filling into crust and bake at 425° for 15 minutes (cover edges with foil if browning too fast[17]). Meanwhile, prepare Crumb Topping.

Remove pie from oven and reduce oven temperature to 325°. Sprinkle Crumb Topping over pie and return to oven. Cover edges and bake 30 more minutes. Remove to rack and cool completely. Serve with small slices of sharp Cheddar cheese.

Crumb Topping: Combine sugar, flour and cinnamon in medium bowl. Cut cold butter into flour mixture with pastry blender until crumbly.

Makes 6 servings   Sandra Travis, Bella Vista, Arkansas

Per serving: 419 calories, 18 g fat, 5 g protein, 63 g carbohydrate, 59 mg cholesterol, 338 mg sodium.

Chess Pie

Eleanor says, "This is an old, old recipe—easy and loved by all."

½	cup (1 stick) butter
1½	cups sugar
1	tablespoon flour
1	tablespoon cornmeal
¼	teaspoon salt

3	eggs, lightly beaten
1	teaspoon vanilla extract
1	tablespoon white vinegar
1	(9-inch) unbaked pie crust

Melt butter in medium saucepan. Remove from heat. Whisk sugar, flour, cornmeal and salt in medium bowl and stir into butter. Whisk in eggs, vanilla and vinegar. Pour filling into crust. Bake at 350° for 15 minutes. Reduce heat to 300° and bake 45 more minutes. Remove to rack and cool completely.

Makes 6 to 8 servings   Eleanor Weathersby, Dawsonville, Georgia

Per serving of 8: 383 calories, 19 g fat, 4 g protein, 50 g carbohydrates, 111 mg cholesterol, 352 mg sodium.

Easy Apple Pie

2   (20-ounce) cans sliced pie apples (not pie filling), drained and rinsed
¾   to 1 cup sugar
2   tablespoons flour
1   teaspoon ground cinnamon
¼   teaspoon ground nutmeg
     Dash of salt
1   (15-ounce) package refrigerated pie crusts
2   tablespoons butter
     Additional sugar

Whisk sugar, flour, cinnamon, nutmeg and salt in large bowl; mix in apples. Set aside 5 to 10 minutes. Place one crust in 9-inch glass pie plate and fill with apple mixture. Dot with butter. Cover filling with remaining crust and flute edges. Make five slits in top crust and sprinkle with sugar. Alternatively, cut second crust into strips, form a lattice top (see *Lattice-Top Apple Pie*) and sprinkle with sugar.[30] Bake at 400° for 45 to 50 minutes. Cover edges with foil[17] if beginning to brown too fast, and reduce temperature to 375°.

Makes 8 servings   Fletcher Bell, Lawrence, Kansas

Per serving: 218 calories, 8 g fat, 1 g protein, 35 g carbohydrate, 19 mg cholesterol, 104 mg sodium.

Strawberry Rhubarb Pie

1   pint fresh strawberries
1   pound fresh rhubarb
1⅓ cups sugar
⅓   cup flour
2   (9-inch) unbaked pie crusts
1   tablespoon butter
      Milk
      Additional sugar

Remove caps, rinse and cut strawberries in half. Trim, rinse and cut rhubarb into ½-inch pieces (slit broad stalks lengthwise before cutting) . Mix sugar and flour in large bowl. Add strawberries and rhubarb. Let stand 30 minutes.

Line 9-inch glass pie plate with one crust, allowing ½- to ¾-inch overhang. Pour strawberry-rhubarb mixture into crust, mounding in center. Dot with butter. Moisten edges of bottom crust with cold water. Cut second crust into nine 1-inch wide strips. Arrange five strips ½ inch apart over filling. Place remaining strips at right angles over first strips to make a lattice. Trim ends of strips even with rim of pie plate and gently press ends into bottom crust. Fold extended bottom crust up and over ends of lattice strips and decoratively crimp edge of crust. Lightly brush lattice top with milk and sprinkle with sugar.[30] Bake at 400° for 50 minutes or until crust is golden and thick juices bubble through lattice. Cover edges with foil if beginning to brown too fast,[17] or tent whole pie with foil. Cool uncovered on rack. Serve with ice cream.

Makes 8 servings

Per serving: 380 calories, 14 g fat, 4 g protein, 62 g carbohydrate, 4 mg cholesterol, 308 mg sodium.

Raisin Crème Pie

Jo's mother-in-law, Mimi, was a tremendous cook. She approached cooking as an art, not a science. Her Raisin Crème Pie was made with "a pinch, a lump, a scoop, or just enough." She died before Jo could nail down the measurements. After several tries Jo arrived at this version.

1½ cups raisins	3 tablespoons evaporated milk or heavy cream
1 cup water	
½ cup (1 stick) butter	¾ teaspoon vanilla extract
3 eggs, lightly beaten	1 (9-inch) unbaked pie crust
1½ cups sugar	Ground nutmeg

Put raisins and water in medium saucepan and simmer 8 to 10 minutes; do not drain. While hot, add butter and stir until melted. Allow mixture to cool (raisins will absorb most of liquid). Whisk eggs, sugar, evaporated milk and vanilla in medium bowl and stir into raisins. Pour mixture into crust and sprinkle with nutmeg. Bake in lower third of oven at 350° for 47 to 50 minutes or until center is almost firm. If browning too fast, cover edges with foil.[17] Transfer to rack. Cool *completely* before serving.

Makes 8 servings   Jo Bain, Bella Vista, Arkansas

Per serving: 365 calories, 14 g fat, 4 g protein, 60 g carbohydrate, 83 mg cholesterol, 167 mg sodium.

Carolina Peach Pie Filling

Lois lives in a peach-growing area. In the summer she makes and freezes pie filling for making pies later. "Best peach pie I've ever had," she says.

5 cups peeled[35] and sliced fresh peaches	1 cup packed brown sugar[1]
	⅓ cup flour
1 tablesoon fresh lemon juice	1 (15-ounce) package refrigerated pie crusts
1 teaspoon almond extract	

Put peaches in large bowl. Add lemon juice (keeps peaches from turning brown) and almond extract. Whisk brown sugar and flour together in a bowl and add to peaches. Mix well. Line 9-inch deep-dish pie plate with one crust. Pour in filling. Make a lattice top with remaining crust (see **Lattice-Top Apple Pie**), or bake without a top crust. Bake at 400° for 1 hour. If browning too fast, lower temperature to 375° and cover edges with foil.[17] Serve with ice cream.

Makes 6 to 8 servings   Lois Dole, West End, North Carolina

Per serving of 8: 270 calories, 6 g fat, 3 g protein, 53 g carbohydrate, 0 mg cholesterol, 157 mg sodium.

Lenore's Peach Pie

Crust:
1½ cups flour
½ teaspoon salt
¼ cup butter
¼ cup shortening
2 teaspoons lemon zest (optional)
3 tablespoons cold water
1 tablespoon fresh lemon juice

Filling:
4 cups peeled[35] and sliced peaches

½ cup sugar
2 tablespoons brown sugar
1 tablespoon cornstarch
1½ teaspoons ground cinnamon
½ teaspoon ground cloves

1 tablespoon butter
1 egg white, lightly beaten
1 teaspoon sugar

Crust: Mix flour and salt in large bowl. Cut ¼ cup butter and shortening into flour with pastry blender until resembling coarse crumbs. Mix in lemon zest. Combine water and lemon juice in small bowl. Add to flour mixture, a tablespoon at a time, stirring with fork until mixture clings together (add 1 teaspoon more water at a time if dry). Form dough into ball. Divide in half and make two thick disks. Wrap each disk in plastic and refrigerate 1 hour.

Filling: Mix peaches, sugars, cornstarch, cinnamon and cloves in large bowl.

Roll out one disk of dough to 12-inch circle. Place in 9-inch pie plate, allowing ½- to ¾-inch overhang. Roll out other disk to 12-inch circle for top crust. Pour filling into crust and dot with butter. Moisten edges of bottom crust with water. Cover with second crust. Seal and flute edges. Cut five 1-inch slits in top crust. Alternatively, make lattice crust—see *Lattice-Top Apple Pie*. Brush with egg white and sprinkle with sugar.[30] Bake at 375° for 40 to 50 minutes. Cool on rack.

Makes 8 servings   Lenore Diem, Bella Vista, Arkansas

Per serving: 218 calories, 8 g fat, 2 g protein, 36 g carbohydrate, 12 mg cholesterol, 91 mg sodium.

Mud Pie

Our friend, George Forsyth, really loves this pie! What's not to love?

½ gallon coffee ice cream
1 (9-inch) chocolate-wafer pie crust
¼ cup purchased fudge topping

Whipped cream
½ cup toasted sliced almonds

Soften ice cream just enough to spread. Spoon ice cream into crust and smooth surface. Freeze until firm. Drizzle fudge topping over pie and freeze again. Remove and slice. Top servings with whipped cream and sprinkle with toasted almonds.

Makes 8 servings

Per serving: 523 calories, 76 g fat, 9 g protein, 60 g carbohydrate, 61 mg cholesterol, 316 mg sodium.

Old-Fashioned Peach Cobbler

1	recipe *Double Cobbler Crust*, or 1 (15-ounce) package refrigerated pie crusts	1	cup packed light brown sugar[1]
4	cups peeled[35] and sliced fresh peaches (about 3 pounds)	½	teaspoon ground nutmeg
		½	teaspoon ground cinnamon
			Dash of salt
¼	cup fresh lemon juice	2	tablespoons flour
½	cup orange juice	⅛	teaspoon almond extract
½	cup (1 stick) butter, cubed	½	teaspoon vanilla extract
1	cup plus 1 tablespoon sugar		Egg wash[30] or milk

Roll out one portion of cobbler crust dough or one refrigerated pie crust on lightly floured surface with floured rolling pin to 11x14-inch rectangle. Fold dough in half and lift carefully with both hands underneath; lay folded edge across middle of sprayed 9x13-inch baking dish and unfold. Pat into bottom and halfway up sides of dish without stretching. Refrigerate 10 minutes. Prick crust with fork in several places. Bake at 375° for 10 minutes (crust should look done but not brown). Meanwhile, prepare peaches.

Put peaches, lemon juice, orange juice and butter in large saucepan. Cook over medium-low heat until butter melts. Remove from heat. Whisk 1 cup sugar, brown sugar, nutmeg, cinnamon, salt and flour in large bowl and stir into peaches. Stir in almond and vanilla extracts. Set aside.

Roll out remaining portion of dough or pie crust to 11x14-inch rectangle. Cut into ten to twelve 1-inch wide strips. Pour peaches into prepared bottom crust (okay if liquid rises above crust). Lay five longest strips lengthwise over peaches. Place shorter strips across long strips at an angle to form a lattice (if pieces break, just overlap or piece together). Use all the dough, putting some in corners or wherever you can find space (makes cobbler good). Brush lattice with egg wash or milk and sprinkle with 1 tablespoon sugar. Bake at 375° for 40 minutes or until top is golden brown and thick juices bubble through lattice. Remove and let stand until warm. Serve with vanilla ice cream.

Makes 10 servings

Per serving: 619 calories, 33 g fat, 4 g protein, 79 g carbohydrate, 52 mg cholesterol, 446 mg sodium.

Blueberry Cobbler variation: Substitute 5 cups fresh blueberries for peaches, use 2 tablespoons lemon juice, ¼ cup orange juice and 3 tablespoons flour. Omit almond extract. Continue as directed above, using remaining ingredients.

Fried Apricot Pies

2 cups dried apricots, or 1 cup dried apricots and 1 cup dried peaches
½ to ¾ cup sugar
1 tablespoon butter
½ teaspoon ground cinnamon
Dash of ground nutmeg
Dash of salt
1 (15-ounce) package refrigerated pie crusts
½ cup canola, safflower or vegetable oil
Confectioners' sugar

Snip fruit into smaller pieces if large. Put in medium saucepan and add just enough water to cover. Bring to boil. Reduce heat and simmer covered 30 minutes or until very tender, stirring occasionally. Remove cover and cook until water evaporates. Puree apricots in blender or use handheld blender (could also mash with potato masher). Blend in sugar, butter, cinnamon, nutmeg and salt.

Working with one crust at a time, roll out to 14-inch circle on lightly floured surface. Cut seven 4-inch circles from each crust (a lid from 16-ounce carton of sour cream works well, or use small saucer as guide). Combine remaining dough scraps from both crusts and roll out to cut two more circles, making a total of sixteen circles.

Place heaping tablespoon of filling in center of each circle. Dip index finger in water and moisten edges. Fold circle in half and press edges together with fingers to seal. Make decorative edge by pressing with fork. Prick tops in about three places to let steam escape–important.

Heat oil in large nonstick skillet over medium-high heat–not too hot or crusts will burn before cooking. Cook several pies at a time about 45 seconds on each side or until golden brown. Drain on paper towels. Sprinkle with confectioners' sugar.

Makes 16 fried pies   Carol Harrison, Bella Vista, Arkansas

Per pie: 216 calories, 10 g fat, 1 g protein, 32 g carbohydrate, 0 mg cholesterol, 121 mg sodium.

French Strawberry Glacé Pie

Glacé:
6 cups small strawberries, *divided*
1 cup water, *divided*
1 cup sugar
3 tablespoons cornstarch
Dash of salt

2 teaspoons fresh lemon juice
2 or 3 drops red food coloring (optional)
3 ounces cream cheese, softened
1 (9-inch) *Prebaked Pie Crust*

Glacé: Rinse strawberries and remove caps. Drain on paper towels. Mash enough strawberries to measure 1 cup (food chopper works well). Combine with ⅔ cup water in medium saucepan and bring to boil. Reduce heat and simmer 3 minutes. Whisk sugar and cornstarch in medium bowl and mix in remaining ⅓ cup water. Stir into strawberries and cook over medium heat, stirring constantly until clear and thickened. Stir in salt, lemon juice and food coloring. Cool.

Stir cream cheese in small bowl until smooth. Spread over bottom of cooled pie crust with back of spoon. Place remaining whole strawberries, points upward, over cream cheese with larger ones in center and smaller ones outside. (If only large strawberries are available, cut in half and arrange in circles with tips pointing toward center.) Carefully spoon Glacé over strawberries. Refrigerate until firm. Serve with sweetened whipped cream.

Strawberry Tart variation: Omit cream cheese. Coat bottom of crust with Glacé to "waterproof" it. Allow to dry. Line crust with whole strawberries. Spoon Glacé over strawberries. Continue as directed above.

Makes 6 servings   Roberta McKay, Bella Vista, Arkansas

Per serving: 368 calories, 14 g fat, 4 g protein, 60 g carbohydrate, 16 mg cholesterol, 240 mg sodium.

Perfect Pumpkin Pie

1 cup packed light brown sugar[1]
1 tablespoon flour
1 tablespoon pumpkin pie spice
1 (12-ounce) can evaporated milk

1 (15-ounce) can pumpkin
1 egg, lightly beaten
½ teaspoon salt
1 (9-inch) unbaked pie crust

Whisk brown sugar, flour and pumpkin pie spice in large bowl. Whisk in evaporated milk, pumpkin, egg and salt until smooth. Pour mixture into crust. Bake at 375° for 55 to 60 minutes or until sharp knife inserted near center comes out clean. If edges brown too fast, tent pie with foil, being careful not to let foil touch filling. Cool on rack before serving.

Makes 8 servings   Katherine Forsyth, Boulder, Colorado

Per serving: 293 calories, 8 g fat, 4 g protein, 44 g carbohydrate, 32 mg cholesterol, 314 mg sodium.

Pecan Pie

1	teaspoon flour	1	teaspoon vanilla extract
1	tablespoon water	¼	teaspoon salt
¼	cup (½ stick) butter, softened	⅔	cup heavy dark corn syrup[16]
⅔	cup sugar	1	(9-inch) *cold* unbaked pie crust
3	eggs, lightly beaten	40	to 45 toasted pecan halves[10]

Mix flour and water in small bowl. Set aside. Beat butter and sugar in medium bowl with mixer until creamed, about 2 minutes. Scrape down sides occasionally. Add eggs, flour mixture, vanilla and salt. Beat until just combined. Pour in syrup and beat until smooth and caramel colored, about 30 seconds. Pour filling into crust. Arrange pecan halves in circles on top, starting at outside edge. Bake at 375° for 5 minutes. Reduce heat to 325° and bake 45 to 50 more minutes or until center is just firm. If edges brown too fast, cover with foil.[17] Cool completely on rack before serving.

Makes 8 servings   Audrey Ward, Burlington, North Carolina

Per serving: 464 calories, 27 g fat, 5 g protein, 49 g carbohydrate, 81 g cholesterol, 337 mg sodium.

Macadamia Nut Pie variation: After blending in syrup, stir in 2 tablespoons coffee-flavored liqueur. Substitute 1¼ cups chopped macadamia nuts for pecan halves, folding into filling. Bake at 375° for 5 minutes. Reduce heat to 325° and bake 50 to 55 more minutes.

Easy Cherry Cobbler

My brother, Lawrence Rabb, loves cherry pie and cherry cobbler. This cobbler is so easy, he whips one up in no time.

2	tablespoons flour	¾	to 1 cup sugar
1	(16-ounce) can tart pie cherries, drained, reserve juice	1	(9-inch) unbaked pie crust, or 1 crust from a 15-ounce package of refrigerated pie crusts
2	tablespoons fresh lemon juice		

Put flour in 8x8-inch baking dish. Gradually stir in reserved cherry juice, lemon juice and sugar until flour and sugar are dissolved. Carefully stir in cherries.

Cut pie crust into 1-inch-wide strips and form a lattice pattern across cherries. Piece shorter strips together and turn under ends of long strips. (Brush strips with milk[30] and sprinkle with sugar, if desired.) Bake at 375° for 35 to 40 minutes or until top is brown and thick juices bubble through lattice (cobbler will set up as it cools). Serve with ice cream or half-and-half.

Makes 4 servings   Lawrence and Clo Ann Rabb, Meridian, Mississippi

Per serving: 463 calories, 12 g fat, 3 g protein, 86 g carbohydrate, 0 mg cholesterol, 301 mg sodium.

Lemon Meringue Pie

1	(9-inch) *Prebaked Pie Crust*	⅓	cup fresh lemon juice
1½	cups sugar	1½	cups hot water
3	tablespoons cornstarch	3	egg yolks
3	tablespoons flour	2	tablespoons butter
¼	teaspoon salt	1	recipe *Meringue for Pies*
½	teaspoon grated lemon zest		

Prebake pie crust. Transfer to rack. Cool completely. Mix sugar, cornstarch, flour and salt in medium saucepan. Whisk in lemon zest, lemon juice and hot water. Cook over medium heat until clear. Remove from heat. Lightly beat egg yolks in small bowl. Gradually stir in hot lemon mixture 1 tablespoon at a time until you have about ½ cup warmed egg yolks. Return to saucepan and whisk until combined. Bring to gentle boil over medium heat, stirring until beginning to thicken. Cook and stir 2 more minutes. Remove from heat and stir in butter. Pour hot filling into prepared crust.

Prepare meringue and spread over warm filling, sealing to crust. Bake at 425° for 5 to 8 minutes or until golden. Cool on rack 1 hour. Refrigerate uncovered 3 to 6 hours (to refrigerate longer, loosely cover with foil, making sure foil does not touch meringue). Cut with wet knife and serve.

Makes 8 servings   Katie Humphreys, Lenexa, Kansas

Per serving: 376 Calories, 11 g fat, 5 g protein, 67 g carbohydrate, 87 mg cholesterol, 274 mg sodium.

Meringue Tips

Separate whites from yolks while eggs are cold. For more volume, let whites come to room temperature before beating and use smaller eggs; they have more concentrated whites with less water content. Egg white is allowed in yolks, but never let *any* yolk or greasy substance get into whites–whites will not beat stiff.

Do not add salt to whites. Salt draws water out of beaten whites and decreases stability. Beating time will be increased. Gradually beat sugar into whites until completely dissolved (usually 2 tablespoons for each egg white). Rub between fingers–meringue should feel smooth. Overbeaten whites will be dull and lumpy.

If meringue is applied to *cold* filling and cooked in too hot an oven, top will be overcooked and will bead; bottom will be undercooked and will leave watery layer between meringue and filling. Sprinkle graham cracker crumbs or dry breadcrumbs over filling before adding meringue. Helps prevent watery layer.

Apply meringue over *warm* pie filling, spreading area around edge first, making sure meringue adheres to crust; otherwise, meringue will shrink away from crust as it bakes. Then fill center. Less beading will occur when meringue is applied over warm filling and baked at a higher temperature for a shorter time; for example, bake at 425° for 5 to 8 minutes.

Meringue for Pies

4 egg whites,[12] room temperature	¼ teaspoon cream of tartar
½ teaspoon vanilla extract	½ cup sugar

In large deep grease-free metal or glass bowl, beat egg whites, vanilla and cream of tartar with mixer on medium until soft peaks form, about 1 minute (longer on humid day). Peaks will curl. Gradually add sugar, *1 tablespoon at a time*, beating on high until sugar completely dissolves and stiff peaks form, 4 to 5 minutes. Peaks will stand straight. Use as directed in recipes that call for meringue. (See *Meringue Tips*.)

Makes meringue for one 9- or 10-inch pie

Per recipe: 463 calories, 0 g fat, 14 g protein, 102 g carbohydrate, 0 cholesterol, 487 mg sodium.

Joye's Meringue Shells

4 egg whites, room temperature[12]	1 teaspoon vanilla extract
¼ teaspoon cream of tartar	1 cup sugar
Dash of salt	

Combine egg whites, cream of tartar, salt and vanilla in large deep grease-free metal or glass bowl. Beat with mixer on low until whites begin to foam, then beat on medium until whites hold soft peaks. Add ¼ cup sugar, 1 tablespoon at a time, while beating with mixer on high. Beat until whites are *very* stiff. Gradually add remaining sugar, beating again until very stiff.

Drop teaspoonfuls of meringue about 1 inch apart onto large parchment- or foil-lined baking sheets, about 24 per sheet. Make mounds and form a well in center of each with back of teaspoon. Bake meringues on separate oven racks, if necessary, at 200° for 1 hour. Turn off oven–do not open door. Leave meringues in oven at least 1 hour, preferably overnight. Remove from oven and transfer to airtight containers–meringues will keep at room temperature and at low humidity for months. Fill meringue shells with fresh fruit, custards, puddings or fillings (see *Joye's Lemon Filling*).

Makes 48 to 50 small meringue shells   Joye Miller, Bella Vista, Arkansas

Per small meringue: 18 calories, 0 g fat, 1 g protein, 4 g carbohydrate, 0 mg cholesterol, 10 mg sodium.

Meringue Tarts and Discs variation: For meringue tart shells, draw ten to twelve 3- to 4-inch circles on large parchment-lined or foil-lined baking sheets, spread meringue over circles and build up sides with back of spoon. To make discs for layered desserts, draw three 8- or 9-inch circles. Spread meringue evenly over circles. Bake as directed above.

His Honor's Lemon Icebox Pie

*My cousin Richard sent a recipe along with a vignette about his introduction to Icebox Pie.
The vignette reads as follows:*
*"One summer after the Second World War when I was a preschooler in rural Mississippi, my
mother put me on a Greyhound bus. A sign pinned to my shirt repeated her instructions to
deliver me to Tchula where my uncle would be waiting at his Lion Oil Service Station when
the bus stopped two hours later. Leaving my three brothers at home, I was soon spoiled by my
aunt and uncle and their two older daughters. My uncle "Windy" was the mayor of the small
Delta town and one evening at dinner my cousin answered the phone, announcing it was for
'His Honor'. Without hesitation I jumped up from the table and headed for the phone, much
to everyone's amusement and my subsequent embarrassment! My aunt softened the blow by
announcing that I could have as much dessert as I wanted before she served everyone else. It so
happened that the dessert was lemon icebox pie (which became popular during the war because
it required no sugar). Later family gatherings verified that I ate that whole pie! From that day
forward, my aunt made two pies when I came to visit."*

Crust:
30 vanilla wafers, *divided*

Meringue:
3 egg whites[12]
5 tablespoons sugar

Filling:
3 egg yolks[12]
1 (14-ounce) can sweetened
   condensed milk
⅓ cup fresh lemon juice

Crust: Finely crush 15 wafers and press into bottom of buttered 9-inch pie
plate. Make rim around the inside by standing remaining 15 whole wafers on
edge, rounded side toward filling.

Meringue: Beat egg whites in medium deep, grease-free metal or glass bowl with
mixer on medium until soft peaks form, about 1 minute. Gradually add sugar,
1 tablespoon at a time, beating on high until stiff peaks form, about 4 minutes.

Filling: Beat egg yolks in medium bowl with same beaters. Beat in condensed
milk. Add lemon juice and beat until smooth.

Pour filling evenly over crushed wafers. Spread meringue over filling, sealing to
standing wafers. Bake at 350° for 10 minutes. Cool on rack 1 hour. Refrigerate
uncovered 3 to 6 hours (to refrigerate longer, loosely cover with foil, making
sure foil does not touch meringue).

Makes 6 servings, except in Richard's case   Richard Darnell, Edmond, Oklahoma

Per serving: 447 calories, 13 g fat, 10 g protein, 73 g carbohydrate, 143 mg cholesterol, 190 mg sodium.

Meringue Swirls
Make swirls in pie meringues, but keep tips low; otherwise,
tips will burn before meringue bakes.

Easy Key Lime Pie

Must be green? Actually it's yellow!

4 egg yolks	½ cup Key lime juice*
1 (14-ounce) can sweetened condensed milk	1 (9-inch) graham cracker of chocolate cookie pie crust
½ teaspoon freshly grated lime zest[61] (optional)	1 (8-ounce) container whipped topping, thawed

Beat egg yolks in medium bowl with mixer on low just until combined. Gradually beat in condensed milk, lime zest and Key lime juice. Pour filling into crust and bake at 350° for 12 minutes. Cool on rack 1 hour. Refrigerate until thoroughly chilled, at least 1 hour. Cover filling with whipped topping and garnish with additional grated lime zest, if desired. Refrigerate until ready to serve.

* Bottled Key lime juice is available in most supermarkets; very good!

Makes 6 servings

Per serving: 245 calories, 13 g fat, 4 g protein, 29 g carbohydrate, 142 mg cholesterol, 233 mg sodium.

Hazel's Pie Crust

2¼ cups flour	⅔ cup vegetable oil
½ teaspoon salt	¼ cup water

Mix flour and salt in large bowl. Make well in center. Pour oil into glass measure and add water–do not stir. Pour all at once into well. Stir gently with fork until flour is mostly moistened; add 1 or 2 more teaspoons water if dry. Form into ball, divide in half and flatten into disks. Place disk between wax paper[80] and roll out from center to edge, making quarter turn after each roll. Roll to 12-inch circle–do not roll edges too thin or dough will tear. To mend, overlap dough and roll across tear.

Peel off top piece of wax paper, turn paper over and loosely place on crust again. Gently turn crust over onto loosened paper. Peel off and discard top wax paper. Turn crust over into pie plate and press in place. Carefully remove and discard loosened wax paper. Finish edge of crust by pressing dough against pie plate rim with fork. Repeat with other disk or freeze.

Makes two 9-inch pie crusts   Hazel Woodson, Farmington, New Mexico

Per crust: 1154 calories, 74 g fat, 15 g protein, 107 g carbohydrate, 0 mg cholesterol, 537 g sodium.

Quiche Crust variation: Mix 2 teaspoons baking powder in with flour and salt. Substitute ¼ cup milk for water. Proceed as directed above. Add milk if dry.

Single Pie Crust

1¼ cups flour	½ cup *cold* shortening
¾ teaspoon salt	3 tablespoons cold water

Whisk flour and salt in large bowl. Cut shortening into pieces over flour. Cut in with pastry blender until coarse crumbs form (okay if some pieces resemble small peas). Sprinkle in water, a tablespoon at a time, while tossing with fork until mixture leaves sides of bowl and looks like small pieces of cauliflower. Gather mixture together and shape into thick disk.

Place disk on lightly floured surface. Give disk a couple of gentle taps with floured rolling pin. Lift dough, rotate quarter turn and tap two or three more times. Roll dough outward from center in all directions (around the clock) until 6 or 7 inches across, flouring rolling pin as needed. Lift and turn dough *over* (dough scraper helps), *lightly* sprinkling flour on rolling surface. Roll dough to 12-inch circle for 9-inch pie or to 13-inch circle for 10-inch pie.

Fold dough in half (dough scraper helps). Lift carefully with both hands underneath and lay folded edge across middle of pie plate. Unfold dough and gently press into bottom and sides without stretching, removing any air pockets underneath. If dough tears, repair with scraps of dough. Trim crust edge, allowing ½- to 1-inch overhang. Turn overhang under even with edge of pie plate to form double-thickness crust. Flute pie crust edge by placing thumb and index finger of one hand in pinched position against outside crust edge and with index finger of other hand inside crust, gently push dough between thumb and index finger. Continue around entire edge. Cover crust with plastic wrap and chill 10 to 15 minutes before baking; will firm shortening and help crust hold its shape.

Makes one 9- or 10-inch pie crust

Per crust: 1589 calories, 104 g fat, 19 g protein, 143 mg carbohydrate, 0 mg cholesterol, 1071 mg sodium.

Double Pie Crust variation: Use 3 cups flour, 1½ teaspoons salt, 1 cup *cold* shortening and 9 to 10 tablespoons cold water. Follow directions for *Single Pie Crust*, but after gathering mixture together, divide in half and shape into two thick disks. Roll out one disk at a time for use in recipes calling for two pie crusts, or refrigerate or freeze one for later use.

Double Cobbler Crust variation: Use 3 cups flour, 1 tablespoon sugar, 1 teaspoon salt, 1 cup *cold* butter-flavored shortening and 9 to 10 tablespoons cold water. Follow directions for *Single Pie Crust*, but after gathering mixture together, divide in half and shape into two thick rectangles. Roll out one rectangle at a time for use in double-crust cobbler recipes.

Using Stick Shortening

Stick shortening saves time, is easy to measure and eliminates messy cleanup.

Partially-Baked Pie Crust

1 unbaked pie crust

Place pie crust in glass pie plate and chill 10 to 15 minutes. Spray piece of foil large enough to extend just over edge of crust. Place foil sprayed-side down into crust, shaping to fit. Add dried beans, rice or ceramic pie weights, just enough for crust to hold its shape while baking–not too full or weight will cause foil to stick to crust. Bake at 400° for 8 to 9 minutes on lower rack of oven. Carefully gather foil edges toward center and lift to remove beans (save beans to use again). Bake crust 2 to 3 more minutes or until set and dry.

Makes 1 partially baked pie crust

Prebaked Pie Crust

1 unbaked pie crust

Follow directions for *Partially-Baked Pie Crust* through point of removing beans. Bake crust 7 or 10 more minutes or until entire crust is golden. If crust forms bubbles during baking, gently press out with back of spoon. Transfer to rack and cool.

Makes 1 prebaked pie crust

Kat's Snails

Make these little jewels with scraps of dough left over from serious pie making.

Pie dough

Sugar
Ground cinnamon

Roll out dough to ⅛ inch and sprinkle generously with sugar and cinnamon. Cut into 2-inch strips about 1 inch wide and roll up from short side. Place seamside down on an ungreased baking sheet and sprinkle with additional sugar, if desired. Bake at 400° for 10 minutes or until golden.

Makes as many as scraps allow   **Katherine Forsyth, Boulder, Colorado**

Pie Crust Tips
Cold pastry that goes into a hot oven becomes extra flaky and delicious!
Pie crust dough containing butter should be refrigerated before rolling.
Add pie filling while baked crust is still warm to help prevent leakage.

Cream Cheese Pastry

4 ounces cream cheese, softened	2 tablespoons half-and-half or milk
½ cup (1 stick) butter, cut into pieces and softened	1¼ cups flour
	¼ to ½ teaspoon salt

Beat cream cheese, butter and half-and-half in large bowl with mixer on low until creamed. Whisk flour and salt in separate bowl and gradually beat into creamed mixture on low until soft dough forms. Shape dough into ball and flatten into disk. Wrap in plastic and refrigerate 1 hour or overnight (if refrigerated overnight, remove and allow to soften). Roll out dough on lightly floured surface. Use for tarts, pastry shells and other recipes that call for cream cheese pastry, such as *Mini Quiches* and *Chicken Wellington*.

Makes dough for 9-inch tart, 24 pastry shells or 4 *Chicken Wellingtons*

Per shell: 75 calories, 6 g fat, 1 g protein, 5 g carbohydrate, 16 mg cholesterol, 75 mg sodium.

Almond Tarts

1 cup (2 sticks) butter or margarine,[50] softened	1½ cups sugar
6 ounces cream cheese, softened	3 eggs, room temperature
2 cups flour	2 tablespoons flour
	½ teaspoon salt
Filling:	1 teaspoon almond extract
1 pound almond paste (not almond filling), grated	1 teaspoon vanilla extract

Blend butter and cream cheese in large bowl with mixer. Mix in flour on low to make soft dough. Cover and chill. Pinch off teaspoonfuls of dough and roll into balls. Press into bottom and up sides of sprayed miniature muffin tins. Put teaspoonful of filling in each cup. Bake at 350° for 20 to 25 minutes or until filling is set and crust is golden. Cool in tins 10 minutes. Carefully run plastic knife around each tart and remove to racks. Cool completely. Store in airtight containers at room temperature. Tarts may be frozen.

Filling: Beat almond paste and sugar in large bowl with mixer until combined. Add eggs one at a time, beating well after each addition. Beat in flour, salt and extracts.

Makes 72 tarts   Dorothy VanderVeen, Delavan, Wisconsin

Per tart: 92 calories, 5 g fat, 2 g protein, 10 g carbohydrate, 12 mg cholesterol, 55 mg sodium.

Waikiki Tart

*Irene's **Waikiki Tart** won 1st place in the Grand Cook-Off sponsored by The **Grand Rapids Press**.*

Crust:
1 cup flour
¼ cup packed brown sugar[1]
½ cup (1 stick) butter
½ cup finely chopped macadamia nuts
1 tablespoon water

Filling:
6 ounces cream cheese, softened
¼ cup sugar
1 teaspoon vanilla extract

½ cup finely chopped macadamia nuts
2 bananas, peeled and sliced
1 (20-ounce) can pineapple tidbits, drained
½ cup flaked coconut

Meringue:
3 egg whites, room temperature[12]
¼ teaspoon cream of tartar
6 tablespoons sugar

Crust: Combine flour and brown sugar in medium bowl. Cut in butter with pastry blender. Add nuts, sprinkle with water and toss with fork until ingredients are moistened. Shape into ball. Press dough evenly into bottom and sides of 11-inch tart pan with removable bottom. Bake at 400° for 10 to 15 minutes or until golden.

Filling: Beat cream cheese, sugar and vanilla in medium bowl with mixer until smooth. Stir in nuts. Spread filling over crust. Add layer of bananas and layer of pineapple. Sprinkle with coconut.

Meringue: In grease-free deep medium metal or glass bowl, beat egg whites and cream of tartar with mixer until soft peaks form. Gradually add sugar, beating on high until stiff and glossy peaks form. Carefully spread meringue over filling, sealing to edge of crust. Bake at 375° for 10 to 12 minutes or until delicately brown. Remove to rack and cool.

Makes 8 to 10 servings   Irene Menninga, Grand Rapids, Michigan

Per serving of 8: 527 calories, 33 g fat, 7 g protein, 55 g carbohydrate, 54 mg cholesterol, 210 mg sodium.

Cream Puffs

1 cup water	1 cup bread flour[63] (may substitute unbleached all-purpose flour)
7 tablespoons butter, cut into pieces	
½ teaspoon salt	3 eggs plus 2 egg whites,[12] room temperature

Preheat oven to 325°. Heat water, butter and salt in large saucepan until butter melts; bring to boil over medium heat. Add flour all at once. Stir vigorously with wooden spoon until mixture leaves sides of pan and almost comes together in a ball. Remove from heat and cool slightly, about 5 minutes, stirring occasionally. Beat in eggs and whites in following order: one egg, another egg, both egg whites and remaining egg. Beat thoroughly with wooden spoon after each addition, 1 to 2 minutes. Dough will look slippery after each addition, but will come together as you beat. Continue to beat vigorously until dough is smooth and satiny. Drop ¼-cupfuls of dough about 3 inches apart onto one large sprayed or parchment-lined (preferred) baking sheet.

Place baking sheet in *lower half* of oven. Immediately raise temperature to 425° and bake 20 minutes. Reduce temperature to 325° (do not open door or puffs will fall) and bake 15 to 18 minutes or until puffed and golden brown. Remove puffs and turn off oven. Make small slit in side of each puff with sharp knife to let moisture escape or run wooden skewer through whole puff. Return to oven for 7 minutes with door ajar to dry out; puffs should sound hollow when thumped. Place on rack away from drafts and cool completely. (May flash freeze when cool.[26] Thaw at room temperature. Place on baking sheets and heat at 250° for 5 minutes or 3 minutes for Mini Puffs.) Slice top third off each puff and discard any webbing inside. Fill bottoms with ½ cup of desired filling and cover with tops.

Makes 10 cream puffs

Per cream puff: 141 calories, 10 g fat, 4 g protein, 10 g carbohydrate, 86 mg cholesterol, 218 mg sodium.

Mini Puffs: Preheat oven to 325°. Drop 2-tablespoon-size scoops of dough about 1½ inches apart onto one large prepared baking sheet. Place in *lower half* of oven. Immediately raise oven temperature to 425° and bake 15 minutes. Reduce temperature to 325° and bake 15 minutes or until puffed and golden (without opening oven door). Remove puffs and turn off oven. Make slit in side of each puff, return to oven for 6 minutes with door ajar. Continue as directed above.

Makes 48 mini puffs

Per mini puff: 71 calories, 52 g fat, 2 g protein, 5 g carbohydrate, 43 mg cholesterol, 109 mg sodium.

Apricot Roll

Our neighbor, Louise, made Apricot Rolls every Christmas. She would always bring one to us.

¾ cup (1½ sticks) butter, softened
½ cup vanilla ice cream, softened
1 teaspoon vanilla extract
2 cups flour, *divided*
½ teaspoon salt
¼ cup sugar

1 cup apricot preserves, *divided*
⅔ cup golden raisins, *divided*
⅔ cup finely chopped toasted pecans, *divided*

Confectioners' sugar

Beat butter in large bowl with mixer until creamed. Mix ice cream and vanilla in small bowl until smooth. Beat into butter until resembling cottage cheese. Mix 1 cup flour, salt and sugar in bowl and beat into butter mixture until smooth. Gradually stir in remaining 1 cup flour with wooden spoon (mixture will get chunky). Gather and gently press mixture into ball, incorporating any flour left in bowl. Divide in half and flatten each portion into 4x6-inch rectangle. Wrap each in plastic and refrigerate overnight.

Remove dough from refrigerator and allow to soften. Meanwhile, puree preserves or cut fruit into smaller pieces with kitchen shears.

Unwrap one rectangle of dough and roll out on lightly floured surface to an 8x12-inch rectangle. With one long side nearest you as bottom, spread ½ cup preserves over surface of rectangle, leaving an unspread border of 1 inch at bottom and sides and 2 inches at top. Sprinkle ⅓ cup raisins and ⅓ cup pecans over preserves. Lift and fold bottom of dough 2 inches over filling. Fold in sides. Roll up like jelly roll, lifting while rolling to keep filling from pushing ahead. Pinch seam and ends and pat pastry back into a roll shape. Place seamside down on sprayed foil-lined baking sheet. Cut halfway through roll at 1-inch intervals. If desired, spray with butter-flavored cooking spray for a golden finish. Bake at 450° for 18 to 20 minutes. Remove and slide foil with roll onto rack. Let roll cool completely. Sprinkle with confectioners' sugar. Cut into 1-inch pieces. Repeat process for remaining rectangle of dough. Rolls may be baked and cut into slices a day before serving. Store at room temperature in airtight containers or freeze for later use.

Makes 2 rolls of 10 pieces each   Louise Augenstein, Berkeley Heights, New Jersey

Per piece: 208 calories, 9 g fat, 3 g protein, 33 g carbohydrate, 14 mg cholesterol, 60 mg sodium.

Banket

Banket, an absolutely delicious almond pastry, was often served at social gatherings in the Dutch communities around Chicago where my husband, Art, grew up. Sylvia Van Poolen introduced banket to me in 1958 when Art and I lived in Glenn Ellyn, Illinois. Dorothy VanderVeen's version is very similar, so I combined the two recipes.

Pastry:
4 cups flour
2 cups (4 sticks) butter, cut into pieces
1 cup cold water

Filling:
16 ounces almond paste (not almond filling)

2 cups sugar
3 eggs, lightly beaten
1 teaspoon vanilla extract
¼ teaspoon almond extract
Dash of salt

1 egg white, lightly beaten

Pastry: Put flour in large bowl. Cut in butter with pastry blender until crumbly. (If desired, since working with such a large amount of butter and flour, use food processor to pulse and cut butter into flour; transfer mixture to large bowl.) Make well in flour mixture and gradually add water, tossing with fork until combined. Crisscross two large pieces of plastic wrap on work surface and place dough in center. Bring ends of plastic up and over top; twist to enclose dough. Press to form into large ball. Refrigerate overnight.

Filling: Crumble or shred almond paste into large bowl. Beat in sugar, eggs, extracts and salt with mixer until combined. Refrigerate 30 minutes. Place filling on lightly-floured surface. Divide into eight portions. Working with floured hands on floured surface, roll each portion into 12-inch-long cylinder the diameter of a dime. Set aside.

Divide pastry dough into four parts. Place one part on lightly floured surface and roll into an 8x13-inch rectangle. Cut in half, lengthwise, making two 4x13-inch strips of dough. Center cylinder of filling on one strip and brush long *top edge* of pastry with water. Fold short sides in over filling. Lift bottom long side of pastry up and roll around filling toward top edge. Press seam to seal. Repeat with remaining strip of dough and another cylinder of filling. Place both rolls seamside down on sprayed foil-lined baking sheet. Brush tops with egg white. Prick top of rolls crosswise with fork at 1-inch intervals. Bake at 400° for 25 to 30 minutes or until lightly browned. Slide foil to racks. Let rolls cool completely. Repeat process with remaining three portions of dough and six cylinders of filling. Cut each roll into 6 or 7 pieces and store in airtight containers at room temperature.

Makes 8 rolls (about 48 pieces)

Sylvia Van Poolen, Wayland, Michigan
Dorothy VanderVeen, Delavan, Wisconsin

Per piece: 165 calories, 10 g fat, 2 g protein, 18 g carbohydrate, 30 mg cholesterol, 80 mg sodium.

Potatoes, Rice & Grains

Potatoes, Rice and Grains

Potatoes

Rice and Grains

Perfect Mashed Potatoes

Potatoes should be beaten until smooth before adding any milk, and milk should be heated.

2 pounds (about 6) medium russet potatoes, peeled and quartered	½ cup (1 stick) butter, cut into pieces, *divided*
	¼ to ½ cup milk or half-and-half

Put potatoes in large saucepan of salted water and bring to boil. Reduce heat and cook until tender, about 20 minutes. Drain off water and return pan to low heat to evaporate any remaining water. Beat potatoes in saucepan with mixer until smooth. Beat in ¼ cup butter. Season with salt and pepper. Heat milk to just below boiling in small saucepan and stir in remaining ¼ cup butter until melted. Gradually beat milk mixture into potatoes until creamy. If stiff, beat in more heated milk. Serve hot.

Makes 6 servings

Per serving: 230 calories, 16 g fat, 3 g protein, 21 g carbohydrate, 21 mg cholesterol, 255 mg sodium.

Make-Ahead Mashed Potatoes

5 pounds (about 15) medium russet potatoes, peeled and quartered	1 teaspoon onion salt
1 (8-ounce) package cream cheese, softened	1 teaspoon seasoned salt
1 cup half-and-half	1 teaspoon salt
¾ cup (1½ sticks) butter, *divided*	¼ teaspoon pepper
	Paprika

Put potatoes in large pot of salted water and bring to boil. Reduce heat and cook until tender, about 20 minutes. Drain off water and return pan to low heat to evaporate any remaining water. Remove from heat and beat potatoes in pot with mixer until smooth. Beat cream cheese and half-and-half in medium bowl with same beaters until smooth; beat into potatoes. Add 1 stick butter cut into pieces, onion salt, seasoned salt, salt and pepper. Beat until combined. Spoon into sprayed 9x13-inch baking dish and spread out evenly. Melt remaining ½ stick butter in small bowl in microwave or in small saucepan on stove. Brush over potatoes. Cool. Cover and refrigerate overnight or up to 24 hours. Remove 30 minutes before baking. Sprinkle with paprika. Bake uncovered at 350° for 35 to 40 minutes or until thoroughly heated.

Makes 12 servings   Tiffany Corbett, Summit, New Jersey

Per serving: 272 calories, 17 g fat, 5 g protein, 27 g carbohydrate, 49 mg cholesterol, 575 mg sodium.

Spinach Mashed Potatoes

3   pounds (about 9) medium russet potatoes, peeled and quartered
1   (8-ounce) package cream cheese, softened and cut into pieces
3   tablespoons butter, *divided*

½   teaspoon garlic salt
2   to 3 tablespoons milk
1   (10-ounce) package frozen chopped spinach, thawed and well drained[43]

Put potatoes in large pot of lightly-salted boiling water. Boil 20 minutes or until tender. Drain. Transfer to large bowl and beat with mixer on low until smooth. Beat in cream cheese, 2 tablespoons butter and garlic salt. Gradually beat in enough milk to make fluffy. Fold in spinach. Spoon mixture into sprayed 9x13-inch casserole. Cover and chill at least 1 hour or up to 24 hours. Bake covered at 325° for 30 minutes; remove and stir potatoes. Dot with remaining 1 tablespoon of butter. Bake uncovered for 30 to 35 more minutes or until hot.

Makes 8 servings   Judy Gianetto, Boulder, Colorado

Per serving: 248 calories, 15 g fat, 6 g protein, 25 g carbohydrate, 31 mg cholesterol, 298 mg sodium.

Scalloped Potatoes

2   pounds (about 6) medium russet potatoes, peeled and sliced ¼-inch thick
½   large sweet onion, thinly sliced and separated into rings
3   tablespoons flour, *divided*

8   ounces Cheddar cheese, shrdded (2 cups) *divided*
3   tablespoons butter, *divided*
1   to 1½ cups milk, or as needed
    Paprika

Put potatoes in large saucepan of salted water and bring to boil. Reduce heat and cook until just tender, about 3 minutes. Carefully drain in colander.

Spray 7x11-inch baking dish or 2-quart casserole. Layer one-third of potatoes in bottom and lightly sprinkle with salt and pepper. Cover with one-third of onion rings. Sprinkle with 1 tablespoon flour and ⅔ cup cheese. Dot with 1 tablespoon butter. Repeat layers two more times, lightly sprinkling potato layers with salt and pepper. Add milk to almost cover. Sprinkle with paprika. Cover with foil. Bake at 350° for 40 to 45 minutes. Uncover and bake until lightly browned, about 7 more minutes. Tent with foil. Let stand 5 minutes before serving.

Makes 6 servings

Per serving: 347 calories, 20 g fat, 14 g protein, 29 g carbohydrate, 60 mg cholesterol, 586 mg sodium.

Twice Baked Potatoes

4 large russet potatoes	¼ cup milk
½ teaspoon salt, or to taste	4 ounces Cheddar cheese, shredded
¼ teaspoon pepper	(1 cup)
½ cup (1 stick) butter, softened, *divided*	Paprika

Wash potatoes and pat dry. Prick with fork and spray with cooking spray. Bake potatoes on oven rack at 375° for 1 hour or until soft. Remove and tent with foil. Turn off oven. When cool enough to handle, cut potatoes in half lengthwise. Scoop out pulp into large mixing bowl, leaving enough in shells to retain shape. Place six best shells on baking sheet and return to warm oven 5 minutes. Discard remaining two or eat as a snack with salt and pepper.

Beat pulp with mixer until smooth. Beat in salt, pepper and ½ stick butter. Heat milk to just below boiling in small saucepan and stir in remaining ½ stick butter. *Gradually* beat milk mixture into potatoes, beating until creamy. If potatoes seem stiff, add *small amount* of heated milk.

Spoon potatoes into shells until full and rounded. Place in sprayed 9x13-inch baking dish. (May prepare to this point early in day. Cover and refrigerate. Remove 30 minutes before baking.) Sprinkle each potato half with cheese. Sprinkle paprika on top. Bake at 350° for 30 to 40 minutes or until thoroughly heated.

Makes 6 servings

Per serving: 593 calories, 22 g fat, 15 g protein, 87 mg cholesterol, 305 mg sodium.

Roasted New Potatoes

2 pounds (about 15) small red potatoes	Salt and pepper
2 tablespoons butter	Finely snipped parsley

Rinse potatoes and peel ½-inch strip from around middle of each. Put in large saucepan of salted water and bring to boil. Reduce heat and boil 10 to 15 minutes or until just tender. Drain.

Melt butter in 7x11-inch baking dish in 350° oven. Remove and add potatoes; roll in butter to coat. Sprinkle with salt, pepper and parsley. Bake 10 minutes or until tender.

Makes 4 to 6 servings

Per serving of 6: 76 calories, 2 g fat, 2 g protein, 14 g carbohydrate, 0 mg cholesterol, 71 mg sodium.

Smashed Red Potatoes

Potatoes may be prepared ahead and kept warm 2 hours or more.

2 pounds small or medium red potatoes, unpeeled	½ cup sour cream
2 tablespoons butter	2 tablespoons prepared horseradish
3 tablespoons finely sliced green onions	Dash of hot pepper sauce
1 garlic clove, minced	¼ cup snipped flat-leaf parsley
½ cup half-and-half or whole milk	1 tablespoon snipped chives or finely sliced green onion tops
1 tablespoon chicken bouillon granules	⅛ teaspoon freshly ground black pepper[90]

Scrub potatoes. Cut in half if small or quarter if medium. Put in large saucepan of salted water and bring to boil. Reduce heat and cook 15 to 20 minutes or until tender. Meanwhile, melt butter in small saucepan and sauté green onion about 2 minutes. Add garlic and cook 30 seconds. Mix in half-and-half and bouillon granules, cooking and stirring over medium heat until granules dissolve and mixture is hot. Remove from heat. Stir in sour cream, horseradish, pepper sauce, parsley, chives and pepper. Set aside.

Drain water off potatoes and return pan to low heat to evaporate any remaining water. Coarsely smash potatoes in saucepan with potato masher. Fold in sour cream mixture. Reheat. Keep potatoes warm 2 hour or more following TIP 85.

Makes 4 to 6 servings

Per serving of 6: 163 calories, 7 g fat, 4 g protein, 23 g carbohydrate, 16 mg cholesterol, 229 mg sodium.

Lite Baked Potato Halves

2 medium russet potatoes	Paprika
2 tablespoons lite ranch or peppercorn ranch salad dressing	

Slice potatoes in half lengthwise and place in sprayed pie plate or shallow baking dish. Spread salad dressing over potatoes and sprinkle with paprika. Bake covered at 400° for 35 minutes or until tender.

Makes 4 servings

Per serving:156 calories, 2 g fat, 4 g protein, 33 g carbohydrate, 0 mg cholesterol, 76 mg sodium.

Baked Red Potatoes

| 6 medium-large red potatoes | Kosher salt or coarse sea salt |

Rinse potatoes and place on small squares of foil. Spray each with cooking spray and sprinkle all over with coarse salt (do not use table salt). Let dry. (I do not prick these potatoes.) Squeeze foil around bottom to catch salt. Bake at 375° for 1 hour or until soft. Serve with steaks or meat loaf. For a meal in itself, cut potatoes in half, squeeze to fluff or cut into pieces. Serve with any or all of following: ranch dressing, sour cream, bacon bits, shredded cheese, salsa or chili.

Makes 6 servings

Per serving: 179 calories, 0 g fat, 5 g protein, 41 g carbohydrate, 0 mg cholesterol, 640 mg sodium.

Hash-Browns variation: Bake extra potatoes. Cool and refrigerate. Shred three potatoes. Heat 2 tablespoons butter, canola oil or bacon drippings in large skillet. Add potatoes and sprinkle with ½ cup chopped onion and ¼ cup chopped bell pepper. Fry until potatoes are brown on bottom and vegetables are tender. Turn and fry other side. Serve portions topped with shredded cheese and sour cream.

Home-Fries variation: In large skillet, sauté ½ cup chopped onion and ¼ cup chopped bell pepper in 3 tablespoons melted butter, oil or bacon drippings until tender, about 2 minutes. Cube three leftover unpeeled baked potatoes and toss with sautéed onion and bell pepper. Fry over medium heat until potatoes are brown, stirring occasionally. Add salt and pepper to taste.

Baked Potato Fries: Bake three extra potatoes. Cool and refrigerate. Slice into ¼-inch unpeeled rounds. Heat 2 tablespoons bacon drippings or oil in large skillet. Add slices and fry until brown on bottom. Turn and fry other side. Drain on paper towels. Salt.

Oven-Baked Fries

5 medium red potatoes, unpeeled	Kosher salt or coarse sea salt
Cooking spray	Freshly ground black pepper
1 teaspoon paprika or chili powder	

Scrub potatoes. Cut in half crosswise and quarter each half. Put in large bowl and spray with cooking spray; toss. Sprinkle with paprika, kosher salt and ground black pepper; toss to coat. Place potatoes in single layer in sprayed foil-lined 9x13-inch jelly-roll pan. Bake at 400° for 10 minutes. Turn with tongs and bake 10 more minutes or until nicely browned and tender. Drain on paper towels. Serve with hamburgers or steaks.

Makes 4 servings

Per serving: 103 calories, 7 g fat, 1 g protein, 10 g carbohydrate, 0 mg cholesterol, 3 mg sodium.

Fried Potatoes

1 pound (about 3) medium russet or red potatoes, unpeeled	½ cup chopped onion (optional)
2 tablespoons bacon drippings, vegetable oil or olive oil	2 tablespoons snipped flat-leaf parsley (optional)

Boil potatoes in medium saucepan of salted water until tender, about 20 minutes. Drain and cool. Cut into cubes.

Heat bacon drippings in large iron skillet or other heavy skillet. Add potatoes and onion. Fry long enough so potatoes and onion will not stick to pan when stirred, about 5 minutes. Stir and fry 7 to 8 more minutes or until all potatoes are brown, stirring occasionally. Drain on paper towels. Season with salt and pepper or favorite seasoning and sprinkle with parsley.

Makes 4 servings

Per serving: 156 calories, 7 g fat, 3 g protein, 22 g carbohydrate, 7 mg cholesterol, 111 mg sodium.

Baked German Potato Salad

8 slices bacon, diced[14]	1½ cups water
3 pounds (about 9) medium red potatoes, peeled and cubed ½ inch (about 8 cups)	1 cup cider vinegar
	⅔ cup sugar
1 cup chopped celery	1 teaspoon salt
1 cup chopped onion	1 teaspoon pepper
3 tablespoons flour	1 cup sliced radishes (optional, but good)

Cook bacon in large nonstick skillet until crisp. Remove with slotted spoon and drain on paper towels. Reserve ¼ cup bacon drippings in skillet. Set aside. Meanwhile, Put potatoes in large saucepan of salted water and bring to boil. Cook until just tender, about 10 minutes. Drain and set aside.

Heat bacon drippings in skillet. Add celery and onion. Sauté until tender, 2 to 3 minutes. Stir in flour. Cook and stir about 1 minute; stir in water and vinegar. Cook until *thick* and bubbly, stirring constantly. Stir in sugar, salt and pepper. Stir until sugar dissolves. Put potatoes and bacon in sprayed 9x13-inch baking dish and cover with sauce. Mix lightly. Bake covered at 350° for 30 to 40 minutes or until hot and bubbly. Remove from oven. Stir in radishes, if desired. Serve at once. Recipe may be halved.

Makes 10 to 12 servings   Mimi Tyte, Bella Vista, Arkansas

Per serving of 12: 211 calories, 9 g fat, 5 g protein, 33 g carbohydrate, 10 mg cholesterol, 301 mg sodium.

German Potato Salad

2 pounds (about 5) medium russet or red potatoes
6 thick slices lean bacon, cut into ½-inch pieces
¾ to 1 cup chopped onion
2 tablespoons flour

1 to 2 tablespoons sugar
1½ teaspoons salt
½ teaspoon celery seeds
¼ teaspoon pepper
¾ cup water
⅓ cup cider vinegar

Boil potatoes in large saucepan of salted water until just tender, 20 to 25 minutes. Drain. When cool, peel and cube potatoes. Set aside. Cook bacon in large iron or other heavy skillet over low heat. Remove with slotted spoon and drain on paper towels. Set aside. Pour off drippings, leaving about 2 tablespoons in skillet. Add onion and sauté until light brown, stirring with wooden spatula to loosen brown bits on bottom. Mix flour, sugar, salt, celery seeds and pepper in small bowl. Stir into onions. Cook and stir over low heat 1 minute (mixture will ball up). Mix water and vinegar in 2-cup glass measure. Pour into skillet. Cook, stirring constantly until smooth and bubbly. Remove from heat and gently stir in potatoes and bacon. Cover and let stand 20 to 25 minutes to blend flavors. Transfer to serving bowl. Serve warm or at room temperature.

Makes 4 to 6 servings   Harold DeWeerd, Delavan, Wisconsin

Per serving of 6: 137 calories, 3 g fat, 4 g protein, 24 g carbohydrate, 5 mg cholesterol, 464 mg sodium.

Arline's Potato Casserole

When Arline asks, "What can I bring?" The answer is always, "Your potato casserole!"

1 cup milk
⅓ cup (5⅓ tablespoons) margarine
⅔ pound pasteurized prepared cheese product, cubed
⅔ cup mayonnaise

1 (2-pound) package frozen hash-brown potatoes
2 tablespoons dried minced onion
Paprika

Combine milk, margarine and cheese in medium saucepan over low heat, stirring until cheese melts. Add mayonnaise and whisk until smooth. Set aside. Spread frozen hash browns in sprayed 9x13-inch baking dish and sprinkle with minced onion. Sprinkle lightly with salt and pepper. Pour cheese mixture over potatoes (will solidify when contacting frozen hash browns so break up with fork to even out). Sprinkle with paprika. Bake uncovered at 350° for 45 to 60 minutes or until hot and bubbly and beginning to brown. Remove from oven and tent with foil. Let stand 10 minutes before serving.

Makes 8 servings   Arline Hutchinson, Bella Vista, Arkansas

Per serving: 457 calories, 37 g fat, 12 g protein, 23 g carbohydrate, 46 mg cholesterol, 840 mg sodium.

Praline Sweet Potato Casserole

I adapted this recipe from a 1970s "Methodist Advocate." It has been a family favorite.

3 pounds (about 5) medium sweet potatoes	¼ teaspoon ground nutmeg
¼ cup (½ stick) butter, cut into pieces	Dash of ground cinnamon
1 cup sugar	Topping:
½ teaspoon salt	½ cup packed brown sugar[1]
3 eggs, lightly beaten	¼ cup flour
½ cup milk	¼ cup (½ stick) butter, cut into pieces
1 teaspoon vanilla extract	¾ cup chopped toasted pecans

Peel and cut potatoes into 1-inch rounds.[7] Cut large rounds in half. Put in large saucepan of cold salted water and bring to boil. Reduce heat and cook until tender, 8 to 10 minutes. Drain off water and return pan to low heat to evaporate any remaining water. Beat potatoes in saucepan with mixer until smooth. Scrape down sides. Beat in butter, sugar, salt, eggs, milk, vanilla, nutmeg and cinnamon. Pour into sprayed 2-quart casserole. (May prepare ahead, cover and refrigerate. Remove 30 minutes before baking.) Sprinkle topping over potatoes and bake at 350° for 30 minutes or until hot and bubbly.

Topping: Mix brown sugar and flour in medium bowl. Cut in butter with pastry blender until crumbly. Stir in pecans. Makes 2 cups.

Makes 8 servings

Per serving: 544 calories, 16 g fat, 6 g protein, 95 g carbohydrate, 83 mg cholesterol, 350 mg sodium.

Note: If preferred, omit topping and sprinkle with miniature marshmallows during last few minutes of baking. Bake until marshmallows are puffy and brown, being careful not to burn.

About Sweet Potatoes & Yams

Sweet potatoes and yams are unrelated, although both are roots of a vine. Sweet potatoes are members of the morning glory family, while yams are members of the lily family. Yams can grow up to seven feet in length.

More than thirty years ago, dark-skinned sweet potatoes with sweet bright-orange flesh were introduced into United States. To distinguish them from the more traditional tan-skinned variety of sweet potato with less-sweet light-colored flesh, the African word "nyami," referring to an edible root, was adopted in its English form "yam" and given to those dark-skinned sweet potatoes. Common usage has made the term acceptable; however, the U. S. Department of Agriculture requires that the label "yam" always be accompanied by "sweet potato."

Southern Sweet Potato Casserole

The marshmallows are undetectable, but they give the sweet potatoes a light fluffy texture.

3	pounds (about 5) medium sweet potatoes	½	teaspoon grated lemon zest
¼	cup (½ stick) butter	1	tablespoon brandy or bourbon
¾	cup packed light brown sugar[1]	1	cup miniature marshmallows
	Dash of ground nutmeg	½	cup crushed cornflakes
2	tablespoons half-and-half or milk		Butter-flavored cooking spray or butter
¼	teaspoon salt		

Peel and cut sweet potatoes into 1-inch rounds.[7] Cut large rounds in half. Boil in large saucepan of salted water until tender. Drain. Mash potatoes in saucepan with potato masher or beat with mixer. Mix in butter, brown sugar, nutmeg, half-and-half, salt, lemon zest and brandy.

Spoon half the potato mixture into sprayed 7x11-inch baking dish. Cover with marshmallows. Add remaining potato mixture and top with cornflakes. Spray with butter-flavored spray or dot with butter.* Bake at 350° for 30 minutes.

* If preferred, omit cornflakes and butter. Sprinkle with miniature marshmallows during last few minutes of baking. Bake until marshmallows are puffy and brown.

Makes 6 servings   Dorothy Rose P. Wright, Orange Park, Florida

Per serving: 360 calories, 8 g fat, 4 g protein, 69 g carbohydrate, 1 mg cholesterol, 368 mg sodium.

Apple-Yam Bake

6	medium tart apples	½	teaspoon salt
2	(15-ounce) cans yams or sweet potatoes, drained	½	teaspoon ground cinnamon
1	tablespoon grated orange zest	6	tablespoons (¾ stick) butter, melted, *divided*
⅓	cup packed light brown sugar[1]		

Core and peel apples. Cut lengthwise into eight wedges.[7] Cut yams in half and combine with apples and orange zest in sprayed 9x13-inch baking dish. Mix brown sugar, salt and cinnamon in small bowl. Sprinkle *half* the mixture over apple-yam mixture and toss lightly. Drizzle 3 tablespoons melted butter over top. Cover with foil and bake at 350° for 1 hour. Remove from oven and gently turn apples and yams in juice. Combine remaining 3 tablespoons melted butter with remaining sugar mixture and sprinkle over apple-yam mixture. Bake uncovered 15 more minutes or until bubbly and well glazed.

Makes 8 servings   Tiffany Corbett, Summit, New Jersey

Per serving: 282 calories, 9 g fat, 2 g protein, 50 g carbohydrate, 23 mg cholesterol, 268 mg sodium.

Roasted Sweet Potato Rounds

2½ pounds (about 4) medium sweet
   potatoes
4 tablespoons butter

2 to 3 tablespoons honey
2 tablespoons water
   Ground cinnamon

Peel and cut sweet potatoes into 1½-inch rounds. Rinse and pat dry. Melt butter in small bowl in microwave; dip rounds in butter, coating all sides to prevent darkening. Put rounds and any remaining butter in sprayed 9x13-inch baking dish. Sprinkle lightly with salt and freshly ground black pepper. Drizzle with honey. Add water to dish and sprinkle rounds with cinnamon. Cover with foil and bake at 350° for 45 minutes or until rounds can easily be pierced with fork. Turn rounds over and raise temperature to 375°. Bake uncovered 15 more minutes or until nicely glazed, basting with liquid in dish after 8 minutes.

Makes 4 to 6 servings

Per serving of 6: 182 calories, 8 g fat, 2 g protein, 27 g carbohydrate, 20 mg cholesterol, 89 mg sodium.

Quick variation: Prepare rounds and put in 10-inch quiche dish or pie plate. Continue through sprinkling with cinnamon as directed above. Cover loosely with plastic wrap and microwave on HIGH 8 to 15 minutes or until potatoes can easily be pierced with fork. Turn rounds over and place uncovered dish in 375° oven for 15 minutes or until potatoes are nicely glazed, basting after 8 minutes.

Candied Sweet Potatoes

2½ pounds (about 4) medium sweet
   potatoes

   Syrup:
½ cup (1 stick) butter
½ cup sugar
½ cup packed brown sugar[1]

¼ teaspoon salt
½ teaspoon ground cinnamon
   Dash of ground nutmeg
1 tablespoon grated orange zest
⅓ cup fresh orange juice

Peel potatoes and cut into ⅜- to ½-inch rounds. Cook in large saucepan of lightly salted boiling water until *just* tender. Drain. Meanwhile, prepare syrup.

Place half the potatoes in sprayed 9x13-inch baking dish. Spoon half the syrup over potatoes. Cover with remaining potatoes and remaining syrup. Bake at 325° until syrup thickens, about 40 minutes, basting occasionally with syrup in dish. Serve with baked ham, turnip greens and cornbread.

Syrup: Melt butter in small saucepan. Add sugars, salt, cinnamon, nutmeg, orange zest and orange juice. Cook over medium heat, stirring until sugars dissolve.

Makes 6 to 8 servings   Christine Howell, Frederick, Oklahoma

Per serving of 8: 276 calories, 12 g fat, 1 g protein, 43 g carbohydrate, 31 mg cholesterol, 197 mg sodium.

Praline Sweet Potato Fries

3 sweet potatoes, unpeeled, (about 2 pounds) use fairly large, long and slender sweet potatoes

Praline Sauce:
2 tablespoons sugar
2 tablespoons brown sugar

1 tablespoon butter
¼ cup water
Dash of ground cinnamon
Dash of ground nutmeg
Dash of salt

Wash and scrub sweet potatoes. Cut off any damaged ends. Cut thin slice from long side of each potato so it will lie flat. Slice potatoes into ⅜-inch-thick planks. Cut planks into ⅜-inch sticks. Put in pan of water to keep from turning dark.

Drain potato sticks and pat dry. Spray with cooking spray, turning to coat. Sprinkle lightly with salt. Arrange sticks in single layer in sprayed 11x17-inch jelly-roll pan. Bake at 450° for 15 minutes. Remove from oven and flip fries with spatula. Return to oven and bake 10 more minutes or until soft but firm. Meanwhile, prepare Praline Sauce.

Remove fries and turn off oven. Transfer fries to sprayed 7x11-inch baking dish and pour Praline Sauce over fries; toss gently to coat. Keep warm in oven until ready to serve, making sure oven is not hot or fries will continue to cook.

Praline Sauce: Spray small saucepan and add sugars, butter, water, cinnamon, nutmeg and salt. Bring to boil. Reduce heat and boil slowly without stirring until syrupy, about 5 minutes, swirling pan occasionally. Makes about ½ cup.

Makes 6 servings

Per serving: 120 calories, 2 g fat, 1 g protein, 25 g carbohydrate, 5 mg cholesterol, 230 mg sodium.

Plain Fluffy White Rice

1 teaspoon canola oil
1 cup long-grain white rice
½ to 1 teaspoon salt

2 cups boiling water
1 teaspoon fresh lemon juice for whiter rice (optional)

Pour oil into 10-inch skillet with tight-fitting lid; stir in rice to coat. Stir salt and lemon juice into boiling water and pour over rice; do not stir. Bring to boil; turn heat to low boil. Cover and cook without lifting lid 20 minutes or until tender and water is absorbed. Turn off heat. Lift lid and place two paper towels across top of skillet; return lid. Let stand 10 to 15 minutes.[40] Gently fluff and serve.

Makes 3 cups (4 servings)

Per serving: 194 calories, 3 g fat, 3 g protein, 37 g carbohydrate, 8 mg cholesterol, 568 mg sodium.

Rice Cooked in Broth variation: Reduce salt to ¼ teaspoon; add 1 teaspoon each chicken and beef bouillon granules to boiling water. Continue as directed.

Fluffy Buttered Rice

Basmati rice, a rice grown in foothills of Himalayas, is a long-grain rice with a nutty flavor and fine texture. It makes this dish special!

1	cup basmati rice	1	teaspoon fresh lemon juice
1	(10½-ounce) can chicken broth	1	tablespoon butter
¾	cup water	1	tablespoon snipped parsley
½	teaspoon salt		

Rinse rice in strainer and drain. Combine chicken broth, water, salt, lemon juice and butter in heavy medium saucepan. Stir in rice and bring to boil. Reduce heat to lowest setting and simmer covered 15 minutes without lifting lid. Check to see if rice is tender and water is absorbed; if not cook longer. Remove from heat. Uncover and place paper towel across top of pan. Return cover and let stand 5 to 10 minutes.[40] Sprinkle with parsley. Gently fluff with fork and serve.

Makes 4 servings

Per serving: 188 calories, 1 g fat, 6 g protein, 38 g carbohydrate, 1 mg cholesterol, 662 mg sodium.

Note: Regular long-grain white rice may be substituted for basmati rice–do not rinse. Simmer covered 20 minutes without lifting lid. Continue as directed above.

Fluffy Buttered Rice Timbales variation: Spray four 6-ounce custard cups with butter-flavored cooking spray. Pack cooked rice firmly into cups. Invert onto individual serving plates and unmold. Rice timbales may also be made with other varieties of cooked rice.

Soy-Sesame Rice

1	tablespoon butter	1	teaspoon sesame oil
½	cup finely chopped onion		Dash of hot pepper sauce
2	cups chicken broth[11]	1	cup long-grain white rice
1	tablespoon sherry	1	tablespoon toasted pine nuts[5]
1	tablespoon soy sauce	⅓	cup sliced green onions

Melt butter in medium saucepan and sauté onion until clear, about 3 minutes. Add chicken broth, sherry, soy sauce, sesame oil and pepper sauce. Stir in rice and bring to boil. Reduce heat to lowest setting and simmer covered 20 minutes without lifting lid. Check to see if rice is tender and water is absorbed; if not cook longer. Remove from heat. Uncover and place paper towel across top of pan. Return cover and let stand 5 to 10 minutes.[40] Add pine nuts and green onion. Gently fluff with fork. Serve with beef, pork or chicken.

Makes 6 servings

Per serving: 182 calories, 5 g fat, 7 g protein, 28 g carbohydrate, 6 mg cholesterol, 736 mg sodium.

Gourmet Rice

Wild Rice:
¾ cup wild rice
1½ cups water
1 teaspoon chicken bouillon granules
1 teaspoon fresh thyme leaves, or ½ teaspoon dried thyme, crushed

Long-grain White Rice:
1⅓ cups water
½ cup long-grain white rice
1 teaspoon chicken bouillon granules

¼ teaspoon salt (optional)
1 teaspoon grated lemon zest
1 tablespoon fresh lemon juice
2 tablespoons snipped fresh chives
2 tablespoons snipped flat-leaf parsley
¼ cup toasted sliced almonds[5]

Butter-flavored cooking spray, or 1 tablespoon butter, softened
½ cup chicken broth[11] or water

Wild Rice: Rinse rice thoroughly in strainer and pour into medium saucepan. Add water, bouillon granules and thyme. Bring to boil. Reduce heat to medium-low and simmer covered 45 minutes or until rice has puffed and most water has been absorbed. Set aside, allowing rice to steam in pan.[40]

Long-grain White Rice: After wild rice has simmered 20 minutes, combine water, long-grain white rice and bouillon granules in separate medium saucepan. Bring to boil. Reduce heat to lowest setting and simmer covered about 20 minutes or until water is absorbed. Set aside and allow rice to steam in pan several minutes.[40] Fluff with fork.

Combine wild rice and long-grain rice in one saucepan. Mix in salt, lemon zest, lemon juice, chives, parsley and almonds. (At this point, rice may be held covered 20 to 30 minutes.) Spray rice with butter-flavored spray or add 1 tablespoon butter. Add chicken broth or water. Heat thoroughly, about 3 minutes. Fluff with fork and serve.

Makes 6 servings

Per serving: 160 calories, 4 g fat, 5 g protein, 24 g carbohydrate, 0 mg cholesterol, 311 mg sodium.

Easy Red Beans and Rice

¾ pound smoked sausage
½ cup water
1 cup coarsely chopped onion
½ cup chopped bell pepper
½ cup chopped celery
2 garlic cloves, minced
¼ teaspoon freshly ground black
   pepper
¼ teaspoon cayenne pepper
2 bay leaves
½ teaspoon dried thyme, crushed
½ teaspoon dried basil, crushed
½ teaspoon creole seasoning
3 (15-ounce) cans red beans, or
   red kidney beans,[19] undrained
1½ cups long-grain white rice

Cut sausage in half lengthwise and slice crosswise into ½-inch pieces. Put sausage, water, onion, bell pepper, celery, garlic, black pepper, cayenne pepper, bay leaves, thyme, basil and creole seasoning in large saucepan. Cover and simmer 8 minutes, adding more water if thick. Add beans. Simmer covered 20 minutes, adding water only if needed (mixture should be fairly thick). Cook rice according to package directions while bean mixture simmers. Remove bay leaves and serve over rice in individual bowls.

Makes 6 servings   Clo Ann Rabb, Meridian, Mississippi

Per serving: 394 calories, 18 g fat, 18 g protein, 37 g carbohydrate, 40 mg cholesterol, 1150 mg sodium.

Mushroom Rice

½ cup (1 stick) butter, melted
1 tablespoon dried minced onion
1 (10½-ounce) can beef broth
1 (10½-ounce) can beef consommé
1 tablespoon Worcestershire sauce
⅛ teaspoon garlic powder
¼ teaspoon salt
⅛ teaspoon pepper
2 cups long-grain white rice
1 (4-ounce) can sliced mushrooms,
   undrained

Pour butter into 2-quart casserole; swirl to coat. Add dried onion, beef broth, beef consommé, Worcestershire sauce, garlic powder, salt, pepper, rice and mushrooms. Stir to combine. Let stand 10 minutes to reconstitute onion. Bake covered at 350° for 1 hour or until rice is tender and liquid is absorbed. Fluff with fork and serve with *Our Favorite Meat Loaf*, *Green Beans* and a salad.

Makes 10 servings   Margaret Ann Nicke, Birmingham, Alabama

Per serving: 233 calories, 9 g fat, 5 g protein, 33 g carbohydrate, 25 mg cholesterol, 678 mg sodium.

Zucchini and Rice

3 medium zucchini, thinly sliced	2 cups sour cream
2 (4-ounce) cans whole green chiles, drained and coarsely chopped	1 teaspoon garlic salt
	2 tablespoons chopped parsley
2 cups cooked long-grain white rice	¼ cup chopped green onions
12 ounces Monterey Jack cheese, shredded (3 cups), *divided*	¼ cup chopped bell pepper
	1 large tomato, sliced

Cook zucchini until crisp tender in just enough water to cover. Drain well. Combine green chiles, rice, 2 cups cheese, sour cream, garlic salt, parsley, green onion and bell pepper in large bowl. Season with salt and pepper. Fold in zucchini. Pour mixture into sprayed 9x13-inch baking dish. Place overlapping tomato slices down middle. Sprinkle remaining 1 cup cheese over top of casserole. Bake uncovered at 350° for 45 to 50 minutes.

Makes 8 servings   Sandra Travis, Bella Vista, Arkansas

Per serving: 365 calories, 25 g fat, 15 g protein, 21 g carbohydrate, 63 mg cholesterol, 586 mg sodium.

Barley Casserole

½ cup (1 stick) butter*	1 (4-ounce) can sliced mushrooms, drained
½ cup chopped onion	
1 cup fine pearl barley	1 (8-ounce) can sliced water chestnuts, rinsed and drained
2 cups chicken broth[11]	
1 (1-ounce) envelope onion soup mix	½ cup slivered almonds

Melt butter in medium skillet. Sauté onion and barley until onion is clear and barley is lightly browned. Transfer to deep, sprayed 2-quart casserole. Stir in chicken broth, soup mix, mushrooms, water chestnuts and almonds. Bake covered at 350° for 1 hour or until barley is tender and liquid is absorbed. Serve with *Roast Turkey Breast* and *Apple Crisp* for dessert.

* Amount of butter may be halved, if desired. Terry likes it buttery.

Makes 6 servings   Terry VanderVeen Bright, Lynchburg, Virginia

Per serving: 377 calories, 22 g fat, 10 g protein, 38 g carbohydrate, 42 mg cholesterol, 1184 mg sodium.

Jack's Wild Rice

Jack and Shirley, like to serve Jack's rice with brats and sauerkraut at their annual Fourth of July celebration on Lake Windsor.

1 (16-ounce) package wild rice	2 (8-ounce) cans mushroom stems and pieces, drained
4½ cups water	
2 tablespoons sugar	2 (8-ounce) cans sliced water chestnuts, rinsed and drained
½ cup cream sherry	
2 (16-ounce) packages regular pork sausage	2 (10¾-ounce) cans cream of mushroom soup
½ cup (1 stick) butter	1 (10¾-ounce) can cream of celery soup
2½ cups chopped green onions, including some tops	½ teaspoon celery salt
4 cups diagonally sliced celery with some leaves (slit broad ribs lengthwise before slicing)	½ teaspoon onion salt
	1 teaspoon white pepper, or to taste

Prepare wild rice for casserole early in the day. Put rice in large saucepan or Dutch oven. Add *cold* water and wash rice thoroughly, swishing grains through your fingers. Drain. Cover rice with *hot* water and swish again. Drain rice through strainer and return to pot. Add 4½ cups water and sugar. Bring to low boil and cook covered until rice is plump and tender, 15 to 20 minutes, stirring occasionally to keep rice from sticking. Stir in sherry. Simmer covered 15 more minutes or until water has cooked down below top of rice. Let rice stand covered until most water is absorbed. Push rice down and turn frequently with spatula. If rice does not absorb all the water after an hour or so, drain off unabsorbed water.

Brown sausage in large skillet, breaking up pieces with wooden spatula. Let stand 5 minutes. Drain off fat, if needed, and transfer sausage to large bowl. Set aside. Melt butter in same skillet. Add green onion and cook over medium heat until tender, about 5 minutes, stirring occasionally. Stir in celery, mushrooms and water chestnuts; cook until tender, about 5 minutes. Mix in soups. Season with celery salt, onion salt and white pepper. Stir soup mixture and sausage into prepared rice. Divide between two buttered 2-quart casseroles. (May prepare ahead. Cover and refrigerate several hours or overnight. Remove 30 minutes before baking.) Bake covered at 350° for 45 minutes. Uncover and fluff with fork. Bake uncovered about 15 more minutes, watching so rice does not dry out. Serve with brats, sauerkraut, baked beans and beer. Recipe may be halved.

Makes 16 servings   Jack Lausen, Bella Vista, Arkansas

Per serving: 410 calories, 25 g fat, 14 g protein, 32 g carbohydrate, 59 mg cholesterol, 1145 mg sodium.

Poultry

Chicken

Turkey

Easy Cooked Chicken

Chicken cooked this way will be moist and tender.

6	(5-ounce) or 7 (4-ounce) frozen boneless, skinless chicken breast halves	½	medium onion, cut into chunks
	Salt and pepper	1	or 2 ribs celery with leaves, broken into large pieces

Cut piece of foil 2½ times the length of jelly roll pan large enough to hold breasts. Center foil lengthwise in pan. Rinse chicken breasts and place on foil. Sprinkle both sides with salt and pepper. Put onion and celery around chicken. Join ends of foil, fold twice and flatten over chicken; fold in sides to seal packet. Cook at 350° for 55 to 60 minutes. (Cook only until breasts are no longer pink in center–check after 55 minutes. Do not overcook–breasts will continue to cook internally in foil.) Remove from oven and let cool in foil 30 minutes. Unfold foil and transfer chicken to plate. Make spout at one end of foil; pour liquid into jar with tight-fitting lid and refrigerate–makes great chicken broth. Discard onion and celery. Refrigerate chicken in covered container if not using immediately. Pull breasts apart along grain into ½-inch strips. Use kitchen shears to cut strips crosswise into bite-size pieces or as called for in recipe. Use in casseroles, salads or other recipes calling for cooked chicken.

Note: I also prepare thawed breasts the same way. Cook 40 to 45 minutes.

Makes about 4 cups

Per cup: 165 calories, 2 g fat, 39 g protein, 0 g carbohydrate, 113 mg cholesterol, 68 mg sodium.

Microwave Easy Cooked Chicken

4	(4-ounce) boneless, skinless chicken breast halves, *thawed*	¼	medium onion, cut into chunks
	Salt and pepper	1	rib celery with leaves, cut into large pieces
⅓	cup water		

Place breasts in medium round casserole. Sprinkle with salt and pepper. Add water, onion and celery. Cover and microwave on HIGH 5 to 6 minutes. Turn breasts over. Cook covered 5 to 6 more minutes or until breasts are no longer pink inside. Let stand covered 10 to 15 minutes to absorb juices before removing. Pull breasts apart along grain into ½-inch wide strips. Cut strips crosswise into bite-size pieces with kitchen shears.

Makes about 2¼ cups

Per cup: 165 calories, 2 g fat, 39 g protein, 0 g carbohydrate, 113 mg cholesterol, 68 mg sodium.

My Very Best Southern Fried Chicken

Brown, crispy and cooked to the bone! Great for picnics and road trips.

3 pounds cut up chicken pieces with skin and bones	1 cup flour
Salt and pepper	¼ teaspoon salt
Milk	2 to 2½ cups canola oil

Rinse chicken well. Drain. Rub each piece *thoroughly* with salt (enough salt is the secret to good fried chicken). Sprinkle with pepper. Put chicken in large bowl, cover with milk and refrigerate covered 1 hour or overnight, turning pieces occasionally. Drain chicken in colander and set aside. Mix flour and salt in ziptop bag. Add chicken, one piece at a time, and shake to coat. Put floured pieces in single layer on large jelly-roll pan. Let dry 10 minutes. (If time does not permit soaking chicken in milk, proceed directly to mixing flour and salt in ziptop bag.)

Heat oil in large electric skillet (oil should come about halfway up sides of chicken pieces). Set skillet temperature to 360°. When oil is hot, add enough chicken pieces skin-side down to fill skillet without crowding. Cover, leaving vent open. Fry 12 minutes *without peeking*. Turn pieces over. Cover and fry 10 to 12 more minutes. Dark meat takes longer to cook, so check small pieces and white meat after 10 minutes. Drain on paper towels. Repeat until all pieces are fried, adding more oil if needed. Serve with ***Mother's Potato Salad***, ***Terry's Baked Beans*** and ***Fudgy Brownies***.

Makes 6 servings

Per serving: 598 calories, 43 g fat, 32 g protein, 19 g carbohydrate, 145 mg cholesterol, 137 mg sodium.

Frying Tip

To prevent smell and mess in kitchen, fry chicken and other foods that spatter outside on deck or patio. Set electric skillet on newspaper-covered counter or table next to electric outlet (household extension cords are not recommended). Heat oil in skillet and fry chicken or other food as directed. When finished, let oil cool and pour into disposable container (coffee can with lid works well). Roll up newspapers and dispose of oil and newspapers.

Savory Grilled Chicken

Tender, juicy grilled chicken.

6 bone-in chicken breast halves with skin	⅓ cup soy sauce
	2 tablespoons fresh lemon juice
Marinade:	3 tablespoons sesame seeds
⅓ cup Italian dressing	2 garlic cloves, mashed

Rinse chicken breasts. Set aside. Reserve ¼ cup marinade for basting. Pour remainder into large ziptop bag and add breasts. Refrigerate at least 2 hours, turning occasionally. About 20 to 30 minutes before grilling, remove chicken and discard marinade. Pat dry. Break bones in breasts with heel of hand to flatten for more even cooking. Transfer to plate and cover.

Set grill rack 5 or 6 inches above heat source. Cover middle of grill rack with heavy duty foil, securing foil around front and rear edges. Leave an area uncovered on each side for heat circulation. Press foil between grill ridges and make small holes all over foil with meat fork. Preheat grill to MEDIUM (see *Grill Tips*).

Spray chicken and foil well with cooking spray. Place skin side down on grill. Close grill and cook 10 minutes. Turn and baste with reserved marinade. Cook 10 minutes. Turn, baste and cook 10 more minutes or until instant-read thermometer registers 160° and juices run clear when pierced with fork. (If breasts are very large, cook 12 minutes instead of 10.)

Marinade: Mix Italian dressing, soy sauce, lemon juice, sesame seeds and garlic in jar with tight-fitting lid. Shake well.

Makes 6 servings   Eleanor Weathersby, Dawsonville, Georgia

Per serving: 130 calories, 3 g fat, 26 g protein, 1 g carbohydrate, 75 mg cholesterol, 249 mg sodium.

Barbecued Chicken variation: Do not marinate chicken. Prepare 1 recipe of *Phyllis's Barbecue Sauce* (or use your favorite barbecue sauce) and use for basting in place of marinade. Rinse chicken, pat dry, rub with salt and pepper and sprinkle with chili powder. Spray foil and breasts well; place on foil *skin side up*. Baste with barbecue sauce. Close grill and cook 10 minutes. Turn, baste and cook 10 minutes. Turn, baste and cook as directed above.

Barbecued Country-Style Pork Ribs variation: Substitute 6 country-style boneless pork ribs for chicken. Prepare 1 recipe of *Phyllis's Barbecue Sauce*. Preheat grill to LOW (see *Grill Tips*). Spray foil and ribs just before grilling. Rinse ribs and pat dry. Sprinkle with salt and pepper. Place ribs on foil, close cover, and grill 40 to 45 minutes on LOW, turning every 10 minutes. Baste frequently with ½ cup *Phyllis's Barbecue Sauce* during last 10 to 15 minutes of grilling time. Serve remaining ¾ cup sauce on the side.

Makes 6 servings

Per serving: 531 calories, 40 g fat, 36 g protein, 5 g carbohydrate, 146 mg cholesterol, 386 mg sodium.

Rotisserie Roasted Chicken

Rotisserie roasting produces very moist and tasty chicken. (Recipe was tested on gas grill.)

1	(3½- to 4-pound) whole broiler-fryer chicken	2 teaspoons coarse salt
1	tablespoon lemon pepper	1 tablespoon herbes de Provence, crushed

Remove and discard any packet from cavity of chicken. Thoroughly rinse chicken inside and out. Pat dry. Mix lemon pepper, salt and herbes de Provence in small bowl. Sprinkle half into cavity and neck area of chicken. (If roasting two chickens, double amount of seasoning mixture.)

Tie legs together with butcher's twine. Wrap twine around chicken to hold wings against sides. Insert spit lengthwise through chicken. (If roasting two chickens, place neck to neck on spit and turn one upside down for balance.) Adjust prongs, balancing weight as much as possible. Tighten clamps. Remove spit with chicken and place across kitchen sink. Spray chicken with cooking spray and sprinkle with remaining herb mixture. Let stand while preparing drip pan.[48]

Remove grill racks. Preheat grill to LOW (see *Grill Tips*). Insert spit in motor and place drip pan below chicken on lava rocks. Start rotisserie and lower lid to vent position (prop open about one inch). Roast chicken 40 to 60 minutes, depending on size, or until instant-read thermometer inserted into inside area of thigh registers 160°. Turn gas off. Let chicken turn on spit 15 to 20 minutes to set juices. Remove chicken to cutting board. Cut chicken in half or into pieces. Serve with *Roasted Sweet Potato Rounds*, *Fresh Asparagus* and *Mandarin Orange Salad*.

Makes 2 to 4 servings

Per serving of 4: 272 calories, 11 g fat, 42 g protein, 0 g carbohydrate, 129 mg cholesterol, 123 mg sodium.

Barbecued Rotisserie Chicken variation: Substitute 1 to 1½ teaspoons barbecue seasoning (dry spice) for 1 tablespoon herbes de Provence in herb mixture and proceed as directed above. During last 15 minutes of roasting baste with *Barbecue Sauce* or with your favorite barbecue sauce. Turn gas off. Let chicken turn on spit 10 to 15 minutes to set juices. Continue as directed above. Serve with potato salad, coleslaw and baked beans.

Baked Chicken Halves

1 (3½- to 4-pound) broiler-fryer,
  split in half
  Seasoned salt or herb seasoning
  Cayenne pepper
  Freshly ground black pepper
  Paprika
4 ribs celery, including leaves
  Several sprigs of flat-leaf parsley

1 large sweet onion, cut into
  wedges
3 or 4 carrots, scrubbed or peeled,
  cut into 1½-inch pieces
1 green, red or yellow bell pepper,
  seeded and cut into chunks
2 unpeeled medium red potatoes,
  rinsed, cut in half and quartered

Trim excess fat from chicken halves. Rinse well and pat dry. Lift wing of each half up and over back and hook it behind top of breast. Spray chicken with cooking spray. Sprinkle with seasoned salt, cayenne pepper, black pepper and paprika. Set aside. Place celery ribs in sprayed 9x13-inch baking dish to form rack for chicken. Put parsley sprigs, onion wedges, carrots, bell pepper and potatoes around celery. Sprinkle lightly with seasoned salt. Place chicken halves skin-side up in opposite directions on top of vegetables. Bake uncovered at 300° for 2 hours or until juices run clear in inside leg area when pierced with fork. Baste occasionally with accumulated juices. Remove and tent with foil. Let stand 7 to 10 minutes. Cut chicken into pieces and serve with vegetables.

Makes 4 servings

Per serving: 609 calories, 40 g fat, 50 g protein, 10 g carbohydrate, 189 mg cholesterol, 207 mg sodium.

Baked Feta Chicken

4 boneless, skinless chicken breast
  halves
  Salt
½ cup seeded and finely diced
  plum tomatoes
1 tablespoon chopped fresh mint,
  or ½ teaspoon dried mint
¼ teaspoon dried oregano, crushed

2 tablespoons snipped flat-leaf
  parsley
  Freshly ground black pepper
2 tablespoons finely diced yellow or
  red bell pepper, or 1 tablespoon
  of each
4 tablespoons crumbled feta cheese
1 teaspoon olive oil

Rinse breasts and pat dry. Lightly salt and place in sprayed 8x8-inch baking dish. Mix tomatoes, mint, oregano, parsley, black pepper, bell pepper and feta cheese in a bowl and spoon equally over each breast. Drizzle with oil. Bake at 375° for 25 minutes or until firm and opaque. Spoon cooking juices over breasts and garnish with sprigs of parsley. Serve with *Rice Cooked in Broth* or pasta.

Makes 4 servings   Theresa Nuzum, Grand Lake, Colorado

Per serving: 166 calories, 5 g fat, 28 g protein, 3 g carbohydrate, 88 mg cholesterol, 208 mg sodium.

Chicken Stir-Fry

4 boneless, skinless chicken breast halves, rinsed and cut into ¾-inch pieces (partially freeze for easier cutting)

¼ cup roasted-garlic teriyaki sauce

2 teaspoons ground fresh ginger (in jar–found in produce section)

1½ tablespoons soy sauce

1 cup chicken broth[11]

1½ teaspoons brown sugar

1 tablespoon cornstarch

3 teaspoons sesame oil, *divided*

3 cups fresh broccoli florets*

2 cups julienned mixed red, yellow and green bell pepper*

½ cup thinly sliced green onions

Put chicken pieces in ziptop bag. Mix teriyaki sauce and ginger in small bowl and pour over chicken. Work marinade over chicken in bag to coat. Refrigerate 2 hours or overnight, turning bag occasionally.

Drain chicken in colander and discard marinade. Mix soy sauce, chicken broth, brown sugar and cornstarch in glass measure or small bowl. Set aside.

Spray nonstick stir-fry skillet or other large nonstick skillet and add 1½ teaspoons sesame oil. Heat over medium-high heat. Add chicken and stir-fry 3 to 4 minutes until white and tender. Remove to plate; set aside. Heat remaining 1½ teaspoons oil in skillet. Add broccoli and stir-fry until crisp-tender, 1 to 2 minutes. Add bell pepper and green onion. Stir-fry 3 to 4 more minutes. Remove vegetables to bowl and set aside.

Stir broth mixture and pour into skillet. Cook and stir until mixture thickens. Return chicken and vegetables. Cook, stirring constantly until thoroughly heated. Serve over hot cooked rice.

May substitute 16-ounce package fresh stir-fry vegetables (containing broccoli, carrots and snow peas) for broccoli and bell pepper. Stir-fry carrots and broccoli florets 2 minutes. Add snow peas with green onion. Stir-fry 3 to 4 more minutes. Set aside and continue as directed above.

Makes 4 to 5 servings

Per serving of 5: 408 calories, 4 g fat, 29 g protein, 63 g carbohydrate, 60 mg cholesterol, 906 mg sodium.

Chicken à la King

½ cup (1 stick) butter, *divided*	⅛ teaspoon paprika
1 large bell pepper, coarsely chopped	¼ cup cream sherry
1 (4-ounce) can sliced mushrooms, drained	4 cups bite-size *Easy Cooked Chicken* or leftover turkey
⅓ cup flour	1 (4-ounce) jar diced pimiento, drained
1⅓ cups chicken broth, *divided*	2 egg yolks
1 cup half-and-half	

Melt 3 tablespoons butter in medium skillet. Sauté bell pepper and mushrooms until bell pepper is crisp tender. Set aside. Melt remaining 5 tablespoons butter in large saucepan over medium heat. Blend in flour and cook to a light roux,ᴳ about 2 minutes, stirring constantly. Stir in 1 cup chicken broth and half-and-half. Cook and stir until sauce is smooth and thick. Stir in sautéed vegetables and add paprika. Season with salt and pepper. Stir in sherry, chicken and pimiento. Cook over medium heat until thoroughly heated, stirring occasionally. Beat egg yolks and ⅓ cup chicken broth together in small bowl. Stir into chicken mixture until combined. Add more broth if thick. Serve over rice, noodles or biscuits, or serve in puff-pastry shells.

Makes 8 servings   Bev Lehmann, Bella Vista, Arkansas

Per serving: 327 calories, 18 g fat, 31 g protein, 11 g carbohydrate, 143 mg cholesterol, 508 mg sodium.

Poulet de Boeuf

1 (26-ounce) can cream of mushroom soup	8 good-size, boneless, skinless chicken breast halves, cut in half crosswise
2 (16-ounce) containers sour cream	8 slices bacon, cut in half
1 teaspoon dried chervil, crushed	Paprika
2 (2¼-ounce) jars sliced dried beef	

Mix soup and sour cream in large bowl. Stir in chervil and set aside. Separate beef slices and put in bowl of warm water for 1 minute. Drain on paper towels. Reserve 16 slices. Line sprayed 9x13-inch baking dish with remaining slices. Arrange chicken pieces over beef layer. Cover with bacon and reserved beef slices, forming 16 mounds. Spoon sauce over and around mounds. Cover and refrigerate several hours or overnight. Remove 30 minutes before baking. Sprinkle with paprika. Bake uncovered at 275° for 1½ to 2½ hours or until chicken is no longer pink in center; check after 1½ hours by cutting into thickest piece of breast. Serve over rice, noodles, mashed potatoes or stuffing.

Makes 8 servings   Jo Bain, Bella Vista, Arkansas

Per serving: 458 calories, 32 g fat, 36 g protein, 9 g carbohydrate, 143 mg cholesterol, 896 mg sodium.

Chicken Wellington

Several steps are required to make Chicken Wellington, but they can be done a day ahead. Final Wellingtons can be assembled and baked in a short time, producing an elegant entrée!

Pastry:
1 recipe *Cream Cheese Pastry*

Chicken:
4 boneless, skinless chicken breast halves
1 tablespoon butter
1 tablespoon vegetable oil
Salt and pepper

Mushroom Duxelles:
3 tablespoons butter
¼ cup minced shallots or green onions, or 2 tablespoons of each
1 small garlic clove, minced
1 pound fresh mushrooms,[3] finely chopped with food chopper
½ cup dry white wine or dry vermouth

2 tablespoons chopped toasted pine nuts[5] (optional, but good)
⅓ cup finely snipped flat-leaf parsley

Madeira Sauce:
2 tablespoons butter
2 tablespoons flour
½ cup chicken broth[11]
½ cup beef broth[11]
⅓ cup dry Madeira
¾ cup Mushroom Duxelles

Egg Wash:
1 egg, lightly beaten
1 tablespoon water
Dash of salt

Pastry: Prepare and wrap pastry dough in plastic. Refrigerate 1 hour or overnight.

Chicken: Remove all fat from breasts (kitchen shears work well). Rinse and pat dry. Heat butter and oil in large skillet and sauté breasts 2 minutes on each side. Drain on paper towels. Lightly sprinkle with salt and pepper. Transfer to plate. Refrigerate covered 15 minutes or overnight.

Mushroom Duxelles: Melt butter in large skillet over medium heat and sauté shallots, garlic and mushrooms 1½ minutes. Raise heat to medium-high (mushrooms will begin to sizzle, then boil, releasing their liquid). Cook until most liquid evaporates, about 5 minutes, stirring frequently. Reduce heat to medium. Stir in wine, pine nuts and parsley. Season with salt and pepper. Cook until reduced and thickened, about 4 minutes. Cool. Put in covered container and refrigerate until ready to use (up to 2 days).

Madeira Sauce: Melt butter in small saucepan. Sprinkle in flour and cook, stirring constantly until hot and bubbly, about 1 minute. Add chicken broth and beef broth. Cook and stir until mixture is smooth and thickened. Stir in Madeira and ¾ cup Mushroom Duxelles. Cook until slightly thickened. Cool. Transfer to covered container and refrigerate until ready to use or overnight. Reheat before serving. Makes 1½ cups.

Assembly: Remove pastry from refrigerator, allow to soften and cut into fourths.

continues

Chicken Wellington (continued)

Working with one portion at a time, roll out on lightly floured surface to 7x8-inch rectangle about ⅛ inch thick. Spoon one-fourth of remaining Mushroom Duxelles in center of pastry rectangle and place a chicken breast upside-down on top. Fold pastry over chicken (like folding a letter) and pinch overlapping dough together to seal. Fold sides in and pinch ends, *making sure of seal*. Turn over. Repeat, making three more. (May assemble Wellingtons several hours ahead. Transfer to large plate, cover and refrigerate. Remove and let stand 1 hour before baking.)

Baking and serving: Place Wellingtons seamside down on parchment-lined or foil-lined baking sheet. Mix egg, water and salt in small bowl. Brush over each Wellington. Prick tops with fork in several places and bake at 425° for 18 to 20 minutes or until golden brown. Let stand 5 to 10 minutes before serving. Serve with warm *Madeira Sauce, Mozzarella Tomatoes* and *Green Beans*.

Makes 4 servings

Per serving: 838 calories, 57 g fat, 37 g protein, 37 g carbohydrate, 259 mg cholesterol, 720 mg sodium.

Chicken Alfredo Marsala

4 boneless, skinless chicken breast halves	1 garlic clove, minced
Salt and pepper	1 (17-ounce) jar creamy Alfredo sauce
2 tablespoons olive oil	¼ cup dry Marsala or dry sherry
1 red bell pepper, cut into thin strips	6 ounces angel hair pasta
2 cups sliced fresh mushrooms[3]	Paprika

Rinse breasts and pat dry. Sprinkle with salt and pepper. Heat oil in large skillet and brown breasts about 2 minutes on each side. Transfer to plate. Add bell pepper and mushrooms to skillet. Cook over medium heat 3 to 4 minutes, stirring frequently. Add garlic and cook about 1 more minute. Reduce heat. Stir in Alfredo sauce and Marsala. Cook over low heat 1 minute, stirring constantly. Return chicken breasts to skillet. Simmer covered 8 to 10 minutes depending on thickness of breasts. Meanwhile, prepare pasta according to package directions. Drain; do not rinse.

Place servings of pasta on four plates. Cover each with a chicken breast and spoon sauce over chicken. Sprinkle with paprika and garnish with parsley. Serve with rolls, *Mandarin Orange Salad* and a glass of Chardonnay,

Makes 4 servings

Per serving: 528 calories, 24 g fat, 36 g protein, 39 g carbohydrate, 145 mg cholesterol, 838 mg sodium.

Sesame Chicken Rolls

8	boneless, skinless chicken breast halves	½	teaspoon salt
	Salt and pepper	1½	tablespoons finely snipped flat-leaf parsley or 1 tablespoon dried parsley flakes, crushed
½	cup (1 stick) butter		
½	teaspoon minced garlic		
½	cup seasoned dry breadcrumbs	3	tablespoons fresh lemon juice
1½	ounces Asiago or Parmesan cheese, grated (½ cup)		Paprika
		1	tablespoon sesame seeds

Trim breasts or any fat, rinse and pat dry. Sprinkle lightly with salt and pepper. Set aside. Melt butter in medium skillet. Add garlic and sauté 30 seconds. Cool. Mix breadcrumbs, Asiago cheese, salt and parsley in shallow dish or pie plate. Dip each chicken breast in butter mixture, then dredge[G] in breadcrumb mixture.[33] Roll breasts tightly from narrow end and secure with toothpick horizontally through center. Place seamside down in sprayed 9x13-inch baking dish. (May prepare ahead early in the day and refrigerate. Remove 30 minutes before baking.) Drizzle lemon juice over chicken. Sprinkle with paprika and sesame seeds. Bake uncovered at 350° for 35 to 40 minutes or until no longer pink in center. (Test by cutting into center of roll with sharp knife. If breasts are small, test sooner.) Baste chicken with liquid in dish. Tent with foil and let stand 5 minutes. Serve with *Spicy Creamed Spinach* and *Candied Sweet Potatoes*.

Makes 8 servings   Terry VanderVeen Bright, Lynchburg, Virginia

Per serving: 269 calories, 15 g fat, 30 g protein, 6 g carbohydrate, 111 mg cholesterol, 611 mg sodium.

Easy Chicken Parmigiana variation: Omit lemon juice, paprika and sesame seeds from recipe. Add 1 (48-ounce) jar spaghetti sauce, 6 ounces mozzarella cheese, shredded (1½ cups) and 1 (16-ounce) package thin spaghetti, cooked according to package directions.

Prepare breasts as directed above through dipping in butter and dredging in breadcrumbs. Place *unrolled* breasts in sprayed foil-lined 10x15-inch jelly-roll pan; do not refrigerate. Bake breasts at 350° for 10 to 15 minutes, depending on size. Turn with tongs and bake 10 to 15 more minutes. (Do not overbake; breasts will be heating in sauce.) Meanwhile, heat spaghetti sauce in a large saucepan.

Spoon 2 to 2½ cups warm spaghetti sauce into sprayed 9x13-inch baking dish. Arrange breasts over sauce. Sprinkle with mozzarella cheese. Bake at 350° for 5 to 10 minutes or until cheese is lightly browned. Place servings of spaghetti in individual pasta bowls. Add chicken breasts and spoon sauce over chicken. Serve with additional warm spaghetti sauce, green salad and garlic bread.

Makes 8 servings

Per serving: 720 calories, 27 g fat, 69 g protein, 74 g carbohydrate, 136 mg cholesterol, 1374 mg sodium.

Chicken Cacciatore

4 (5- to 6-ounce) boneless, skinless chicken breast halves
Paprika
1 tablespoon olive oil
Salt and pepper
1 medium onion, sliced
1 bell pepper, cut into ¼-inch strips
1 cup sliced fresh mushrooms,[3] or 1 (4-ounce) can sliced mushrooms, drained
1 garlic clove, minced, or ¼ teaspoon garlic salt
1 tablespoon flour
1 cup beef broth[11]
¾ cup red wine (optional)

1 (8-ounce) can tomato sauce
1 (14½-ounce) can whole tomatoes, undrained, snipped[73]
1 teaspoon dried oregano, crushed
½ teaspoon dried basil, crushed
½ teaspoon dried rosemary, crushed
¼ teaspoon dried thyme, crushed
1 bay leaf
⅛ teaspoon fennel seeds (optional)
½ teaspoon salt
⅛ teaspoon freshly ground black pepper
Pinch of red pepper flakes, crushed
Pinch of sugar

Trim breasts of any fat, rinse and pat dry. Sprinkle both sides with paprika. Heat oil in large nonstick skillet. Add breasts. Sauté 2 minutes on each side over medium-high heat. Remove from heat. Transfer breasts to plate and sprinkle with salt and pepper. Set aside. Return skillet to heat (without cleaning) and add onion and bell pepper. Sauté 3 minutes. Add mushrooms and garlic and sauté 1 more minute, or until mushrooms are soft. Sprinkle in flour. Cook and stir about 1 minute. Pour in beef broth and wine. Stir in tomato sauce, tomatoes, oregano, basil, rosemary, thyme, bay leaf, fennel seeds, salt, pepper, pepper flakes and sugar. Stir well and bring to boil. Return chicken and any juices to skillet. Spoon sauce over breasts. Simmer covered 10 to 15 minutes. (May hold at this point 30 minutes, in which case simmer only 10 minutes and reheat.) Remove bay leaf and serve over rice or pasta.

Makes 4 servings

Per serving: 234 calories, 7 g fat, 31 g protein, 12 g carbohydrate, 85 mg cholesterol, 1353 mg sodium.

Overnight Chicken Casserole

Kat and I prepared many recipes of this casserole for the post-election victory party for volunteers when George Forsyth ran for Boulder County Treasurer.

1	(6-ounce) box long grain and wild rice mix	1	teaspoon chicken bouillon granules
¼	cup (½ stick) butter	2	tablespoons Madeira or dry sherry
½	cup chopped onion		
⅓	cup chopped bell pepper or celery	1	(8-ounce) can sliced water chestnuts, rinsed and drained
¼	cup flour		
⅔	cup chicken broth[11]	1	(4-ounce) can sliced mushrooms, drained
1½	cups half-and-half, or 1 (12-ounce) can evaporated milk	3	cups bite-size *Easy Cooked Chicken*
	Dash of hot pepper sauce	1	(2-ounce) jar diced pimiento, drained
½	teaspoon seasoned salt		
¼	teaspoon pepper	¾	cup sliced almonds, *divided*

Prepare rice mix according to package directions. Pour into large bowl and set aside. Melt butter in large skillet and sauté onion and bell pepper until tender. Stir in flour and cook about 1 minute. Add chicken broth and half-and-half; stir until combined. Add pepper sauce, seasoned salt, pepper and bouillon granules. Cook and stir until thickened. Mix in Madeira. Stir in water chestnuts, mushrooms, chicken, pimiento and ½ cup sliced almonds. Combine with rice mixture. Pour into sprayed 9x13-inch baking dish. Cover and refrigerate overnight.

Remove casserole 30 minutes before baking. Sprinkle remaining ¼ cup sliced almonds on top. Bake at 350° for 35 to 40 minutes or until hot and bubbly. Serve with *Strawberry Tossed Salad* and *Herb Roll-ups* or croissants.

Makes 6 servings   Katherine Forsyth, Boulder, Colorado

Per serving: 505 calories, 24 g fat, 36 g protein, 42 g carbohydrate, 83 mg cholesterol, 747 mg sodium.

About Celery

To wash and store celery, cut off enough end of stalk to separate ribs. Soak in cold water 30 minutes. Brush ribs with vegetable brush to remove dirt. Drain and wrap in kitchen towels to absorb water. Unwrap and let dry. Wrap 2 or 3 ribs together in separate pieces of foil. Refrigerate. Celery will keep fresh for several weeks. *Theresa Nuzum, Grand Lake, Colorado*

Chicken Artichoke Casserole

6	(5- to 6-ounce) boneless skinless chicken breast halves	½	cup dry vermouth, or ¾ cup other dry white wine
	Salt	1	(10½-ounce) can chicken broth
	Freshly ground black pepper	¼	teaspoon dried thyme, crushed
	Paprika	4	ounces cream cheese, cubed
3	tablespoons butter	1	teaspoon chicken bouillon granules
1	tablespoon vegetable oil		
1	cup chopped onion	1	(13¾-ounce) can quartered artichoke hearts, drained
1	garlic clove, minced		
1½	cups sliced fresh mushrooms[3]	2	tablespoons drained diced pimiento
2	tablespoons flour	½	cup toasted sliced almonds[5]

Trim any excess fat from chicken breasts (kitchen shears work well). Rinse and pat dry. Lightly sprinkle both sides of each breast with salt, pepper and paprika. Heat butter and oil in large nonstick skillet and brown chicken over medium heat, about 3 minutes per side. Transfer to sprayed 9x13-inch baking dish. Set aside.

Sauté onion, garlic and mushrooms in same skillet in pan drippings until tender. Sprinkle in flour. Cook and stir about 1 minute (mixture will ball up). Add vermouth, chicken broth and thyme. Cook over medium heat, stirring constantly until bubbly and saucelike. Add cream cheese and whisk until cheese melts and mixture thickens slightly. Whisk in bouillon granules. Season with salt and pepper if needed. Remove from heat. Arrange artichoke quarters around chicken and sprinkle with pimiento. Pour sauce over casserole. (May prepare ahead to this point. Cool. Cover and refrigerate overnight. Remove casserole 30 minutes before baking.) Bake covered at 350° for 45 to 50 minutes or until hot and bubbly. Uncover and sprinkle with toasted almonds. Return to oven 3 to 4 minutes. Remove and let stand 5 to 10 minutes before serving. Serve with timbales[6] of *Rice Cooked in Broth* (see *Fluffy Buttered Rice Timbales*), *Raspberry Salad* and sourdough rolls.

Makes 6 servings

Per serving: 429 calories, 25 g fat, 33 g protein, 13 g carbohydrate, 123 mg cholesterol, 1033 mg sodium.

Deluxe Chicken Casserole

2 cups bite-size *Easy Cooked Chicken*, or cooked turkey or ham
1 cup thinly sliced celery cut on diagonal
1 tablespoon grated onion[55]
1 (8-ounce) can sliced water chestnuts, drained
½ recipe *Rice Cooked in Broth*
1 (10¾-ounce) can cream of chicken or cream of mushroom soup
¾ cup mayonnaise
1 tablespoon fresh lemon juice
Dash of hot pepper sauce
1 (4-ounce) can sliced mushrooms, drained
1 (2-ounce) jar diced pimientos, drained
3 hard-cooked eggs,[18] chopped
½ cup toasted slivered almonds[5]
15 round buttery crackers, crushed
2 tablespoons butter or use butter-flavored spray

Combine chicken, celery, grated onion, water chestnuts and rice in large bowl. Whisk soup, mayonnaise, lemon juice and pepper sauce together in separate bowl; fold in mushrooms, pimiento and eggs. Combine with chicken mixture and season with salt and pepper. Spoon mixture into sprayed 2-quart round casserole. Sprinkle top with almonds and crushed crackers; dot with butter. Bake at 350° for 30 to 35 minutes or until hot and bubbly. Serve with fresh fruit and croissants.

Makes 6 servings

Per serving: 599 calories, 42 g fat, 28 g protein, 33 g carbohydrate, 182 mg cholesterol, 888 mg sodium.

About Lettuce

Buy a lightweight head of iceberg lettuce with nice green leaves; a heavy one will have a large, dense core. To wash and store iceberg lettuce, hold head with both hands and hit stem end on edge of sink to break core loose from leaves. Pull out and discard core. Rinse head inside and out with cold water and drain in colander. Spin whole head in lettuce spinner if possible. Push paper towel into cavity and wrap head in paper towels. Store in ziptop bag in refrigerator. Change paper towels when damp. For romaine lettuce, break off leaves, put in sink of cold water and let stand 30 minutes or more, swishing occasionally. Drain in colander and spin in lettuce spinner, if possible. Put paper towels in large ziptop bag, add layer of romaine leaves, more paper towel and remaining leaves. Store in refrigerator. Lettuce will remain nice and crisp.

Quick Chicken Curry

¼ cup (½ stick) butter	1 (14-ounce) can chicken broth
1 cup chopped onion	½ cup half-and-half
½ cup chopped celery with some leaves	Dash of ground cinnamon
	Dash of ground cumin
⅓ cup chopped bell pepper	Dash of hot pepper sauce
½ to 1 tablespoon curry powder	4 cups bite-size *Easy Cooked Chicken*
½ teaspoon ground ginger	
2 (10¾-ounce) cans cream of chicken soup	⅔ cup peeled and chopped apple

Melt butter in large saucepan over medium heat. Add onion, celery, bell pepper, curry powder (start with a little and add more, if desired) and ginger. Cook and stir about 5 minutes. Stir in soup, chicken broth, half-and-half, cinnamon, cumin and pepper sauce. Heat thoroughly without boiling. Mix in chicken and apple. Season with salt and pepper. Add broth or water if thick. (May prepare to this point a day ahead and refrigerate. Reheat.) Serve over hot cooked rice with uneven number of condiments sprinkled or spooned on top. Choose from chutney, sliced bananas, golden raisins, toasted coconut, pineapple tidbits, chopped roasted peanuts and chopped onion or other condiments you prefer.

Makes 8 servings   Clo Ann Rabb, Meridian, Mississippi

Per serving: 264 calories, 10 g fat, 31 g protein, 13 g carbohydrate, 90 mg cholesterol, 743 mg sodium.

Crunchy Chicken Casserole

2 cups bite-size *Easy Cooked Chicken*	1 cup finely chopped onion
	1 (2-ounce) jar diced pimientos, drained
½ cup regular or light mayonnaise	
½ cup regular or light sour cream	1 tablespoon fresh lemon juice
1 (4-ounce) can sliced mushrooms, drained	Dash of hot pepper sauce
	1½ cups chow mein noodles
1 (10¾-ounce) cream of mushroom soup	20 round buttery crackers, crushed
	Butter-flavored spray
1 cup finely chopped celery	

Mix chicken, mayonnaise, sour cream, mushrooms, soup, celery, onion, pimientos, lemon juice, pepper sauce and noodles in large bowl. Pour mixture into sprayed 7x11-inch baking. Top with crushed crackers and spray with butter-flavored spray. Bake at 350° for 25 to 30 minutes or until hot and bubbly.

Makes 6 servings

Per serving: 302 calories, 17 g fat, 16 g protein, 24 g carbohydrate, 48 mg cholesterol, 785 mg sodium.

Chicken Spaghetti

2 tablespoons butter	1 (10¾-ounce) can cream of celery soup
1 cup chopped onion	
½ cup chopped celery	4 ounces pasteurized prepared cheese product, cubed (½ cup)
1 cup chopped bell pepper	
3½ to 4 cups bite-size *Easy Cooked Chicken* or cooked turkey	2 (14-ounce) cans chicken broth
	8 ounces thin spaghetti
1 (10-ounce) can diced tomatoes and green chilies, undrained	½ cup grated Asiago cheese
	Paprika

Melt butter in large saucepan and sauté onion, celery and bell pepper until tender, about 4 minutes. Stir in chicken, tomatoes and green chillies, soup, cubed cheese and lemon juice. Season with salt and pepper. Cook until cheese melts, gently folding occasionally. Bring chicken broth to boil in medium saucepan. Break spaghetti into thirds and add to pan. Return to boil. Cook 8 minutes, stirring occasionally to keep spaghetti from sticking together. Do not drain. Let stand 5 minutes. Stir spaghetti into chicken mixture. Pour into sprayed 9x13-inch baking dish. Sprinkle with Asiago cheese. Bake covered at 350° for 30 minutes or until hot and bubbly. Let stand 10 minutes. Freezes well.

Makes 6 to 8 servings

Per serving of 8: 360 calories, 10 g fat, 39 g protein, 29 g carbohydrate, 105 mg cholesterol, 1091 mg sodium.

Chicken Tetrazzini

2 tablespoons butter	1 (10¾-ounce) can cream of mushroom soup
1 cup chopped bell pepper	
¾ cup chopped onion	2 ounces Cheddar cheese, shredded (½ cup)
1 cup chopped celery	
3 cups bite-size *Easy Cooked Chicken*	3¼ cups chicken broth
	8 ounces thin spaghetti, broken
2 tablespoons diced pimiento	½ cup grated Parmesan cheese

Melt butter in large saucepan. Sauté bell pepper, onion and celery until tender, 3 to 4 minutes. Stir in chicken, pimiento, mushroom soup and Cheddar cheese. Cook spaghetti in chicken broth in separate large saucepan until al dente, about 8 minutes, stirring occasionally to prevent sticking together. Do not drain. Mix *half* the spaghetti into chicken mixture. Put in sprayed 9x13-inch baking dish and cover with remaining spaghetti. Sprinkle with Parmesan cheese. Cover and bake at 375° for 30 minutes. Let stand 10 minutes. May make ahead.

Makes 6 to 8 servings   **Eleanor Irish, Annandale, Virginia**

Per serving of 8: 314 calories, 10 g fat, 29 g protein, 27 g carbohydrate, 59 mg cholesterol, 715 mg sodium.

Turkey Tetrazzini

8	ounces thin spaghetti, broken into thirds	3	cups bite-size cooked turkey or *Easy Cooked Chicken*
½	cup (1 stick) butter	1	(7.3-ounce) jar small whole mushrooms, drained
1	cup chopped onion		
6	tablespoons flour	2	tablespoons drained sliced ripe olives (optional)
4	cups chicken broth		
1	teaspoon seasoned salt	2	to 3 tablespoons drained sliced pimiento
	Dash of hot pepper sauce (optional)	1½	ounces Parmesan cheese, freshly grated (½ cup, optional)
4	ounces pasteurized prepared cheese product, cubed (½ cup)	2	tablespoons snipped parsley Paprika

Cook spaghetti according to package directions until al dente, 7 to 8 minutes (spaghetti will continue to cook in casserole). Drain, but do not rinse. Set aside in large bowl. Meanwhile, melt butter in large saucepan over medium heat and sauté onion until tender. Sprinkle in flour. Cook and stir until mixture is bubbly and beginning to brown, about 2 minutes. Add chicken broth, seasoned salt and pepper sauce. Bring almost to boil and simmer until slightly thickened. Add cubed cheese, stirring until melted and smooth. Mix in turkey, mushrooms, olives and pimiento. Stir into spaghetti and pour into sprayed 9x13-inch baking dish. Sprinkle with Parmesan cheese, parsley and paprika. Bake uncovered at 350° for 30 to 35 minutes or until hot and bubbly. Let stand 5 to 10 minutes. Serve with *Autumn Pear and Pomegranate Salad* and *Joey's Holiday Rolls.*

Makes 6 to 8 servings   Mona Bell, Lawrence, Kansas

Per serving of 8: 403 calories, 24 g fat, 32 g protein, 18 g carbohydrate, 119 mg cholesterol, 1255 mg sodium.

Alternative Topping: Mix 4 tablespoons dry breadcrumbs, 1 teaspoon vegetable oil and 2 tablespoons grated Parmesan or Asiago cheese together in small bowl until evenly blended. Sprinkle over Tetrazzini mixture. Bake at 350° for 25 to 35 minutes or until crumbs are golden brown and edges are bubbling.

Roast Turkey Breast

1	(4- to 7-pound) bone-in turkey breast, thawed
	Salt and pepper
	Fresh lemon juice
2	tablespoons butter, melted
¼	teaspoon paprika
⅛	teaspoon dried thyme, crushed
⅛	teaspoon dried basil, crushed
¼	teaspoon salt

⅛	teaspoon pepper
1	teaspoon chicken bouillon granules
½	cup Rosé wine, or water
2	cups small whole fresh mushrooms[3] (optional)
1	(16-ounce) package frozen pearl onions, or 1 pound pearl onions, peeled (optional)

Thoroughly rinse turkey breast and pat dry. Lightly sprinkle inside and outside with salt and pepper. Squeeze lemon juice on both sides. Place breast skin-side up in sprayed roasting pan without rack. Mix butter, paprika, thyme, basil, salt and pepper in small bowl and brush over outside of breast. Dissolve bouillon granules in wine in small bowl or glass measure. Set aside for basting.

Roast breast uncovered with neck area toward rear of oven at 400° for 20 minutes. Extend rack and turn pan around. Baste breast with wine mixture. Reduce heat to 325° and bake 18 to 20 minutes per pound minus 20 minutes already baked at 400°. Baste with wine mixture and pan drippings frequently. Turn breast around in oven occasionally. If pan drippings begin to fry, add ¼ cup water to pan. During last 30 minutes of roasting, add mushrooms and onions to pan. Add another ¼ cup water if dry. Bake until instant-read thermometer inserted in thickest part of breast reads 165°. If turkey gets done before vegetables, remove turkey to cutting board and tent with foil. Let stand 15 minutes or until vegetables are tender. Remove mushrooms and onions with slotted spoon to serving bowl. Cover with foil and keep warm in turned off oven. Carve breast into slices[60] and transfer to serving platter. Garnish with parsley.

Use liquid in pan to make gravy. If needed, add about ½ cup water or chicken broth[11] to increase amount of liquid. Pour into small saucepan and heat over medium heat. To thicken gravy, stir 1 tablespoon flour into ¼ cup water in small bowl until flour dissolves. Quickly whisk into gravy. Cook and whisk until thickened. Add salt and pepper if needed. Serve gravy over turkey slices.

Makes 8 servings   **Pauline Friend, Chandler, Arizona**

Per serving: 429 calories, 14 g fat, 70 g protein, 3 g carbohydrate, 137 mg cholesterol, 1752 mg sodium.

To Peel Pearl Onions

Put 1 pound pearl onions in medium saucepan and add about 2 cups boiling water or enough to cover. Let stand covered about 5 minutes. Drain and rinse with cold water. Cut off root ends and peel (squeeze onions out of their skins). Snip off any stringy tops with kitchen shears.

Roast Turkey

1 fresh or frozen turkey (figure 1- to 1½-pounds per serving)	Onion, celery and parsley
Salt and pepper	Vegetable oil
	Paprika

Place frozen turkey on newspapers in refrigerator to thaw. Allow 24 hours for each 5 pounds of turkey. *Do not thaw at room temperature or in warm water.* To rapidly thaw, place packaged bird in sink or large pan of cold water. Change water every 30 to 40 minutes and allow 30 minutes per pound to thaw.

Weigh neck and giblets–could weigh a pound. Subtract from total weight to determine roasting time. Start Giblet Broth for gravy (see *Turkey Gravy*).

Release legs from under wire clasp if present. Thoroughly rinse turkey with cold water inside and out. Pat dry. Lightly rub cavity with salt and pepper. Put whole peeled medium onion, several celery pieces with leaves and several sprigs of parsley in cavity. Secure neck skin to back skin with toothpick. Rub turkey with oil or spray with cooking spray. Sprinkle with salt and pepper. Slip drumsticks back under wire clasp or through slits in skin in tail area. Lift wings up and across back with tips touching.

Use sturdy roasting pan large enough to hold turkey–one with good handles. Cover inside of V-shaped wire rack with double thickness of heavy-duty foil. Put rack in roasting pan. Place turkey *breast down* on rack. Sprinkle back with paprika. Put pan in preheated 400° oven with legs toward rear. (If oven is not deep enough, put pan in sideways and rotate 180° after roasting 20 minutes.) Roast turkey 45 minutes. Remove roasting pan from oven. Using turkey lifters or several thicknesses of paper towels, lift turkey and remove foil from rack. Return turkey *breast up* to rack. Sprinkle with paprika. Cut piece of heavy-duty foil 10 inches longer than width of pan and fold in half crosswise. Open foil and place fold lengthwise over bird. Crimp sides of foil to sides of pan without letting foil touch turkey. Leave ends open for heat circulation. No need to baste. Return roasting pan to oven. *Reduce temperature* to 325°. Roast for *remaining* time according to following table (takes into account 45 minutes already roasted):

10 to 12 pounds – 2½ to 3 hours	16 to 18 pounds – 3¼ to 4 hours
12 to 14 pounds – 2¾ to 3¼ hours	18 to 20 pounds – 3½ to 4¼ hours
14 to 16 pounds – 3 to 3¾ hours	20 and over – 3¾ to 4½ hours

With 30 minutes of roasting time left, remove tent and free legs, allowing inside of thighs to cook thoroughly. Now baste turkey with pan drippings. Turkey is done when instant-read thermometer inserted into inner thigh reads 175° to 180°, legs wiggle easily and juices run clear when fork is inserted into deepest part of leg joint. Transfer turkey to cutting board and tent with foil. Let turkey stand 20 minutes before carving.[60] Set pan with drippings aside for making *Turkey Gravy*. Serve with *Cornbread Dressing* and *Turkey Gravy* or *Giblet Gravy*.

Per pound: 564 calories, 28 g fat, 73 g protein, 0 g carbohydrate, 280 mg cholesterol, 240 mg sodium.

Turkey Gravy

Giblet Broth:

Turkey neck, gizzard and liver
2 ribs of celery, broken into pieces
1 small onion, quartered
½ teaspoon salt

¼ teaspoon pepper

Pan of drippings from
Roast Turkey
3 tablespoons flour

Giblet Broth: Remove any skin from turkey neck. Thoroughly rinse neck, gizzard and liver. Refrigerate liver (I discard heart). Put neck, gizzard, celery, onion, salt and pepper in medium saucepan and add water to cover. Bring to boil. Reduce heat and simmer covered 45 minutes to 1 hour or until tender. Add water or broth as needed to keep neck and giblets covered. During last 15 minutes add liver, if used (its taste is not universally enjoyed). Strain broth into medium bowl and cover. Discard vegetables. When neck is cool enough to handle, pull off meat, discarding bones. Coarsely chop neck meat and giblets. Put in bowl and cover. Refrigerate broth and giblets until ready to make gravy.

Pour *Roast Turkey* drippings from roasting pan through strainer into 4-cup glass measure or bowl. Set aside.

Add 1 cup Giblet Broth to roasting pan. Stir over low heat to loosen any brown bits on bottom. Pour into drippings in 4-cup glass measure. Let stand 10 minutes, allowing fat to rise to surface. Spoon 3 tablespoons of surface fat into medium saucepan; set aside. Skim off and discard any remaining fat from liquid in glass measure. Add remaining giblet broth to glass measure and add canned chicken broth or water to make 3½ cups.

Heat fat in saucepan over medium heat. Whisk in flour. Cook 1 to 2 minutes, whisking constantly until golden. Gradually whisk in 3½ cups liquid from glass measure. Cook and whisk over medium heat until gravy is smooth and slightly thickened. Add *small* amount of browning and seasoning sauce, if desired. Season with salt and pepper if needed.

Makes 3½ cups.

Per ¼ cup: 70 calories, 3 g fat, 9 g protein, 1 g carbohydrate, 84 mg cholesterol, 276 mg sodium.

Giblet Gravy: Prepare Turkey Gravy as directed above. Stir giblets, 2 chopped hard-cooked eggs and, optionally, 2 tablespoons uncooked cornbread dressing (reserved from making *Cornbread Dressing*) into saucepan of Turkey Gravy. Heat thoroughly. Makes about 4 cups.

Salads & Salad Dressings

Salads

Salad Dressings

Chicken and Strawberry Tossed Salad

One of my favorite salads, especially for lunch. The Poppy Seed dressing is outstanding.

Poppy Seed Dressing:
¼ cup cider vinegar
½ cup sugar
2 teaspoons minced onion
¼ teaspoon garlic powder
1 teaspoon salt
1 teaspoon dry mustard[9]
1 tablespoon poppy seeds
2 tablespoons orange juice

¾ cup vegetable oil
3 cups bite-size spinach[28]
3 cups bite-size romaine lettuce
2½ cups bite-size *Easy Cooked Chicken*
2 cups halved or quartered strawberries
2 cups cubed honeydew melon
½ cup toasted sliced almonds[5]

Poppy Seed Dressing: Mix vinegar, sugar, onion, garlic powder, salt, dry mustard, poppy seeds and orange juice in blender. Slowly pour oil through top and blend until emulsified. (Alternatively, put all ingredients except oil in jar with tight-fitting lid and shake well. Add oil and shake to emulsify.) Refrigerate until ready to serve. Makes 1½ cups.

Prepare salad ingredients and put in separate covered containers. Refrigerate all ingredients except almonds. Just before serving, mix spinach, romaine, chicken, strawberries, melon and almonds in large salad bowl. Drizzle with desired amount of dressing (not too much, you can always add more). Toss and serve.

Makes 8 servings   Faye Netzer, Denver, Colorado

Per serving: 344 calories, 23 g fat, 14 g protein, 23 g carbohydrate, 40 mg cholesterol, 274 mg sodium.

Strawberry Tossed Salad variation: Omit chicken. Proceed as directed above.

Creamy Tuna or Chicken Twist

1½ cups spiral pasta
1 cup mayonnaise
2 tablespoons cider vinegar
Dash of pepper
1 cup chopped celery
¼ cup chopped red onion

1 teaspoon dried dill weed, crushed
½ cup frozen baby green peas
Dash of hot pepper sauce
1 (9-ounce) can albacore tuna, drained and flaked, or 1½ cups bite-size *Easy Cooked Chicken*

Cook pasta according to package directions. Rinse in cold water.[57] Drain. Whisk mayonnaise, vinegar and pepper in large bowl. Stir in celery, onion, dill, peas, pepper sauce and tuna. Add pasta and toss. Cover and refrigerate. If dry, stir in more mayonnaise. Add salt and pepper if needed. Recipe may be doubled.

Makes 4 servings   Patsy Minter, Destin, Florida

Per serving: 611 calories, 48 g fat, 22 g protein, 29 g carbohydrate, 38 mg cholesterol, 579 mg sodium.

My Favorite Chicken Salad

4 cups bite-size *Easy Cooked Chicken*	⅛ teaspoon pepper
	¾ cup mayonnaise
1 cup chopped celery	2 tablespoons fresh lemon juice
2 tablespoons chopped green onions or chopped sweet onion	⅛ teaspoon hot pepper sauce
	4 hard-cooked eggs,[18] chopped
½ teaspoon salt	Paprika
¼ teaspoon celery salt	

Combine chicken, celery, green onion, salt, celery salt and pepper in large bowl. Stir in mayonnaise, lemon juice and pepper sauce. Gently mix in eggs.[49] Cover and refrigerate 2 hours or overnight. Stir. Add more mayonnaise if dry. Serve in glass salad bowl. Sprinkle with paprika. Fill **Mini Puffs** with salad for a great appetizer!

Makes 6 servings

Per serving: 492 calories, 36 g fat, 39 g protein, 5 g carbohydrate, 479 mg cholesterol, 923 mg sodium.

Shrimp Salad variation: Substitute 4 cups cut-in-half, peeled, boiled shrimp for chicken. Prepare salad as directed above. Serve on individual lettuce-lined plates. Garnish with tomato wedges, quartered hard-cooked eggs, slice of sweet onion, ripe olives and pepperoncini.[G] Serve with round buttery crackers.

Sardi's Salad

4 cups bite-size *Easy Cooked Chicken*	1 cup finely snipped parsley
	1 cup chopped toasted pecans
3 tablespoons chopped green onions	1 cup sour cream
	1 cup mayonnaise
¾ cup chopped celery, including some leaves	½ teaspoon salt
	¼ teaspoon pepper
3 teaspoons small capers, rinsed and drained	Dash of hot pepper sauce
1 cup frozen baby green peas	8 romaine lettuce leaves

Combine chicken, green onion, celery, capers, peas, parsley and pecans in large bowl. Cover and refrigerate. Mix sour cream, mayonnaise, salt, pepper and pepper sauce in separate bowl. Cover and refrigerate. (May prepare to this point early in the day.) About an hour before serving, combine mixtures and refrigerate to allow flavors to blend. Serve on lettuce-lined plates with toasted rye crackers or **Herb Pita Toast**.

Makes 8 servings   Midge Bartlett, Boulder, Colorado

Per serving: 480 calories, 41 g fat, 24 g protein, 9 g carbohydrate, 86 mg cholesterol, 663 mg sodium.

Midge's Layered Chicken Salad

4 cups shredded iceberg lettuce	4 cups bite-size *Easy Cooked Chicken*
1 (8-ounce) can sliced water chestnuts, rinsed and drained	1 cup shredded Cheddar cheese
1 cup fresh bean sprouts	Dressing:
½ cup thinly sliced green onions, including some tops	2¼ cups mayonnaise
½ cup thinly sliced peeled cucumber	1 teaspoon curry powder
2 cups frozen baby green peas, thawed	1 tablespoon sugar
	⅛ teaspoon white pepper

Place lettuce in bottom of 10x15-inch baking dish. Layer with water chestnuts, bean sprouts, green onion, cucumber, peas and chicken. Put dollops of dressing over chicken and spread out evenly to cover and seal layers. Refrigerate covered at least 24 hours. Sprinkle with Cheddar cheese and garnish with dry-roasted peanuts, cherry tomatoes and parsley. Serve by cutting into squares and lifting out layered portions. Serve with *Cranberry Sherbet Salad* and warm croissants.

Dressing: Mix mayonnaise, curry powder, sugar and pepper in medium bowl.

Makes 10 to 12 servings   Midge Bartlett, Boulder, Colorado

Per serving of 12: 450 Calories, 39g Fat, 23g Protein, 9g Carbohydrate, 76 mg Cholesterol, 354mg Sodium.

Rhona's Chicken Salad

1 cup salad dressing	5 cups bite-size *Easy Cooked Chicken*
1 tablespoon milk	
2 teaspoons sugar	½ cup chopped bell pepper
1 tablespoon grated onion[55]	2 tablespoons drained diced pimiento
½ teaspoon salt	4 hard-cooked eggs,[18] chopped
¼ teaspoon pepper	1½ to 2 cups chow mein noodles
1¾ cups diagonally sliced celery	

Mix salad dressing, milk and sugar in small bowl until smooth. Stir in onion, salt and pepper. Put celery, chicken, bell pepper and pimiento in large bowl. Fold in salad dressing mixture. Gently stir in eggs.[49] Chill. Stir in chow mein noodles just before serving. Serve with *Raspberry Salad* and croissants.

Makes 10 servings   Rhona Hulst, Zeeland, Michigan

Per serving: 216 calories, 12 g fat, 31 g protein, 10 g carbohydrate, 173 mg cholesterol, 381 mg sodium.

Variation: Substitute mayonnaise for salad dressing. Add 1 teaspoon fresh lemon juice and dashes of hot pepper sauce to mayonnaise mixture. Omit noodles. Mix and chill as directed above. Serve on lettuce or make *Chicken Salad Melts*.

Chicken Napa Cabbage Salad

3 cups bite-size *Easy Cooked Chicken*

1 large head napa cabbage

6 green onions, thinly sliced

24 snow peas, washed, drained, tips removed and cut diagonally into thirds (about ½ cup)

½ cup sliced water chestnuts, rinsed and drained

Dressing:

¼ cup seasoned rice vinegar

1 tablespoon soy sauce

¼ cup sugar

1 tablespoon fresh lemon juice

½ cup canola oil

Ramen Noodle Mixture:

3 tablespoons butter

2 (3-ounce) packages chicken-flavored or Oriental-flavored ramen noodle soup mix (discard seasoning packets)

½ cup pine nuts

½ cup roasted salted sunflower kernels, or ¼ cup toasted sesame seeds[5]

Prepare chicken. Remove center and any brown parts from cabbage. Soak in cold water 20 minutes and drain upside down in colander. Insert paper towels into cavity. Wrap in paper towels and put in ziptop bag. Put snow peas and water chestnuts in separate ziptop bags. Refrigerate all ingredients until ready to assemble. Meanwhile, prepare Dressing and Ramen Noodle Mixture. (May prepare ahead to this point and assemble following day.)

Dressing: Mix vinegar, soy sauce, sugar and lemon juice in jar with tight-fitting lid. Shake well. Add oil and shake until emulsified. Set aside or refrigerate.

Ramen Noodle Mixture: Melt butter in large pie plate or medium shallow pan in 350° oven. Remove. Crush noodles into small pieces in bowl and mix in pine nuts and sunflower kernels. Pour mixture into pie plate and toss with the melted butter. Return to oven. Bake at 350° for 6 to 7 minutes. Drain on paper towels. Cool.

About 15 minutes before assembling salad remove paper towels from cabbage. Turn cabbage on its side and slice into ribbons. Drain in colander. Combine cabbage, green onion, snow peas, water chestnuts and chicken in large bowl. Add desired amount of dressing and toss gently. Mix in baked noodle mixture and serve immediately.

Makes 6 to 8 servings

Per serving of 8: 475 calories, 30 g fat, 23 g protein, 34 g carbohydrate, 80 mg cholesterol, 410 mg sodium.

Wild Woodland Salad

Dressing:
1 or 2 garlic cloves, minced
1 tablespoon Dijon mustard
¼ teaspoon salt
¼ teaspoon sugar
¼ teaspoon pepper
¼ cup white wine vinegar or seasoned rice vinegar
⅓ cup vegetable oil

1 (6.7-ounce) box brown and wild rice (mushroom recipe)

1 cup chicken broth[11]
1 cup water
1 tablespoon fresh lemon juice
3 cups bite-size *Easy Cooked Chicken*
¼ cup chopped green onions
½ cup diced red bell pepper
48 snow peas, washed, drained, tips removed and cut diagonally into thirds (about 1 cup)
2 avocados, peeled and diced[29]
1 cup chopped toasted pecans

Dressing: Mix garlic, mustard, salt, sugar, pepper and vinegar in jar with tight-fitting lid. Shake well. Add oil and shake until emulsified. Dressing may be made several days ahead. Refrigerate until ready to use. Shake well before using.

Stir rice, contents of seasoning packet, chicken broth and water together in medium saucepan. Bring to boil. Reduce heat and simmer covered 25 minutes. Remove from heat. Let stand covered 10 minutes or until most liquid is absorbed. Fluff with fork and transfer to large glass salad bowl. Mix in lemon juice, chicken, green onion, bell pepper and snow peas. Pour dressing over chicken mixture and mix well. Refrigerate 2 to 4 hours. Just before serving, add avocado and pecans. Toss gently and serve.

Makes 6 servings   Virginia Holmes, Longmont, Colorado

Per serving: 558 calories, 38 g fat, 26 g protein, 34 g carbohydrate, 57 mg cholesterol, 1041 mg sodium.

Crunchy Mandarin Chicken Salad

1 cup regular or light mayonnaise
1 teaspoon soy sauce
½ to 1 teaspoon curry powder
½ teaspoon ground ginger

2 cups bite-size *Easy Cooked Chicken*
½ cup chopped cashew nuts
1 (11-ounce) can Mandarin oranges, drained

Mix mayonnaise, soy sauce, curry powder and ginger in small bowl; set aside. Combine chicken and cashews in medium bowl; fold in oranges. Stir in dressing. Chill. Serve on croissants with lettuce leaf or in lettuce-lined salad bowl.

Makes 4 servings

Per serving: 477 calories, 31 g fat, 30 g protein, 20 g carbohydrate, 98 mg cholesterol, 418 mg sodium.

Apple Walnut Salad

Cranberry Vinaigrette:
½ cup whole-berry cranberry sauce
1 tablespoon chopped red onion
2 tablespoons sugar
¼ teaspoon salt
1 teaspoon dry mustard[9]
⅓ cup red wine vinegar
⅔ cup canola oil

1 small tart apple, unpeeled

1 small Golden or Red Delicious apple, unpeeled
10 cups bite-size mixed greens: romaine and iceberg lettuce and spinach, or 2 (10-ounce) bags mixed greens
½ red onion, thinly sliced and separated into rings
¾ cup broken toasted walnut pieces[5]
¼ cup crumbled blue cheese

Cranberry Vinaigrette: Combine cranberry sauce, onion, sugar, salt, dry mustard and vinegar in food processor, blender, or in 2-cup glass measure with handheld blender. Process or blend until smooth. Gradually add oil and blend until emulsified. Pour into jar with lid and refrigerate. Shake well before using. Makes 1⅓ cups.

Core apples and thinly slice lengthwise. Cut slices in half and put in medium bowl.[7] Put greens in large salad bowl. Add apples. Toss salad with just enough vinaigrette to coat greens. Place onion rings on top and sprinkle with walnuts and blue cheese. (Alternatively, toss salad with vinaigrette. Place individual portions on salad plates. Arrange several onion rings on top. Sprinkle each with walnuts and blue cheese.) Recipe may be halved.

Makes 10 servings

Per serving: 183 calories, 15 g fat, 4 g protein, 12 g carbohydrate, 3 mg cholesterol, 80 mg sodium,

Cucumbers and Onions

3 medium cucumbers, peeled and thinly sliced
1 sweet medium onion, thinly sliced and separated into rings
1 teaspoon salt

½ cup sugar
⅔ cup white wine vinegar
1 teaspoon dried chervil, crushed
⅛ teaspoon pepper

Put cucumbers and onions in deep bowl. Sprinkle with salt and toss. Cover with small inverted saucer that will fit inside bowl. Weight down with heavy object (like can of beans). Refrigerate at least 1 hour. Remove and drain without rinsing. Stir sugar and vinegar in small bowl until dissolved and pour over cucumbers and onions. Mix in chervil and pepper. Refrigerate in covered container.

Makes 6 servings   Terry VanderVeen Bright, Lynchburg, Virginia

Per serving: 116 calories, 1 g fat, 3 g protein, 28 g carbohydrate, 0 mg cholesterol, 363 mg sodium.

Autumn Pear and Pomegranate Salad

Pears, unlike most fruit, ripen best off the tree.[97] *Pomegranates are available during October and November in the United States.*

2 or 3 ripe Bosc, Anjou, or Bartlett pears, unpeeled	¾ cup broken toasted walnut pieces[5]
10 cups bite-size mixed greens: spinach, romaine and iceberg lettuce, or 2 (10-ounce) bags mixed greens	¼ cup crumbled blue cheese
	Seeds of 1 pomegranate, or 3 tablespoons snipped dried cranberries (freeze cranberries to prevent sticking to kitchen shears)
1 recipe *Balsamic Vinaigrette, Raspberry Vinaigrette* or *Cranberry Vinaigrette*	

Cut pears into wedges and remove seeds (apple wedger works well). Cut wedges in half or into thirds.[7] Combine greens and pears in large salad bowl. Toss gently with just enough vinaigrette to coat. Sprinkle walnuts, blue cheese and pomegranate seeds on top. (Alternatively, make as many individual composed[G] salads as needed using one pear for every two or three salads. Slice into wedges; peel and remove seeds. Line each salad plate with bed of greens and arrange uneven number of wedges on top. Drizzle with vinaigrette. Sprinkle with walnuts, blue cheese and pomegranate seeds.)

Makes 10 servings

Per serving: 149 calories, 12 g fat, 3 g protein, 10 g carbohydrate, 3 mg cholesterol, 88 mg sodium.

Fairhope Spinach Salad

Dressing:	1¼ pounds fresh spinach, washed, drained and stems removed[28] (about 10 cups)
2 tablespoons balsamic vinegar	
2 tablespoons honey	
1 tablespoon snipped fresh parsley	1 small red onion, thinly sliced and separated into rings
2 garlic cloves, crushed	
Freshly ground black pepper	4 ounces feta cheese, crumbled (½ cup)
¼ to ⅓ cup extra-virgin olive oil	⅓ cup toasted pine nuts[5]

Dressing: Combine vinegar, honey, parsley, garlic and pepper in jar with tight-fitting lid. Shake well. Add olive oil (¼ cup for tarter dressing) and shake well.

Place whole spinach leaves on individual plates. Add onion rings and sprinkle with feta cheese. Pass dressing and pine nuts.

Makes 6 servings   Jeff Vadakin, Fairhope, Alabama

Per serving: 330 calories, 29 g fat, 10 g protein, 19 g carbohydrate, 25 mg cholesterol, 376 mg sodium.

Almond Citrus Salad

Dressing:

⅓ cup orange juice

2 tablespoons white wine vinegar

1 tablespoon honey

2 teaspoons grated fresh ginger

¼ teaspoon salt

⅛ teaspoon red pepper flakes

2 tablespoons vegetable oil

2 grapefruit, segmented[47]

2 navel oranges, peeled and sliced

¼ cup finely chopped red onion

6 cups lightly packed fresh spinach leaves, torn into bite-size pieces[28]

⅓ cup toasted slivered almonds[5]

Dressing: Combine orange juice, vinegar, honey, ginger, salt, pepper flakes and oil in blender or in jar with tight-fitting lid. Blend or shake until emulsified.

Combine grapefruit, oranges and onion with dressing in medium bowl. Let stand 10 minutes or up to 1 hour. Line individual salad plates with spinach. Spoon fruit mixture with dressing over spinach and sprinkle with almonds.

Makes 4 servings   **Lois Flavin, Boulder, Colorado**

Per serving: 215 calories, 12 g fat, 6 g protein, 25 g carbohydrate, 0 mg cholesterol, 202 mg sodium.

Unusual Spinach Salad

Jessie often stayed at the Holiday Inn in Jefferson City, Missouri on business trips and frequently ordered this salad from the menu. When it was removed from the menu, she sent a comment card asking why. Later the recipe arrived in the mail. Now her guests ask for "her" recipe.

Dressing:

½ cup sour cream

¼ cup sugar

2 tablespoons cider vinegar or herb-flavored vinegar

½ teaspoon dry mustard[9]

2 tablespoons prepared horseradish

¼ teaspoon salt

10 ounces fresh spinach, torn into bite-size pieces[28]

½ cup broken toasted pecan pieces[5]

1 (12-ounce) container small curd cottage cheese, drained, or dry curd cottage cheese

1 (8-ounce) package fresh mushrooms, sliced[3] (about 3 cups)

Dressing: Whisk sour cream, sugar, vinegar, dry mustard, horseradish and salt in medium bowl until blended. Cover and refrigerate at least 1 hour.

Combine spinach, pecans, cottage cheese and mushrooms in large salad bowl. Pour dressing over mixture and toss lightly but thoroughly to coat.

Makes 8 servings   **Jessie Patterson, Bella Vista, Arkansas**

Per serving: 156 calories, 9 g fat, 97 g protein, 13 g carbohydrate, 10 mg cholesterol, 281 mg sodium.

Mandarin Orange Salad

This is a "mix and match" type of recipe with many tips. Use some or all ingredients. Add more greens and dressing to increase number of servings.

3 cups bite-size baby spinach[28]
3 cups bite-size iceberg lettuce
3 cups bite-size romaine lettuce
1 medium red onion, thinly sliced and separated into rings
1 (8-ounce) can sliced water chestnuts, rinsed and drained
½ cup diagonally sliced celery
1 cup sliced fresh mushrooms[3]

1 chilled (11-ounce) can Mandarin oranges, drained
1 or 2 avocados, peeled and diced[29]
2 kiwis, peeled and sliced[76]
¼ to ½ cup *Praline Topping* (optional)
1 recipe *Poppy Seed Dressing, Cranberry Vinaigrette* or purchased poppy seed dressing

Put greens, onion, water chestnuts, celery, mushrooms, Mandarin oranges, avocado, kiwi and *Praline Topping* in large salad bowl. Toss with desired amount of dressing (not too much, you can always add more).

Makes 6 to 8 servings

Per serving of 8: 107 calories, 4 g fat, 2 g protein, 18 g carbohydrate, 0 mg cholesterol, 27 mg sodium.

Mock Caesar Salad

2 hearts of romaine lettuce

Mock Caesar Dressing:
1 garlic clove, minced, or to taste
2 tablespoons mayonnaise
½ teaspoon Dijon mustard
1 tablespoon fresh lemon juice
½ teaspoon Worcestershire sauce
¼ teaspoon salt

Freshly ground black pepper
¼ teaspoon sugar
2 tablespoons water
¼ cup extra-virgin olive oil
1½ ounces Asiago or Parmesan cheese, finely shredded (½ cup)

1 cup Caesar croutons

Wash and drain lettuce. Tear into large pieces and put in salad bowl. Pour dressing over salad and toss. Add croutons and mix gently. Serve at once.

Mock Caesar Dressing: Combine garlic, mayonnaise, mustard, lemon juice, Worcestershire sauce, salt, pepper, sugar and water in 2-cup glass measure. Whisk thoroughly. Slowly whisk in oil until emulsified. Stir in cheese. Makes ¾ cup.

Makes 4 to 6 servings

Per serving of 6: 190 calories, 17 g fat, 5 g protein, 6 g carbohydrate, 8 mg cholesterol, 371 mg sodium.

Napa Cabbage Salad

Napa cabbage, or Chinese cabbage, is actually more like lettuce than cabbage—its leaves are thin, crisp and mild. Look for tightly packed heads with crisp green-tipped leaves.

1 large head napa cabbage	1½ cups mayonnaise
1 (8-ounce) package fresh mushrooms, sliced[3]	3 tablespoons soy sauce
½ cup sliced green onions	1½ cups chow mein noodles

Remove center and any brown parts from cabbage. Soak in cold water 20 minutes and drain upside down in colander. Insert paper towels into cavity. Wrap in paper towels and put in ziptop bag. Put mushrooms and green onion in separate ziptop bags. Mix mayonnaise and soy sauce in small bowl with cover. (May prepare ahead to this point. Refrigerate all ingredients until ready to assemble.)

About 15 minutes before serving remove paper towels from cabbage, turn cabbage on its side and slice into ribbons. Drain in colander. *Just before serving,* mix cabbage, mushrooms and green onion in large bowl. Fold in mayonnaise mixture. Mix in noodles and serve immediately.

Makes 8 servings   Linda Sellers, Bella Vista, Arkansas

Per serving: 367 calories, 37 g fat, 4 g protein, 12 g carbohydrate, 14 mg cholesterol, 539 mg sodium.

Tuna Salad

2 (6-ounce) cans albacore tuna, well drained, or 1 (7-ounce) foil pouch and 1 (3-ounce) foil pouch albacore tuna, contents patted dry	⅛ teaspoon seasoned salt
	⅓ cup mayonnaise
	Dash of hot pepper sauce
½ teaspoon fresh lemon juice	1 tablespoon sweet pickle relish (optional)
½ teaspoon prepared mustard	
1 tablespoon sliced green onions	½ tart apple, peeled and diced (optional)
⅓ cup chopped celery	
¼ teaspoon lemon pepper	3 hard-cooked eggs,[18] chopped

Flake tuna with fork in medium bowl. Add lemon juice, mustard, green onion, celery, lemon pepper, seasoned salt, mayonnaise, pepper sauce, pickle relish and apple. Mix well. Gently mix in eggs.[49] Add salt and pepper if needed. Cover and refrigerate. Serve on lettuce-lined plates with crackers or *Cranberry Cornbread Muffins,* or serve on toast with lettuce for sandwiches.

Makes 6 servings

Per serving: 274 calories, 20 g fat, 23 g protein, 1 g carbohydrate, 186 mg cholesterol, 466 mg sodium.

Shrimp Rémoulade

Rémoulade Sauce:
- 1 garlic clove, minced
- ¾ cup Creole mustard
- ⅓ cup olive oil
- ¼ cup white wine vinegar
- 1 tablespoon chopped fresh chives or chopped green onion tops
- ½ cup finely chopped celery
- 2 tablespoons finely snipped parsley
- 2 tablespoons paprika
- ½ teaspoon salt
- ¼ teaspoon freshly ground black pepper[90]
- ½ teaspoon sugar
- Dash of Worcestershire sauce
- Dash of hot pepper sauce
- ¼ cup dry sherry
- 2 pounds medium *Boiled Shrimp*, peeled, deveined and tails removed (about 2⅔ cups)
- Shredded iceberg lettuce or unshredded romaine leaves

Rémoulade Sauce: Combine garlic, mustard, oil, vinegar, chives, celery, parsley, paprika, salt, pepper, sugar, Worcestershire sauce, pepper sauce and sherry in medium bowl. Mix well. Cover and refrigerate 4 hours (preferably overnight) to blend flavors. Makes about 2 cups.

Put shrimp in covered container and refrigerate. Do not combine shrimp with sauce until ready to serve or shrimp will lose their firm texture.

For buffet offering, place bed of shredded lettuce on serving platter, add shrimp and cover with Rémoulade Sauce. For individual servings, serve portion of shrimp on individual plates lined with leaf of romaine. Spoon generous serving of sauce over shrimp. Garnish platter or individual plates with wedges of hard-cooked eggs, tomato wedges and whole ripe olives. Serve with round buttery crackers.

Makes 4 to 6 servings

Per serving of 6: 227 calories, 12 g fat, 20 g protein, 4 g carbohydrate, 243 mg cholesterol, 1236 mg sodium.

Tomate Vinaigrette

- 3 medium tomatoes, cut into ¼-inch slices
- 1 medium sweet onion, thinly sliced (optional)
- 1 garlic clove, minced
- 1 tablespoon cider vinegar
- 2 tablespoons olive oil or vegetable oil
- Salt and pepper
- Snipped parsley or basil

Alternate slices of tomato and onion in a circle on serving plate, or just make circle of tomatoes. Sprinkle with garlic. Drizzle with vinegar, then oil. Sprinkle with salt, pepper and parsley. Cover and let stand 15 minutes before serving.

Makes 4 servings   Katherine Forsyth, Boulder, Colorado

Per serving: 59 calories, 3 g fat, 1 g protein, 9 g carbohydrate, 0 mg cholesterol, 76 mg sodium.

Cucumber Boats

Louis Dressing:		Dashes of hot pepper sauce
¼	cup heavy cream	½ teaspoon sugar
1	cup mayonnaise	¼ cup finely chopped bell pepper
1	cup sour cream	2 tablespoons finely chopped
½	cup chili sauce	green onions
1	to 1½ teaspoons prepared horseradish	2 pounds medium *Boiled Shrimp*, peeled, deveined and tails removed (about 2⅔ cups)
¼	teaspoon celery salt	
2	tablespoons fresh lemon juice	3 medium cucumbers
1	tablespoon Worcestershire sauce	Italian dressing

Louis Dressing: Whisk heavy cream, mayonnaise, sour cream, chili sauce, horseradish, celery salt, lemon juice, Worcestershire sauce, pepper sauce and sugar together in medium bowl. Stir in bell pepper and green onion. Add salt and pepper to taste. Refrigerate. Makes about 3 cups.

Put shrimp in covered container and refrigerate until ready to serve. Peel cucumbers and cut in half lengthwise. Cut thin slice from bottom of each half so "boats" will lie flat. Scoop out seeds and some pulp (grapefruit spoon works well). Brush boats inside and out with Italian dressing to coat. Place upside down on paper-towel-lined plates to drain. Cover and chill until ready to serve.

Mix shrimp with 2 cups of Louis Dressing. Place cucumber boats on lettuce-lined plates and fill each with a portion of shrimp. Garnish with cherry tomatoes, quartered hard-cooked eggs, sweet onion slices, ripe olives and pepperoncini.[G] Serve with remaining Louis Dressing and round buttery crackers.

Makes 6 servings   Martha Tompkins, Greenville, South Carolina

Per serving: 404 calories, 35 g fat, 9 g protein, 13 g carbohydrate, 144 mg cholesterol, 743 mg sodium.

Cranberry Salad

1½	cups boiling water	1	(16-ounce) can whole-berry
2	(4-serving size) packages raspberry-flavored gelatin		cranberry sauce
		1	(16-ounce) container sour cream

Stir boiling water into gelatin in large bowl until completely dissolved, about 2 minutes. Mash cranberry sauce slightly and stir into gelatin. Cool. Fold in sour cream. Pour mixture into 9x13-inch baking dish. Refrigerate until firm. Cut into squares and serve.

Makes 8 servings   Phyllis Myers, Bella Vista, Arkansas

Per serving: 214 calories, 12 g fat, 3 g protein, 26 g carbohydrate, 25 mg cholesterol, 69 mg sodium.

Cucumber Cream Salad

1 (8 serving-size) package lime- or lemon-flavored gelatin
1 teaspoon salt
2 cups boiling water
1 tablespoon vinegar
1 teaspoon grated onion[55]
2 cups sour cream

½ cup mayonnaise
1½ cups seeded and finely chopped cucumber, drained
½ teaspoon dried dill weed, crushed
Mayonnaise
Paprika

Place gelatin and salt in a large bowl and add boiling water. Stir until completely dissolved, about 2 minutes. Add vinegar and onion. Refrigerate until syrupy. Whisk sour cream and mayonnaise together in a medium bowl and fold into chilled gelatin. Stir in cucumber and dill. Pour mixture into sprayed 5-cup mold, 10 individual ½-cup molds or 8x8-inch baking dish. Refrigerate until firm.

Unmold[54] or cut into squares. Serve on lettuce-lined plates. Top each serving with teaspoon of mayonnaise and sprinkle with paprika, if desired.

Makes 9 or 10 servings   Willie McCaleb Rabb, Lexington, Mississippi

Per serving of 10: 248 calories, 19 g fat, 3 g protein, 19 g carbohydrate, 24 mg cholesterol, 346 mg sodium.

Fresh Cranberry Apple Salad

1 (4-serving size) package raspberry-flavored gelatin
1 (4-serving size) package black-cherry-flavored gelatin
½ cup sugar
2 cups boiling water
¼ teaspoon fresh lemon juice

Dash of salt
2 medium Red Delicious apples, unpeeled
1 (12-ounce) package fresh cranberries
1 (8-ounce) can crushed pineapple in juice, drained

Pour gelatins and sugar into large bowl. Add boiling water and stir until completely dissolved, about 2 minutes. Stir in lemon juice and salt. Set aside.

Core and quarter apples. Chop into medium-size pieces (food chopper works well). Put in large bowl. Rinse cranberries and pat dry. Finely chop and add to apples. Mix in pineapple. Stir fruit mixture into gelatin mixture. Pour into sprayed 7x11-inch baking dish. Cover with plastic wrap and refrigerate until firm or overnight. Cut into squares. Serve on lettuce-lined plates. Salad will keep several days covered and refrigerated.

Makes 8 servings

Per serving: 188 calories, 0 g fat, 2 g protein, 46 g carbohydrate, 0 mg cholesterol, 92 mg sodium.

Raspberry Shimmer

A shimmering beauty to serve for a holiday brunch or buffet.

2   cups boiling water
3   (4-serving size) packages raspberry-flavored or strawberry-flavored gelatin

3   (10-ounce) packages frozen sweetened raspberries,* *partially thawed*
24 ounces original low-fat red raspberry yogurt*

Stir boiling water into gelatin in large bowl until completely dissolved, about 2 minutes. Stir in raspberries until thawed (gelatin will begin to thicken). Stir yogurt until creamy and fold into gelatin mixture. Spray 12-cup mold or Bundt pan, two 6-cup molds, or twelve to sixteen individual molds and fill with gelatin mixture. Cover and refrigerate until firm, preferably overnight. Unmold onto appropriate serving platter[54] or unmold smaller molds onto individual lettuce-lined plates. Serve with *Overnight Chicken Casserole*.

* Must use sweetened raspberries and low-fat or full-fat yogurt—not no-fat!

Makes 12 to 16 servings   Judy Gianetto, Boulder, Colorado

Per serving of 16: 140 calories, 0 g fat, 3 g protein, 31 g carbohydrate, 3 mg cholesterol, 63 mg sodium.

Strawberry Shimmer variation: Substitute frozen sweetened sliced strawberries for raspberries and original low-fat strawberry yogurt for raspberry yogurt. Proceed as directed above.

Strawberry Salad

1½ cups boiling water
2   (4-serving size) packages strawberry-flavored gelatin
1   (16-ounce) package frozen sweetened sliced strawberries, *partially thawed*

1   (8-ounce) can crushed pineapple in juice, undrained
½   cup chopped toasted pecans[5] (optional)
1   cup sour cream

Stir boiling water into gelatin in medium bowl until completely dissolved, about 2 minutes. Add strawberries and mix until separated. Refrigerate until partially set (will not take long). Add pineapple and stir in pecans. Pour 2 cups into sprayed 6-cup ring mold or other fancy 6-cup mold, or into 9x9-inch baking pan. Chill slightly. Fold or whisk sour cream into remaining gelatin mixture. Gently pour over chilled layer. Refrigerate until firm. Unmold[54] or cut into squares. Serve on crisp salad greens.

Makes 9 to 12 servings   Ruth Hartman, Springfield, Virginia

Per serving of 12: 166 calories, 7 g fat, 2 g protein, 25 g carbohydrate, 9 mg cholesterol, 49 mg sodium.

Champagne Salad

1 (8-ounce) package cream cheese, cut into pieces and softened	1 (10-ounce) package frozen sweetened sliced strawberries, thawed
¾ cup sugar	1 cup chopped toasted nuts[5]
1 (20-ounce) can crushed pineapple in juice, drained	1 (8-ounce) container whipped topping, thawed
2 bananas, peeled and sliced[7]	

Beat cream cheese and sugar in medium bowl with mixer until smooth. Combine pineapple, bananas, strawberries and nuts in large bowl. Fold in cream cheese mixture, then fold in whipped topping. Spoon mixture into sprayed 7x11-inch baking dish, or into muffin tins lined with paper baking cups for individual servings. Freeze until firm. Let thaw slightly before serving. Slice into squares or remove liners from individual servings. Line silver platter with lettuce leaves, place servings of salad on lettuce and serve. Pretty for a buffet.

Makes 12 servings   Nancy Owens, Annandale, Virginia

Per serving: 66 calories, 0 g fat, 0 g protein, 17 g carbohydrate, 0 mg cholesterol, 0 mg sodium.

Colorful Corn Salad

½ cup cider vinegar	1 (15-ounce) can French-cut green beans
1 tablespoon water	1 (4-ounce) can sliced mushrooms
⅔ cup sugar	1 (2-ounce) jar diced pimiento
½ teaspoon salt	2 cups chopped celery
¼ cup vegetable oil	½ cup chopped onion
Dash of paprika	½ cup chopped green bell pepper
1 (15-ounce) can young early green peas	½ cup chopped yellow bell pepper
1 (15-ounce) can shoe peg corn	½ cup chopped orange bell pepper

Mix vinegar, water, sugar, salt, oil and paprika in small saucepan. Bring to boil. Remove from heat. Cool. Drain peas, corn, beans, mushrooms and pimientos in colander and pour into large bowl. Add celery, onion and bell pepper. Pour vinegar mixture over vegetables. Mix well. Refrigerate covered overnight or up to 2 days. Serve in glass salad bowl with slotted spoon.

Makes 6 servings   Myrtice Frieburg, Tulsa, Oklahoma

Per serving: 190 calories, 1 g fat, 4 g protein, 47 g carbohydrate, 0 mg cholesterol, 833 mg sodium.

Raspberry Salad

Easy. A winner everytime!

1½ cups boiling water	1 (12-ounce) package frozen unsweetened raspberries, partially thawed
2 (4-serving size) packages raspberry-flavored gelatin	
2 tablespoons fresh lemon juice	2 cups applesauce

Stir boiling water into gelatin in large bowl until completely dissolved, about 2 minutes. Add lemon juice and raspberries. Gently stir until raspberries are thawed. Fold in applesauce. Pour mixture into sprayed 7x11-inch baking dish. Refrigerate until firm. Cut into squares and serve on lettuce-lined plates. Garnish with fresh raspberries and mint leaves, if desired.

Makes 8 servings   Women's Association, Valley Presbyterian Church
Scottsdale, Arizona

Per serving: 203 calories, 0 g fat, 2 g protein, 51 g carbohydrate, 0 mg cholesterol, 58 mg sodium.

Broccoli Salad

4 cups small-cut fresh broccoli pieces including some tender stalks (broccoli crowns are good)	¼ cup roasted and salted sunflower kernels
	½ cup raisins
1 cup diagonally-sliced celery	1 (8-ounce) can sliced water chestnuts, rinsed and well drained
½ cup sliced green onions, including some tops	
1 cup halved red seedless grapes	Dressing:
8 slices bacon, cooked and crumbled[14] (about ⅔ cup)	1 cup mayonnaise
	⅓ cup sugar
¾ cup toasted slivered almonds[5]	2 tablespoons red wine vinegar

Mix broccoli, celery, green onion and grapes in large covered container. Refrigerate several hours or overnight. About 1 hour before serving, pour dressing over broccoli mixture. Toss well and return to refrigerator. Just before serving, mix bacon, almonds, sunflower kernels, raisins and water chestnuts in medium bowl. Add to salad and toss.

Dressing: Whisk mayonnaise, sugar and vinegar together in small covered container. Refrigerate several hours or overnight to dissolve sugar. Stir well before adding to salad.

Makes 6 to 8 servings   Gay Hendricks, Cumberland, Wisconsin
(contributed by Jo Bain, Bella Vista, Arkansas)

Per serving of 8: 415 calories, 33 g fat, 8 g protein, 29 g carbohydrate, 10 mg cholesterol, 419 mg sodium.

Cranberry Sherbet Salad

Perfect for Thanksgiving. Nancy Gamble and I have been friends since the early 1970's, when we lived in Berkeley Heights, New Jersey.

1½ cups boiling water	1 (16-ounce) can whole-berry cranberry sauce
2 (4-serving size) packages raspberry-flavored gelatin	½ cup chopped toasted nuts
1 pint raspberry sherbet	1 cup finely chopped celery
1 tablespoon fresh lemon juice	

Stir boiling water into gelatin in large bowl until completely dissolved, about 2 minutes. Whisk in sherbet and lemon juice. Chill until mixture mounds. Mash cranberry sauce slightly and fold into gelatin mixture along with nuts and celery. Pour into sprayed 6-cup mold or 9x13-inch baking dish and chill. Unmold onto lettuce-lined platter or cut into squares and serve on lettuce.

Makes 8 servings   Nancy Gamble, Auburn, Alabama

Per serving: 288 calories, 6 g fat, 4 g protein, 57 g carbohydrate, 25 mg cholesterol, 110 mg sodium.

Broccoli and Chicken Salad Valentino

2 cups small broccoli florets	Dressing:
4 cups bite-size *Easy Cooked Chicken*	½ cup sour cream
1 red bell pepper, julienned	½ cup mayonnaise
12 slices bacon, cooked and crumbled[14]	3 tablespoons Dijon mustard
6 croissants	3 tablespoons raspberry vinegar or cider vinegar
6 lettuce leaves	4 tablespoons chopped fresh dill weed, or 1 tablespoon dried dill weed, crushed

Blanch[G] broccoli by cooking in boiling salted water until crisp-tender, about 3 minutes, and plunging into bowl of ice water about 2 minutes to stop cooking. Drain well. Combine chicken, bell pepper, broccoli and bacon in large bowl. Pour dressing over salad and toss; refrigerate. Split each croissant, add lettuce leaf and serving of chicken salad. Serve with fresh fruit for a nice lunch.

Dressing: Whisk sour cream, mayonnaise, mustard, vinegar and dill in a small bowl and refrigerate covered until ready to use.

Makes 6 servings   Kaylene Miller, Granby, Colorado

Per serving: 414 calories, 29 g fat, 33 g protein, 7 g carbohydrate, 111 mg cholesterol, 899 mg sodium.

Aunt Mabel's Sweet Onion Slaw

Crisp and delicious.

4	large sweet onions	½	cup mayonnaise
1½	cups cider vinegar	1	teaspoon celery seeds
½	cup cold water	1	avocado, peeled and sliced
2	tablespoons sugar	2	plum tomatoes, cut into wedges

Cut onions in half stem to root.[68] Remove skin and place cutside down on cutting board; slice ¼-inch thick. Separate half-slices and put in large covered container. Mix vinegar, water and sugar in medium bowl. Stir until sugar dissolves. Pour over onions. Cover and refrigerate 8 hours or overnight, tossing occasionally. Just before serving *drain well* in colander; return to container. Stir mayonnaise and celery seeds together in small bowl and gently mix into onions. Transfer to serving bowl and attractively arrange sliced avocado and tomato wedges on top.

Makes 8 servings   Mabel McCaleb McKinney, Indianola, Mississippi

Per serving: 184 calories, 16 g fat, 2 g protein, 13 g carbohydrate, 5 mg cholesterol, 86 mg sodium.

Spaghetti Slaw

Feeds a lot of people–good for a cookout.

Dressing:
- 2 cups mayonnaise
- ½ cup sugar
- ¼ cup cider vinegar
- 1 tablespoon prepared mustard[G]
- 1 teaspoon celery salt
- 1 teaspoon celery seeds
- 1 teaspoon salt, or to taste
- Dashes hot pepper sauce

- 1 pound thin spaghetti
- 2 (16-ounce) packages 3-color coleslaw mix
- 1 cup chopped sweet onion
- 1 cup chopped bell pepper (optional)
- 1 tablespoon chopped seeded jalapeño (optional)
- 1 cup frozen baby green peas, thawed (optional)

Dressing: Mix mayonnaise, sugar, vinegar, mustard, celery salt, celery seeds, salt and pepper sauce in bowl. Stir well to dissolve sugar. Cover and refrigerate.

Break spaghetti into thirds. Cook to al dente[G] according to package directions. Rinse with cold water;[57] *drain well*. Mix spaghetti, cole slaw mix, onion, bell pepper, jalapeño and peas in large bowl. Stir in dressing. Cover and refrigerate 2 hours or overnight. Keeps well in refrigerator several days. Recipe may be halved.

Makes 7 quarts, 16 to 20 servings   Vera Larimer, Scottsdale, Arizona

Per serving of 20: 281 calories, 19 g fat, 4 g protein, 26 g carbohydrate, 8 mg cholesterol, 333 mg sodium.

Mother's Potato Salad

3	pounds (about 9) medium red potatoes
1	teaspoon salt
¼	teaspoon pepper
3	to 4 tablespoons diced small sweet pickles
2	tablespoons sweet pickle juice
¼	cup chopped sweet onion, or chopped green onions

1	cup chopped celery
½	cup chopped bell pepper
¼	teaspoon celery seed
1	cup mayonnaise
1	tablespoon prepared mustard
4	hard-cooked eggs,[18] chopped
2	hard-cooked eggs, sliced
	Paprika

Boil potatoes in large pot of boiling salted water, 25 to 30 minutes. Remove as they become tender but still firm. When cool enough to handle, remove skins and cut into irregular pieces into large bowl. Sprinkle with salt and pepper. Mix in pickles, pickle juice, onion, celery, bell pepper and celery seed. Stir mayonnaise and mustard together in small bowl and fold into potatoes. Gently mix in chopped eggs.[49] Spoon salad into 2-quart casserole and place sliced eggs on top. Sprinkle lightly with paprika and extra celery seed. Cover and refrigerate. Garnish with parsley just before serving.

Makes 8 servings   Willie McCaleb Rabb, Lexington, Mississippi

Per serving: 408 calories, 28 g fat, 9 g protein, 36 g carbohydrate, 171 mg cholesterol, 556 mg sodium.

Em's German Potato Salad

9	or 10 medium red potatoes
1½	cups finely chopped parsley leaves–no stems
¾	cup finely chopped onion

	Salt
	White pepper
½	cup corn oil, *divided*
¼	cup white vinegar

Boil potatoes in large saucepan of salted water until just tender, 15 to 20 minutes. Do not overcook–test with fork after 15 minutes (they will continue to cook as they cool). Drain. When cool enough to handle, peel and thinly slice.

Make several layers of potatoes in 7x11-inch baking dish, sprinkling parsley, onion, salt and pepper between layers. Pour half the oil, all the vinegar and then the remaining oil over layers. Cover and refrigerate overnight. Remove at least 30 minutes before serving. Toss gently. Adjust seasoning by adding salt, pepper, oil and vinegar if needed.

Makes 8 servings   Mimi Lyons, Baldwinsville, New York

Per serving: 294 calories, 21 g fat, 3 g protein, 26 g carbohydrate, 0 mg cholesterol, 281 mg sodium.

Marinated Asparagus

Marinade:

1 teaspoon fresh French tarragon, snipped, or ¼ teaspoon dried tarragon, crushed

¼ teaspoon garlic salt

¼ cup tarragon vinegar

½ cup Italian salad dressing

1 tablespoon diced pimiento

3 cups water

1 teaspoon salt

1 pound fresh asparagus, rinsed, snapped and drained[34]

¼ cup mayonnaise

Boston lettuce leaves

Paprika

Marinade: Put tarragon, garlic salt and vinegar in jar with tight-fitting lid and shake well. Add Italian dressing and shake until emulsified. Stir in pimiento.

Bring water and salt to boil in large nonstick skillet. Add asparagus in single layer if possible and return to boil. Reduce heat and simmer covered 5 minutes or until crisp-tender. Plunge asparagus into bowl of ice water for about 4 minutes. Drain. Place asparagus in shallow container long enough to hold spears without bending and pour in marinade. Cover and refrigerate 8 hours or overnight, gently turning occasionally.

Drain asparagus, reserving 1 tablespoon marinade. Mix mayonnaise and reserved marinade in small bowl to make dressing. Place lettuce leaf on each individual salad plate and arrange about four asparagus spears over lettuce. Spoon teaspoon of dressing on top. Sprinkle with paprika.

Note: Canned asparagus spears may be used. They will be tasty, but not crunchy.

Makes 4 servings

Per serving:184 calories, 19 g fat, 2 g protein, 5 g carbohydrate, 5 mg cholesterol, 262 mg sodium.

Balsamic Vinaigrette

¼ cup balsamic vinegar

2 teaspoons soy sauce

1 teaspoon sugar

2 garlic cloves, minced

½ teaspoon dried parsley flakes, crushed

½ cup canola oil

Put vinegar, soy sauce, sugar, garlic and parsley flakes in jar with tight-fitting lid. Shake well. Add oil and shake until emulsified.

Makes about ¾ cup

Per 2 tablespoons: 168 calories, 18 g fat, 0 g protein, 2 g carbohydrate, 0 mg cholesterol, 115 mg sodium.

Rabb Family Vinaigrette

1 garlic clove	Pepper to taste
⅓ cup cider vinegar	⅓ cup vegetable oil or olive oil
¾ teaspoon salt	

Crush garlic through garlic press into glass measure or small bowl. Add vinegar. Whisk in salt until dissolved. Add pepper and stir in oil. Strain out any garlic pieces, if desired. Stir vigorously with fork or pour into jar with tight-fitting lid and shake well. Serve over tossed salad.

Makes about ⅔ cup   **Lawrence Rabb, Meridian, Mississippi**

Per 2 tablespoons: 110 calories, 12 g fat, 0 g protein, 1 g carbohydrate, 0 mg cholesterol, 267 mg sodium.

Basil Lemon Vinegar

Drizzle over salads as a dressing or use in vinaigrettes.

2 cups white vinegar	4 (1-inch long) strips lemon zest
3 (5-inch long) sprigs fresh basil	

Microwave directions: Put vinegar, basil and lemon zest in microwave-safe bowl or 2-cup glass measure. Microwave on HIGH 2½ to 3 minutes or until mixture reaches 140° to 150° on instant-read thermometer. Pour into pint jar and cover with lid. Let stand in cool, dark place several days or up to two weeks. Strain into slender decorative bottles with caps or corks. Add sprig of fresh basil and one or two strips of lemon zest.

Conventional directions: Heat vinegar to boiling in small stainless steel saucepan. Place silver or stainless steel spoon in pint jar to absorb heat and carefully pour hot vinegar over back of spoon into jar. Add basil and lemon zest. Cover with lid. Let stand to blend flavors. Proceed as directed above.

Makes 1 pint

Per 2 tablespoons: 5 calories, 0 g fat, 0 g protein, 2 g carbohydrate, 0 mg cholesterol, 0 mg sodium.

Note: For nice gifts, I use small juice bottles with resealable caps, cut small squares from colorful material with pinking shrears, hold square over cap, wrap a rubber band around neck of bottle and tie a pretty ribbon around material to hide the rubber band.

Vinaigrette Tip
A small amount of Dijon mustard or dry mustard[30] added to vinaigrettes will help emulsify ingredients. Mustard binds oil and vinegar and helps blend flavors.

Raspberry Vinaigrette

½	cup seedless raspberry jam	¼	teaspoon pink peppercorns, or ground white pepper
¾	cup red wine vinegar	⅛	teaspoon salt
¾	cup cranberry juice	¼	teaspoon dry mustard
¼	cup sugar	1	cup canola oil
¼	teaspoon minced garlic		

Blend raspberry jam, vinegar, cranberry juice, sugar, garlic, peppercorns, salt and dry mustard in blender or food processor. Slowly pour oil in stream through top while continuing to blend. Store in jar with tight-fitting lid and keep refrigerated up to 3 months. Shake well before using.

Makes 2½ cups

Per 2 tablespoons: 132 calories, 11 g fat, 0 g protein, 10 g carbohydrate, 0 mg cholesterol, 17 mg sodium.

Flagstaff's Honey Mustard Dressing

The Flagstaff House Restaurant, situated a few thousand feet up Flagstaff mountain, has a beautiful view overlooking the city of Boulder. Don Monet, owner, featured this dressing as the house dressing in the late 1970s when we lived in Boulder. This recipe is one-eighth of the restaurant's original 2-quart recipe.

½	cup mayonnaise	¼	cup honey
¼	cup prepared mustard[G]	⅛	cup creamy Italian dressing

Whisk mayonnaise, mustard, honey and Italian dressing in medium bowl and refrigerate. Serve over fresh baby spinach or tossed young greens. Top with sliced fresh mushrooms, sprouts, crumbled bacon and shredded hard-cooked eggs.

Makes about 1 cup   Don Monet, Boulder, Colorado

Per 2 tablespoons: 123 calories, 11 g fat, 1 g protein, 8 g carbohydrate, 4 mg cholesterol, 161 mg sodium.

Sweet Cream Cheese Topping

1	(3-ounce) package cream cheese	¼	teaspoon clear imitation vanilla extract[22]
1	cup sour cream	1	tablespoon fresh lemon juice
⅓	cup sugar		

Beat cream cheese, sour cream, sugar, vanilla and lemon juice in medium bowl with mixer or handheld blender until smooth. Refrigerate until ready to use. Spoon over fresh fruit or sweet gelatin salads.

Makes about 1 cup

Per 2 tablespoons: 132 calories, 10 g fat, 2 g protein, 10 g carbohydrate, 24 mg cholesterol, 47 mg sodium.

Sauces, Pickles & Potpourri

Sauces

Pickles

Potpourri

Aïoli

In September 1999, we spent two delightful days in southern France at Le Clos des Saumanes, a Bed and Breakfast owned by Phillippe and Elisabeth Lambert. Elisabeth wrote out this aïoli (garlic mayonnaise) recipe for me; garlic is a passion among the people of Provence.

4 to 5 full and firm garlic cloves*	1 tablespoon Dijon mustard
¼ to ½ teaspoon coarse salt	1 tablespoon white wine vinegar
1 very fresh egg, room temperature	1 cup extra-virgin olive oil

Peel[20] and mince garlic (food chopper works well). Mash garlic and salt with mortar and pestle in circular motion, forming as smooth a paste as possible. (Alternatively, mince garlic on cutting board and add salt. Crush with flat side of chef's knife, moving blade in circular motion to form paste.) Transfer paste to blender or food processor. Add egg, mustard and vinegar. Puree until smooth. With machine running, add oil, a few drops at a time, through top–not too much or mixture will not emulsify. Stop and scrape down sides occasionally. As mixture thickens, add remaining oil in slow steady stream. Aïoli is best served within 24 hours but may be refrigerated several days; bring to room temperature and stir before serving. Serve with *Sole en Papillote*, other fish, meats, hot or cold vegetables and eggs.

* Two or three garlic cloves are more than enough for the usual palate–you would have to be a passionate garlic lover to enjoy four or five cloves in this recipe.

Makes 1⅓ cups   **Elisabeth Lambert, Châteauneuf de Gadagne, Provence, France**

Per tablespoon: 92 calories, 10 g fat, 1 g protein, 1 g carbohydrate, 10 mg cholesterol, 98 mg sodium.

Tips: Although I had no problems with Elisabeth's recipe, these tips may be helpful: If mixture becomes too thick, add 1 or 2 tablespoons warm water at a time to adjust consistency. If runny, egg may be old; add tablespoon mayonnaise or start again with fresher egg. Make sure mortar, pestle and all ingredients are at room temperature; temperature differences can cause aïoli to separate. If concerned about using raw egg, use recommended amount of egg substitute. This recipe was tested using a fresh egg.

Quick Aïoli

3 garlic cloves, minced[20]	⅔ cup mayonnaise
2 teaspoons fresh lemon juice	

Puree garlic and lemon juice in small food processor or in bowl with handheld blender. Add mayonnaise and mix well. Cover and chill.

Makes ⅔ cup

Per tablespoon: 97 calories, 11 g fat, 0 g protein, 1 g carbohydrate, 5 mg cholesterol, 76 mg sodium.

Velouté Sauce or Béchamel Sauce

Velouté sauce is a light sauce made with chicken, veal or fish stock. By substituting milk for stock, you have béchamel, a basic white sauce. Many sauces can be made from these two basic recipes! For good sauce, add cold liquids to hot roux or add hot liquids to cold roux.

3 tablespoons butter	¼ teaspoon salt
3 tablespoons flour	⅛ teaspoon black or white pepper
2 cups chicken stock or broth, or 2 cups milk for béchamel	

Melt butter in medium saucepan. Remove from heat and whisk in flour, making smooth paste (roux^G). Return to heat. Add cool stock or milk, all at once, whisking and cooking until thickened (for thicker sauce, use less stock or milk). Stir in salt and pepper.

Makes about 2 cups

Per ¼ cup: 52 calories, 4 g fat, 1 g protein, 3 g carbohydrate, 11 mg cholesterol, 198 mg sodium.

Mornay Sauce variation: Add ½ cup shredded Swiss cheese to *Béchamel Sauce*. Stir until melted. Alternatively, use 1 cup milk and 1 cup chicken broth instead of 2 cups milk.

Lemon-Sherry Sauce variation: After returning roux to heat, add 1 cup chicken broth and 1 cup half-and-half to roux. Cook and whisk until thickened. Stir in 2 tablespoons dry sherry, 2 tablespoons fresh lemon juice and ¼ teaspoon sugar. Season with salt and pepper. Serve over fresh steamed broccoli and sprinkle with toasted slivered almonds.

Makes 2 cups

Per ¼ cup: 94 calories, 8 g fat, 2 g protein, 4 g carbohydrate, 23 mg cholesterol, 134 mg sodium.

Lite Alfredo Sauce

1 tablespoon butter	Dash of ground nutmeg
¼ cup flour	¾ cup freshly grated Parmesan cheese
3 cups reduced-fat milk	

Melt butter in medium saucepan and stir in flour until bubbly, about 1 minute. Whisk in milk and nutmeg. Cook until sauce begins to thicken. Add grated cheese and stir until melted and smooth. Add salt and black or white pepper to taste. If thick, add more milk. Serve sauce over hot cooked egg noodles and sprinkle with snipped fresh parsley.

Makes 3 cups

Per ½ cup: 154 calories, 8 g fat, 10 g protein, 10 g carbohydrate, 24 mg cholesterol, 315 mg sodium.

Madeira Sauce

2	tablespoons butter	½	teaspoon cracked black peppercorns[21]
2	tablespoons finely chopped shallots	1	teaspoon beef base or 2 teaspoons beef bouillon granules
2	tablespoons finely chopped green onions	½	cup hot water
¾	teaspoon fresh thyme leaves, or ¼ teaspoon dried thyme, crushed	½	cup dry Madeira
		¼	cup heavy cream

Melt butter in medium skillet. Sauté shallots, green onion, thyme and cracked peppercorns over medium heat until shallots and green onion are clear, 1½ to 2 minutes. Mix beef base with hot water in glass measure and add to skillet. Stir in Madeira. Simmer uncovered 5 to 6 minutes, reducing mixture to about half. Strain, if desired, discarding shallots and green onion. Return liquid to skillet. (May prepare to this point and hold until ready to finish and serve.) Add heavy cream and heat without boiling. If thicker sauce is desired, mix 1 tablespoon flour with ¼ cup water in small bowl and stir into sauce. Cook and stir until thickened. Serve warm over *Elegant and Easy Pork Tenderloin.*

Makes about 1 cup

Per tablespoon: 23 calories, 2 g fat, 1 g protein, 1 g carbohydrate, 4 mg cholesterol, 70 mg sodium.

Clarified Butter

½ cup (1 stick) butter

Melt butter in saucepan over low heat. Pour into small shallow bowl. Place plastic wrap directly on surface of butter. Refrigerate until solidified.

Remove plastic wrap–most foamy milk solids will adhere to plastic. Wipe off any solids that remain on butter with paper towel. Run knife around sides of bowl and invert clarified butter onto plate. Gently wipe off any milky mixture on bottom. Clarified butter may be used immediately or may be refrigerated three to four weeks. (Be sure butter is stored in an airtight container; otherwise, it will absorb odors from other foods.)

Makes about ⅓ cup

Per tablespoon: 127 calories, 15 g fat, 0 g protein, 0 g carbohydrate, 37 mg cholesterol, 0 mg sodium.

Hollandaise Sauce

2	egg yolks		Dash of ground nutmeg
2	tablespoons water		(optional)
⅓	cup *Clarified Butter*		Dash of cayenne pepper
⅛	teaspoon salt	1	to 2 teaspoons fresh lemon juice
⅛	teaspoon white pepper		

Whisk egg yolks and water in small saucepan until light and frothy using whisk small enough to get into curve of saucepan. Whisk over low heat until yolks are pale yellow and slightly thickened, about 30 seconds. Remove from heat to prevent boiling and continue whisking 10 to 20 seconds. Cool slightly. Warm *Clarified Butter* in microwave or in small saucepan on stove; whisk *slowly* into egg yolks until sauce is creamy (handheld blender works well). Whisk in salt, white pepper, nutmeg, cayenne pepper and lemon juice. Cover and keep warm.[51] Serve over *Fresh Asparagus* and eggs Benedict. Recipe may be doubled.

Makes about ⅔ cup

Per tablespoon: 39 calories, 4 g fat, 1 g protein, 0 g carbohydrate, 28 mg cholesterol, 51 mg sodium.

Béarnaise Sauce

⅓	cup *Clarified Butter*	½	teaspoon dried chervil, crushed
2	tablespoons minced shallots, or green onions (white part only)		(optional)
2	tablespoons white wine vinegar	¼	teaspoon freshly ground black pepper
2	tablespoons water	2	egg yolks
1½	teaspoons minced fresh French tarragon leaves, or ½ teaspoon dried tarragon, crushed		Salt
			Dash of cayenne pepper
			Dash of ground nutmeg

Warm *Clarified Butter* in 1-cup glass measure in microwave or in small saucepan on stove. Remove any white foam and let cool slightly. Combine shallots, vinegar, water, tarragon, chervil and black pepper in separate small saucepan. Bring to boil. Cook until most liquid evaporates, 2 to 3 minutes. Cool. Add egg yolks and whisk briskly over low heat until thickened and fluffy. Let pan cool down until just warm. When *Clarified Butter* and egg mixture have cooled to about the same temperature, *slowly* pour butter into egg mixture, whisking (almost whipping) constantly, until all butter is incorporated (handheld blender works well). Season to taste with salt, cayenne pepper and nutmeg. Cover and keep slightly warm up to 2 hours.[51] If sauce separates, whisk in a few drops of cold water to restore its creamy consistency.

Makes ¾ cup

Per tablespoon: 64 calories, 7 g fat, 1 g protein, 1 g carbohydrate, 51 mg cholesterol, 24 mg sodium.

Microwave Hollandaise Sauce

¼	cup (½ stick) butter	⅛	teaspoon white pepper
2	tablespoons heavy cream		Dash of ground nutmeg
2	egg yolks		Dash of cayenne pepper
2	tablespoons water	1	to 2 teaspoons fresh lemon juice
⅛	teaspoon salt		

Put butter in 2-cup glass measure. Microwave on HIGH 30 to 40 seconds just until butter melts–not hot. Stir in heavy cream. Mix egg yolks and water in small bowl and stir into butter mixture. Stir in salt, white pepper, nutmeg, cayenne pepper and lemon juice. Microwave 1 minute on MEDIUM, stir, heat 1 more minute on MEDIUM and stir. (Sauce should be slightly thickened; if not, heat 30 more seconds on MEDIUM and stir.) Beat sauce with whisk, mixer or handheld blender until fluffy. Cover and set aside until ready to serve, or refrigerate. If refrigerated, reheat sauce in microwave on MEDIUM just before serving.

Makes ⅔ cup

Per tablespoon: 57 calories, 6 g fat, 1 g protein, 0 g carbohydrate, 54 mg cholesterol, 69 mg sodium.

Microwave Béarnaise Sauce

Microwave Béarnaise sauce can be refrigerated. Reheat just before serving.

¼	cup (½ stick) butter	2	tablespoons water
2	tablespoons minced shallots or green onions (white part only)	2	egg yolks
		2	tablespoons heavy cream
1½	teaspoons minced fresh French tarragon leaves, or ½ teaspoon dried tarragon, crushed	¼	teaspoon salt
		¼	teaspoon freshly ground black pepper
½	teaspoon dried chervil, crushed (optional)		Dash of cayenne pepper
			Dash of ground nutmeg
1½	tablespoons white wine vinegar		

Put butter in 2-cup glass measure and microwave on HIGH 30 to 40 seconds. Remove and stir. Add shallots, tarragon, chervil and vinegar. Mix water and egg yolks in small bowl and add to butter mixture. Stir in heavy cream, salt, black pepper, cayenne pepper and nutmeg. Microwave 1 minute on MEDIUM, stir, heat 1 more minute on MEDIUM and stir. (Sauce should be slightly thickened; if not, heat 30 more seconds on MEDIUM). Beat with whisk, mixer or handheld blender until fluffy. Cover and set aside until ready to serve, or refrigerate. If refrigerated, reheat sauce in microwave on MEDIUM just before serving.

Makes ¾ cup

Per tablespoon: 54 calories, 6 g fat, 1 g protein, 1 g carbohydrate, 49 mg cholesterol, 63 mg sodium.

Crème Fraîche

Crème fraîche is easy to make. Good to add to hot sauces and soups. Unlike sour cream, Crème fraîche can be boiled without curdling.

1 tablespoon buttermilk[42]	1 cup heavy cream

Mix buttermilk and cream in glass jar. Cover loosely with foil. Let stand at room temperature 8 to 24 hours or until very thick. Stir well, cover with lid and refrigerate. Crème fraîche will keep about one week refrigerated. Stir before using. Serve over fruit tarts, puddings and cobblers. Sweeten slightly to serve over fresh fruit.

Makes 1 cup

Per tablespoon: 52 calories, 6 g fat, 1 g protein, 1 g carbohydrate, 20 mg cholesterol, 7 mg sodium.

Applesauce

12 Jonathan or Granny Smith apples, or 6 of each	¾ cup packed brown sugar[1]
¾ cup sugar	Dash of salt
	1 quart water

Core, peel and slice apples. Put in large bowl of lemon water.[7] Drain and transfer to Dutch oven or large pot. Add sugars, salt and water. Cook uncovered over medium-low heat 1 to 1½ hours or until reduced, stirring occasionally. Mash with potato masher to desired consistency–smooth or chunky. Place in covered containers and refrigerate or freeze.

Makes 6 cups   Jean Curby, Tulsa, Oklahoma

Per cup: 346 calories, 1 g fat, 0 g protein, 90 g carbohydrate, 0 mg cholesterol, 16 mg sodium.

Cranberry Sauce

1 (12-ounce) package fresh cranberries	1½ cups sugar
1 cup water	1 teaspoon margarine

Rinse and drain cranberries. Put in medium saucepan and add water. Cook until skins pop, about 5 minutes. Force cranberries and juice through food mill or sturdy strainer into another saucepan. Add sugar and margarine. Cook 10 to 15 minutes or until thickened, stirring occasionally. Pour into mold or covered container. Refrigerate until ready to serve.

Makes 8 servings   CharLee Bright Hollinger, Westminster, Maryland

Per serving: 170 calories, 1 g fat, 0 g protein, 43 g carbohydrate, 0 mg cholesterol, 7 mg sodium.

Mushroom Sauce

¼ cup (½ stick) butter
¼ cup flour
1⅓ cups chicken broth[11]
1 teaspoon browning and seasoning
    sauce

2 (4-ounce) cans mushrooms
    pieces and stems, drained,
    reserve ⅔ cup juice
1 teaspoon beef bouillon granules
    Salt and pepper

Melt butter in medium saucepan and stir in flour. Cook 2 to 3 minutes or until flour begins to brown, stirring frequently. Mix in chicken broth, browning sauce, reserved mushroom juice and bouillon granules. Cook and stir until thickened. Stir in mushrooms and season with salt and pepper if needed. Serve hot over stuffing, mashed potatoes, hamburger steak, or just about anything that needs sauce or gravy.

Makes about 3½ cups

Per ½ cup: 99 calories, 7 g fat, 3 g protein, 6 g carbohydrate, 19 mg cholesterol, 674 mg sodium.

Meatballs in Mushroom Sauce variation: Add 25 to 30 precooked meatballs (and a little burgundy or red wine, if desired) to sauce. Heat. Serve over mashed potatoes or cooked noodles. Quick and hearty.

Makes 4 servings

Per serving; 443 calories, 33 g fat, 19 g protein, 15 g carbohydrate, 79 mg cholesterol, 1839 mg sodium.

Tartar Sauce

2 petite kosher dill gherkins or
    cornichons, finely chopped
    (about 2 tablespoons)
1 tablespoon small capers, rinsed,
    drained and chopped
¼ cup finely chopped sweet onion
    or green onions

1 garlic clove, minced[20]
¼ cup finely snipped flat leaf
    parsley
1 cup regular or light mayonnaise
1 teaspoon Dijon mustard
    Dash of hot pepper sauce

Combine gherkins, capers, onion, garlic, parsley, mayonnaise, mustard and pepper sauce in medium bowl and mix well. Cover and refrigerate. Stir and serve with *Salmon Croquettes* or crab cakes.

Makes 1 cup

Per tablespoon: 103 calories, 12 g fat, 0 g protein, 1 g carbohydrate, 5 mg cholesterol, 103 mg sodium.

Sweet Basil Pesto

4	cups fresh sweet basil leaves	½	cup pine nuts
1½	teaspoons minced garlic	6	ounces Asiago cheese, grated (2 cups)
¼	teaspoon freshly ground black pepper	2	ounces provolone or mozzarella cheese, shredded (½ cup)
1	teaspoon kosher salt	¾	cup extra-virgin olive oil
½	cup coarsely chopped toasted pecans[5]		

Wash, drain and coarsely chop basil leaves in blender or food processor. (It is most important that leaves get chopped before adding any other ingredients. Otherwise nuts will just grind up on bottom. If all leaves do not fit in blender, chop those that fit and add more as room permits.) Add garlic, pepper, kosher salt, pecans and pine nuts. Process until finely chopped. Add cheeses and process into *fairly smooth* paste. Scrape down sides. With machine running, slowly pour oil through top in steady stream until incorporated. Transfer to one or more covered containers. Pesto can be covered with thin layer of oil and refrigerated one week or frozen several months.

Pesto is good served over pasta. Thin ½ to ¾ cup of pesto with small amount of heavy cream. Combine with ½ to ¾ pound cooked linguine, fettuccine or other pasta. Also, add small amount of pesto to vinaigrettes.

Makes about 2 cups

Per tablespoon: 109 calories, 10 g fat, 4 g protein, 2 g carbohydrate, 7 mg cholesterol, 185 mg sodium.

Creamy Horseradish Sauce

½	cup sour cream	1½	teaspoons fresh lemon juice
1	to 2 tablespoons prepared horseradish	1	tablespoon mayonnaise
			Pinch of sugar
1½	teaspoons Worcestershire sauce	1	tablespoon snipped flat-leaf parsley
1½	teaspoons Dijon mustard with mustard seeds		

Combine sour cream, horseradish, Worcestershire sauce, mustard, lemon juice, mayonnaise, sugar and parsley in small bowl. Season with salt and pepper. Mix well. Cover and refrigerate. Serve with *Steamed Corned Beef and Cabbage* or prime rib.

Makes ⅔ cup

Per tablespoon: 34 calories, 3 g fat, 1 g protein, 1 g carbohydrate, 5 mg cholesterol, 47 mg sodium.

Spicy Cocktail Sauce

1 cup ketchup	2 to 3 tablespoons prepared horseradish (not creamed)
1 to 2 teaspoons fresh lemon juice	
2 teaspoons Worcestershire sauce	

Mix ketchup, lemon juice, Worcestershire sauce and horseradish in small bowl. Taste. If too spicy, add ¼ to ½ cup additional ketchup.

Makes 1¼ cup   Matt Bright, Lynchburg, Virginia

Per 2 tablespoons: 28 calories, 0 g fat, 1 g protein, 7 g carbohydrate, 0 mg cholesterol, 300 mg sodium.

Cucumber Dill Sauce

1 large cucumber	1 tablespoon fresh lemon juice
¾ cup sour cream	¼ teaspoon salt
⅛ teaspoon paprika	1 teaspoon dried dill weed, crushed
1 teaspoon chopped fresh chives	

Peel cucumber and cut in half. Remove seeds and grate into strainer. Let drain 30 minutes. Gently press out any excess liquid and put grated cucumber in medium bowl.[43] Stir in sour cream, paprika, chives, lemon juice, salt and dill. Cover and refrigerate. Stir before serving. Serve with salmon and other fish.

Makes 1½ cups

Per 2 tablespoons: 33 Calories, 3 g fat, 1 g protein, 1 g carbohydrate, 6 mg cholesterol, 52 mg sodium.

Dill Sauce

1 (8-ounce) container plain yogurt	2 teaspoons finely chopped onion
¼ cup mayonnaise	2 teaspoons dried dill weed, crushed
2 teaspoons prepared horseradish	

Mix yogurt, mayonnaise, horseradish, onion and dill in bowl. Cover and refrigerate. Stir before serving. Serve over grilled salmon or other fish.

Makes 1¼ cups

Per 2 tablespoons: 56 calories, 5 g fat, 1 g protein, 2 g carbohydrate, 5 mg cholesterol, 46 mg sodium.

Barbecue Sauce

Great on ribs or chicken!

1 tablespoon vegetable oil	¼ teaspoon black pepper
½ cup finely chopped onion	⅛ teaspoon cayenne pepper
1 garlic clove, minced[20]	¾ cup water
2 tablespoons light brown sugar	1 (8-ounce) can tomato sauce
1 teaspoon dry mustard[9]	2 tablespoons Worcestershire sauce
½ teaspoon chili powder	2 tablespoons fresh lemon juice
½ teaspoon paprika	2 tablespoons cider vinegar
½ teaspoon salt	⅛ to ¼ teaspoon hot pepper sauce
½ teaspoon celery salt	1 teaspoon liquid smoke (optional)

Heat oil in medium saucepan. Sauté onion until tender, stirring occasionally. Remove from heat and stir in garlic, brown sugar, dry mustard, chili powder, paprika, salt, celery salt, black pepper and cayenne pepper. Mix in water. Stir in tomato sauce, Worcestershire sauce, lemon juice, vinegar, pepper sauce and liquid smoke. Return to heat and bring to boil. Reduce heat and simmer uncovered 20 to 25 minutes. Puree sauce, if desired. Mix in small amount of water or vinegar, if thick. Refrigerate in covered container.

Makes 2 cups

Per 2 tablespoons: 24 calories, 1 g fat, 1 g protein, 4 g carbohydrate, 0 mg cholesterol, 223 mg sodium.

Phyllis's Barbecue Sauce

½ cup finely chopped onion	⅛ teaspoon cayenne pepper
2 tablespoons brown sugar	2 tablespoons Worcestershire sauce
1 tablespoon paprika	¼ cup cider vinegar
1 teaspoon salt	¼ cup ketchup
1 teaspoon dry mustard[9]	½ cup water
¼ to ½ teaspoon chili powder	

Mix onion, brown sugar, paprika, salt, dry mustard, chili powder, cayenne pepper, Worcestershire sauce, vinegar, ketchup and water in small saucepan. Bring to boil. Reduce heat and simmer uncovered 15 minutes, stirring occasionally. Blend with handheld blender or in blender, if desired. Recipe may be doubled; simmer 20 to 25 minutes.

Makes 1¼ cup   **Phyllis McKinney, Frannie, Wyoming**

Per 2 tablespoons: 26 calories, 0 g fat, 1 g protein, 6 g carbohydrate, 0 mg cholesterol, 316 mg sodium.

Jezebel Sauce

Good with roast beef or for dunking chicken nuggets and cubed ham. Pour over cream cheese and serve with crackers for a quick appetizer.

4 tablespoons dry mustard	1 (18-ounce) jar apple jelly or grape jelly
¼ cup cold water	
1 (5-ounce) jar prepared horseradish (not creamed)	1 tablespoon cracked black peppercorns[21]
1 (18-ounce) jar pineapple, apple, rhubarb or apricot preserves	

Mix dry mustard and water in glass measure[9] and let stand several minutes. Transfer to large bowl and add horseradish. Beat with mixer until combined. Blend in preserves, jelly and cracked peppercorns. Refrigerate in covered containers. Sauce will keep several months in refrigerator.

Makes about 4 cups   Dr. Kenneth Ubbens, Rogers, Arkansas

Per 2 tablespoons: 94 calories, 1 g fat, 1 g protein, 22 g carbohydrate, 2 mg cholesterol, 25 mg sodium.

Note: I tested the sauce using apricot preserves and apple jelly. It was delicious—great for dipping egg-rolls. (I used the preserves and jelly jars to store most of the sauce.)

Jezebel Spread variation: Mix 4 ounces softened cream cheese with *Jezebel Sauce* to spreading consistency. Spread on sandwich bread cut into desired shapes for open-face tea sandwiches. Sprinkle with snipped parsley.

Fresh Tomato and Basil Sauce

4 tablespoons olive oil, *divided*	¼ teaspoon freshly ground black pepper
2 medium garlic cloves, minced	
¼ cup sliced green onions	6 slices lean bacon, cooked and crumbled, or 1 cup chopped cooked ham or chicken (optional)
3 large ripe tomatoes, peeled,[98] cored and cut into ½ inch pieces	
3 tablespoons chopped fresh basil	½ pound angel hair pasta
1 teaspoon salt	½ cup grated Parmesan cheese

Heat 3 tablespoons oil in large skillet. Sauté garlic and green onion 1 minute. Stir in tomatoes, basil, salt and pepper. Cook about 2 minutes, stirring frequently. Stir in bacon, if used. Prepare pasta according to package directions in large saucepan. Drain, reserving ¼ cup cooking water. Return pasta to pan. Mix in reserved water, tomato mixture and remaining 1 tablespoon oil. Toss well. Sprinkle cheese over each serving. Serve with French bread and *Mock Caesar Salad*.

Makes 4 servings   Bev Lehmann, Bella Vista, Arkansas

Per serving: 425 calories, 19 g fat, 14 g protein, 52 g carbohydrate, 10 mg cholesterol, 788 mg sodium.

Mom Walton's Pickled Beets

Theresa is famous for these pickled beets in Grand Lake. Her grandmother, Theresa Walton, passed this recipe on to her namesake.

10	pounds fresh medium beets	1	cup cider vinegar
2	cups sugar	2	teaspoons salt
4	cups water		

Cut off leafy stems ½-inch above beet tops–do not trim roots. Wash and gently scrub beets with vegetable brush to remove any dirt, being careful not to break skin. Place beets in large pot and cover with water. Bring to boil. Reduce heat and simmer covered 40 minutes (longer, if beets are large) or until easily pierced with knife. Peel beets over sink by cutting off stems and roots and slipping off skins. Halve beets or quarter, if large. Pack in hot sterilized jars.[83]

Meanwhile, combine sugar, 4 cups water, vinegar and salt in large saucepan. Bring to rolling boil. Skim off any foam and pour liquid over beets. Seal jars and place in boiling water bath 15 to 20 minutes.[52]

Makes 3½ to 4 quarts   Theresa Nuzum, Grand Lake, Colorado

Per ½ cup: 32 calories, 0 g fat, 1 g protein, 7 g carbohydrate, 0 mg cholesterol, 93 mg sodium.

Note: Baking is an easy alternative to boiling beets and will intensify their flavor. Wash and put beets in two or more 9x13-inch baking dishes. Add ½-inch water to each dish and cover with foil. Bake at 350° for 1 to 1½ hours, depending on size of beets. Test for doneness with sharp knife. Strain baking water through cheesecloth or paper towel[41] and reserve for making sugar-vinegar mixture, adding additional water to make 4 cups. Also good way to cook beets for other recipes.

Pickled Peaches

Traditional Thanksgiving dinner at our house includes pickled peaches. These are quick and a good substitute for whole peach pickles.

½	cup cider vinegar	2	(15½-ounce) cans peach halves
½	cup packed brown sugar[1]		in heavy syrup, drained,
1	stick cinnamon, broken in half		reserve syrup
1	teaspoon whole cloves		

Combine vinegar, brown sugar, cinnamon, cloves and reserved peach syrup in medium saucepan. Bring to boil. Reduce heat and simmer uncovered 5 minutes. Add peaches and bring to full boil. Remove from heat. Cool peaches in syrup and refrigerate overnight. Drain. Serve with turkey or ham.

Makes 8 servings

Per serving: 159 calories, 0 g fat, 1 g protein, 43 g carbohydrate, 0 mg cholesterol, 15 mg sodium.

Cinnamon Cucumber Pickle Rings

If you grow your own cucumbers, those large seedy ones you were going to throw away are perfect for making these pickle rings. The process is a little involved, but the pickles are worth the effort.

7	pounds large, seedy cucumbers	1	teaspoon alum*
2	cups fresh pickling lime	8	to 10 cinnamon sticks
4½	cups water, *divided*	11	cups sugar, *divided*
3	cups vinegar, *divided*	9	ounces red cinnamon candy
1	tablespoon red food coloring		Whole cloves

Wash, peel and cut cucumbers in half crosswise. Core out seeds from each half (grapefruit spoon works well) and slice into ½-inch rings. Put in large plastic container or enameled pail with cover. Dissolve pickling lime in 2½ cups water in saucepan. Pour over cucumbers, adding water to cover, if needed. Soak covered 24 hours at room temperature, stirring occasionally with wooden spoon. Drain and rinse. Soak 3 hours in enough ice water to cover. Drain again. At this point, you may cover and refrigerate overnight or proceed with next step.

Put cucumbers in large kettle and add cold water to cover. Mix 1 cup vinegar, food coloring and alum in glass measure and stir into cucumbers. Bring to boil. Reduce heat and simmer 2 hours. Drain cucumbers in colanders. Set aside. Discard solution. Clean kettle.

Mix cinnamon sticks, remaining 2 cups water, 8 cups sugar, cinnamon candy and remaining 2 cups vinegar in kettle. Bring to boil, stirring well to dissolve sugar and candy. Add cucumbers and more water to cover, if needed. Bring to boil. Remove from heat, cover and let stand 24 hours.

Drain off syrup from cucumbers into large saucepan. Add 1 cup sugar to syrup, stir and bring to boil. Pour syrup back over cucumbers and cinnamon sticks in kettle. Let stand another 24 hours. Repeat this procedure *two more times*–draining off syrup into saucepan, adding a cup of sugar, boiling, pouring back over cucumbers and letting stand 24 hours each time.

Sterilize jars.[83] Heat cucumber rings in syrup to boiling. Spoon rings into jars, cutting some in half, if necessary to fit. Put 1 cinnamon stick and 4 cloves in each jar. Add syrup to cover. Seal jars. (I place jars in boiling water bath[52] for 15 minutes right after sealing–Nita and Lenore do not.)

* Alum makes pickles crispier; it can be found at pharmacies.

Makes 8 to 10 pints   **Nita May and Lenore Diem, Bella Vista, Arkansas**

Per 2 tablespoons: 27 calories, 0 g fat, 0 g protein, 7 g carbohydrate, 0 mg cholesterol, 0 mg sodium.

Uncooked Green Tomato Relish

4	quarts green tomatoes	1	teaspoon ground cinnamon
10	bell peppers, seeded	1	teaspoon ground allspice
6	medium onions	1	teaspoon whole mustard seeds
1	small cabbage, shredded	1	quart white vinegar
1	teaspoon ground turmeric	5	cups sugar
1	teaspoon dry mustard[9]	⅓	to ½ cup salt

Finely chop green tomatoes, bell peppers and onions (food processor works well–chop separately). Drain green tomatoes in colander. Shred cabbage with shredder blade in food processor or on shredder side of hand grater. Combine tomatoes, bell pepper, onion and cabbage in large glass, plastic, enameled or other nonreactive container. Add turmeric, dry mustard, cinnamon, allspice, mustard seeds, vinegar, sugar and salt. Mix well. Let stand covered at room temperature 10 to 12 hours or overnight. Pack into hot sterilized jars;[83] seal at once. Store in cool place. Refrigeration is not required.

Makes about 12 pints   Charlene Holeman, Bentonville, Arkansas

Per 2 tablespoons: 24 calories, 0 g fat, 0 g protein, 6 g carbohydrate, 0 mg cholesterol, 216 mg sodium.

Yellow Squash Relish

Use in deviled eggs, pasta salads, potato salads and tartar sauce. Also good spooned over black-eyed peas as chowchow or over bean soup. Don't forget the cornbread.

10	cups finely chopped or shredded unpeeled medium yellow summer squash	2¼	cups white vinegar
		1	tablespoon ground turmeric
2	cups finely chopped bell pepper	3½	cups sugar
5	cups finely chopped onion	1	tablespoon cornstarch
1	(2-ounce) jar diced pimiento, drained	1	teaspoon ground nutmeg
⅓	cup salt	2	tablespoons celery seeds

Prepare vegetables separately (shredder blade in food processor works well for squash). Combine squash, bell pepper, onion and pimiento in large bowl. Mix in salt. Cover and refrigerate 24 hours. Rinse well in colander. Drain. Pour squash mixture into large kettle or Dutch oven. Stir in vinegar, turmeric, sugar, cornstarch, nutmeg and celery seeds. Bring to boil. Reduce heat and simmer uncovered 30 minutes, stirring frequently. Pour into sterilized jars[83] and seal.

Makes 5 pints   Jackie Hughett, Lynchburg, Virginia

Per 2 tablespoons: 44 calories, 0 g fat, 0 g protein, 11 g carbohydrate, 0 mg cholesterol, 28 mg sodium.

Easy Candied Dill Pickles

1 tablespoon pickling spice	2 cups sugar
1 quart whole dill pickles, drained (use an inexpensive brand)	1 cup cider or tarragon vinegar
	¼ teaspoon alum (optional)

Tie pickling spice in cheesecloth or put in brew bag[G] or tea ball. Set aside. Quarter pickles lengthwise into spears. Return spears to jar. Combine sugar, vinegar, alum (makes crispier pickles) and pickling spice in saucepan. Bring to full boil, stirring until sugar dissolves. Remove from heat. Cool 10 minutes. Remove spice bag. Pour mixture over spears in jar. Tightly screw on lid. Refrigerate at least 5 days (longer is better). Serve with pimento cheese sandwiches.

Makes 1 quart, about 20 servings

Per serving: 88 calories, 0 g fat, 0 g protein, 23 g carbohydrate, 0 mg cholesterol, 607 mg sodium.

Rum Pecan Pumpkin Butter

2 (15-ounce) cans pumpkin[19] (not pumpkin pie filling)	½ cup chopped toasted pecans[5]
1 teaspoon finely grated lemon zest	1 (1¾-ounce) package powdered pectin (not liquid pectin)
2 teaspoons fresh lemon juice	4 cups sugar
1 tablespoon pumpkin pie spice	½ cup packed brown sugar[1]
¼ teaspoon salt	⅓ cup dark rum (optional)

Combine pumpkin, lemon zest, lemon juice, pumpkin pie spice, salt and pecans in large pot or Dutch oven. Sprinkle in pectin and mix well. Bring to full boil (will take about 5 minutes), stirring frequently at first and stirring constantly later to prevent burning. Stir in sugars, all at once. Return to constant boil (will take about 4 minutes). Boil for exactly 1 minute, stirring constantly. Remove from heat and stir in rum. Quickly ladle into hot sterilized jars,[83] leaving about ¼-inch headspace (a canning funnel helps). Wipe rims and threads with damp paper towels, cover with flat lids and tightly screw on bands. Place jars upside-down on towel-covered jelly roll pan for 5 minutes. Turn upright. (Lids should pop shortly, indicating jars have sealed.) After jars cool, check seals by pressing middle of lids–if lids spring back, jars did not seal and will need to be refrigerated. Let sealed jars stand at room temperature 24 hours. Store in cool, dark, dry place up to one year. Serve with English muffins or bagels.

Makes 6 or 7 (8-ounce) jars

Per 2 tablespoons: 79 calories, 1 g fat, 0 g protein, 18 g carbohydrate, 0 mg cholesterol, 11 mg sodium.

Parsley Butter

Good on grilled steaks or fish.

½ cup (1 stick) butter, softened
2 teaspoons fresh lemon juice
1 teaspoon salt, or to taste

Dash of hot pepper sauce
¼ cup finely snipped parsley
¼ cup finely chopped green onions

Beat butter in medium bowl with mixer until creamed. Blend in lemon juice, salt and pepper sauce. Stir in parsley and green onion. Place on wax paper and roll into a log. Refrigerate until firm. Slice into pats and layer between wax paper in covered container. Refrigerate or freeze. Logs may also be frozen.

Makes 16 pats   Theresa Nuzum, Grand Lake, Colorado

Per pat: 52 calories, 6 g fat, 0 g protein, 0 g carbohydrate, 15 mg cholesterol, 125 mg sodium.

Tarragon Butter variation: Omit lemon juice and onion. Substitute 1 tablespoon finely chopped fresh French tarragon for parsley. Continue as directed above.

Sweet Basil Butter

½ cup (1 stick) butter, softened
¼ cup *Sweet Basil Pesto*

1 tablespoon fresh lemon juice

Blend butter, pesto and lemon juice in bowl with mixer or handheld blender until smooth (or use small food processor). Place in covered container. Chill. May also make into pats (see *Parsley Butter*). Bring to room temperature before serving. Serve over steamed vegetables or poached fish.

Makes about ¾ cup

Per tablespoon: 103 calories, 11 g fat, 2 g protein, 1 g carbohydrate, 23 mg cholesterol, 139 mg sodium.

Strawberry or Raspberry Butter

½ cup (1 stick) butter, softened
⅓ cup strawberry jam or
    seedless red raspberry jam

1 teaspoon fresh lemon juice
2 teaspoons confectioners' sugar
2 drops red food coloring (optional)

Beat butter, jam, lemon juice, confectioners' sugar (helps keep butter from separating) and food coloring in medium bowl with mixer on high until blended and fluffy. Refrigerate in covered container. Spread on sweet breads, toast, biscuits or crackers.

Makes ¾ cup

Per tablespoon: 90 calories, 8 g fat, 0 g protein, 6 g carbohydrate, 20 mg cholesterol, 81 mg sodium.

Hot Pepper Peach Preserves

Make Hot Pepper Peach Preserves or Almond Peach Pecan Preserves when fresh peaches are plentiful. They make nice hostess gifts for the holidays.

3 pounds (about 10) medium firm ripe peaches	½ teaspoon butter
⅓ cup chopped jalapeños with seeds (about 2 medium jalapeños)	1 (1¾-ounce) package powdered pectin (not liquid pectin)
2 tablespoons fresh lemon juice	5½ cups sugar

Measure ingredients accurately. Sterilize jars.[83] Meanwhile blanch peaches to remove skins.[35]

Slice and finely chop peaches (should have exactly 4 cups). Put peaches, jalapeños, lemon juice and butter (butter reduces foaming) in large pot or 4- to 5-quart Dutch oven. Sprinkle in pectin and mix well. Bring to full rolling boil (one that cannot be stirred down) over high heat, stirring occasionally (will take about 5 minutes). Stir in sugar all at once with strong wooden spoon. Mix well. Return to rolling boil, stirring frequently (will take about 5 minutes but will suddenly begin to boil vigorously). Boil exactly 1 minute, stirring constantly, reducing heat if needed, but keeping a rolling boil. Remove from heat and skim off foam with metal spoon. Immediately ladle peaches into sterilized jars, leaving ½-inch headspace. Wipe rims and threads of jars with damp paper towels and cover with lids. Tightly screw on bands. Place jars upside-down on towel-covered jelly roll pan for 5 minutes. Turn upright. (Lids should pop shortly, indicating jars have sealed.) After jars cool, check seals by pressing middle of lids–if lids spring back, jars did not seal and will need to be refrigerated. Let sealed jars stand 24 hours at room temperature. Store in cool, dark, dry place up to one year. Heat and serve as dipping sauce for chicken nuggets and egg rolls, as basting sauce for ham and roast chicken, or pour over cream cheese and serve with crackers.

Makes eight 8-ounce jars

Per 2 tablespoons: 85 calories, 0 g fat, 0 g protein, 22 g carbohydrate, 0 mg cholesterol, 1 mg sodium.

Almond Peach Pecan Preserves variation: Omit jalapeños and cook as directed above. After skimming off foam, quickly stir in ⅓ cup almond-flavored liqueur and ¼ cup finely chopped toasted pecans. Ladle into jars, seal and let stand as directed above.

Ginger's Blue Ribbon Chutney

Ginger's cranberry chutney won a blue ribbon and a Grand Champion ribbon at the county fair in Kremmling, Colorado.

4	cups fresh or frozen cranberries, rinsed and drained	1	unpeeled tart apple, chopped[7]
1	cup water	1	unpeeled pear, chopped[7]
2½	cups sugar	¼	cup chopped onion
2	cinnamon sticks, broken in half	½	cup sliced celery
6	whole cloves	1	cup raisins
½	teaspoon salt	½	cup sliced almonds
		1	tablespoon grated lemon zest[61]

If cranberries are frozen, decrease water to ½ cup and sugar to 2 cups. Rinse large saucepan with water–do not dry.[38] Add cranberries, water, sugar, cinnamon sticks, cloves and salt; bring to boil over high heat. Reduce heat to gentle boil and cook uncovered 10 minutes or until most berries pop, stirring occasionally. Add apple, pear, onion, celery and raisins to saucepan. Cook uncovered 15 more minutes, stirring occasionally. Stir in almonds and lemon zest. Cool. Pour into covered containers and refrigerate or freeze. Serve with pork, chicken or turkey. (Makes 5 cups with frozen cranberry adjustments.)

Makes 6 cups   **Ginger Meerbott McCabe, Houston, Texas**

Per ½ cup: 282 calories, 4 g fat, 2 g protein, 64 g carbohydrate, 0 mg cholesterol, 105 mg sodium.

Mango Chutney

I wanted a mango chutney recipe, so I used Ginger's Blue Ribbon Chutney recipe as a basis.

4	or 5 firm ripe mangos,[67] chopped (3 to 3½ cups)	1	Asian pear, cored, peeled and chopped[7]
½	cup water	¼	cup chopped onion
1½	cups sugar	½	cup sliced celery
2	cinnamon sticks, broken in half	1	cup golden raisins
6	whole cloves	½	cup sliced almonds
½	teaspoon salt	1	tablespoon grated lemon zest[61]
1	unpeeled tart apple, chopped[7]	1	to 2 tablespoons fresh lemon juice

Rinse large saucepan with water–do not dry.[38] Add mangoes, water, sugar, cinnamon sticks, cloves and salt; bring to boil. Reduce heat to gentle boil and cook uncovered 10 minutes. Add apple, pear, onion, celery and raisins. Cook uncovered 20 to 25 more minutes or until reduced and syrupy. Stir in almonds, lemon zest and lemon juice. Cool. Refrigerate or freeze in covered containers.

Makes about 5 cups

Per ½ cup: 252 calories, 5 g fat, 3 g protein, 56 g carbohydrate, 0 mg cholesterol, 115 mg sodium.

Soups & Sandwiches

Soups

Sandwiches

Vegetable Beef Soup

I usually have this soup ready to serve the first night our family comes for Christmas.

6	cups water	1	cup chopped celery
2¼	cups tomato juice	1	(8¾-ounce) can whole kernel corn, drained
3	teaspoons salt, *divided*		
4	teaspoons Worcestershire sauce	1	(14½-ounce) can whole tomatoes, undrained, snipped into pieces[73]
½	teaspoon chili powder		
2	bay leaves	1	(10-ounce) package frozen baby lima beans
⅓	cup chopped onion		
3	pounds crosscut beef shanks		Pinch of sugar
1	cup sliced carrots	1	teaspoon beef bouillon granules (optional)
1	cup peeled and diced potatoes		

Combine water, tomato juice, 2 teaspoons salt, Worcestershire sauce, chili powder, bay leaves and onion in large pot or Dutch oven. Rinse and add beef shanks. Bring to boil. Reduce heat and simmer covered 2 hours. Remove meat from pot and cut into large cubes, discarding fat. Strain stock into large bowl and cool slightly. Skim off any fat and return stock and meat cubes to pot. (May cover pot and refrigerate overnight at this point. Next day remove any solidified fat from surface.[77]) Add carrots, potatoes, celery, corn, tomatoes, lima beans, sugar and bouillon granules. Mix well and bring to boil. Reduce heat and simmer covered 1 hour or until vegetables are tender. Stir in remaining 1 teaspoon salt. Remove cover toward end of cooking time to allow soup to cook down, if desired.

Makes 8 servings   Fletcher Bell, Lawrence, Kansas

Per serving: 325 calories, 12 g fat, 28 g protein, 27 g carbohydrate, 49 mg cholesterol, 1057 mg sodium.

Chicken Rice Soup

2	(14-ounce) cans chicken broth	½	cup chopped onion
2	soup cans of water	½	cup chopped carrots
2	teaspoons chicken bouillon granules	½	cup long-grain white rice
1	teaspoon beef bouillon granules	2	cups bite-size *Easy Cooked Chicken*
1	cup chopped celery	1	teaspoon fresh lemon juice

Pour chicken broth and water into large saucepan. Stir in bouillon granules, celery, onion, carrots and rice; bring to boil. Reduce heat; cover and simmer 15 minutes. Add chicken and simmer covered 10 to 15 more minutes or until rice is tender. Stir in lemon juice; add salt if needed. Let stand 10 minutes.

Makes 4 to 6 servings

Per serving of 6: 242 calories, 4 g fat, 23 g protein, 29 g carbohydrate, 57 mg cholesterol, 1273 mg sodium.

Spicy Black Bean Soup

3 (15-ounce) cans black beans, undrained, *divided*
1 (14-ounce) can chicken broth
1 (14½-ounce) can stewed tomatoes (Mexican recipe), undrained
1 (10-ounce) can Mexican Festival or regular diced tomatoes and green chilies, undrained

1 tablespoon vegetable oil
½ cup chopped onion
1 to 2 garlic cloves, finely chopped[20]
½ teaspoon salt
2 tablespoons fresh lime juice
3 teaspoons ground cumin, *divided*
¼ to ½ teaspoon red pepper flakes, crushed (optional)

Pour two cans of beans into blender or food processor. Rinse cans with chicken broth and add to blender. Pulse until smooth. Pour mixture into 2-quart glass measure or large bowl. Without cleaning blender, add stewed tomatoes and diced tomatoes and green chilies to blender. Pulse until mixture resembles salsa. Pour into bean mixture. Stir in remaining can of beans. Set aside.

Heat oil in Dutch oven or large saucepan over medium-high heat and sauté onion for 1 minute. Add garlic and sauté 30 seconds. Add bean mixture, salt, lime juice, 2 teaspoons cumin and pepper flakes. Bring to boil. Reduce heat and simmer covered 15 minutes. Stir in remaining 1 teaspoon cumin. Simmer covered 15 more minutes, stirring occasionally. Top individual servings of soup with sour cream, if desired. Serve with warm tortillas or *Cornbread*.

Makes 6 servings

Per serving: 258 calories, 4 g fat, 14 g protein, 17 g carbohydrate, 1 mg cholesterol, 1107 mg sodium.

Handheld Blender Method: Pour 2 cans of beans into large saucepan or medium soup kettle, rinse cans with chicken broth and add to pan. Blend with handheld blender until smooth. Add stewed tomatoes and diced tomatoes and green chilies. Blend until chunky. Stir in remaining can of beans.

Heat oil in small skillet. Sauté onion 1 minute. Add garlic and sauté 30 seconds. Add to bean mixture in saucepan along with salt, lime juice, 2 teaspoons cumin and pepper flakes. Bring to boil. Reduce heat and simmer covered 15 minutes. Stir in remaining 1 teaspoon cumin. Simmer covered 15 more minutes, stirring occasionally. Top servings and serve as directed above.

Slow Cooker Split Pea Soup

1 (16-ounce) package split peas	½ teaspoon dry mustard[9]
1 (49½-ounce) can chicken broth	½ teaspoon salt
1 teaspoon chicken bouillon granules	¼ teaspoon coarsely ground black pepper
1 cup chopped celery	¼ teaspoon red pepper flakes
½ cup chopped onion	¼ teaspoon dried oregano, crushed
½ cup chopped carrots	1 meaty ham bone or 1½ cups cooked ham pieces
1 jalapeño, seeded and chopped	

Rinse and drain peas in large strainer. Pour into sprayed 3½- or 4-quart slow cooker. Stir in chicken broth, bouillon granules, celery, onion, carrots, jalapeño, dry mustard, salt, black pepper, red pepper flakes and oregano. Add ham bone. Cook on HIGH 2 hours or until ham pulls away from bone. Cut meat into pieces and return to pot. Discard bone and any fat. Cook on HIGH 2½ to 3½ more hours or until peas are tender. Soup may separate after several hours of cooking; mash and stir with potato masher to puree peas and combine ingredients before serving. Serve with *Cornbread* or crackers.

Makes 6 servings

Per 1½ cups: 360 calories, 6 g fat, 27 g protein, 51 g carbohydrate, 20 mg cholesterol, 1597 mg sodium.

Walterspiel Potato Soup

2 pounds (about 3) large red or russet potatoes	3 (10½-ounce) cans condensed beef broth
2 to 3 medium leeks	1 (14-ounce) can beef broth
4 slices lean bacon, diced	2 egg yolks, lightly beaten
¼ cup chopped onion	1 cup regular or lite sour cream
2 tablespoons flour	1 tablespoon minced parsley

Peel and thinly slice potatoes.[7] Thoroughly wash leeks[96] and thinly slice white and light-green parts only. Drain well. Set aside. Sauté bacon in large soup pot or Dutch oven 5 minutes. Add leeks and onion. Sauté 5 more minutes. Sprinkle in flour. Cook and stir 1 minute. Gradually add beef broths, stirring constantly. Add potatoes and bring to boil. Reduce heat. Simmer covered 30 to 35 minutes or until potatoes are tender. Do not mash—potatoes will break into pieces with stirring. Combine egg yolks and sour cream in medium bowl. Stir in ½ cup soup from pot to help prevent curdling. Stir in another ½ cup and return sour cream mixture to pot. Simmer uncovered 10 minutes, stirring constantly. Stir in parsley. Season with salt and pepper. Serve with toasted buttered baguette slices.

Makes 4 to 6 servings   Sandra Travis, Bella Vista, Arkansas

Per serving of 6: 349 calories, 19 g fat, 12 g protein, 39 g carbohydrate, 98 mg cholesterol, 1506 mg sodium.

Beer Cheese Soup

Beer cheese soup has become a Christmas Eve tradition at the Taylor house. Lois served it to our bridge group and we all wanted the recipe!

1	(12-ounce) can of beer	1½	cups peeled and cubed potatoes
2½	cups water	1	(16-ounce) package frozen broccoli, cauliflower and carrots
4	teaspoons chicken bouillon granules	2	(10¾-ounce) cans regular or low-fat cream of chicken soup
1	cup finely chopped celery	1	pound regular or light pasteurized prepared cheese product, cubed
1	cup finely chopped carrots		
1	cup finely chopped onion		

Combine beer and water in large pot or Dutch oven. Whisk in bouillon granules until dissolved. Add celery, carrots, onion and potatoes. Bring to boil. Reduce heat and simmer 15 minutes. Add frozen vegetable mixture and simmer uncovered about 5 minutes. Add soup and cheese; cook and stir until cheese melts and soup is thoroughly heated–do not boil. May prepare and refrigerate a day ahead; however, soup does not freeze well.

Makes 8 servings   Lois Taylor, Bella Vista, Arkansas

Per serving: 333 calories, 15 g fat, 16 g protein, 32 g carbohydrate, 56 mg cholesterol, 1788 mg sodium.

Chicken and Wild Rice Soup

2	tablespoons butter	2	cups milk
½	cup chopped onion	½	pound pasteurized prepared cheese product, cubed
½	cup chopped celery	2	(10¾-ounce) cans cream of potato soup
2	(14-ounce) cans chicken broth		
1	(6-ounce) box long grain and wild rice mix, original recipe (discard seasoning packet)	2	to 3 cups bite-size *Easy Cooked Chicken*

Melt butter in Dutch oven or large pot. Sauté onion and celery until tender, 2 to 3 minutes. Stir in chicken broth and rice mix. Bring to boil. Reduce heat and simmer covered 20 to 25 minutes or until rice is tender. Set aside.

Heat milk and cheese in large saucepan, stirring until cheese melts and mixture is creamy. Stir in potato soup. Add to rice mixture and stir in chicken. Heat thoroughly. Add additional cheese to thicken, if desired. Season with salt and pepper. Serve with *Herb Pita Toast*.

Makes 8 servings   Jackie Nicewander, Bella Vista, Arkansas

Per serving: 313 calories, 12 g fat, 26 g protein, 26 g carbohydrate, 70 mg cholesterol, 1364 mg sodium.

Zucchini and Italian Sausage Soup

1   pound sweet or hot Italian sausage, casings removed, or use ½-pound sweet and ½-pound hot

2   cups diagonally-sliced celery with some leaves

1   cup chopped onion

2   (28-ounce) cans diced tomatoes, undrained

2   teaspoons sugar

2   teaspoons salt

½   teaspoon dried basil, crushed

1   teaspoon dried oregano, crushed

¼   teaspoon garlic powder

1   teaspoon Italian seasoning, crushed

2   pounds small unpeeled zucchini, quartered lengthwise and cut crosswise into ½-inch pieces (about 6 cups)

2   cups chopped bell pepper

1   (8-ounce) package fresh mushrooms,[3] sliced (optional)

1   teaspoon beef bouillon granules (optional)

Freshly grated Asiago or Parmesan cheese

Crumble and brown sausage in Dutch oven. Drain if there is excess fat; however, some drippings will add flavor. Add celery and onion. Cook until tender, about 5 minutes, stirring occasionally. Stir in tomatoes, sugar, salt, basil, oregano, garlic powder, Italian seasoning and zucchini. Bring to boil, reduce heat and simmer covered 20 minutes. Stir in bell pepper, mushrooms and bouillon granules. Cover and simmer 10 more minutes. Top individual servings with grated cheese. Serve with *Natchez Bread* or *Cornbread Muffins*. (Soup is even better if prepared a day ahead and refrigerated. Does not freeze well.)

Makes 8 to 10 servings   Harold and Hildi VanderVeen, Wheaton, Illinois

Per serving of 10: 223 calories, 14 g fat, 10 g protein, 13 g carbohydrate, 34 mg cholesterol, 983 mg sodium.

Strawberry Soup

1   (16-ounce) container frozen sweetened sliced strawberries

2   cups *Crème Fraîche*, or 1 (16-ounce) container regular or lite sour cream

½   teaspoon clear imitation vanilla extract[22]

1   teaspoon grenadine syrup (optional)

½   cup half-and-half

Puree strawberries in blender. Add crème fraîche and blend until smooth. Blend in vanilla and grenadine. (Blending can also be done in medium bowl with handheld blender.) Mix in half-and-half until just combined. Pour into covered container and refrigerate. Stir before serving. Serve in sherbet or wine glasses. Garnish with fresh strawberry slices and sprig of mint. Freezes well.

Makes 4 to 6 servings

Per serving: 131 calories, 4 g fat, 3 g protein, 23 g carbohydrate, 13 mg cholesterol, 72 mg sodium.

Sausage Tortellini Soup

A "quick fix" for lunch. Our daughter calls it a lifesaver! Keep smoked sausage in the freezer and dry tortellini in your cabinet. You will probably have the other ingredients on hand. Leave out sausage for a tasty vegetarian soup.

2   cups dry cheese-filled tortellini
½   teaspoon prepared minced garlic
1   (14-ounce) can chicken broth[11]
1   (14-ounce) can beef broth[11]
1   (14½-ounce) can diced tomatoes, undrained
    Pinch of sugar

1   cup ½-inch-thick smoked sausage slices, halved, or ½ cup pepperoni slices, halved
1   teaspoon dried basil, crushed
2   tablespoons freshly grated Parmesan cheese (optional)

Combine tortellini, garlic and broths in large saucepan. Bring to boil. Reduce heat and simmer covered 10 minutes. Stir in tomatoes, sugar, sausage and basil. Cover and simmer 5 more minutes or until tortellini are tender and soup is hot; do not overcook or tortellini will fall apart. Sprinkle individual servings with Parmesan cheese. Serve with French bread or Texas toast.

Makes 4 servings

Per serving: 208 calories, 8 g fat, 15 g protein, 15 g carbohydrate, 17 mg cholesterol, 1772 mg sodium.

Spinach Tortellini Soup

A delicious, colorful soup that would give a festive flair to any yuletide occasion.

1   tablespoon butter
2   small garlic cloves, minced
2   (14-ounce) cans chicken broth
1   (9-ounce) package fresh cheese-filled tortellini
1   teaspoon chicken bouillon granules

1   (14½-ounce) can stewed tomatoes, undrained, snipped[73]
1   (5-ounce) package fresh prepared baby spinach, or 1 (10-ounce) package frozen leaf spinach, thawed and drained
    Freshly grated Parmesan cheese

Melt butter in large saucepan. Add garlic and cook 30 seconds. Stir in chicken broth and tortellini. Bring to boil. Reduce heat and simmer covered 5 minutes. Stir in bouillon granules, tomatoes and spinach. Heat until fresh spinach is wilted or thawed frozen spinach is heated thoroughly and tortellini are tender, about 4 minutes. Add salt and pepper to taste. Sprinkle Parmesan cheese over individual servings. Serve with French bread.

Makes 4 servings   Melissa Shaw O'Connor, Round Hill, Virginia

Per serving: 309 calories, 9 g fat, 19 g protein, 35 g carbohydrate, 36 mg cholesterol, 1198 mg sodium.

Tomato Soup Base

40	large or 60 medium tomatoes	2	cups (4 sticks) butter
4	large onions, chopped	1	rounded cup of flour
1	large bell pepper, chopped	1¾	cups sugar
1	large bunch of celery with leaves, chopped	2	tablespoons salt
		1	teaspoon curry powder

Wash, core and quarter tomatoes. Put in large pot or Dutch oven. Add onions, bell pepper and celery. (As tomatoes cook, they will make their own liquid.) Bring to boil. Reduce heat and simmer 20 to 30 minutes or until celery is tender. Cool. Blend or process vegetables in blender or food processor, a portion at a time. Run mixture through food mill or press through heavy strainer into large bowl, reserving juice. Discard skins and seeds.

Wash pot. Add butter and melt over medium-low heat. Whisk in flour, sugar, salt and curry powder. Cook about 1 minute, stirring constantly. Gradually add reserved juice. Cook and stir over medium heat until thick and bubbly. Remove from heat. Blend or process mixture again until smooth, if desired.

Pour soup base into pint-size containers and freeze. Thaw and mix one pint of tomato soup base with one pint of milk to serve four. (Vera runs it through the blender again to make it really smooth.) Heat without boiling, stirring frequently.

Makes 12 to 15 pints   Vera Larimer, Scottsdale, Arizona

Per pint: 347 calories, 25 g fat, 5 g protein, 31 g carbohydrate, 65 mg cholesterol, 1133 mg sodium.

Tomato Leek Mushroom Soup

2	medium leeks	¼	teaspoon pepper
½	cup (1 stick) butter	1	(14-ounce) can chicken broth
4	cups sliced fresh mushrooms[3]	2	(14½-ounce) cans diced tomatoes, undrained
¼	cup flour	1	cup half-and-half
1	teaspoon salt		

Slice leeks into thin rings using white and pale-green parts only, about 2 cups.[96] *Rinse well* and drain. Melt butter in large saucepan or Dutch oven. Sauté leeks and mushrooms until tender, about 5 minutes. Stir in flour, salt and pepper. Gradually stir in chicken broth and add tomatoes. Bring to boil. Simmer uncovered about 20 minutes, stirring occasionally. (May prepare ahead to this point and refrigerate. Reheat.) Pour half-and-half into 2-cup glass measure. Stir in ½ cup hot soup to prevent curdling and return mixture to soup in pan. Heat thoroughly without boiling, stirring occasionally. Serve with *Herb Roll-ups*.

Makes 6 servings   Vera Larimer, Scottsdale, Arizona

Per serving: 274 calories, 20 g fat, 5 g protein, 18 g carbohydrate, 15 mg cholesterol, 996 mg sodium.

Hearty Beef and Vegetable Stew

⅓	cup flour	1	(14½-ounce) can Italian style stewed tomatoes, undrained
1	tablespoon Cajun seasoning	2	teaspoons beef bouillon granules
2	pounds sirloin, cut into ¾- to 1-inch cubes	1	teaspoon Worcestershire sauce
5	tablespoons extra virgin olive oil, *divided*	1	teaspoon salt
1	cup chopped bell pepper	1	teaspoon soy sauce
2	cups chopped sweet onion	1	teaspoon vinegar
2	to 3 garlic cloves, minced	½	teaspoon dried thyme, crushed
1	cup burgundy wine	½	teaspoon dried basil, crushed
1½	cups sliced carrots	1	bay leaf
2	cups sliced celery	1	(10-ounce) package frozen baby lima beans, thawed
1	(10-ounce) can diced tomatoes and green chilies, undrained	1½	cups frozen whole-kernel yellow corn, thawed

Mix flour and Cajun seasoning in ziptop bag. Shake well. (Try not to inhale Cajun seasoning!) Put several beef cubes in bag and shake to coat. Transfer to plates without stacking. Continue until all cubes are coated.

Heat 3 tablespoons oil in Dutch oven. Brown one-third of beef over medium-high heat,[84] turning after about 2½ minutes (do not turn too soon or flour will stick to pan and not to beef). Cook another 2½ minutes. Roll cubes to brown sides. Drain on paper towels without stacking. Brown half the remaining beef, adding 1 tablespoon oil. Drain. Repeat for remaining cubes, adding remaining tablespoon oil. Set aside.

Without cleaning pot, add bell pepper and onion. Sauté about 1½ minutes. Add garlic and sauté 30 seconds. Brown bits on bottom of pot will release with moisture from vegetables; scrape up with wooden spatula. Add wine, stirring until all brown bits are dissolved. Add carrots and celery. Cook 2 minutes. Stir in tomatoes and green chilies, tomatoes, bouillon granules, Worcestershire sauce, salt, soy sauce, vinegar, thyme, basil, bay leaf and lima beans. Return beef to pot and bring to boil. Reduce heat and simmer covered 30 minutes. Add corn and simmer 30 more minutes or until beef is very tender. Remove bay leaf. Serve with French bread or *Cornbread* and green salad.

Makes 8 to 10 servings

Per serving of 10: 303 calories, 11 g fat, 23 g protein, 24 g carbohydrate, 55 mg cholesterol, 763 mg sodium.

Brunswick Stew

¼ cup flour
⅛ teaspoon cayenne pepper
1 teaspoon salt
¼ teaspoon dried thyme, crushed
¼ teaspoon freshly ground black pepper
1 teaspoon paprika
2 tablespoons vegetable oil, or 1 tablespoon vegetable oil and 1 tablespoon bacon drippings
1 cup chopped bell pepper
½ cup chopped celery (optional)
1 cup chopped onion
1 to 2 garlic cloves, minced
1½ cups diced cooked lean ham

3 (14-ounce) cans chicken broth, *divided*
4 medium red potatoes, peeled and diced (2½ to 3 cups)
1 (28-ounce) can diced tomatoes, undrained
⅓ cup prepared barbecue sauce (optional)
1 teaspoon Worcestershire sauce
1 bay leaf (optional)
1 cup frozen baby lima beans, thawed
1 cup frozen shoe peg or yellow corn, thawed
2 cups bite-size, *Easy Cooked Chicken*

Mix flour, cayenne pepper, salt, thyme, black pepper and paprika in small bowl. Set aside.

Heat oil in large Dutch oven and sauté bell pepper, celery and onion until tender. Add garlic and cook 30 seconds. Stir in ham and cook about 3 minutes. Sprinkle in flour mixture. Cook and stir with wooden spatula about 1 minute, being careful not to burn (mixture will ball up). Pour in 2 cans chicken broth. Bring to boil, scraping up any brown bits on bottom. Continue to cook until flour dissolves and mixture thickens slightly. Add potatoes, tomatoes, barbecue sauce, Worcestershire sauce and bay leaf. Simmer uncovered 10 minutes. Stir in remaining can of chicken broth and add lima beans. Cook 15 more minutes. Add corn and chicken. Cook until potatoes are tender and stew is thoroughly heated, about 5 minutes. Remove bay leaf and serve.

Note: Brunswick stew, like other stews, is better, if made a day ahead. Cool. Cover and refrigerate. Reheat when ready to serve.

Makes 8 to 10 servings

Per serving of 10: 226 calories, 6 g fat, 17 g protein, 25 g carbohydrate, 38 mg cholesterol, 1353 mg sodium.

Ground, Dried or Fresh Herbs

Substitute ¼ teaspoon ground herbs or 1 teaspoon dried herbs
for 1 tablespoon finely chopped fresh herbs. Dried herbs
should be crushed to release their flavor.

Michelle's Chili

1½ pounds lean ground beef
¼ cup chopped onion, or use 2 tablespoons dried minced onion
1 (1¼-ounce) packet mild chili seasoning
1 (28-ounce) can crushed tomatoes, undrained
1 (10-ounce) can chili fixin's, or use 1 (10-ounce) can tomatoes and green chilies, undrained

1 (16-ounce) can chili beans in mild sauce
1 teaspoon beef bouillon granules
½ cup water
½ teaspoon vinegar (optional)
Chopped onion (optional)
Shredded Cheddar cheese

Brown beef in large skillet with onion. Mix in chili seasoning. Spray 3½- to 4-quart slow cooker and add meat mixture. Stir in tomatoes, chili fixin's, chili beans and bouillon granules. Rinse all cans with water and add. Cook covered 7 to 8 hours on LOW. Stir in vinegar just before serving to give zip to chili. Top servings with chopped onion and shredded cheese. Serve with *Cornbread*.

Makes 4 to 6 servings

Per serving (6): 443 calories, 25 g fat, 27 g protein, 26 g carabohydrate, 85 mg cholesterol, 1347 mg sodium.

Turkey Chili

1 pound ground turkey
½ cup chopped onion
½ cup chopped bell pepper
½ cup chopped celery
1 teaspoon chicken bouillon granules
1 (16-ounce) can kidney beans (or chili beans for spicier flavor), undrained
2 (8-ounce) cans tomato sauce

1 (14½-ounce) can stewed tomatoes, undrained[73]
½ cup water
1 tablespoon Worcestershire sauce
½ teaspoon ground cumin
½ teaspoon chili powder
¼ teaspoon garlic salt
1 fresh jalapeño, seeded and chopped (optional)

Spray large nonstick skillet or electric skillet. Add ground turkey, onion, bell pepper and celery. Sprinkle in bouillon granules. Cook and stir over medium heat until meat is no longer pink. Add beans, tomato sauce and tomatoes. Rinse tomato cans with water and add. Stir in Worcestershire sauce, cumin, chili powder, garlic salt and jalapeño. Bring to boil. Reduce heat and simmer uncovered 5 minutes, stirring occasionally. Serve with shredded cheese, chopped onion, chopped ripe olives, diced tomatoes and shredded lettuce.

Makes 6 servings   Terry VanderVeen Bright, Lynchburg, Virginia

Per serving: 230 calories, 7 g fat, 19 g protein, 24 g carbohydrate, 60 mg cholesterol, 1198 mg sodium.

White Bean Chili

*I made twenty recipes of this chili to serve 160 people at a church supper. Everyone raved about it. There was not a drop left. I prefer to use soaked dry beans, but to save time, use canned beans and **Microwave Easy Cooked Chicken** in quick version below.*

2 cups dry great Northern beans	1 (49½-ounce) can chicken broth
1 tablespoon dried oregano, crushed (Mexican oregano preferred)	1 (14-ounce) can chicken broth
	2 teaspoons chicken bouillon granules
2 teaspoons ground cumin	1 to 2 garlic cloves, minced[20]
1½ teaspoons seasoned salt	1 (4-ounce) can chopped green chiles, undrained
Freshly ground black pepper	
1 tablespoon canola oil	3 cups bite-size *Easy Cooked Chicken**
1 cup chopped onion	

Soak beans overnight;[66] rinse and drain. Combine oregano, cumin, seasoned salt and pepper in small bowl. Heat oil in large Dutch oven. Sauté onion until clear, about 3 minutes. Add *half* the spice mixture. Cook and stir 1 minute over *low* heat. Pour in chicken broth (I also add broth from *Easy Cooked Chicken*). Mix in bouillon granules and garlic. Add beans and bring to boil. Reduce heat and simmer covered 60 to 70 minutes or until beans are almost tender. Stir in remaining spice mixture, green chiles and chicken. Cook until beans are tender, about 15 more minutes. Season with salt and pepper if needed. For thicker chili, mix 1 tablespoon flour with ¼ cup water in small bowl and stir into chili (or stir in ¼ cup instant potato flakes). Cook and stir until thickened. Serve with fresh lime wedges and *Cornbread Muffins*, French bread or warm flour tortillas. Freezes well.

** May substitute **Slow-Cooked Pork** for **Easy Cooked Chicken**.*

Makes 10 servings

Per serving: 237 calories, 3 g fat, 28 g protein, 26 g carbohydrate, 47 mg cholesterol, 976 mg sodium.

Quick White Bean Chili variation: Use *Microwave Easy Cooked Chicken*. Canned beans are already seasoned, so reduce amount of seasoned salt and bouillon granules to taste. Sauté onion in oil. Add chicken broth and half the spice mixture. Mix in bouillon granules and garlic. Bring to boil. Add green chiles and chicken. Gently stir in 3 (15.8-ounce) cans of great Northern beans (rinsed and drained) and remaining spice mixture. Cover and simmer about 15 minutes or until thoroughly heated.

Kat's Chili

1	tablespoon shortening	1	(16-ounce) can dark red kidney
1	pound ground round		beans, undrained[19]
½	cup chopped onion	2	teaspoons beef bouillon granules
1	(14½-ounce) can Italian style	1	to 1½ teaspoons chili powder
	stewed tomatoes, undrained[73]	1	garlic clove, minced
1	tomato can of water		

Heat shortening in Dutch oven or heavy skillet. Brown meat until no longer pink. Drain, if necessary. Add onion and cook until soft. Stir in tomatoes, water, kidney beans, bouillon granules, chili powder and garlic. Simmer uncovered 1 hour or until thick, stirring occasionally. Add salt and pepper if needed.

Makes 4 servings   Katherine Forsyth, Boulder, Colorado

Per serving: 428 calories, 23 g fat, 29 g protein, 27 g carbohydrate, 78 mg cholesterol, 1145 mg sodium.

Roasted Red Pepper Bisque

1	(13-ounce) jar roasted red peppers, drained	½	cup flour
2	large portabella mushroom caps	2	(10½-ounce) cans chicken broth
2	tablespoons extra virgin olive oil	3	tablespoons anisette liqueur*
2	cups finely chopped yellow onion	1	teaspoon chicken bouillon granules
1	to 2 garlic cloves, minced	½	cup water
1	cup (2 sticks) butter, cut into pieces		Dash of hot pepper sauce
		½	cup heavy cream (optional)

Slice open roasted peppers and remove any seeds. Cut into julienne strips. Set aside on plate. Clean mushrooms. (see *About Portabella Mushrooms*). Dice and set aside on separate plate.

Heat oil in large saucepan and sauté onion, about 4 minutes. Add peppers and mushrooms, sautéing 5 more minutes. Add garlic and cook 30 seconds. Stir in butter until melted. Sprinkle in flour and cook 2 to 3 minutes, stirring constantly to prevent sticking. Gradually add chicken broth. Stir until mixture thickens and begins to bubble. Remove from heat and stir in anisette, bouillon granules, water and pepper sauce. Puree mixture with handheld blender or in blender. Blend in cream, if desired. Heat thoroughly without boiling. Ladle into cups and serve with crackers. Bisque freezes well.

* May substitute ¼ to ½ teaspoon anise extract, adding more to taste.

Makes 4 to 6 servings

Per serving of 6: 504 calories, 43 g fat, 4 g protein, 21 g carbohydrate, 113 mg cholesterol, 1260 mg sodium.

California Clam Chowder

6	thick slices smoked bacon, cut into small pieces
1½	cups chopped onion
4	cups peeled or unpeeled diced russet potatoes
1	(8-ounce) bottle clam juice
3	to 4 (6½-ounce) cans *minced* clams, drained, reserve juice
1½	cups snipped flat-leaf parsley
1½	teaspoons dried thyme, crushed
1	teaspoon dried basil, crushed
1	teaspoon salt
½	to 1 teaspoon coarsely ground black pepper
¼	to ½ teaspoon cayenne pepper
2	to 3 garlic cloves, smashed
5	large tomatoes pureed in blender, or 2 (14½-ounce) cans stewed tomatoes, undrained, snipped[73]
1	pint half-and-half

Cook bacon in large skillet until crisp. Remove with slotted spoon and drain on paper towels. Sauté onion in drippings until tender, 4 to 5 minutes. Drain on paper towels and set aside. Put potatoes in Dutch oven. Add bottled and reserved clam juice and just enough water to cover potatoes. Cook until barely tender. Mix in bacon, sautéed onion, parsley, thyme, basil, salt, black pepper, cayenne pepper, garlic and tomatoes. Bring to boil. Stir in clams and half-and-half. Heat without boiling until clams are thoroughly heated. For richer flavor and thicker chowder, let soup cool down and reheat. (Chowder will be even better, if refrigerated overnight and reheated just before serving.) For even thicker chowder, mix 1 tablespoon flour and ¼ cup water in small bowl and stir in while reheating (or stir in ¼ cup instant potato flakes). Serve with French bread or cornbread, or serve with beer and saltine crackers.

Makes 8 servings   Theresa Nuzum, Grand Lake, Colorado

Per serving: 362 calories, 12 g fat, 17 g protein, 48 g carbohydrate, 47 mg cholesterol, 742 mg sodium.

About Portabella Mushrooms

Mushrooms are either cultivated or wild. Portabellas are cultivated mushrooms. They are actually fully matured crimini mushrooms, a brownish variation of the commonly cultivated white or button mushroom. They were probably discovered by accident when criminis were left to grow. They are dark brown in color, have a flat cap and tough woody stem. They are often 6 inches across. With this growth their gills become fully exposed causing moisture loss, which gives them a dense, meaty texture that makes them great for grilling.

Remove stem close to base of cap with a knife. Remove gills with a spoon. Be careful not to damage cap. It is okay to leave gills, they add a wonderful flavor, but they will turn sauces and whatever else you cook dark. Clean these mushrooms by wiping caps with damp paper towels or quickly rinse off any stubborn dirt. Pat dry.

Gingered Chicken Salad Sandwiches

3 cups bite-size *Easy Cooked Chicken*
⅓ cup toasted chopped walnuts or pecans
½ cup finely chopped celery
⅓ cup regular or light mayonnaise
⅓ cup regular or light sour cream
1 teaspoon Dijon mustard

1 teaspoon grated orange zest
1 teaspoon finely chopped candied ginger^G
¼ teaspoon salt
½ teaspoon sugar
12 slices raisin bread, toasted
5 butter or Boston lettuce leaves

Lightly toss chicken, walnuts and celery in large bowl. Mix mayonnaise, sour cream, mustard, orange zest, ginger, salt and sugar in medium bowl until combined; add to chicken mixture, stirring to coat. Cover and refrigerate several hours to blend flavors.

Spread about ½-cup chicken mixture over each of 6 toast slices. Add lettuce leaves and cover with remaining toast slices. Cut sandwiches in half or in quarters. Serve on individual plates and garnish with orange wedges and grapes.

Makes 6 sandwiches   Kaylene Miller, Granby, Colorado

Per sandwich: 352 calories, 12 g fat, 32 g protein, 31 g carbohydrate, 84 mg cholesterol, 430 mg sodium.

Chicken Salad Sandwiches

3 cups bite-size *Easy Cooked Chicken*
1 cup light mayonnaise
1 tablespoon Dijon mustard
Dashes of hot pepper sauce
2 to 3 tablespoons milk

8 slices multi-grain bread
4 or 8 slices tomato
4 leaves leaf lettuce
4 slices red onion
Alfalfa sprouts

Put chicken in large bowl. Mix mayonnaise, mustard and pepper sauce in medium bowl and stir into chicken. Gradually stir in milk until creamy. Cover and refrigerate. Spread ½-cup chicken salad on each of 4 bread slices. Add 1 or 2 tomato slices. Sprinkle with salt and pepper to taste. Cover with lettuce leaf and slice of onion. Add alfalfa sprouts as desired and cover with remaining bread slices; cut in half. Serve with dill pickle spears and potato chips.

Makes 4 sandwiches

Per sandwich: 456 calories, 16 g fat, 47 g protein, 36 g carbohydrate, 140 mg cholesterol, 700 mg sodium.

Chunky Pimento Cheese

"Pimento" is the usual spelling for this pimiento and cheese mixture.

1 (10-ounce) foil-wrapped brick extra-sharp Cheddar cheese	¼ teaspoon sugar Salt and freshly ground black pepper to taste
1 cup mayonnaise	
2 teaspoons Worcestershire sauce	1 (4-ounce) jar plus 1 (2-ounce) jar diced pimientos, drained
2 to 3 dashes of hot pepper sauce	
1 tablespoon grated sweet onion	

Shred cheese in food processor* using shredder blade. Remove cheese and place steel blade in work bowl. Return cheese to work bowl and add mayonnaise, Worcestershire sauce, pepper sauce, onion, sugar, salt and pepper. Pulse until *almost* to desired consistency. Add pimientos and pulse until chunky as desired. (Make a day ahead and refrigerate for best consistency and flavor.) Spread pimento cheese on toasted or untoasted white or whole wheat bread. Grill untoasted sandwiches in skillet (like grilled-cheese sandwiches). Serve with *Easy Candied Dill Pickles.*

* Alternatively, shred cheese with hand grater and mix ingredients in bowl with mixer. Continue as directed above.

Makes 2 cups

Per 2 tablespoons: 78 calories, 6 g fat, 4 g protein, 3 g carbohydrate, 19 mg cholesterol, 136 mg sodium.

Hot Crab Sandwiches

2 (6-ounce) cans crabmeat, well drained and flaked	1¼ cups shredded Swiss cheese
¼ cup chopped green onions	1¼ cups shredded Monterey Jack cheese
1 teaspoon dried dill weed, crushed	4 English muffins, split in half
1 tablespoon dry sherry	Paprika
1 cup mayonnaise	

Mix crabmeat, green onion, dill, sherry, mayonnaise and cheeses in bowl. Cover and refrigerate 2 to 3 hours. Remove about 15 minutes before making sandwiches. Spread crab mixture amply on each muffin half and sprinkle with paprika. Place on large foil-lined baking sheet and bake at 450° for 10 minutes or until hot, watching so they do not burn.

Makes 8 servings   Sally Streamer, Boulder, Colorado

Per serving: 318 calories, 21 g fat, 15 g protein, 17 g carbohydrate, 67 mg cholesterol, 629 mg sodium.

Chicken Salad Melts

1	recipe *Rhona's Chicken Salad* variation	16	slices Swiss cheese
8	English muffins, split in half		Paprika

Prepare variation version of **Rhona's Chicken Salad** recipe. Lightly toast muffin halves and cover each with ample amount of chicken salad. Top with cheese slice and sprinkle with paprika. Place on foil-lined baking sheets and bake at 375° for 10 minutes. Place two melts on each plate along with a square of **Raspberry Salad** on a lettuce leaf. Serve **Death by Chocolate Brownie Dessert** for dessert.

Makes 8 servings

Per serving: 203 calories, 14 g fat, 20 g protein, 6 g carbohydrate, 108 mg cholesterol, 203 mg sodium.

Tuna Melts

1	(6-ounce) can albacore tuna, well drained and flaked, or 2 (3-ounce) foil pouches	¼	teaspoon seasoned salt
		⅓	cup mayonnaise
2	tablespoons finely chopped celery		Dash of hot pepper sauce
2	tablespoons finely chopped onion	3	hard-cooked eggs,[18] chopped
2	tablespoons sweet pickle relish	3	English muffins, split in half
¼	cup salad olives, well drained, or sliced pimiento-stuffed olives	6	slices Swiss or sharp Cheddar cheese
¼	teaspoon fresh lemon juice		Paprika

Mix tuna, celery, onion, pickle relish, olives, lemon juice and seasoned salt in medium bowl. Stir in mayonnaise, pepper sauce and eggs. Season with salt and pepper. Cover and refrigerate, if not using immediately.

Lightly toast English muffin halves. Cover each with an ample amount of tuna mixture. Top with slice of cheese and sprinkle with paprika. Place on foil-lined baking sheet and bake at 375° for 10 minutes.

Makes 6 tuna melts

Per serving: 307 calories, 20 g fat, 16 g protein, 17 g carbohydrate, 134 mg cholesterol, 842 mg sodium.

Reubens

8 slices rye bread, or sourdough rye bread	1 pound thinly sliced corned beef
¼ cup (½ stick) butter, softened	1 cup sauerkraut, well drained
1 cup Thousand Island dressing	2 cups shredded Swiss cheese, or 4 slices Swiss cheese

Spread each bread slice with butter. Turn over and spread other sides evenly with Thousand Island dressing. Layer corned beef amply over dressing side of four slices without overhanging edges. Sprinkle with sauerkraut and Swiss cheese. Cover with remaining bread slices, buttered side up.

Heat large griddle or iron skillet and grill two sandwiches at a time (or use two skillets). Press sandwiches down with spatula and cook 3 to 4 minutes. Turn and press again; cook until cheese melts. Turn once more to make sure sandwiches are golden brown and thoroughly heated. Cut each sandwich in half and serve with potato chips and dill pickles.

Makes 4 sandwiches

Per sandwich: 787 calories, 53 g fat, 39 g protein, 40 g carbohydrate, 146 mg cholesterol, 1735 mg sodium.

Joye's Asparagus Roll-ups

1 (15-ounce) can extra-long asparagus spears (about 18)	Butter, softened
Soft white sandwich bread	Mayonnaise
	Seasoned salt

Carefully remove asparagus spears from can. Drain well on paper towels, about 1 hour. Trim crusts from enough bread slices to wrap asparagus (put slices in ziptop bag to keep soft).

Work with six bread slices at a time and spread each with butter. Spread generous layer of mayonnaise over butter and sprinkle lightly with seasoned salt. Place an asparagus spear on each slice with tip exposed (if long enough). Roll bread to enclose spear. Place roll-ups seamside down in single layer in wax-paper-lined covered container. Repeat with remaining bread slices and spears. Cover roll-ups with plastic wrap. Place slightly-dampened paper towel over plastic. Cover and refrigerate several hours or overnight.

Cut roll-ups in half. Stand on cut ends on doily-lined serving plate. Garnish with chive blossoms and long pieces of chives.

Makes 32 to 36 rolls   Joye Miller, Bella Vista, Arkansas

Per roll: 50 calories, 3 g fat, 1 g protein, 6 g carbohydrate, 3 mg cholesterol, 130 mg sodium.

Strawberry and Onion Tea Sandwich

An unusual combination!

1 (8-ounce) package cream cheese, softened	Strawberry jam
½ teaspoon grated onion, or to taste	1 (16-ounce) loaf firm white sandwich bread, crusts removed

Beat cream cheese in small bowl with mixer until fluffy; add onion and beat until smooth. Add enough jam to make mixture pink but not runny. Refrigerate. Cut bread into rounds or strips and spread with cream cheese mixture. Put sandwiches in covered container, separating layers with wax paper. Cover and refrigerate until ready to serve. Top each sandwich with small dab of strawberry jam just before placing on serving plate. Garnish plate with fresh mint or parsley.

Makes about 60 sandwiches   Rae Hunter, Columbia, South Carolina

Per tea sandwich: 31 calories, 2 g fat, 1 g protein, 4 g carbohydrate, 4 mg cholesterol, 39 mg sodium.

Cucumber Sandwiches

2 small firm cucumbers	3 tablespoons mayonnaise
½ cup water	½ to 1 tablespoon grated onion
½ cup vinegar	1 tablespoon fresh lemon juice
½ teaspoon salt	Dash of hot pepper sauce
⅛ teaspoon pepper	1 (16-ounce) loaf firm white sandwich bread
1 (8-ounce) package cream cheese, softened	Paprika

Peel and slice cucumbers into very thin rounds. Mix water, vinegar, salt and pepper in medium bowl. Add cucumber slices. Cover and refrigerate overnight.

Beat cream cheese in medium bowl with mixer until fluffy. Add mayonnaise, onion, lemon juice and pepper sauce and beat until smooth. Cut four circles from each bread slice with 1½-inch biscuit cutter or shot glass. Spread each bread circle with cream cheese mixture. Place in covered container, separating layers with wax paper and covering top layer with plastic wrap. Place slightly dampened paper towel over plastic wrap and refrigerate until 30 minutes before serving. Drain cucumbers. Pat dry on paper towels. Place cucumber slice on each sandwich and sprinkle with paprika.

Makes about 60 sandwiches   Rae Hunter, Columbia, South Carolina

Per sandwich: 30 calories, 2 g fat, 1 g protein, 2 g carbohydrate, 4 mg cholesterol, 33 mg sodium.

Vegetables

Vegetables

Green Bean Bundles

Prepare ahead. Good for a dinner party or holiday dinner.

1	quart water	1	teaspoon soy sauce
1	teaspoon salt	1	teaspoon Worcestershire sauce
1	pound fresh whole young green beans, tips removed and rinsed	1	tablespoon butter
		⅛	teaspoon garlic salt
8	to 10 slices bacon	1	tablespoon brown sugar[1]
1	teaspoon wasabi powder (optional, but good)	⅛	teaspoon red pepper flakes
		1	teaspoon toasted sesame seeds[5]
1	(14-ounce) can beef broth		Diced pimiento

Bring 1 quart water and salt to boil in large saucepan. Add beans and cook uncovered until crisp-tender, 8 to 10 minutes. Drain and plunge into bowl of ice water about 4 minutes to stop cooking. Drain and set aside up to one hour.

Partially cook 4 or 5 slices of bacon at a time in large nonstick skillet about 1 minute on each side. Do not overcook–will be hard to wrap around beans. Drain on paper towels. Cut slices in half.

Mix wasabi powder with 1 teaspoon water in small bowl. Combine with beef broth, soy sauce, Worcestershire sauce, butter, garlic salt, brown sugar and pepper flakes in medium saucepan. Bring to boil. Reduce heat and simmer uncovered about 10 minutes, stirring occasionally (sauce will be thin). Set aside.

Tightly wrap bacon piece around 5 or 6 green beans and secure with toothpick. Place in 9x13-inch baking dish. Continue until beans and bacon are used, making 3 rows of 6 to 7 bundles. Pour sauce over beans. (May prepare to this point early in the day. Cover and refrigerate. Remove 30 minutes before baking. Baste with sauce.) Sprinkle sesame seeds and pimiento over bundles. Bake at 350° for 30 to 35 minutes or until bacon is cooked and bundles are hot–do not overcook or beans will wilt. Baste, being careful not to wash off sesame seeds and pimiento. Serve with slotted spoon.

Makes 6 servings

Per serving: 77 calories, 5 g fat, 4 g protein, 5 g carbohydrate, 9 mg cholesterol, 358 mg sodium.

Green Beans

1½ to 2 pounds fresh green beans	½ small onion, cut into wedges, or
1½ to 2 cups water	1 teaspoon dried minced onions
3 to 4 small pieces cooked ham, *or*	1 teaspoon salt
2 tablespoons butter or bacon	½ to 1 teaspoon beef bouillon
drippings for flavor (optional)	granules

If beans are small, leave whole and trim stem ends only. Otherwise, trim and snap beans to desired lengths. (It is usually not necessary to remove strings from green beans as most varieties are now stringless.) Wash beans thoroughly in cool water and drain.

Pour water in Dutch oven or large saucepan and bring to boil. Add beans, ham, onion, salt and ½ teaspoon bouillon granules. Cook uncovered 5 minutes (will help preserve bean's green color). Cover and cook until tender, 10 to 15 more minutes, stirring occasionally. Add additional bouillon granules if needed. Remove cover and drain, or cook until liquid is reduced. Serve with ham, beef or chicken and *Roasted New Potatoes*.

Makes 4 to 6 servings

Per serving of 6: 91 calories, 5 g fat, 3 g protein, 13 g carbohydrate, 4 mg cholesterol, 260 mg sodium.

Green Beans with Toasted Pecans

2 pounds fresh young green beans	½ teaspoon salt, or to taste
2 tablespoons butter	⅛ teaspoon pepper
⅓ cup chopped shallots or	¼ cup chopped toasted pecans
chopped green onions	

Trim ends and rinse beans. Bring large pot of salted water to boil. Add beans. Return to boil and cook uncovered over medium heat 6 to 8 minutes or until crisp-tender. Drain. Plunge beans into bowl of ice water for 4 minutes. Drain. Let stand at room temperature 1 hour or cover and refrigerate several hours or overnight (if refrigerated, bring to room temperature). Melt butter in large skillet and sauté shallots until tender, about 2 minutes. Add beans, salt and pepper. Toss and heat thoroughly. Stir in pecans and serve.

Makes 6 to 8 servings

Per serving of 8: 88 calories, 5 g fat, 3 g protein, 10 g carbohydrate, 8 mg cholesterol, 170 mg sodium.

Green Beans, Pine Nuts and Basil variation: Substitute ¼ cup toasted pine nuts[5] for pecans and stir in ¼ cup snipped fresh basil. Heat and serve.

Fresh Asparagus

1	to 1½ pounds fresh asparagus spears	Pinch of sugar
3	cups water	2 tablespoons butter, melted, or use butter-flavored spray
1	teaspoon salt	Fresh lemon juice (optional)

Snap, rinse and drain asparagus.[34] Pour water into large nonstick skillet and add salt and sugar. Bring to boil. Add asparagus in single layer if possible and return to boil. Cook covered 5 minutes or until crisp-tender. Drain off water and return to heat to evaporate any remaining water. Drizzle with melted butter and lemon juice. Shake skillet to coat spears. Heat thoroughly and serve at once.

Makes 4 servings

Per serving: 30 calories, 1 g fat, 3 g protein, 5 g carbohydrate, 1 mg cholesterol, 7 mg sodium.

Asparagus with Sesame Mayonnaise variation: Prepare asparagus as directed above, draining and evaporating water, but omit drizzling butter and lemon juice. Place spears in flat serving dish. Meanwhile, whisk ½ cup mayonnaise, 3 tablespoons sour cream and ½ teaspoon sesame oil together in small bowl. Spoon over asparagus. Sprinkle with 1 tablespoon toasted sesame seeds.[5]

Makes 4 servings   Dody Martin, Boulder, Colorado

Per serving: 259 calories, 28 g fat, 3 g protein, 5 g carbohydrate, 14 mg cholesterol, 164 mg sodium.

Broiled Tomato Rounds

These are absolutely delicious!

	Topping:	½ cup finely snipped flat-leaf parsley
2	cups mayonnaise	Salt and pepper
1	cup freshly shredded Parmesan or Asiago cheese	
½	cup chopped green onions, including some tops	3 or 4 firm ripe tomatoes (about ½-pound each)

Topping: Combine mayonnaise, cheese, green onion and parsley in medium bowl. Mix in salt and pepper to taste. Topping may be prepared ahead. Cover and refrigerate.

Cut tomatoes into ½-inch slices and place on foil-lined baking sheet. Spread generous amount of topping on each. Broil 4 to 5 minutes, watching carefully for a light brown color. Transfer to serving plate and serve.

Makes 6 to 8 servings   Jeff Vadakin, Fairhope, Alabama

Per serving of 8: 261 calories, 23 g fat, 5 g protein, 9 g carbohydrate, 27 mg cholesterol, 524 mg sodium.

Mozzarella Tomatoes

2 to 3 medium tomatoes	¾ to 1 cup shredded mozzarella
Mayonnaise	cheese
Creole seasoning or seasoned salt	Paprika

Slice tomatoes ½-inch thick and place in single layer in sprayed shallow baking dish or pie plate. Spread thin layer of mayonnaise over each slice and sprinkle lightly with Creole seasoning. Sprinkle generously with mozzarella cheese. Add dashes of paprika for color. Bake at 350° for 25 to 30 minutes or until hot and cheese begins to brown.

Makes 4 servings   Jackie Andrishok, Destin, Florida

Per serving: 108 calories, 8 g fat, 5 g protein, 4 g carbohydrate, 20 mg cholesterol, 156 mg sodium.

Kat's Peas

2 tablespoons butter	1 (15-ounce) package frozen
¼ cup chopped onion	baby green peas
1 cup sliced fresh mushrooms[3]	1 teaspoon Worcestershire sauce

Melt butter in medium saucepan and sauté onions and mushrooms. Add frozen peas. Cover and cook over low heat until peas thaw (no water needed–peas will produce moisture as they thaw). Stir in Worcestershire sauce. Cover and cook over medium heat until peas are hot and just tender. Season with salt and pepper.

Makes 4 to 6 servings   Katherine Forsyth, Boulder, Colorado

Per serving of 6: 94 calories, 4 g fat, 4 g protein, 11 g carbohydrate, 10 mg cholesterol, 171 mg sodium.

Brown Sugar Carrots

1 pound carrots with green tops	2 tablespoons brown sugar[1]
2 tablespoons butter	¼ teaspoon salt
¼ cup water	

Remove tops and peel carrots. Rinse and thinly slice diagonally. Put carrots, butter, water, brown sugar and salt in heavy saucepan. Cook covered over low heat 10 to 15 minutes or until tender, stirring occasionally. Pour into serving dish and garnish with fresh parsley or fresh mint.

Makes 4 servings

Per serving: 120 calories, 6 g fat, 1 g protein, 17 g carbohydrate, 15 mg cholesterol, 230 mg sodium.

Orange Glazed Carrots

3 pounds carrots with green tops, or use sliced baby-cut carrots
1 cup water*
½ cup fresh orange juice*
1 tablespoon sugar
1 teaspoon salt
2 tablespoons butter

Glaze:
4 tablespoons butter

¼ cup maple syrup or honey[16]
1 tablespoon light brown sugar
Dash of ground nutmeg
1 teaspoon orange zest
3 tablespoons orange-flavored brandy liqueur or other brandy

⅓ cup toasted sliced almonds
2 to 3 tablespoons snipped flat-leaf parsley or mint

Remove tops and peel carrots. Rinse and cut on extreme diagonal into ¼-inch thick slices (9 to 10 cups). Combine carrots, water, orange juice, sugar, salt and butter in Dutch oven or large pot. Bring to boil. Reduce heat and simmer covered until just tender, 7 to 10 minutes, stirring occasionally. Meanwhile, prepare glaze.

Drain carrots well, reserving liquid. Return carrots to pot. Pour glaze over carrots and toss to coat. (May prepare to this point early in the day. Cover and refrigerate.) Heat carrots over medium heat before serving, adding some reserved liquid, if desired. Transfer to serving dish and sprinkle with almonds and parsley. Recipe may be halved.

Glaze: Heat butter, syrup, brown sugar, nutmeg and orange zest in small saucepan over medium-high heat, stirring constantly until butter melts and sugar dissolves. Remove from heat and stir in brandy liqueur.

* To preserve carrot's natural sweet flavor, cook in as little liquid as possible, adding water or orange juice only if absolutely necessary—uncooked carrots will cook down into liquid as they simmer.

Makes 8 servings   **Adapted from recipe by Bev Lehmann, Bella Vista, Arkansas**

Per serving: 219 calories, 9 g fat, 3 g protein, 31 g carbohydrate, 15 mg cholesterol, 180 mg sodium.

Sherried Acorn Squash

When selecting winter squash, such as acorn, butternut or Hubbard, choose heavy, dull-skinned squash for sweeter meat. Keep in cool, dark, dry place if not using immediately.

2 medium acorn squash	2 teaspoons grated orange zest (optional)
Salt	
4 tablespoons butter	4 tablespoons brown sugar[1]
4 tablespoons sherry	

Scrub squash and cut in half lengthwise. Remove fiber and seeds. (If squash are hard to cut, microwave each 1 to 2 minutes on HIGH to soften rind. Then cut and remove fiber and seeds. *Squash will be hot!*) Put halves, cutside down, in large shallow baking dish. Spray skins with nonstick spray. Add ½ inch of water to baking dish. Cover with foil and bake at 350° for 20 to 30 minutes or until soft. Remove foil, avoiding steam, and pour off water. Turn halves over and prick well with fork. Sprinkle with salt. Add 1 tablespoon butter to each well and drizzle with 1 tablespoon sherry. Sprinkle each with ½ teaspoon orange zest and 1 tablespoon brown sugar. Bake uncovered at 350° for 5 minutes. Baste with syrup that forms in wells and bake 5 more minutes. Remove from baking dish and serve in individual bowls.

Makes 4 servings

Per serving: 261 calories, 12 g fat, 2 g protein, 37 g carbohydrate, 0 mg cholesterol, 146 mg sodium.

Baked Acorn Squash and Cranberry Sauce variation: Prepare squash as directed above through pricking insides with fork and sprinkling with salt. Brush insides of each squash half with 2 tablespoons melted butter. Mix ½ cup jellied cranberry sauce, 1 teaspoon ground cinnamon and 2 tablespoons honey in small bowl. Spoon equally into squash halves. Bake uncovered at 350° for 15 to 20 minutes.

CharLee's Sauerkraut

1 (2-pound) package refrigerated sauerkraut, drained	1 cup finely chopped onion
	2 teaspoons caraway seeds
1 medium Granny Smith apple, peeled and finely chopped	¼ teaspoon salt, or to taste
	¼ teaspoon pepper
1 to 2 tablespoons bacon drippings	1½ tablespoons sugar

Put sauerkraut in 3-quart saucepan and add water to almost cover. Mix in apple, bacon drippings, onion, caraway seeds, salt, pepper and sugar. Bring to boil. Reduce heat and simmer covered 1 to 1½ hours, stirring occasionally.

Makes 6 servings   CharLee Bright Hollinger, Westminster, Maryland

Per serving: 87 calories, 5 g fat, 1 g protein, 11 g carbohydrate, 4 mg cholesterol, 391 mg sodium.

Creamed Onions

Good at Thanksgiving.

2 pounds boiler onions	1 teaspoon chicken bouillon granules
1 (14-ounce) can chicken broth	2 tablespoons dry sherry
3 tablespoons butter, *divided*	Dash of hot pepper sauce (optional)
2 tablespoons flour	2 tablespoons snipped fresh parsley
½ teaspoon salt	2 tablespoons dry breadcrumbs
Dashes of white pepper	Paprika
Dash of ground nutmeg	
1½ cups half-and-half	

Put onions in large saucepan and add about 6 cups boiling water or enough to cover. Let stand covered about 5 minutes. Drain and rinse with cold water. Cut off root ends and peel (squeeze onions out of their skins). Snip off any stringy tops with kitchen shears. Return onions to saucepan and add chicken broth. Bring to boil and cook covered 8 to 10 minutes or just until tender. Drain, reserving ½ cup liquid. Set aside.

Melt 2 tablespoons butter in same saucepan. Whisk in flour, salt, pepper and nutmeg. Cook and stir until bubbly, about 1 minute. Stir in reserved onion liquid and half-and-half. Add bouillon granules and bring to boil, stirring constantly. Reduce heat, but continue boiling about 1 minute. Stir in sherry and pepper sauce. Mix in onions and simmer until thickened. Stir in parsley. Pour mixture into 1½-quart casserole. (May prepare a day ahead to this point. Cool. Cover and refrigerate. Remove 30 minutes before baking.) Melt remaining tablespoon butter in small skillet and mix in breadcrumbs. Sprinkle over onions and sprinkle top with paprika. Bake uncovered at 350° for 35 to 40 minutes or until hot and bubbly.

Makes 4 to 6 servings

Per serving of 6: 153 calories, 8 g fat, 4 g protein, 16 g carbohydrate, 24 mg cholesterol, 755 mg sodium.

Onion Casserole

2 to 4 tablespoons butter	20 drops of Worcestershire sauce
3 medium sweet onions, sliced ¼-inch thick and separated into rings	2 cups shredded Swiss cheese or enough to cover
1 (10¾-ounce) can cream of celery or cream of chicken soup	2 cups cubed fresh French bread Butter-flavored cooking spray

Melt butter in large skillet and sauté onion rings until soft. Place in sprayed 7x11-inch baking dish. Spread soup over onions. Dot with Worcestershire sauce and sprinkle with cheese. Cover and bake at 350° for 30 to 35 minutes. Spray bread cubes with cooking spray and sprinkle around edge of casserole. Return to oven and bake uncovered until bread cubes are lightly browned. Let stand 5 to 10 minutes before serving. Serve with beef or pork.

Makes 6 servings   Vera Larimer, Scottsdale, Arizona

Per serving: 315 calories, 22 g fat, 14 g protein, 17 g carbohydrate, 57 mg cholesterol, 632 mg sodium.

Variation: Defrost 1 (12-ounce) package frozen spinach soufflé. Spread over onion layer in place of soup. Continue as directed above. Yum!

Aunt Maude's Corn Casserole

Aunt Maude was a good cook. In fact, all my aunts were good cooks. I wish I had more of their recipes.

¼ cup (½ stick) butter	½ teaspoon sugar
2 tablespoons chopped bell pepper	1 cup milk
½ cup chopped onion	1 (14¾-ounce) can cream style corn
2 tablespoons flour	1 (11-ounce) can whole kernel corn, drained
2 eggs, lightly beaten	
½ teaspoon salt	15 saltine crackers, *divided*
⅛ teaspoon pepper	1 tablespoon butter

Melt butter in large nonstick skillet and sauté bell pepper and onion until tender, about 3 minutes. Sprinkle in flour. Cook and stir 1 minute. Mix eggs, salt, pepper, sugar and milk in medium bowl and stir into skillet. Stir in both cans of corn. Remove from heat. Crumble 10 crackers over bottom of sprayed1½- to 2-quart casserole and pour corn mixture over crumbs. Crumble remaining 5 crackers on top and dot with butter. Bake at 350° for 1 hour.

Makes 6 servings   Maude McCaleb Hayles, Cleveland, Mississippi

Per serving: 242 calories, 12 g fat, 7 g protein, 29 g carbohydrate, 77 mg cholesterol, 852 mg sodium.

Squash and Pearl Onion Casserole

Ordinarily, I would say this recipe makes eight servings, but it is so good that six will not want to share it with two more people!

2	pounds (about 6) medium yellow summer squash	1	(10-ounce) can diced tomatoes and green chilies, undrained
1	(15-ounce) jar whole pearl onions, drained	1	pound pasteurized prepared cheese product, cubed

Quarter squash lengthwise and cut into ½-inch pieces. Sprinkle squash into sprayed 9x13-inch baking dish and cover with onions. Heat tomatoes and green chiles in medium saucepan and stir in cheese until melted. Spread evenly over squash and onions. Bake uncovered at 350° for 30 minutes or until hot and bubbly. Let stand 10 minutes before serving.

Makes 6 servings   Eleanor Weathersby, Dawsonville, Georgia

Per serving: 347 calories, 24 g fat, 19 g protein, 14 g carbohydrate, 71 mg cholesterol, 1366 mg sodium.

Eggplant Casserole

2	large firm eggplants	2	(8-ounce) cans tomato sauce
1	bay leaf	1	tablespoon brown sugar
		1	teaspoon celery salt (optional)
	Sauce:		
2	tablespoons butter or oil	½	cup dry bread crumbs
1	cup chopped bell pepper	½	cup grated Cheddar cheese
1	cup chopped onion	½	cup grated Parmesan cheese
1	cup chopped celery		Paprika

Peel eggplants. Slice crosswise ½-inch thick and cut slices into 1-inch squares. Put eggplant and bay leaf in large pot of enough boiling salted water to cover. Boil partially covered 10 minutes or until eggplant turns pale green. Meanwhile, prepare sauce.

Drain eggplant and discard bay leaf. Put eggplant in sprayed 1½- or 2-quart casserole. Add sauce and toss gently. Mix bread crumbs and grated cheese in small bowl and sprinkle over casserole. Sprinkle with paprika. Bake at 350° for 35 minutes or until hot and bubbly.

Sauce: Melt butter in large nonstick skillet and sauté bell pepper, onion and celery until tender. Stir in tomato sauce, brown sugar and celery salt. Add salt and pepper if needed. Cook over medium-low heat about 5 minutes to blend flavors, stirring occasionally.

Makes 6 to 8 servings   Ada Walker, Bradenton, Florida

Per serving of 8: 165 calories, 8 g fat, 7 g protein, 17 g carbohydrate, 12 mg cholesterol, 424 mg sodium.

Spicy Creamed Spinach

2 (10-ounce) packages frozen chopped spinach
1 tablespoon olive oil or canola oil
½ cup finely chopped sweet onion
1 garlic clove, minced
1 jalapeño, seeded and chopped[44]
1½ tablespoons flour
¾ cup chicken broth[11]
1 (5-ounce) can evaporated milk, or ½ cup half-and-half
1 cup shredded sharp Cheddar cheese
¾ teaspoon salt
¼ teaspoon seasoned salt or your favorite food seasoning
1 tablespoon anisette, anise-flavored liqueur, or ½ teaspoon anise extract
   Dash of ground nutmeg
1 teaspoon fresh lemon juice
¼ cup unseasoned dry breadcrumbs
2 tablespoons grated Asiago or Parmesan cheese
2 tablespoons toasted salted sunflower kernels
   Butter-flavored cooking spray or butter

Thaw spinach and drain well.[43] Heat oil in large skillet and sauté onion, garlic and jalapeño over medium heat until onion is clear. Sprinkle in flour and cook 1 to 2 minutes, stirring constantly. Pour in chicken broth and bring to boil. Cook and stir until thickened. Stir in evaporated milk, Cheddar cheese, salt, seasoned salt, anisette, nutmeg, lemon juice and spinach, mixing well. Pour into sprayed 1½-quart casserole. (May prepare to this point early in the day; refrigerate. Remove 30 minutes before baking. If mixture separates, stir before proceeding.)

Mix breadcrumbs, Asiago cheese and sunflower kernels in small bowl and sprinkle over spinach mixture. Spray or dot with butter. Bake at 350° for 30 minutes or until hot and bubbly. Let stand a few minutes before serving.

Makes 4 to 6 servings

Per serving of 6: 116 calories, 5 g fat, 5 g protein, 10 g carbohydrate, 2 mg cholesterol, 352 mg sodium.

Terry's Baked Beans

3 (15-ounce) cans pork and beans
¾ cup ketchup
1 teaspoon Worcestershire sauce
¼ cup packed brown sugar[1]
1 teaspoon dried minced onion
1 teaspoon dry mustard[9]

Mix pork and beans, ketchup, Worcestershire sauce, brown sugar, dried onion and mustard in 1½- to 2-quart casserole. Stir in salt and pepper to taste. Bake uncovered at 350° for 45 minutes to 1 hour or until hot, bubbly and thickened.

Makes 12 servings   Terry VanderVeen Bright, Lynchburg, Virginia

Per serving: 161 calories, 1 g fat, 6 g protein, 39 g carbohydrate, 0 mg cholesterol, 612 mg sodium.

Asparagus Casserole

1	tablespoon butter	24	round buttery crackers, *divided*
½	cup chopped bell pepper	2	(15-ounce) cans asparagus *tips*, drained, any woody pieces removed
½	cup chopped onion		
1	(10¾-ounce) can cream of mushroom soup	1	(2-ounce) jar diced pimientos, drained
1	(10¾-ounce) can cream of chicken soup	4	hard-cooked eggs,[18] sliced
1	cup milk	1	cup slivered almonds, *divided*

Heat butter in large nonstick skillet and sauté bell pepper and onion until tender. Whisk soups and milk together in medium bowl until smooth and stir into sautéed vegetables. Simmer covered 15 minutes. Crush 18 crackers and spread over bottom of sprayed 9x13-inch baking dish. Cover with layer of asparagus and sprinkle with pimientos. Make layer of sliced eggs and sprinkle with ¾ cup almonds. Pour soup mixture over layers. (May prepare to this point early in the day. Cover and refrigerate. Remove 30 minutes before baking.) Crush remaining 6 crackers and sprinkle over casserole. Sprinkle with remaining ¼ cup almonds. Bake at 350° for 35 to 45 minutes or until hot and bubbly.

Makes 10 servings

Per serving: 216 calories, 13 g fat, 8 g protein, 18 g carbohydrate, 92 mg cholesterol, 527 mg sodium.

Smoky Baked Beans

5	slices bacon	⅓	cup molasses
¾	cup chopped bell pepper	1½	tablespoons Dijon mustard
1	cup chopped onion	½	teaspoon Cajun seasoning
2	(28-ounce) cans vegetarian baked beans	1	tablespoon Worcestershire sauce
½	cup smoky barbecue sauce	¼	teaspoon salt
⅓	cup ketchup	½	teaspoon freshly ground black pepper

Cook bacon in medium skillet. Drain and set aside, reserving 1 tablespoon of drippings. Sauté bell pepper and onion in reserved drippings 3 or 4 minutes or until tender. Mix baked beans, barbecue sauce, ketchup, molasses, mustard, Cajun seasoning, Worcestershire sauce, salt and pepper in 2½-quart deep casserole. Crumble bacon and mix into bean mixture along with sautéed vegetables. Bake uncovered at 350° for 1½ hours or until thickened. Serve with ham and potato salad or with hamburgers and hot dogs.

Makes 8 servings

Per serving: 207 calories, 2 g fat, 6 g protein, 40 g carbohydrate, 3 mg cholesterol, 891 mg sodium.

Pinto Beans

Mary does not soak her beans. I was always an advocate of soaking beans overnight. I cooked the beans without soaking and they were tender and delicious.

1	pound (about 2½ cups) dry pinto beans	1	garlic clove, minced (optional)
6	cups water	2	cups boiling water
1	cup diced salt pork, or 3 slices bacon, cut into pieces, or 1 tablespoon bacon drippings	1½	teaspoons salt
		¼	teaspoon freshly ground black pepper

Remove any debris from beans and rinse thoroughly. Put beans in Dutch oven and add 6 cups water. Add salt pork and garlic. Bring to boil. Reduce heat and simmer covered 45 minutes. Add 2 cups *boiling* water (cold water will split beans). Simmer covered 45 more minutes. Stir in salt and pepper. Cook covered until beans are almost tender, adding more boiling water if needed. Remove cover and turn up heat. Cook until most liquid is absorbed. Mary recommends serving with fried potatoes and cornbread.

Makes 6 servings   Mary Richardson, Bella Vista, Arkansas

Per serving: 347 calories, 3 g fat, 21 g protein, 61 g carbohydrate, 3 mg cholesterol, 600 mg sodium.

Slow Cooker Beans and Ham

2	cups dry pinto beans	2	tablespoons dried parsley flakes, crushed
1	meaty ham bone, or 2 or 3 smoked ham hocks	¼	teaspoon red pepper flakes, crushed
1	bay leaf	2	teaspoons beef bouillon granules
1	to 2 tablespoons dried minced onion		Water

Rinse and drain beans–do not soak. Place ham bone in sprayed 4-quart slow cooker. Add beans, bay leaf, dried onion, parsley flakes, pepper flakes, bouillon granules and enough water to cover. Cook on HIGH 6 to 8 hours, adding water if needed. Remove ham bone and cut meat into bite-size pieces. Return pieces to pot. Discard bone and any fat. Remove bay leaf. Serve with *Jalapeño Cornbread.*

Makes 4 servings

Per serving: 486 calories, 12 g gat, 33 g protein, 63 g carbohydrate, 60 mg cholesterol, 347 mg sodium.

Jalapeño Black-Eyed Peas

1 pound (about 2¾ cups) dry black-eyed peas	1 cup finely chopped onion
2 (10½-ounce) cans beef broth	1 large garlic clove, minced
2 beef broth cans of water	2 jalapeños, seeded and finely chopped[44]
1 meaty ham bone, or 1 ham steak cut into large pieces	1 bay leaf
¼ cup chopped bell pepper	2 teaspoons Cajun seasoning

Remove any debris from peas and rinse thoroughly. Put peas in large bowl and add plenty of cold water.[66] Remove any peas that float. Soak overnight or at least 6 hours. Rinse and drain.

Pour beef broth and water into Dutch oven or large heavy saucepan. Add peas and ham bone. Stir in bell pepper, onion, garlic, jalapeño, bay leaf and Cajun seasoning. Bring to boil. Reduce heat and simmer covered 45 to 60 minutes or until peas are tender, stirring occasionally. Season with salt and pepper to taste. Add additional Cajun seasoning, if desired. Remove ham bone and bay leaf. Cut ham into bite-size pieces and return to pot. Discard bone and any fat. Thoroughly heat peas. Serve with salsa. Also serve with sliced ham, *Praline Sweet Potato Fries* and *Cornbread*.

Makes 6 servings

Per serving: 312 calories, 2 g fat, 25 g protein, 54 g carbohydrate, 98mg cholesterol, 1079 mg sodium.

Quick Jalapeño Black-eyed Peas variation: Substitute 4 (15-ounce) cans black-eyed peas for dry peas. Drain, reserving liquid. Set aside. Substitute 2 (14-ounce) cans beef broth for 10½-ounce cans (14-ounce cans are less concentrated). Omit water. Use ham steak instead of ham bone. Pour beef broth and reserved liquid from peas into Dutch oven. Add cut-up ham steak. Stir in bell pepper, onion, garlic, jalapeño, bay leaf and Cajun seasoning. Bring to boil. Reduce heat and simmer uncovered 30 to 40 minutes or until peppers and onions are tender and mixture is reduced to desired thickness. Remove bay leaf. Add black-eyed peas. Heat thoroughly, adding salt and pepper if needed. Serve as directed above.

Makes 6 servings

Per serving: 314 calories, 3 g fat, 21 g protein, 51 g carbohydrate, 21 mg cholesterol, 2534 mg sodium.

Baked Cauliflower

1 head cauliflower	½ cup half-and-half
1 egg, lightly beaten	½ cup grated Asiago, Cheddar or Swiss cheese
¼ teaspoon salt	
¼ teaspoon pepper	2 tablespoons butter
⅛ teaspoon ground nutmeg	Paprika

Remove cauliflower leaves and cut out core. Rinse head and put in large non-aluminum pot of boiling salted water. Boil about 5 minutes or until crisp-tender. Drain and immediately plunge head into bowl of ice water for 7 to 8 minutes to stop cooking. Drain. Break cauliflower into florets. Place in sprayed shallow baking dish, pie plate or gratin dish.ᴳ Whisk egg, salt, pepper, nutmeg and half-and-half in medium bowl. Pour over florets and toss to coat. Sprinkle cheese on top and dot with butter. Sprinkle with paprika. Bake at 400° for 20 minutes or until hot and golden.

Makes 4 to 6 servings

Per serving: 115 calories, 10 g fat, 4 g protein, 2 g carbohydrate, 63 mg cholesterol, 210 mg sodium.

Ritzy Mushrooms

½ cup (1 stick) butter, *divided*	3 tablespoons flour
1½ to 2 pounds whole fresh medium mushrooms[3] (cut any large ones in half)	1 egg yolk
	1 cup half-and-half
1 tablespoon snipped flat-leaf parsley	¼ teaspoon paprika
	2 tablespoons fresh lemon juice
½ teaspoon salt	25 round buttery crackers, crushed

Melt ½ stick butter in large saucepan and sauté mushrooms 3 minutes. Sprinkle with parsley, salt and flour. Stir until combined. Cover and cook over *very low* heat about 10 minutes, stirring once or twice. Remove from heat. Put egg yolk in 2-cup glass measure or bowl and whisk in half-and-half, paprika and lemon juice. Stir into mushroom mixture. Cook over low heat until slightly thickened. Add salt and pepper if needed. Pour mixture into sprayed 1-quart casserole or 8x8-inch baking dish. Cover and refrigerate several hours or overnight. Remove 30 minutes before baking. (If time does not permit, bake without refrigerating.)

Melt remaining ½ stick butter in small saucepan and mix in crushed crackers. Sprinkle over mushrooms. Bake at 350° for 30 minutes or until hot and bubbly.

Makes 6 servings   **Leighanne Minter Davis, Birmingham, Alabama**

Per serving: 337 calories, 25 g fat, 6 g protein, 25 g carbohydrate, 109 mg cholesterol, 428 mg sodium.

Appendixes

Tips are listed here to provide shortcuts and helpful information. They are referenced in the recipes by superscript numbers near the point at which they apply.

[1] To measure packed brown sugar, buy or store in plastic ziptop bags; using dry measure cup for amount needed, scoop sugar into cup with one hand inside bag and press full measure against other hand outside bag to pack and level.

[2] For best baking results, whisk dry ingredients (flour, baking powder, baking soda and salt) together in a bowl before adding to creamed or liquid mixture.

[3] Store mushrooms in open paper bag in refrigerator (storage in plastic will cause condensation and decay). Clean just before using; wipe with damp paper towels. To remove stubborn dirt, fill ziptop bag half full with water, add mushrooms, *quickly* swish around to prevent absorbing water and drain in colander; pat dry on paper towels. Do not peel mushrooms; there is much flavor in the skin. Trim ends and slice button mushrooms upside down in egg slicer.

[4] If using dark or treated (nonstick) baking pans, muffin tins, loaf pans, layer-cake pans, Bundt pans, tube pans, etc., bake 25° lower than called for in recipe and add 3 to 5 minutes to baking time. Test *for doneness* to be sure.

[5] Toast slivered or sliced almonds, flaked coconut, pine nuts, or seed spices, such as coriander, cumin or sesame seed, in dry nonstick skillet over medium heat until they begin to release their fragrance, 2 to 4 minutes, lifting and shaking skillet frequently. (Do not overbrown sesame seeds or they will become bitter; cook only about 1 minute after they begin to pop.)

[6] To make foil liners for baking pans, invert pan on counter and form sheet of foil over bottom and around sides; remove and place liner inside pan and press into corners. When baking bars, brownies and sheet cakes, liners help prevent hard and crusty edges, making cutting easier. Also saves pans from knife scratches.

[7] Sprinkle lemon juice over cut or peeled fruit (apples, peaches, pears, bananas and other fruit that turn dark). Put peeled potatoes and sweet potatoes in pan of cold water (without lemon juice) to keep from darkening; drain before using.

[8] Transfer cakes in Bundt or tube pans to cooling racks covered with wet kitchen towel to help release cake. Gather towel up and around pan as much as possible. Wet towel again with cold water as it warms. *Marlene Gillette, Bella Vista, Arkansas*

[9] Dry mustard and wasabi powder are easily combined with other ingredients if mixed with an equal amount of water in bowl. Stir until smooth and add. (Mix smaller amounts in teaspoon or tablespoon with toothpick.)

[10] Toast nuts on small jelly roll pan to bring out flavor. Bake 5 to 7 minutes, depending on size, at 325° (or in toaster oven), stirring frequently.

[11] To make 1 cup chicken broth or beef broth: Stir 1 generous teaspoon chicken bouillon granules or beef bouillon granules into 1 cup of boiling water.

[12] Eggs separate easier when cold. However, egg whites at room temperature yield larger volume when beaten.

[13] Unless otherwise stated in stove manual or recipe, set oven selector and temperature to BROIL (550°). Broil in upper third with door ajar at broil stop.

14 Instead of crumbling cooked bacon, stack several uncooked slices and dice or snip into ½-inch pieces with kitchen shears. Cook in skillet, separating pieces with two forks. Remove with slotted spoon and drain on paper towels.

15 The following stages and temperatures of boiling sugar syrup used in candy making will be determined by the effect of dropping syrup into a cup of cold water: **soft-ball stage** (234°-240°)–a drop of boiling syrup immersed in cold water forms a soft ball that flattens of its own accord when removed; **firm-ball stage** (244°-248°)–a drop of boiling syrup immersed in cold water forms a firm but pliable ball; **hard-ball stage** (250°-265°)–a drop of boiling syrup immersed in cold water forms a rigid, somewhat pliable ball; **soft-crack stage** (270°-290°)–a drop of boiling syrup immersed in cold water separates into hard but pliable threads; **hard-crack stage** (300°-310°)–a drop of boiling syrup immersed in cold water separates into hard brittle threads.

16 Spray the glass measure to ease removal of syrup, molasses or honey.

17 Make a pie crust shield from a disposable, foil pizza pan. Place on thick pad of newspapers and score a circle on bottom, slightly smaller than inside upper edge of pie plate to be covered. Cut out circle with pointed paring knife–caution: edge will be sharp. Invert shield over pie crust to prevent overbrowning edges.

18 To hard-cook eggs, place in saucepan, cover with cold water and bring to full boil; turn off heat, cover and let stand 12 minutes (up to 20 minutes at higher altitudes). Drain and run cold water over eggs. To peel, break egg in middle on counter and gently press and roll, breaking shell all over. Remove *shell and membrane* from round end and peel in one direction around egg. Peeling under running water helps. Warm eggs peel easiest; very fresh eggs do not peel well.

19 Open bottoms of canned beans, chili, condensed milk and other cans whose contents may have settled to the bottom. For drawn cans, whose bottoms cannot be opened, store upside down.

20 Make garlic cloves easier to peel by microwaving each clove 3 to 5 seconds on HIGH, depending on size. Peel and cut lengthwise; remove any green area in center–it is bitter.

21 To crack or crush cumin seeds, peppercorns, peanuts and other nuts and seeds, put in ziptop bag, place on hard surface and strike with a meat mallet.

22 Use *clear* imitation vanilla extract in place of pure vanilla extract to prevent darkening batter, glazes and frostings. In flavorings, pure (as in pure vanilla extract) means pure essence, while imitation means the flavor is imitation. Extracts contain alcohol; flavorings without the word "extract" have no alcohol.

23 Keep frosting off cake plate by sliding strips of wax paper under edges of cake before frosting. When finished, lift and pull out wax paper.

24 Flour, though presifted, settles in transit. If a recipe calls for 1 cup flour, fluff with *scoop* and transfer to 1-cup dry measure. Sweep off excess with knife or pastry scraper (do not scoop flour with dry measure). If recipe calls for 1 cup sifted flour, fluff and sift in coarse-mesh strainer over wax paper, fold wax paper, pour into 1-cup dry measure, sweep off excess, and return excess flour to cannister.

25 Divide batter equally among pans by counting the number of spoonfuls put into each pan. Spoon-shaped rubber spatulas work well for spooning batter.

26 To flash freeze fruits, berries, pastries or appetizers, place in single layer or separate them on foil-lined jelly-roll pans. Freeze uncovered until solid. Berries will separate easily. Store in suitable containers in freezer.

27 To prevent wire-rack imprints in breads and cake layers, place folded kitchen towel and sprayed piece of wax paper over racks before turning out to cool.

28 To wash fresh spinach: Fill kitchen sink with cold water, add 1 tablespoon salt and spinach leaves. Swish leaves well. Drain and wash again in cold water without salt. Drain in colander or spin in lettuce spinner. Place spinach in ziptop bag, add paper towels and refrigerate. To remove stems from large spinach leaves, hold leaf together wrong side out with thumb and forefinger of one hand, and pull stem from leaf with other hand. Tear into bite-size or larger pieces, if desired.

29 Cut unpeeled avocados in half lengthwise to the pit; slightly twist and remove one half. Carefully strike pit with sharp edge of knife and twist knife to dislodge pit. Score flesh into cubes, run knife around inside of peel, and scoop out cubes.

30 Egg wash is used on pies, pastries and certain breads to enhance glazing and browning. Also used to seal bottom pie crust from juices in fillings. Beat whole egg with pinch of salt and 1 tablespoon water in small bowl with fork. Brush on pie crusts to seal bottom, or brush lattice or top crust of pies. Sprinkle top with 1 tablespoon sugar (or brush on 1 tablespoon milk instead of egg wash). Avoid getting egg wash, milk or sugar on rim of pie or edge will burn while baking.

31 It is essential to remove silver skin, the tough, pearly membrane found on pork and beef tenderloins, brisket, lamb or other meats; if left on, the membrane becomes tough and chewy and can cause meat to curl. Slip a sharp knife under skin, angle up slightly, and move knife back and forth horizontally. Use your other hand to pull silver skin taut to separate skin from meat. Remove as much silver skin as possible. The job is tedious, but worth the effort.

32 Wash and flash freeze blueberries. Do not thaw blueberries or cranberries when using in baking; blueberries will bleed and cranberries will become mushy.

33 To prevent having two messy, sticky hands when breading floured or unfloured meat cutlets, chicken breasts, fish or vegetables, beat eggs in shallow bowl and put dry coating (breadcrumbs or cracker crumbs) in separate shallow bowl; use one hand to dip item into egg and transfer to coating, and use the other hand to coat, shake off excess and place on plate, Continue until all are coated. Cover with plastic wrap and refrigerate 15 minutes to help coating adhere.

34 Bend asparagus spears until they snap; discard bottom ends. Soak spears in cold water with a sprinkling of salt for 10 to 15 minutes, swishing spears around several times to remove grit. Drain well in colander. (Some cooks prefer to peel tough ends of asparagus and leave spears whole.)

35 To remove peach skins, put peaches in boiling water about 1 minute or until skins split; then plunge into ice water to stop the cooking. Slip off skins. (Some varieties of peaches may not release their skins and will have to be peeled.)

36 Bread dough and roll dough will rise faster in warm place. Set oven to lowest setting and heat about 1 minute; *turn off oven.* Place dough in bowl, cover with sprayed plastic wrap or sprayed lid (foil pizza pan works well) and place on center rack of oven. Allow dough to rise as directed by recipe. (Alternatively, set heating pad on low, cover with folded kitchen towel and place prepared bowl of dough on top. *Charlene Holeman, Bentonville, Arkansas)*

37 Custard pies and quiches should be baked just until sharp knife inserted near center comes out clean. Overbaking will cause curdling.

38 To help prevent sugar from crystallizing around sides of saucepan when making frostings and candies, spray inside of pan with cooking spray or rub sides with butter before adding any ingredients. May also rinse with water and leave wet.

39 Cake layers will be less crumbly and easier to spread with filling or frosting if chilled or frozen first. Leave wax paper or parchment paper liners on layers while chilling; remove before frosting.

40 For fluffy rice, turn off heat after rice has cooked, remove lid and place paper towel across top of pan; replace lid and let stand 5 to 10 minutes. Paper towel will prevent steam from condensing inside lid and dripping back into rice and will help keep grains dry and separate. Fluff rice with fork just before serving.

41 Strain broths, sauces and vegetable juice by filtering through coffee filter, dampened cheesecloth or paper towels. Fold paper towel in fourths and open to make a filter; put in strainer over bowl and pour liquid through filter.

42 To make 1 cup buttermilk or sour milk, mix 1 tablespoon lemon juice or white vinegar with enough milk to make one cup. Let stand 10 minutes.

43 Thaw frozen chopped spinach in microwave-safe bowl on HIGH 3 minutes. Thoroughly drain thawed chopped spinach, chopped broccoli or shredded fresh cucumber by wrapping in double-thickness of paper towels and gently squeezing out moisture. *Theresa Nuzum, Grand Lake, Colorado*

44 When working with jalapeños and onions, keep hands away from face and eyes. Wash hands thoroughly when finished.

45 To make soft breadcrumbs, let bread dry out 1 or 2 hours. Hold slice in one hand and rake or shred with fingers of other hand; discard crust. (Or shred frozen slice across large-hole hand grater.) One slice fresh or frozen bread will make ½ cup soft breadcrumbs. If allowed to dry, makes about ⅓ cup. To make 1 cup buttered soft breadcrumbs, melt 1 tablespoon butter in nonstick skillet, stir in 1 cup soft breadcrumbs and cook over medium heat until lightly browned.

46 To make a strong onion sweet, slice and separate into rings, place in bowl and sprinkle with 1 teaspoon sugar or more, depending on size of onion. Cover with ice cubes and let stand 30 minutes. Drain when ready to use.

47 To segment oranges or grapefruit, cut away top and bottom of unpeeled fruit with sharp knife, cut peel and white pith away from flesh, going from top to bottom around fruit, and holding fruit in one hand over bowl, slice down to the core on each side to free segments from membrane; let segments fall into bowl. Squeeze membranes for additional juice.

48 To make a 6x12x1½-inch foil drip pan, cut piece of 18-inch-wide heavy-duty aluminum foil 24 inches long. Fold in half to make a 12x18-inch, two-ply rectangle. Fold in all sides 1½ inches and crease folds; fold all sides over again 1½ inches. Unfold sides once to stand up vertically, pull out corners into triangles and fold triangles against sides. Place one or two bread slices in pan after dripping begins to prevent spattering and to absorb drippings.

49 Chopped hard-cooked eggs are fragile. Add last to salads to prevent overmixing.

50 Use stick margarine containing 100 calories per tablespoon, or use vegetable-oil spread with at least 60% oil (stated on package), when making recipes whose amount of oil or fat is critical (as in cookies, cakes and candies). Very-low-fat spreads are not suitable for baking or frying–they have too much water content.

51 Béarnaise or hollandaise sauce should be served warm, not hot. Sauce can be held warm in saucepan up to two hours by placing saucepan in larger pan of hot tap water–never in boiling or simmering water.

52 Prepare boiling water bath for canning, by placing rack in bottom of large, deep pot, kettle or Dutch oven and filling half-full with hot or boiling water. Place hot sealed jars in pot without touching sides of pot or other jars. Add hot or boiling water to cover tops by about 1 inch without pouring directly on jars. Bring water to rolling boil; reduce heat, maintaining gentle boil. Cover and boil jars at least 5 minutes or as specified in recipe. Carefully remove jars with tongs and place an inch or so apart on a towel-covered surface to cool.

53 Remove seeds from tomatoes by cutting in half crosswise, turning upside down and gently squeezing each half. Most seeds will fall out, and any remaining seeds can be removed with grapefruit spoon or with swipe of your finger.

54 To unmold gelatin, dip a metal spatula or table knife in warm water and run it around upper edge of mold. Soak kitchen towel in hot water and hold it around bottom of mold for about 10 seconds. Place moistened serving plate on top of mold, invert and gently shake to loosen gelatin. Carefully lift mold while positioning gelatin on serving plate.

55 To grate onion, cut onion in half and rub against ceramic ginger grater[G] in a circular motion. Brush onion into measuring spoon with a pastry brush.

56 When making salmon croquettes and salmon loaf, remove any dark skin from canned salmon. Bones need not be removed because they are soft and will mix with salmon when combined with other ingredients.

57 Only rinse pasta when used in cold dishes or when it will be refrigerated to use later. Rinse under cold water to stop the cooking process and drain well. When using pastas in salads, cook until al dente[G] (will allow pasta to absorb dressing and still remain firm).

58 Use stove-to-oven, flameproof or metal bakeware when dishes are to be baked at high temperatures or browned under broiling element. Glass baking dishes are not recommended for use in oven temperatures above 375°.

59 Do not overmix ground beef for meat loaves, hamburgers or meatballs or meat will become mushy.

60 For tender, juicy turkey slices, cut roasted turkey breasts away from each side of breast bone with long sharp knife, pulling and prying breast as you cut. Slice breasts crosswise across the grain–not in the usual lengthwise manner.

61 Grate only colored part of peel from citrus fruit to get zest.ᴳ A fine microplane nutmeg or spice grater is perfect for the purpose; go over entire surface–zest will collect in trough. Use a zester to make thin strands of zest; chop strands into short pieces. Zest may be frozen.

62 Use a tart tamper to make miniature tart shells. Place a small ball of dough in center of mini-muffin-tin cup, dust small, round end of tamper with flour and press down gently with circular motion, pushing dough up sides of cup. Dust tamper with additional flour and press dough against sides all around until dough rises even with, or slightly above, top edge of cup.

63 Bread flour, a high protein flour, produces high, light popovers, cream puffs and other chouxᴳ pastries.

64 Two pans are needed for water bath cooking, one to hold ingredients and one about 2 inches larger for water bath. Place folded kitchen towel in water-bath pan to prevent sloshing when moving pans. Place pan on oven rack, set ingredient pan on towel and add water to outer pan until halfway up sides of ingredient pan. (Add cream of tartar to aluminum water-bath pan to prevent discoloration.)

65 To prevent streaks in blueberry muffins, especially when berries are very ripe, pour half the amount of batter needed for each muffin into bottom of cup, add a few blueberries and cover with remaining amount of batter for each cup.

66 Rehydrate 1 pound of dry beans by soaking in 6 to 8 cups water in large bowl overnight. For quick soaking, put beans in large saucepan, add 6 to 8 cups water and bring to boil; cook covered 2 minutes. Remove from heat and let stand covered for 1 hour. Either way, drain and rinse before using.

67 Select ripe mangoes with unblemished yellow skin blushed with red. To peel and dice, slice off whole side of unpeeled mango lengthwise along both sides of long slim pit. Score flesh into cubes, flip peel inside out and slice off cubes onto plate. Remove flesh from sides of pit, peel and dice or chop.

68 To slice onion, cut off stem end only and cut onion in half vertically. Remove outer skin, leaving root end intact. Place onion half on cutting board and slice crosswise. To chop onion, place skinned onion-half on cutting board, slice vertically almost to root (root holds onion together) and slice across cuts.

69 If shortening is called for when melting chocolate for coating or dipping, do not substitute butter or margarine, which have water content that can cause chocolate to "seize" and become grainy. Oil should not be substituted either; it can make coating thin and may prevent chocolate from setting up.

70 Prepare basil chiffonade just before using to keep strips from turning dark. Roll several basil leaves together like a little cigar and thinly slice across roll into narrow strips. To finely chop small herb leaves, like rosemary and thyme, when called for along with basil, strip rosemary and thyme leaves from stems and roll up in basil leaves; cut across roll and finely chop.

71 Slice fat on steaks and chops vertically in several places to prevent meat from curling while frying or grilling.

72 To julienne carrots, peel and cut into 2½-inch-long pieces; cut in half lengthwise. Place cutside down on cutting board and slice into matchsticks.

73 Snip canned tomatoes into pieces with kitchen shears while still in can.

74 To truss a roast, make a slipknot with a 2-inch tail out of butcher's twine, loop around roast 1 inch from end, and tighten slightly. Loop twine, twisting loop, and slip over other end of roast; position loop 1 inch from original loop and tighten to take up slack. Continue twisting and positioning loops 1 inch apart down length of roast. Bring twine over end of roast, roll roast over, slip twine under and around end loop, and tighten; secure the twine to each successive loop down roast. Bring twine around original end, roll roast over again, and secure twine to original loop at slipknot; cut twine and knot with tail of slipknot.

75 To easily remove marshmallow creme or peanut butter from jar, remove lid and seal from jar and microwave on HIGH 30 seconds.

76 To peel kiwi fruit, slice off both ends, exposing flesh, use a teaspoon to work around inside of peel, gently releasing flesh from skin and push fruit out of skin. Slice kiwi fruit with an egg slicer.

77 Remove fat from soup, stew, chili or liquids by placing plastic wrap directly on surface and refrigerate. Congealed fat will adhere to plastic. To remove light layer of fat without refrigerating, lay paper towel on liquid and push onto surface around edges with handle of wooden spoon. Carefully remove and discard towel.

78 Well-kneaded dough is smooth and elastic. Knead bread dough with pressing-folding-turning action. Press heels of both hands down into dough, pushing away from body. Fold dough in half toward you, give quarter turn and repeat process. Kneading can take 5 to 15 minutes, depending on dough.

79 To make liners for round cake pans, place pan on piece of wax paper or parchment paper, trace around bottom of pan with a ballpoint pen and cut just inside circle. To grease paper, spray inside of pan, press liner into bottom, turn over, and press liner down into bottom again.

80 When rolling out pastry dough between wax paper, sprinkle a few drops of water on counter to prevent wax paper from slipping.

81 To slice filled roll dough, like cinnamon rolls, place piece of thread underneath roll, cross ends over top and pull thread–will cut slices without flattening roll.

82 Use water instead of milk in preparing omelets or scrambled eggs. Water evaporates into steam, leaving eggs fluffy with no milky residue.

83 To sterilize jars for canning, wash jars, lids and bands in hot soapy water. Rinse well. Boil enough water to cover jars in large kettle. Put jars and bands (not lids) in kettle and boil 10 minutes; turn off heat and add lids. Remove and drain jars. Place upright on foil-lined jelly roll pan and fill, leaving recommended head space: ⅛ inch for jellies and preserves, ¼ inch for fruit juices and pickles and ½ inch for fruit and tomatoes. Wipe jar rims and threads with wet paper towel, add lids and screw bands on tight.

84 Brown cubed meat in small batches. Meat will turn grey if crowded.

85 Hold and keep smashed or mashed potatoes warm for 30 minutes or several hours by placing prepared potatoes in mixing bowl and covering with foil; put an inch of water in a saucepan smaller than mixing bowl and place bowl with potatoes on top. Set over low heat and maintain water level.

86 Keep lid on slow cooker if possible. Each peak costs valuable cooking time.

87 To melt baking morsels or broken baking bars for drizzling, put in small heavy-duty ziptop bag and close without fully sealing. Microwave on HIGH 35 to 40 seconds and knead contents. Microwave additional 20- to 30-second intervals and knead until smooth. Cut tiny corner in bag and squeeze to drizzle chocolate.

88 Warm eggs to room temperature by putting in bowl of warm water 5 minutes.

89 Trimming fat from meat will be easier if meat is partially frozen.

90 To measure freshly ground black pepper, grind pepper over wax paper, fold paper diagonally and slide ground pepper into measuring spoon.

91 For soups or other dishes that require long periods of cooking, use half the spices initially and add remaining spices during last half of cooking time.

92 Form cheesecake crust ½-inch up sides of springform pan by pouring a ring of crumb mixture next to sides; push and press crumbs against sides with the side of a ½-cup dry measure or side of flat-bottom glass. Press remaining crumbs evenly into bottom of pan.

93 Add 1 teaspoon pepper sauce (not hot pepper sauce, but a mixture of vinegar and hot peppers) to bowl of soup to give it "zip," or add 1 teaspoon vinegar.

94 To prevent stringy cheese in sauces and casseroles, especially when using Swiss, mozzarella and Cheddar cheese, squeeze about 1 teaspoon fresh lemon juice over each cup of shredded cheese or sprinkle with white wine; fluff with fork.

95 If concerned about uncooked egg whites in recipes, substitute 2 teaspoons meringue powder mixed with 2 tablespoons water for each egg white.

96 Leeks grow like rolled-up newspapers, hiding dirt and grit. Cut off green tops an inch above white part and trim roots without cutting off root end (keeps ribs intact). Cut leeks in half lengthwise; swish several times in sink of water and soak 15 minutes. Rinse with cold water; rinse again after chopping. Drain well.

97 Ripen pears in paper bag at room temperature. Pears are ripe when flesh yields slightly under gentle pressure near base of stem.

98 To remove skin from tomatoes, immerse in large pot of boiling water 5 to 15 seconds and remove with slotted spoon. Slip off skins with tip of sharp knife. (Or stick with meat fork and swish over gas flame, turning quickly; pull off skins with sharp knife when cool.)

99 To eliminate raw taste of spinach in cooked dishes calling for frozen chopped spinach, precook spinach following package directions (microwave preferred).

100 Thaw whipped topping in refrigerator–microwaving is not recommended. Thaw completely before measuring or using and do not overstir–topping will deflate, losing its fluffy texture.

101 If soup sticks in pan or scorches, pour what can be saved into another saucepan without disturbing scorched bottom. Rescued soup should not taste burned.

102 To get more juice from lemons, roll on counter with palm of hand and warm in microwave 10 to 15 seconds on HIGH.

103 Use parchment paper on baking sheets for easy cleanup. Parchment paper may be wiped off, turned over and reused when baking cookies.

104 To butterfly shrimp, devein and split shrimp down center of back, cutting almost through; shrimp will resemble a butterfly when opened flat. For pork tenderloin filets, slice tenderloin into 2-inch sections and slice almost through across middle of each; open flat to form 1-inch thick filets, resembling butterflies.

105 Salt and acidic foods (tomatoes, wine and citrus juices) should not be added early while cooking dried beans–beans will be tougher and slower to cook; stir in acidic foods 15 to 30 minutes before end of cooking time.

106 To prevent a metallic taste, use nonmetal containers for acidic foods like lemon, lemon juice, tomatoes or pineapples.

107 To help remove tomato stains from plastic or rubber utensils, sprinkle dishwashing detergent into bowl of hot water and soak utensils.

108 Clear up cloudy iced tea by adding ½ cup hot water to pitcher of tea.

109 To make dried orange or lemon peel, remove in strips around circumference using a zester that will cut long, shallow single strands. Remove any white pith from strips with a sharp knife, leaving only yellow or orange zest. Let stand one or two days on jelly-roll pan. Store in small spice jar with lid.

110 For 1 tablespoon finely chopped fresh herbs, you may substitute ¼ teaspoon ground herbs or 1 teaspoon dried herbs (crush dried herbs to release flavor).

111 To chop fresh fennel, remove and discard tough outer stems and wash bulb thoroughly; split bulb lengthwise and discard core. Cut remaining fennel crosswise into ⅛-inch thick slices and coarsely chop.

112 Use distilled water to float candles in clear glass containers–prevents rings.

113 Rinse and drain basmati rice; cook 5 minutes less than other long grain rice.

114 Cool crockery pot of slow cooker adequately before washing; temperature differences may crack pot.

115 Wipe mold from cheese with paper towel dipped in vinegar.

116 Make superfine sugar by blending granulated sugar in blender.

117 An egg slicer works well to slice fresh mushrooms, strawberries and kiwis.

118 To keep parsley fresh, rinse and drain well. Cut off inch of stems at an angle and stand in jar two-thirds full of water with 1 teaspoon of sugar added. Cut off plastic produce bag and place loosely over parsley, making a mini-hothouse. Refrigerate. Every few days, cut off stems and change water. Keeps for weeks.

119 To prevent tortillas from drying out, keep in package until needed in recipe.

120 Wrap cooled muffins in foil individually and freeze; reheat in foil at 325° for about 10 minutes or until warm.

This glossary presents terminology used in the cookbook. Some terms are used mainly in culinary circles or in special regions of the country, while some are foreign cooking terms. Words or expressions that bear a superscript "ᴳ" have an entry here.

adobo sauce [ah-DOH-boh] – a dark-red rather pungent sauce made from ground chiles, herbs and vinegar. Of Mexican origin, it is used as a marinade as well as a serving sauce. Chipotle chiles are often packed in adobo sauce.

aïoli [ay-OH-lee] – the French word for garlic is "ail." Aïoli is a strong garlic-flavored mayonnaise. It is used to spread generously on fish, meats, hot or cold vegetables and eggs, or maybe swirled into a bowl of bouillabaisse (seafood stew).

al dente [al-DEN-tay] – an Italian phrase meaning "to the tooth," used to describe pasta or other food cooked to the correct degree of noneness. Pasta should have a slight resistance, when bitten into, but should have no hard center.

alternately – combining two or more ingredients into a mixture by adding a portion of one and then a portion of the other until both ingredients are added.

anisette [AN-ih-seht; an-ih-SEHT] – a clear, very sweet liqueur made with anise seeds and tasting of licorice.

Asiago [ah-SYAH-goh] – a semi-firm Italian cheese with a rich, nutty flavor. When aged over a year, it becomes hard and suitable for grating.

au gratin [oh-GRAH-tin] – *see* gratin.

baguette [bag-EHT] – A French bread formed into an elongated narrow loaf with browned crust and chewy center.

benne [BEHN-ee] – the sesame seed was brought to America by West African slaves in the 17th and 18th centuries. The slaves called them *benné seed*; they were thought to bring good luck.

beurre manié [burr mahn-YAY] – the French term for kneaded softened butter and flour in equal parts; it is used to thicken sauces.

blanch – partially cooking vegetables in boiling water for a few minutes, then plunging into ice water to stop the cooking.

bouquet garni [boo-KAY gahr-NEE] – herbs typically consisting of sprigs or leaves of thyme, bay leaf and sprigs of parsley tied in a cheesecloth bag or brew bag and used to flavor broths, soups and stews.

brew bag – *see* **bouqet garni**.

butterfly – to split or cut shrimp down center of back almost through and spread apart to resemble a butterfly when opened flat. Pork tenderloin filets are butterflied by cutting into 2-inch sections and slicing almost through across middle of each and opening flat to form 1-inch thick filets resembling butterflies.

candied ginger – *see* **crystallized ginger**.

canola oil – lower in saturated fat than any other oil, it is suitable for cooking and for salads.

capers [KAY-pers] – small flower buds of the Mediterranean caper bush, which are picked, sun-dried and pickled in a vinegar brine. Rinse to remove excess salt.

caramelize [KEHR-ah-meh-lyz] – to heat sugar until it liquefies into a clear syrup from golden in color to dark brown, depending on temperature.

chiffonade [shihf-uh-NAHD] – strips or shreds of vegetables, generally basil and lettuce. Basil leaves are layered, rolled like little cigars and cut crosswise into thin strips. Cut just before using to prevent turning brown.

chop – to cut food into irregular ¼- to ½-inch pieces.

chipotle [chih-POHT-lay] – this hot chile is actually a dried, smoked jalapeño. Available dried whole, powdered and pickled, they are also available canned in adobo sauce. They are added to stews and sauces. To reconstitute dried chipotles, soak in boiling water until soft, about 10 minutes. Pull off and discard stems, veins and seeds to reduce heat. Rinse canned chipotles, if desired, and discard stems, veins and seeds. Wear rubber gloves or wash your hands thoroughly after touching chipotles.

choux [SHOO] – cream puff pastry made with a high gluten, high protein flour, such as bread flour, which causes the cream puffs to be lighter.

citron [SIHT-ron] – a very sour citrus fruit, not suitable for eating raw. It is grown primarily for its thick peel, which is candied and used in baking. Chopped candied citron is often found in fruitcakes.

crème caramel [krehm kehr-ah-MEHL] – custard baked in a caramel-coated mold or ramekin.G When unmolded, the custard is automatically sauced with the caramel in the mold.

creaming, creamed – the technique of blending shortening or butter with sugar by beating the ingredients until a fluffy consistency is achieved.

crostini [kroh-STEE-nee] – small thin slices of toasted bread usually brushed with olive oil and often used as a base for appetizers such as tapas.

crystallized ginger – ginger that has been cooked in a sugar syrup and coated with coarse sugar; also called candied or preserved ginger.

cube – to cut foods into ½-inch cubes.

dash – half of a ⅛-teaspoon measure.

deglaze [dee-GLAYZ] – to heat a small amount of liquid in sauté pan after fat has been removed and to stir or scrape with spatula to loosen browned bits on bottom.

dice – to cut food into ¼-inch uniform pieces.

dredge – to lightly coat food to be fried, as with flour, cornmeal or breadcrumbs.

egg wash – one egg yolk or white beaten with small amount of milk or water; use to brush over pies, pastries and breads to enhance glazing and browning.

emulsify [eh-MUHL-suh-fy] – to combine two liquids which normally do not mix, such as oil and vinegar, by shaking vigorously as in vinaigrettes

flambé [flahm-BAY] – to pour warm brandy or liqueur over food and ignite.

flan [FLAHN} – Spanish baked custard coated with caramel.

flat-leaf parsley – also called Italian parsley, flat-leaf parsley has stronger-flavor than curly-leaf parsley.

fold – to combine by gently lifting heavier ingredients, like whipped cream or custard over lighter ones such as egg whites.

ginger grater – a shallow ceramic dish having many rows of fine, sharp teeth protruding from surface. Grate gingerroot over teeth in circular motion.

gratin – any dish topped with cheese or breadcrumbs mixed with butter and heated or broiled until brown and crispy.

gratin dish – shallow casserole dish used to increase surface area for gratin.

handheld blender – a tall slender portable electric blender having a rotary blade. End of blender may be immersed directly into a pot, cup or bowl to purée or chop contents. Also called stick blender or immersion blender.

haricot vert [ah-ree-koh VERT] – French for "green bean." The term has become associated with the variety of tender, slender green beans.

Herbsaint – developed and made primarily in New Orleans, Herbsaint is an anise-flavored liqueur used in such specialties as oysters Rockefeller.

immersion blender – see **handheld blender**.

Italian parsley – see **flat-leaf parsley**.

jicama [HEE-kah-mah] – a large brown bulbous root vegetable having a sweet nutty flavor, often referred to as Mexican potato. Jicama must be peeled; it can be eaten raw or cooked.

julienned [joo-lee-EHN] – to cut food into very thin strips.

lukewarm – moderately warm or tepid.

marinade – a liquid, usually containing herbs and spices, in which meat, fish or vegetables are soaked to improve flavor and tenderness.

marbling – flecks or thin streaks of fat running throughout piece of meat, enhancing flavor, tenderness and juiciness.

minced – to cut food into very small irregular-shaped pieces.

mirepoix [mihr-PWAH] – mixture of diced onion, carrot and celery (½ onion, ¼ carrots and ¼ celery) sautéed in butter. Used to season sauces, soups and stews or as a bed for braised meats.

Mouli grater [MOO-lee] – a two-piece French rotary grater for grating small amounts of cheese, chocolate or nuts.

pasteurize [PAS-chuh-rize; PAS-tuh-rize] – to kill bacteria by heating liquid foods to high temperatures for a short period of time.

pepperoncini [pep-per-awn-CHEE-nee] – pepperoncini are yellow, green or sometimes red pickled chiles. They are about 2 to 3 inches long and are usually packed in vinegar. Also called Tuscan peppers, they are often used as part of an antipasto.

plum tomatoes – also called Italian plum or Roma tomatoes, they are flavorful, egg-shaped tomatoes,

pots de crème [poh duh KREHM] – French for "pot of cream," a rich, creamy custard served in little pot-shaped cups.

prepared mustard – American-style mustard made of ground white mustard seed and flavored with sugar, vinegar and turmeric, which makes it yellow.

puree [pyuh-RAY] – *n.* food finely mashed or blended into a smooth, thick consistency; *v.* blending food into a paste or liquid until smooth.

ramekin [RAM-ih-kihn] – a small individual casserole dish.

reduce – to simmer or boil liquid until its volume is reduced by evaporation. Reduction causes liquids to thicken and flavors to intensify.

Roma tomatoes [ROH-mah] – *see* **plum tomatoes.**

roux [ROO] – a mixture of flour and fat or oil in equal parts that is slowly cooked over low heat to various stages–light, medium or dark. It is used to thicken soups and sauces and is the basic ingredient in gumbo and étouffée.

sauté [saw-TAY] – to cook food quickly in a small amount of oil in skillet over direct heat.

scald [SKAWLD] – to heat milk to just below boiling with tiny bubbles around edge of saucepan.

seasoned salt – regular salt combined with other flavoring ingredients such as onion salt, garlic salt and celery salt.

shallot [SHAL-uht] – a relative of onion and garlic, shallots have a mild, onion-like flavor.

simmer – to cook food in liquid at low temperature with tiny bubbles just breaking the surface.

spatula – rubber, steel or wooden utensil for turning, flipping or folding.

spoom – wine or fruit juice mixed with egg whites, whipped and frozen to create a frothy iced dessert.

spray, sprayed – in this cookbook, indicates use of nonstick cooking spray.

stick blender – see **handheld blender**

steam – cooking food on a rack over boiling water by temperature of hot steam.

strata – in culinary usage, strata refers to casseroles of several layers of ingredients.

tapas [TAH-pahs] – appetizers popular in Spain to accompany wine, apéritifs or cocktails. They range from simple items such as cheese cubes and olives and miniature sandwiches to more elaborate entrées.

toast points - toast slices cut diagonally into halves or fourths.

timbale [tihm-BAHL] – cooked rice packed in custard cup and unmolded.

tomate [TOE-maht] – French for tomato.

velouté [veh-loo-TAY] – a stock-based white sauce made from a white roux combined with chicken, veal or fish stock. Velouté also serves as a base for a number of other sauces.

wasabi [WAH-sah-bee] – a variety of green horseradish grown only in Japan. The powder has a sharp, pungent, fiery flavor. It is available in specialty and Asian markets in both paste and powder form. The latter is mixed with water much like dry mustard.

Measuring Liquids and Dry Ingredients

Measure liquids and dry ingredients accurately, using appropriate cups. Measure liquids in marked glass or plastic cups with head space to prevent spillage; dry ingredients are measured using nested cups without head space so they can be leveled off for accurate measurement.

Casserole Dishes, Baking Dishes and Baking Pans

Using the correct pan or dish is important to the success of the recipe. Differences in depth of batter or ingredients will cause shorter or longer baking times. Substitution of pans having equal volume and depth will not affect baking.

Measure pan dimensions from inside edge to inside edge. Measure depth vertically from inside bottom center of pan to underside of something flat (like another ruler) placed across top of pan. Volume is determined by filling pan with cup measures of water until filled to brim.

Casserole dishes may be round, square with rounded corners, oblong or oval. Most have glass lids.

8 x 2¾-inch round	½-quarts	non-flameproof oven ware
6½ x 6½ x 1¾-inch	1 quart	flameproof, range-to-oven ware
6½ x 6½ x 2½-inch	1½-quart	flameproof, range-to-oven ware
8 x 8 x 2-inch	2-quart	flameproof, range-to-oven ware
9½ x 12½ x 2-inch	2½-quart	non-flameproof oven ware
10½ x 12¼ x 2½-inch	3-quart	flameproof, range-to-oven ware

Baking dishes are usually square or rectangular and made of tempered glass. They do not normally have lids; use aluminum foil if necessary to cover.

8 x 8 x 2-inch	2-quart	glass, ovenproof
7 x 11 x 1½-inch	2-quart	glass, ovenproof
7½ x 11¾ x 1¾-inch	2½-quart	glass, ovenproof
9 x 13 x 2-inch	3-quart	glass, ovenproof
10 x 15 x 2-inch	4 quart	glass, ovenproof

Baking pans are usually made of anodized aluminum or coated steel. Some have flanges on the short ends for easier handling.

8 x 8 x 2-inch
9 x 9 x 2-inch
9 x 13 x 2-inch

Jelly-roll pans are rectangular with shallow sides.

9 x 13 x ⅝
10 x 15 x ¾
11 x 17 x ⅞

Loaf pans are rectangular with deep sides.

5 x 3 x 2   miniature loaf pan
8 x 4 x 2½-inch
9 x 5 x 3-inch   standard loaf pan
8¾ x 5 x 2¼-inch   glass ovenproof loaf baking dish

Brownie pan
7 x 11 x 1¼

Cake pans are round for layer cakes and rectangular for sheet cakes.
8 x 1½-inch round   8-inch layer cake pan
9 x 1½-inch round   9-inch layer cake pan
12½ x 17½ x 1-inch   half-sheet cake pan

Roasting pans
9 x 14 x 2¼-inch
11 x 17 x 2¼-inch
11 x 17½ x 2⅝-inch
12¼ x 18 x 2½-inch

Saucepans
Small   1-quart
Medium   2-quart
Large   3-quart

Index

Notes

Through the Years – A Lifetime of Good Food

Please send ___ copies of *Through The Years*   @ $22.95 each $_____

Arkansas residents add 5.625% sales tax   @ $1.30 each $_____

Shipping & Handling $3.00 first copy plus $1.50 each addl. $_____

(to same address)   Total: $_____

Name: _____

Address: _____

City: _____ State: _____ Zip: _____

Make check or money order payable to VanderVeen Publishing

Visa/MasterCard#_____ Expires _____

Signature: _____

Telephone:_____

Mail to:

VanderVeen Publishing, 11916 Hickory Drive, Bentonville, AR 72712-8789

(479) 273-3388   Fax: (479) 273-3883   1-800-982-2568

Through the Years – A Lifetime of Good Food

Please send ___ copies of *Through The Years*   @ $22.95 each $_____

Arkansas residents add 5.625% sales tax   @ $1.30 each $_____

Shipping & Handling $3.00 first copy plus $1.50 each addl. $_____

(to same address)   Total: $_____

Name: _____

Address: _____

City: _____ State: _____ Zip: _____

Make check or money order payable to VanderVeen Publishing

Visa/MasterCard#_____ Expires _____

Signature: _____

Telephone:_____

Mail to:

VanderVeen Publishing, 11916 Hickory Drive, Bentonville, AR 72712-8789

(479) 273-3388   Fax: (479) 273-3883   1-800-982-2568